THE COLONIAL ELITE OF EARLY CARACAS

The Colonial ✝ Elite ✝ of Early Caracas

Formation & Crisis 1567∞1767

by

ROBERT J. FERRY

University of California Press
Berkeley · Los Angeles · London

The publisher gratefully acknowledges the contribution from the Eugene M. Kayden Fund of the University of Colorado toward the publication of this book.

University of California Press
Berkeley and Los Angeles, California

University of California Press, Ltd.
London, England

Copyright © 1989
by The Regents of the University of California

Library of Congress Cataloging-in-Publication Data

Ferry, Robert J.
  The colonial elite of early Caracas : formation and crisis. 1567–1767 / Robert J. Ferry.
    p. cm.
  Bibliography: p.
  Includes index.
  ISBN: 978-0-520-30200-6 (pbk. : alk. paper).
  1. Elite (Social sciences)—Venezuela—Caracas—History—17th century. 2. Elite (Social sciences)—Venezuela—Caracas— history—18th century.
  3. Caracas (Venezuela)—Commerce—History.
  I. Title.
HN370.Z9E435 1989
305.5'2'09877—dc19   88-29089
                                                   CIP

*To the memory of José Ignacio Rodríguez,
who showed me the best of Venezuela
To my friend Loren George Deutz
And to Melvid, who is everything*

Contents

Acknowledgments — ix
Introduction — 1

PART ONE THE SEVENTEENTH CENTURY

1. Commerce and Conflict: The First Caracas Elite, 1567–1620 — 13
2. Cacao in the Seventeenth Century: The First Boom — 45
3. Wheat Farm and Cacao Hacienda: Agricultural Business and Elite Families — 72

PART TWO THE EIGHTEENTH CENTURY

4. The Tuy Valley Frontier — 105
5. León's Rebellion — 139
6. The Protest of the Caracas Elite — 177
7. First Families — 216
8. The King in Caracas: The Bourbon Reforms — 241

Appendixes — 255
Notes — 289
Glossary — 325
Bibliography — 329
Index — 337

Acknowledgments

This book has been quite a long time in the making, and over the course of the years I have received the assistance of many people and several institutions. I first went to Venezuela in 1974 with a fellowship from MUCIA, a consortium of Midwestern universities centered at Indiana University. In Venezuela I was the beneficiary of several years of financial support from the Biblioteca Nacional. More recently, the Graduate School of the University of Colorado provided funds for summer research and writing.

From the beginning, no one has provided more direction, help, and inspiration than Stuart Schwartz. John Lombardi read the manuscript several times and offered both his critical judgment and broad knowledge of colonial Venezuela. In Seville, John R. Fisher shared with me his generous company and his considerable experience in the Archivo General de Indias. At the University of Colorado, Phil Mitterling, my undergraduate thesis advisor two decades ago, has again given me the benefit of his own strong sense of effective prose. His infectious enthusiasm for the historical profession has not flagged, and I am fortunate to still be his student. I am also grateful for the no-holds-barred criticisms of several other Colorado colleagues: Fred Anderson, Steve Epstein, Gloria Main, and Ralph Mann.

I am especially grateful to Virginia Betancourt, director of the Biblioteca Nacional, Caracas. Thanks to her interest in my project, I was a research associate with the Biblioteca Nacional from 1976 to 1980. In an unusual reversal of our customary practice of receiving funds from North American agencies for study abroad, during the year 1978 the Biblioteca provided me with very generous support so that I could return to the University of Minnesota to do the computer-assisted family reconstitutions that are an essential part of this study.

In Venezuela I benefited from the companionship and professional friendship of many people, among them Ralph and Carmen Rosa Van Roy, Steve Ellner, Aurelio Alvarez Juan, Ana María Rodríguez, Kathy Waldron, Susan Berglund, Mike McKinley, Rob and Polly Wright and, in particular, Judy Ewell. It is also my good fortune to have had the support, assistance, and friendship of three pillars of Venezuelan historical scholarship: Germán Carrera Damas, Pedro Grases, and Manuel Pérez Vila.

Introduction

The Spanish town of Santiago de León de Caracas was founded in 1567. Located high above the Caribbean Sea in a temperate valley, Caracas flourished early because of its moderate climate and its ideal geographical setting, both near enough to the coast for commerce and yet far enough away to discourage attacks by foreign buccaneers. However, in 1567 the conquistadores who forced the Indian inhabitants of this valley to submit to their will and the authority of the Castilian monarchy were little concerned with climate or geography. In the decades before the foundation of Caracas the most dynamic enterprises on this coast had been the pearl fisheries of the islands of Margarita and Cubagua. The oyster beds in these places played out in the 1520s, and the enterprise was followed by an active slave trade as the natives who had dived for pearls were sold to Panama, where they were employed as carriers in the isthmus crossing. Until at least the 1550s ships carrying Indian slaves passed along the coast in the vicinity of the future settlement of Caracas, and it may have been at this time that the modest potential of the region, perhaps as a source of natives to enslave, attracted the tardy attention of Spanish adventurers.

The first Hispanic settlement in the vicinity of Caracas was established in 1558 by Francisco Fajardo, the mestizo son of a Spaniard and an Indian noblewoman from the island of Margarita. In that year he and a handful of Margariteños settled in a place that they called Panezillo, located some ten leagues east (upwind, or *arriba* in the contemporary idiom) of the site of the future port of La Guaira. Driven off by indigenous coastal people after a year spent trading along the coast, Fajardo returned from Margarita in 1560 with a larger armed force and, in 1560, with permission of the governor Pablo Collado, he founded a town eight or nine leagues west (*abajo*) from Panezillo. This community, named Collado after the governor, would also fail, but not before Fajardo had divided the subjugated Indians of the region into permanent labor units, *encomiendas*, which he distributed to his followers so that they might put the natives to work in any way that they saw fit. These encomiendas were the first created on the central coast.

Yet the push from the seaside settlements of eastern Venezuela went no further west than Collado, and the foundation of the town of Caracas, located about three leagues further downwind and another three leagues south into the mountains away from the coast, would be done by men who came from the other direction. Beginning in the late 1520s, bands of men looking for Indians and gold went south and east from the tiny town of Santa Ana de Coro on the western fringe of present-day Venezuela. Coro was the headquarters of the concession made by Charles V to his Augsburg bankers, the Welsers, and until the early 1540s the exploring and raiding done in the region of the modern boundary of Colombia and Venezuela was directed by Germans: Ambrose Alfinger and Georg Spira. The Welser possession of Venezuela lasted nominally until 1556, but from the late 1540s effective governance was in the hands of Spaniards. A string of successful Hispanic settlements was then established extending eastward from El Tocuyo, founded in 1545 at the crossroads of the north–south axis of the Venezuelan Andean cordillera and the east–west chain of mountains that follows the Caribbean coast to Caracas and beyond. Many of the same individuals participated in the successive creation of El Tocuyo (1545), Barquisimeto (1552), Valencia (1556), and finally Caracas (1567). The peripatetic behavior of these settler–adventurers demonstrates that the ambition of many of them was greater than the resources of the hinterland of towns they founded, but the fact that the towns survived, their native populations divided into encomiendas, indicates that the era of simple exploitation of the Welser period, of Indian slavery and gold hunting, had begun to give way to more permanent colonization.

Located closer to the sea than the residents of other central Venezuelan towns, and with a moderate force of Indian labor, the first permanent settlers of Caracas soon found a place for themselves in a simple commercial network. Linked to the east with Margarita, still a source of pearls and merchandise brought from Spain, Caracas residents traded these items with the interior settlements of *tierra adentro*, where rough cotton cloth (*lienzo*), hammocks, and beeswax could be had. Caracas contributed directly to the exchange with certain foodstuffs that were easily grown or raised in the valley's favorable environment: wheat, maize, pork, beef, and cheese. Yet this modest trade could satisfy only a very few traders, agriculturalists, and ranchers, and until the 1580s the permanent population of the town remained small.

By the second decade following the town's creation Caraqueños had begun to sell significant quantities of wheat to Cartagena, where it was used to supply the Tierra Firme fleet. Sent from Spain to collect the silver of Peru, the fleet waited at Cartagena, the best fortress on the Caribbean coast of South America, until Peruvian silver could be brought up the Atlantic Coast and across the Panamanian Isthmus to Portobelo. Once the silver was in place, the great fair could take place at Portobelo, but that hot and unhealthy site remained occupied only for as long as it took to trade for the silver with the merchandise of Europe. The fleet arrived there ready to depart quickly for Havana and home, having already made repairs and taken on provisions during its stay at Cartagena. In the 1580s, stimulated by the sharply increasing price of wheat in peninsular Spain, Caracas owners of wheat farms known as *estancias* began to expand production and to transport bread and flour to Cartagena for consumption by the sailors of the silver fleet. Almost insignificant in comparison to the frenzied exchange of Peruvian silver for European commodities on which it depended, the wheat trade to Cartagena nevertheless brought Caracas directly into the commercial world of Spain's American empire, and in the process substantially transformed the character of social relations in the town.

For more than thirty years after 1580, wheat, and an occasional shipment of tobacco or cattle hides, provided Caracas residents with profitable exports. Sometime during the 1620s Caraqueños discovered that cacao beans, which grew on trees indigenous to the Venezuelan coast, could be sold for profit to Indian consumers in Mexico. The market for Caracas cacao proved to be vast, and the cacao trade across the Caribbean early and permanently fixed Caracas as a colony of the silver-rich and economically powerful viceroyalty of New Spain. The cacao trade was directly responsible for the transformation of the labor base in the Caracas province from Indian encomienda to African slavery. Alone of Spain's American colonies in the seventeenth century, Caracas came early to depend on slave labor. Sustained for several generations by steadily expanding sales of cacao, slavery had a profound effect on the character of Caracas society.

The combined impact of earthquake, crop blight, and reorganization of the silver economy in New Spain caused the Caracas economy to slump from the late 1640s through the 1660s. Profitable exports resumed in the 1670s, and a surging, booming business in cacao production and commerce followed, expanding virtually without a pause until the 1740s. Before the end of the seventeenth century the original cacao groves of most of the coastal valleys had been expanded to the physical limits of those valleys, and the vigorous planting of new haciendas shifted south and east of Caracas to the fertile valleys of the Tuy River and its several tributary streams. The Tuy boom attracted both established planters, who sent their younger and stronger slaves there to plant new haciendas, and more humble Spanish immigrants, especially Canary Islanders, who came to the colony looking to follow the pattern of the earlier settlers and become hacienda owners and slave masters themselves. The cacao prosperity of Caracas also finally attracted the attention of the Bourbon state. Ignored by the crown for more than a century, beginning in the late 1720s the colony was subject to new and comprehensive policies which were designed to increase royal revenues and to acquire much greater quantities of cacao for Spanish and European consumers and markets. The principal instrument for the implementation of these policies was the *Real Compañía Guipuzcoana de Caracas*, Spain's first royally chartered commercial monopoly company.

From its headquarters in San Sebastián in the Basque province of Guipúzcoa, the Guipuzcoana Company enjoyed exclusive rights to carry cacao from Caracas to Spain. Reflecting the general autonomy of the Basque provinces, which were united with the crown of Castile only through the person of the king, Company ships could leave for Caracas directly from San Sebastián without paying any duty whatsoever, and, after stopping to pay royal taxes at Cádiz, they could return there to unload.[1] By condition of its royal license, granted in 1728, only Company ships could carry cacao to Spain, but the traditional trade with New Spain was not altered in any way. The Company was not supposed to compete for cacao cargoes with those merchants and hacienda owners who preferred to ship their beans to Mexico. Rather, as the Basques who advocated the monopoly had argued in their initial request for a royal charter, Company profits were to come from two other sources: a substantial increase in cacao production, which would naturally follow the commercial stimulus provided by the Company, and a sharp reduction in cacao smuggling, which Company proponents claimed was widespread. To prevent the illicit trade, which would channel cacao by way of the royal monopoly into the legal (and taxable) market, the crown charged the Company with the responsibility of creating an effective coast guard.

In the event, the Guipuzcoana Company did not cause cacao production to increase substantially and, in an effort to increase their portion of cacao exports, aggressive Company factors did interfere with the traditional trade to Mexico. Basque governors who administered the province in the 1730s and 1740s favored the Company and collaborated with their monopolist countrymen, much to the disgust of many Caraqueños of all classes. Discontent reached a crisis in 1749, when Canary Islander cacao farmers, supported surreptitiously by members of the provincial elite, left their fledgling haciendas in the Tuy Valley and marched to Caracas to protest. Although it was not their intention, the protesters became rebels against the authority of the king when the governor fled in fear of the mob and took refuge in the fort at La Guaira. The royal reaction to this threat was swift and the king's justice did not equivocate. First crown troops from both Santo Domingo and Spain overwhelmed the rebels and punished the ringleaders, and then, during the 1750s, a series of military governors established the firm presence of the king in Caracas. Before the end of the decade a brigade of soldiers was permanently quartered in the town, taxation was revamped, and a myriad of lesser policies were enforced to make royal authority more immediately evident. These significant changes, which have until now gone unnoticed by historians, constitute the first steps in what would become a comprehensive effort by the Spanish monarchy to strengthen control of its American empire. That the Bourbon Reforms were originally implemented in the wake of a popular uprising in Caracas in the 1750s, and not in Havana after the English occupation a decade later, is an important new discovery that suggests the need to reconsider more than one aspect of the history of Spanish America in the eighteenth century.

The rebellion of 1749 and its aftermath mark the end of a distinct epoch in the history of early Caracas. Cacao would continue to be the motor force of the provincial economy until the end of the colonial period, but after midcentury agricultural expansion would be at a much slower pace. The century-long cacao boom was over, and the particular features of Caracas society which such sustained growth had fostered would undergo substantial adjustments.

One of these features, in my opinion the most distinctive aspect of colonial Caracas society, was the continuation in status and wealth of many of its elite families from one generation to the next without decline. It has become conventional wisdom to regard elite status in Spanish America as a volatile condition characterized by "a high rate of change in the composition of the elites on individual and, to some extent, family levels."[2] Once acquired by individual initiative or good fortune, wealth was difficult to multiply because economic activities either produced low incomes, as in the case of agriculture, or were subject to high risks, which was generally true in commerce, mining, or industry. Equally problematic for longer-term status maintenance, wealth rarely survived the passing of the generations. Castilian inheritance law did not allow primogeniture, and those individuals who died wealthy were obliged to divide their estates more or less equally among their often many heirs. Yet many families of the Caracas gentry were able to preserve their wealth and elite status for, in a good number of cases, as many as six and seven generations. The most famous of all colonial Caraqueños, Simón Bolívar, was a seventh-generation native son, and his case is not exceptional.

The success of the Caracas gentry depended directly on the steadily expanding demand for cacao in two very distinct markets, Mexico and Europe. Also of essential importance was the regular supply to Caracas of African slaves, which, with intermittent but short interruptions, was constant to the late 1730s. The steady demand for cacao and constant supply of slave labor coincided with an abundance of land suitable for cacao haciendas. The combined benefits of cacao markets, slaves, and available land sustained a score of families in local elite status from the middle of the seventeenth century through the first several decades of the eighteenth. The collapse of the slave trade in 1739 and the control over cacao commerce exercised by the Guipuzcoana Company in the 1730s and 1740s brought the prolonged cacao boom to a standstill. Although the second half of the eighteenth century is beyond the scope of this book, the Caracas elite obviously made adjustments that allowed foremost families such as the Bolívar to retain their status during the last decades of the colonial period and to emerge as leaders in the wars for independence. The first phase of these adjustments, which included cooperation with both the Guipuzcoana Company and a forceful royal authority in exchange for assistance in forging a free-labor replacement for slavery, is discussed in the last section of this book.

The research for *Early Caracas* was done in Caracas archives, in particular the little-used depository of notarial records, the Archivo del Registro Principal, and in the Archivo General de Indias in Seville. Much of the analysis is based either on sources that have traditionally formed the documentary core of colonial histories—governors' reports, royal *cédulas*, *actas* of the town cabildo, and so forth—or on sources, such as wills and notarial data, that have been used by researchers with increasing frequency and sophistication over the course of the last decade. The method of analysis is for most part traditional as well, formed usually by a close reading of discrete documents in an effort to come to an understanding of the particular problem at hand. In one detail, however, the methodology is sufficiently innovative to merit a comment here.

One obviously distinctive characteristic of colonial Caracas was the fact that the same elite families were able to counter the effects of bipartible inheritance (male and female heirs received an equal share of the estate; no primogeniture) and to thereby retain both wealth and political power for many generations. An understanding of how this longevity was accomplished seemed central to the internal dynamics of this society; therefore, to allow me to follow the Caracas elite over the course of several generations, all the families identified as having been of high status and influence were reconstituted from the first immigrant ancestor who arrived in Caracas in the sixteenth or early seventeenth century to his or her descendants who lived in the city at the turn of the nineteenth century. These family histories confirmed genealogical linkages, and complete demographic data (birth date, marriage date, death date) were obtained for many individuals.

Studied in isolation, this collective genealogical history of Caracas elite families made it possible to examine such facets of elite social life as strategies of marriage (including nonmarriage). The rapidly expanding literature on colonial elites emphasizes the importance of marriage in the maintenance of elite status. Much is made of the value of marriages of prominent creole women to peninsular Spaniards, who brought both prestige and new commercial contacts to the family. In addition, patriarchal authority is almost universally credited with the direction of family marriage strategies.[3] Again in these particulars the Caracas elite differed significantly from the Spanish American norm. The several clans that made up the Caracas gentry were decidedly self-contained with regard to marriage. It is clear that marriage between first cousins was common among prominent families, and that strict endogamy increased as a proportion of all elite marriages during the course of the eighteenth century. It is also evident that elite Caracas fathers, because they typically married in their late thirties and died in their middle fifties, were not often alive when their children married. Because mothers did survive to witness the weddings of their children, and for a number of other reasons discussed in the text, it would seem that elite women played a more instrumental part than men in arranging marriages and in several ways directing and determining the membership of the family, or rather the lineage, from one generation to the next. This study attempts to link these patterns to the general course of Caracas economic and social history.

Studied in conjunction with other materials, such as the censuses of haciendas made in 1684, 1720, and 1744, and the household census of Caracas taken in 1759, the reconstituted family data allowed me to trace the generational transfer of agricultural wealth and to make some observations about the matrix of kinship and residence for Caracas elites at midcentury. The results of this form of inquiry appear throughout part II of the text, dealing with the eighteenth century. As an example of the way elite family reconstruction can be used to inform the general history of Caracas society, it is my understanding that many of the Caracas elite were particularly desperate to end the Guipuzcoana Company monopoly by the 1740s because the number of living individuals by then with claims to elite status was increasing at a much faster rate than the cacao economy. Those elites who were most vociferous in their opposition to the Company usually belonged to large and rapidly expanding families whose members, on a per capita basis, owned fewer cacao trees in 1744 than their parents had held a quarter-century earlier. Unable to provide for their children as they had been provided for, they protested, and some, surreptitiously, even backed the rebellion of the lower classes in 1749.

The terminal date for this history of early Caracas is 1767. It is not entirely satisfactory as an ending point in that no particularly significant event occurred in that year which might be used to mark the end of a precise epoch or a clearly delimited phase in the history of the town and province. Yet it was chosen to suggest that the first two centuries after the foundation of Caracas can be seen as a coherent period. In 1767, after twenty years of protest and repression, elite young men took the opportunity to demonstrate their loyalty to the newly emphatic authority of the Bourbon monarchy, and joined the Company of Noble Adventurers, an honorary king's militia of cavalry created in that year. By that time the elite had come to terms with the Guipuzcoana Company, for more than a decade they had been paying new taxes without protest in support of the contingent of regular army troops quartered in the plaza, and they had begun to make adjustments to the end of the long, often remarkably dynamic, boom in cacao agriculture and commerce. As an example of this adjustment, a long hiatus in slave imports—there was virtually no trade at all from the end of the English *asiento* in 1739 until the 1780s—obliged elite hacendados to turn increasingly to wage laborers to work their cacao estates.

By the middle of the eighteenth century Caracas had experienced a fundamental change for the middling class of Hispanic residents as well for the elite. For several generations Caracas had been a true frontier where wealth and slaveholder's status awaited the ambitious immigrant, but failure of the 1749 revolt signaled the end of the long bonanza and the closing of opportunity for those who were not already well established as slave and hacienda owners. The reforms of the 1750s, including the vagrancy laws that served to help elites in their search for an alternative to slave labor, provided the mechanisms needed to enforce the new order, which would last for another fifty years.

Finally, the history of revolutionary Caracas lies beyond the scope of this book, but it is worth noting that most of the colony's leaders in the movement for independence were members of families whose elite status of nearly two centuries had not been diminished by the crisis of 1749 and its aftermath. At that time the Caracas elite established a modus vivendi with the Bourbon regime which allowed them two more generations of profit from their haciendas and, along with the profit, significant local prestige and authority. This arrangement lasted until the end of the century, when the markets of the empire once again became inadequate to fulfill the needs and aspirations of the colony's foremost families. From the perspective of the internal dynamics of early Caracas, the primary impetus for independence seems to have come from elites who were again desperate to preserve their traditional place in the local society. Needless to say, the second crisis of the Caracas elite, that of 1810, was resolved in a manner very different from that of the first.

By way of definition: the concept of *elite* used in this book is based on families, or more exactly family lineages, rather than on individuals. Granted that certain individuals, governors and bishops for example, were given elite status from the moment of their arrival in Caracas, but the primary interest here is the resident, permanent, planter and slaveholding elite. Colonial Caracas was characterized by the long tenure of elite status maintained by a number of families, and this tenure is included here in the definition of elite, in as much as such *antigüedad* counted for a great deal to early Caraqueños. Therefore, an elite individual, a *mantuano* as he or she would have been referred to in eighteenth-century Caracas, was someone whose paternal and maternal ancestors in most cases had been in Caracas since the middle of the seventeenth century or earlier, whose male relatives and ancestors served and had served on the town council, and whose family members appear on lists of cacao haciendas taken in 1684, 1720, and 1744. It is my belief that all those colonials who would have been considered mantuanos by their contemporaries have been included in the analyses that are presented in these pages.

PART I

THE SEVENTEENTH CENTURY

1

Commerce and Conflict: The First Caracas Elite, 1567–1620

A band of adventurers led by Diego de Losada broke the fierce resistance of the Carib Indians and established in 1567 the town of Santiago de León de Caracas. Caracas evidently either failed to fulfill the ambitions of these men or they had no intention of giving up the conquistador's freebooting lifestyle, for only 18 of the 136 men who accompanied Losada were still present in the town in 1578. At that time there were some 4000 Indian tributaries divided into forty encomiendas, more native labor than was available in any other Venezuelan town at that time, but, significantly, this was only about one-third the number of Indians who had inhabited the region just ten years earlier. With little besides shrinking encomiendas to offer, it is not surprising that Caracas did not excite many imaginations in Spain. To the end of the sixteenth century Venezuela continued to be the least popular destination for Spaniards who crossed the Atlantic.[1]

Dreams of El Dorado were for many the only tolerable alternative to the poverty of early Caracas. Of course, neither grand illusions nor the bold exploits of those who actually looked for fabled Indian cities in the Guayana jungles would alter the barrenness of this land that seemed to betray the promise of the Indies.[2] The only practical way for Caraqueños to improve their economic condition to any significant degree was to acquire an encomienda, or, if they were already *encomenderos*, to add Indian laborers to the one they held. On several occasions the first generation of Caracas *vecinos*, permanent residents who had not moved on to seek their fortunes elsewhere, sallied out from the town in search of Indians much in the same way that a century earlier their countrymen had gone out to raid Muslim villages from wooden *fortalezas* on the Barbary and Atlantic coasts of Africa.[3] From shortly after its foundation in 1567,

Caracas was the permanent residence of the provincial governor, who was responsible for defending and extending the colony's frontiers and, as a consequence, Caraqueños had more opportunities than did vecinos of other towns to participate in these raids. Such slave hunting was illegal, but in Caracas these forays were disguised as defensive expeditions made to protect existing settlements. They were appealing, both for the slaves that could be made of Indians who resisted in such supposedly "just" wars, and for the royal favors that could be claimed, such as the grant of a vacated encomienda, on the basis of military services rendered. These were the motives behind the campaign led by Garci González de Silva against the Cumanagoto Indians of the Tuy River valley in 1579 and 1580, and the venture organized by Sebastián Díaz de Alfaro, which resulted in the establishment of the frontier town of San Sebastián de los Reyes in 1584.[4] At the same time, the frequent uprisings of the Indians of Nirgua, which were said to have threatened the settlements in the western part of the province and disrupted traffic on the road to New Granada, were suppressed by bands of men sent out by the governor from distant Caracas, and not, as might have been expected if the threat to them had been truly serious, by vecinos from towns much nearer to Nirgua such as Barquisimeto and Valencia.[5]

In these circumstances the urban functions of Caracas remained little different from the primitive ones of an armed camp. Since fully forty of the settlement's sixty vecinos held at least a small Indian labor grant in 1578, encomendero status was not a primary social distinction or a source of local influence. Rather, for men like Garci González de Silva and Sebastián de Alfaro who held it, power was rooted in the personal charisma and other leadership qualities that made it possible for them to assemble and lead a *cabalgada*, or Indian raiding party.[6] The only other possible source of local influence, a position on the town council, the *cabildo*, was limited to the formation and execution of rules concerning the use of existing or finite wealth, such as the setting of food prices or the provision of meat for the town. Indian raids, on the other hand, held the hope of increasing that wealth, the only such hope for about two decades after 1567. Even so, they did not produce much profit, for there were simply not many Indians available for capture. But the raids were imbued with social meaning retained from the archaic traditions of frontier wars with Islam, and for twenty years no other economic activity had the appeal of the organized hunt for Indian slaves.

In the late 1580s, a fortuitous combination of climatic, geographic, and economic factors brought Caracas belatedly into Spain's New World empire. The much quicker pace of the commercial world of the sixteenth century brought noticeable changes to the once-rustic, thatch-roofed village. As producers and exporters of wheat grain and flour, newly prosperous Caracas vecinos added tile roofs and second storys to their churches, homes, and community buildings. With new wealth to administer and an increased opportunity to govern, the cabildo replaced the cabalgada as the town's most important political institution. Coming of age as a colonial town created new tensions and conflict, however, and the controversies that emerged at this time of transition provide a revealing look at the social relations of the powerful and not-so-powerful farmers and traders of early Caracas.

The value of Spain's Atlantic shipping more than doubled during the first fifteen years following the foundation of Caracas, and during this time, with the world's richest commercial highway passing just behind the narrow range of mountains to the north, the town's enterprising vecinos discovered profitable alternatives to hit-and-run Indian raids. The best alternatives came as Caracas was drawn into the market network centered on the annual trade fair at Portobelo. Before landing at Portobelo, the Tierra Firme fleet made port at Cartagena, and from there news of its arrival in America was sent south to Peru by way of Panama. Then, while the Portobelo merchants made preparations for their fair and the wealth of Peru was brought up the Pacific Coast, the waiting fleet, secure beneath the walls of the Cartagena fortress, traded for the gold and emeralds of New Granada and for Venezuelan pearls.[7] The galleons also needed provisions; their sailors, good Spaniards, insisted on wheat bread, and from the early 1580s ships loaded with Caracas wheat grain and flour made the easy, trade-winds assisted sail west along the Caribbean coast to Cartagena.

The transition from raiding to farming could take place because of the particularly mild Caracas climate. Repeated attempts to grow grapes and citrus trees met with little success in the valley, but wheat flourished. Even though the settlement was located near the equator at about ten degrees north latitude, cereal cultivation was possible in Caracas because its high elevation, about 800 meters in the immediate vicinity of the town, provided moderate temperatures. In addition, although it was never abundant and in time there would be sharp conflicts over rights to its use, during the early years enough water was available to sustain a modest boom in wheat farming and grain milling.

Losada had situated the Caracas plaza in an ideal spot above where the Guaire River makes a wide bend, on the ridge of a broad plain at the base of the high mountains which stood as a barrier between the settlement and the sea. This plain is divided by streams carrying rainwater runoff from the mountains to the Guaire, and the early importance of these streams is made evident by their prominence on the well-known map of the town and environs prepared by Governor Juan Pimentel in 1578 or shortly thereafter (see Map 1). From the text of the detailed report that this sketch accompanied, part of the *Relaciones Geográficas* ordered by Philip II, it is clear that by this date wheat farming was underway, and that for its cultivation Caracas farmers relied both on rainfall and on irrigation water taken from these streams.[8]

Within little more than a decade after the Pimentel report an increase in the need for water resources became noticeable in the town council record—petitions to the cabildo, for pastures and for cornfields to sustain the Indian population in the 1570s and 1580s, had given way to requests for water rights and wheat mill sites by the 1590s. Other documents indicate that by then wheat had become an important part of the economic life of the town. Business was particularly brisk during the months of September and October, the principal planting season, during March and early April when the grain was harvested (although the harvest occasionally came as early as mid-February), and again in late May and June when it was ground into flour and sent to La Guaira for shipment to Cartagena and other Caribbean ports. During these periods farmers and traders, both vecinos and *forasteros*, outsiders, from Spain, the Canary Islands, and other Indies towns, appeared at the Caracas notaries' offices to register their wheat sales, to sign promises to pay for merchandise or labor with the next year's harvest, or to make shipping arrangements.[9] Business was so good, in fact, that it attracted the English buccaneer Aymas Preston, who raided the

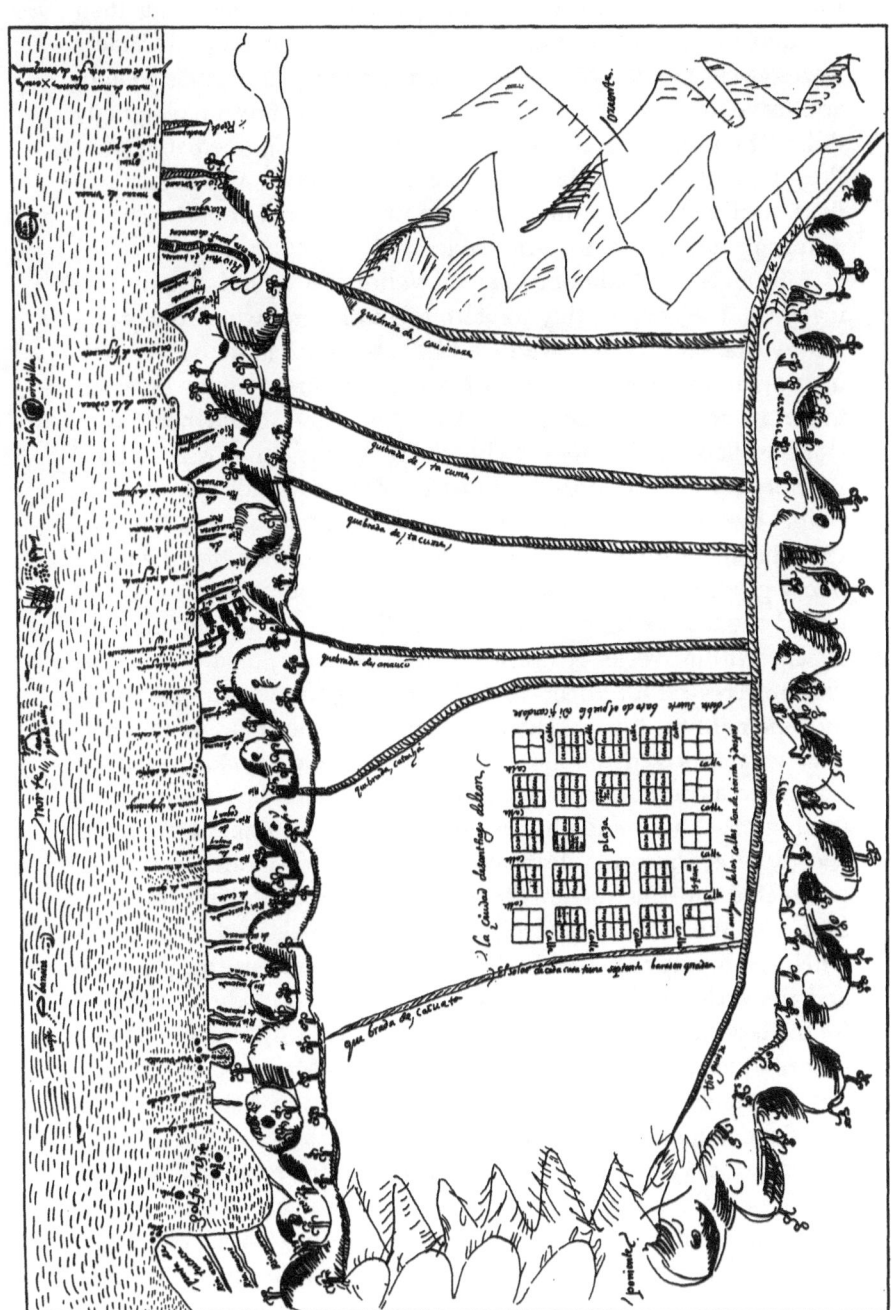

Map 1. Pimentel Map

town in 1595. Ten years earlier Cartagena residents had paid the huge sum of 110,000 ducats to Francis Drake in ransom for their city and its warehouses full of merchandise, but in modest Caracas it was easier to flee, carrying away the greater part of one's wealth, and leave the town to be sacked and burned, as Preston obligingly did.[10] The flurry of reconstruction that followed immediately after Preston's attack, also clearly visible in the cabildo and notary records, indicates that by then the town had acquired importance and a strong commitment to permanence.

Although the bishopric see for Venezuela would remain formally until 1637 in the tiny western town of Coro, where the cathedral was a very modest wattle-and-daub edifice ("the best church of straw in the Indies"), Caracas, where the first bishops invested in land and actually spent most of their time, could boast of a stone-walled and tile-roofed church from 1584. In 1595 the pirate Preston burned the timbers of this building and those of a similar chapel then under construction in the Franciscan convent. Eager to reestablish the solid and secure presence in the town that the prosperity generated by wheat had allowed them, the church's agents joined the town's foremost citizens as the first to rebuild after the attack. Within weeks of Preston's departure, Bartolomé de la Canal, church vicar for fifteen years prior to 1595, made arrangements for repairs to his house. The lieutenant governor Juan de Riberos, who was criticized for his absence during the attack, may have expressed a commitment to the future defense of the settlement by trading his straw-roofed house and 350 pesos for one roofed in tile shortly after Preston's destructive visit. So many other residents contracted for construction labor that by 1596 the town's few artisans and the local supply of building materials had been overwhelmed by the rush to rebuild. As a result, the wealthier vecinos and the ecclesiastical establishment sought to outbid one another for the few craftsmen and scarce resources. This indecorous competition, which was ended by a cabildo order in May 1596, is perhaps the best measure of the wheat-driven transition from transience and slave raiding to permanent settlement.[11]

For Caracas craftsmen the wheat trade meant booming opportunity for employment. Equally important, flour and grain became the principal in-town medium of exchange for transactions of all kinds, and by the turn of the seventeenth century many vecinos were doing much of their business in wheat and wheat futures. In June 1597, *capitán* Juan de Guevara agreed to pay mason Francisco Benítez the equivalent of 276 gold pesos in flour and carpenter Juan García Cabeza 130 pesos, also in flour, to construct a second story on the house he had purchased the year before. The following month Benítez was promised 125 pesos, this time in gold coin, to finish the masonry work on the Franciscan chapel, but such transactions in specie were rare.[12] Negotiations of all kinds were both regulated by the annual rhythms of the wheat harvest and dependent on a successful crop to satisfy outstanding obligations. In February 1599 blacksmith Juan Muñoz pledged to pay Pascual Pérez 69 pesos in wheat for a year's service as his assistant. At the time of the March harvest of that year Manuel Díaz, master shoemaker, advanced 160 arrobas of flour worth 70 pesos to Juan Pérez, who agreed to work for one year as the cobbler's helper. With the September planting of 1599, Díaz, in return for leather work to be done during the following six months, took a promise to pay in wheat flour worth 89 pesos, to be delivered in March of 1600, from Alonso García Pineda, mill owner, slaveholder, and government notary. Some years later, in July of 1605, shoemaker Díaz's widow, María de Medina, married Baltasar García, who had been growing wheat in the valley since 1593 when the cabildo granted him vecino status and twelve *fanegadas* (one fanegada was equal to about 1.6 acres) of land. The day after their wedding the couple arranged to buy a townhouse and lot from Diego Díaz León, the Portuguese slave factor. They paid 50 pesos in cash and promised to pay the remaining debt of 130 pesos in flour the following March. Juan Césaro, a Sicilian merchant who had lived in Caracas since the early 1590s, signed a contract in October 1605 with Francisco de Medina, master carpenter, who agreed to put a storeroom and living quarters in a second story that was to be built above Césaro's present shop. The value of the entire project was set at 167 gold pesos, payment to be made half in dry goods at the beginning of construction, half in wheat flour after the first harvest following its conclusion.[13]

While the original significance of Caracas wheat was its export value, perhaps as much as one-half of the wheat grown circulated as an exchange medium and was sooner or later consumed in the town. This ratio can be estimated because the legal exports for the

Table 1 Caracas Wheat and Tobacco Exports, 1603–1607,
Totals, by Vecino Status of Traders

	Wheat (1603–1607)	Tobacco (1604–1607)
ALL TRADERS		
Quantity Exported (arrobas)	68,220	8,952
Number of Traders	111	93
Average Quantity per Trader	614	96
HISPANIC VECINOS		
Quantity Exported	26,326	4,561
Number of Traders	33	38
Average Quantity per Trader	797	120
FOREIGN VECINOS		
Quantity Exported	4,420	1,379
Number of Traders	9	12
Average Quantity per Trader	491	114
NON-VECINOS		
Quantity Exported	37,474	3,012
Number of Traders	69	43
Average Quantity per Trader	543	70

Source: AGN, Real Hacienda, legs. 3, 5, 6. See chap. 1, nn. 14 and 49.

Wheat was valued for export tax purposes at 4 reales the arroba; tobacco at 25 reales the arroba. At this rate the total value of Caracas wheat exports for these four years was 34,110 pesos (8527 pesos/year). Tobacco exports for three years were worth 27,975 pesos (9325 pesos/year).

period 1603 to 1607 are known exactly (see table 1),[14] and because the cabildo declared after the 1604 harvest that 2500 fanegas of wheat grain then remaining in the town could not be sold for export. Of this quantity 1000 *fanegas* were needed as seed for the next planting, and 1500 fanegas were needed for local consumption during the coming year. Ground into flour, 2500 fanegas of grain would yield about 15,000 arrobas of flour,[15] and this amount, which represents the quantity of wheat kept in Caracas every year, is approximately equal to the average annual export of wheat made from Caracas during the short period for which complete data are available (13,644 arrobas, one-fifth of the five-year total of 68,220 arrobas).

During the dry "summer" months from November to March or April, the scant rainfall collected on the mountainsides north of Caracas provided irrigation for the wheat farms of the fortunate few growers who owned land along the streams leading to the Guaire River. Most wheat destined for export was brought to har-

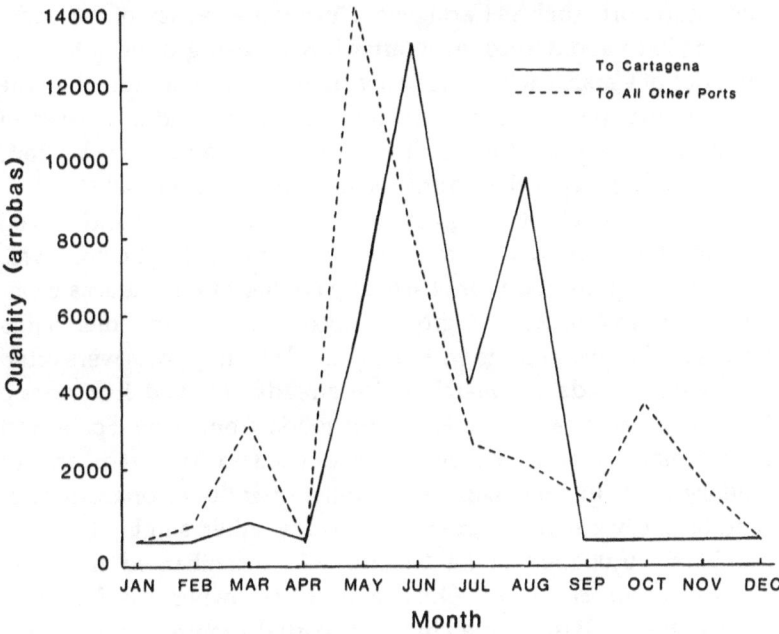

Fig 1. Caracas Wheat Flour to Indies Ports by Month and by Destination, 1603–1607

vest at the dry season's end, and the fact that this grain could then be ground into flour in water-powered mills driven by the heavy "winter" rains of May and June made it possible to have Caracas wheat flour in Cartagena well in advance of the flota, which generally departed Spain in August[16] (fig. 1). This was a climatological-commercial coincidence of singular benefit to Caracas growers, but it is likely that the Caracas wheat trade flourished not so much because of favorable local circumstances, but rather because of agricultural problems in Spain. In his classic study of the Mediterranean, Fernand Braudel informs us that by 1560 "flour from Andalusia was no longer sufficient to make biscuit for the fleets, and the Spanish crown had to go in search every year, good or bad, for 100,000 fanegas of grain. . . . In 1583 the shortage spread to the whole economy."[17] As the price of Andalusian wheat skyrocketed, the Caracas-grown grain became an important cash crop, for ships could load in Seville only the biscuit that was needed by their crews for the Atlantic crossing and then buy the rest of their wheat in

American ports such as Cartagena. During the heyday of the trade, from 1580 to about 1620, even after it had been ground into flour the price of Caracas wheat was only about 15 percent more than the average price paid for wheat grain in Andalusia, and in thirteen of the thirty-three years for which we have information Caracas flour was actually cheaper than Andalusian wheat in the kernel.[18]

Although much of the grain was consumed locally and served an important exchange function in the absence of hard coin, it was as an export commodity that wheat gave life to the Caracas economy. Artisans as well as grower–encomenderos and merchants traded in Caribbean ports with the grain. Wheat exports were often in payment made for merchandise already received in Caracas. Vecino-owned vessels loaded with goods from New Spain and from China by way of New Spain docked in May 1601 and in January 1602. In July 1602 a substantial quantity of Spanish merchandise, several times greater than any other single shipment previously unloaded at La Guaira, was disembarked from the *Nuestra Señora del Soccoro*, whose master and owner was Sebastián Bengoechea, a Basque merchant. In partial remuneration for his cargo, Bengoechea arranged to have 6090 arrobas of flour, about one-fifth of the rich 1603 wheat harvest, shipped to Cartagena. Promises to pay in wheat flour seem to have increased in amount in accordance with the availability of imported goods to buy; credit for 100 pesos, common in 1595, was given for 600 or 700 pesos in 1605. To secure this merchandise growers were willing to "mortgage the harvest," as the contracts aptly phrased it, not only for the following year's crop, but in some cases for the crop two years distant as well. The Sicilian merchant Césaro granted extended credit of this sort to royal accountant and encomendero Simón Bolívar in November 1605.[19]

During the early seventeenth century a few merchants, attracted by wheat, invested their commercial capital in farming and became resident growers, millers, and encomenderos. In the late 1590s, before he was twenty years old, Nofre Carrasquer established residence in Caracas as agent to the Sevillian merchant Fernán Pache de Sárate, who was a wholesaler to several Caracas importers. Most of early Caracas's European imports were transshiped from the island of Margarita, the first landfall after the Atlantic crossing,[20] and in his own name and that of his associate, Carrasquer traded for such goods there with Caracas foodstuffs, particularly dried fish and wheat flour. To the west along the Caribbean coast his commercial ties and credit extended to Cartagena, where he preferred that all of his debtors make payment, and in the interior his accounts reached as far as the settlement of El Tocuyo, seventy leagues to the southwest of Caracas, where he exchanged European merchandise for *lienzo*, the rough cotton fabric used, among other things, to make flour bags. By 1610 he had become a vecino and an encomendero privileged with the labor of 120 Indian tributaries in the Baruta Valley near Caracas, but even before he became a wheat grower in his own right he was an important manager of local agricultural produce: in March 1600, as the annual harvest was just beginning, merchant Carrasquer could guarantee delivery of 1000 arrobas of flour within five weeks.[21]

With the turn from the conquest of the land and its indigenous inhabitants to a more intensive form of colonization and the formation of an agrarian society dependent on seaborne commerce, the exclusive overlordship of the region's remaining conquistadors became diluted and a new, more complex elite was formed. Membership in this elite was expanded from the old soldiers, the first founders and their children, to include several successful merchants who had become vecinos and encomenderos, wheat growers and millers. The authority of the older generation, formerly based on the cabalgada and the heroics of conquest, was now channeled through the municipal law of the cabildo. Most importantly, the rejuvenated cabildo found that its jurisdiction included authority that could directly affect the wheat trade. For the most part town-council policies such as the fixing of bread prices and the work levy assigned to vecinos to upgrade and maintain the road to La Guaira met with no opposition. On other occasions, however, certain powerful wheat growers and traders manipulated the town council, bending its laws to fit their particular needs and private interests.

In an early analysis of Spanish American cabildo politics, Frederick Pike made it clear that social justice was not always the principal objective of town authorities. Pike perceived an agrarian interest in many council decisions. This emphasis was not the outcome of a conscious plot, but rather it was "another manifestation of the glorification of agrarian and rural values over those of trade and manufac-

ture, in short of urban life, which had become an ingrained part of Spanish character as a result of centuries of historical experience."²²
There was no dichotomy of town versus rural, or of urban entrepreneurial versus landed oligarchy, in early seventeenth-century Caracas, for the same prominent individuals were both traders and owners of agricultural estates. However, a close examination of two cases reveals that powerful trader–farmers in Caracas quite consciously did manipulate municipal law in order to extend and to protect their investments in wheat agriculture and commerce.

The devious maneuvering of Garci González de Silva, who used the town council to deprive weaker opponents of the land and water that he wanted, is indeed a simple example of petty greed, but it is useful because it illustrates both the stress that was created as Caracas responded to the booming demand for wheat and the self-serving use of the cabildo on the part of those with access to its authority. In the second detailed case study, a wheat–grower faction is first identified from among the principal planters and traders. This faction used the cabildo authority to restrict tobacco commerce because it attracted pirates and thus interfered with their own wheat interests. Demonstrated is the effective capacity of local Caracas authority, skewed as it was to favor certain individuals and interests, to influence the regional economy during the earliest years of commercial exports. This was characteristic of Caracas only during the period when wheat was king. Tobacco was first to threaten local influence in commerce; cacao, as will be seen, was far too dynamic an export commodity to be regulated in any way by town authority. Not until the 1760s, after a social rebellion that shook the colony to its foundations, would the cabildo be given a voice in the determination of cacao prices. In the interim, a period of 150 years, the dicta of distant markets and the royal will would determine the nature of the Caracas economy. The 1580 to 1620 period is unique, then, for the strength of local interests in the economic life of the Caracas region.

These examples of self-interest on the part of the elite also serve to correct a misconception about the integrated and harmonious nature of early Caracas society. In an often-cited essay, the first detailed study of the Caracas community during its earliest years, historian Stephanie Blank argued that the men of the Caracas elite, because they held prestige and power as municipal officials, and because they conducted business in the larger world of Spain's empire, were able to perform an essential integrative role in the community as social brokers and patrons for less-privileged vecinos.[23] Blank observed that there were a variety of mechanisms, including kinship and ritual kinship, or *compadrazgo*, that provided links between Caracas residents, and she believed that these links were used for vertical social integration that affected almost everyone in the town. However, her study lacks the all-important evidence of the service actually rendered the clients of the grandees who were dependent on them for protection and advancement. In fact, rather than the tendency toward consensus that Blank observed, the internal history of Caracas during the early commerical period reads best as a series of petty struggles and at times violent, socially disintegrative adjustments to rapid changes. What most often prevailed was the simple will of strong men concerned with the profits to be realized from their wheat crop and the financing of imports with the anticipated return from future harvests. Rather than benign leaders of an integrated social organism, the members of this elite did what they could to advance their own interests as a class, or, perhaps better, as a kin-linked faction, without much concern for those who were neither powerful nor influential. Willing to incur considerable personal risk by defying the governor, placing him under arrest and sending him under guard to Spain, as they did in 1624 to prevent enforcement of the encomienda law,[24] it was not difficult for them to use the cabildo for their own benefit, even at the expense of poorer vecinos who, in earlier times, had enjoyed the patronage of many of these same Indian raiders now turned wheat traders.

The wheat commerce with Cartagena and other Caribbean ports brought the construction of flour mills on the banks of the Anauco, Catuche, and Chacao streams where they crossed the plain above the town to the north and east. Although their owners' principal income came from the commercial sale of flour, operating these mills was evidently profitable, and their possession was both a privilege and a source of conflict which fell within the dominion of the cabildo to give and to resolve. In 1591 Alonso García Pineda received eight fanegadas of land from the cabildo. The only condition of ownership of this land, which was located on the banks of the Chacao stream, was that García Pineda fence the parcel to keep out the cattle that were still permitted to roam freely in the valley.

By the end of the following year he had obtained two more land grants on the Chacao, and until January 1593 he shared the stream with only one other individual, Sebastián Díaz de Alfaro, a companion of Losada in the foundation of Caracas, an *alcalde ordinario* in the cabildo, cabalgada leader on occasion, and founder in his own right of the town of San Sebastián de los Reyes. Then, on the same day, *capitán* Francisco de Olalla and the royal treasurer don Francisco Gomes de Ubierna petitioned for land and water rights along the Chacao. They were followed in May by three other petitioners, including the powerful old soldier Garci González de Silva. The cabildo granted these requests as well, despite García Pineda's claim that his prerogatives were being infringed upon. To protect themselves, in June he and Sebastián Díaz de Alfaro asked for and received guarantees to first water rights to the run-off carried by the stream.[25]

Rights to water usage of the other streams were quickly granted thereafter; the recipients were most often encomenderos. The normal pattern seems to have been that of the Chacao, where several mills were constructed one below the other by growers who also drew water from the same source to irrigate the wheat that they grew on contiguous land. The mill that the lieutenant governor Juan de Riberos began to build on the Anauco in 1594 was different in that his fields were not close at hand. The Anauco passed near the town and most of the irrigable land on its banks was already owned by Garci González de Silva. Located on municipal or *ejido* land below González de Silva's wheatfields, Riberos's mill was not a threat to the other's water needs and there was no objection made to its establishment. By 1597 the best wheat land in the Caracas Valley had been allocated and the cabildo had begun to grant mill sites to those who were willing to take title to land parcels located along the Guaire River. In many cases these recipients were encomenderos and were therefore at no significant disadvantage with respect to the labor force which they could put to work in their fields, but notary records and the records of taxes paid on wheat exports indicate that vecinos who grew wheat on the banks of the Guaire were not as successful as those growers who had earlier secured preferred land adjacent to the hillside streams. What is more, there is no evidence that it proved possible to divert water from the Guaire for the purpose of grinding flour.[26]

There were no more than five or six wheat mills in the Caracas Valley at the beginning of the seventeenth century, their numbers more limited by the shortage of favorable sites than by construction costs. They were not inexpensive, however. Juan de Riberos claimed that the mill he planned to build would be "of great utility for the *republica*, for there are few mills, so few that the wheat cannot be ground due to the lack of them, which is because they are so expensive to build, each one costing more than three hundred ducats [equal to 412 pesos]."[27] Yet it may be that Riberos, who could afford the building costs, overstated his case so that the cabildo would be sure to grant him a millsite; we know that encomendero Esteban Marmolejo purchased his mill for only 200 pesos in 1598.[28]

In any event, the mills were probably profitable, and all the more so if they were limited in number. A rough estimate of milling income is made possible on the basis of a provision of the cabildo which stipulated that millers were to receive in payment for the milling service one *almud* of wheat for every *fanega* of grain ground in their mills. In Andalusian measure, the almud was equivalent to the eighth part of one fanega,[29] and if each fanega produced six arrobas of flour, then the miller was paid three-fourths of one arroba for every six arrobas ground in his mill. With flour valued in Caracas at seven reales the arroba, the portion that went to millers of the 24,370 arrobas exported and some 6000 arrobas consumed in the town during the boom year of 1603 can be estimated at 3796 arrobas, worth 3321 pesos. If this amount were divided among six mill owners, each would have received 553 pesos or the equivalent value in flour in 1603, some 34 percent more than the total value of Riberos's mill, in that year alone.

The annual flour production in Caracas was much less than that of 1603, however. For the period 1604–1607 the average amount taken in fees by each of six mill owners would have been 230 pesos, about what it would have cost to pay the wages of an overseer and maintenance costs. Thus, as long as the mills remained few in number and wheat harvests and prices remained steady, the cabildo in effect guaranteed that the almud-per-fanega fee would at least pay operating costs. Indeed, this was most likely the intention of the provision, although in a very good year the miller might make a profit that surpassed the purchase price of his mill. Of course his principal profits, like those of all growers, came from the commercial sale of his flour, either on consignment to his account in Cartagena and other ports, or to *forastero* merchants and captains of passing ships. The profits from these sales cannot be estimated until price schedules for other Indies ports are available, but we can be sure that before their flour entered the Caribbean market the Caracas millers' had at least one advantage over encomendero-growers without mills: as mill owners they were not obliged to leave one-eighth of their grain at the mill door in order to have the remainder converted to flour. Also, and most importantly, unlike the encomienda, the mill was alienable property and could be sold or inherited without restriction.

While the wheat trade remained active, then, the ownership of a flour mill was desirable and, consequently, a source of competition and conflict. As in other aspects of town life, the sorting out of these problems fell to the cabildo, and here the distinction between public and private interest occasionally blurred. The following account is particularly useful because, although selected by Blank to demonstrate how uncertainty and the potential for violence in the fledgling town were ameliorated by the patron–client relationships between the powerful and the weak,[30] it is more convincing as an example of the propensity of these social bonds to break when burdened with the pressures of booming commercial agriculture.

During the last decades of the sixteenth century and the first decade of the seventeenth there was no single individual in Caracas who was more influential, and therefore more likely to serve as patron to several clients, than Garci González de Silva. Aided by his early arrival in the region and a fortunate marriage to the daughter of a Caracas conquistador, he successfully combined the qualities of cabalgada leader, encomendero, merchant, and town councilman. Such was his prestige in the community that in 1593 he was commissioned by the cabildo to take testimony from the conquistadors and first settlers who were still in the town so that an official history of the conquest of Caracas might be written.[31] Already owner of irrigated wheat farms on the Chacao and the Anauco streams as well as other property in the Caracas valley and cattle ranches elsewhere in the province, his desire to build a mill on the Catuche stream north of the town initiated a struggle that shows clearly that the martial society of the 1560s and 1570s was indeed past history and in need of its historian.

The Caracas community first formally determined the limits of its ejido in 1594. Twenty-five years had passed since the town's founding before this was done, perhaps because there had been land in abundance until the wheat boom made it scarce and valuable. The *ejido* was land that was to be used communally, for the common pasture of mules and horses, for instance, or rented to individuals for the benefit of the municipal treasury. Juan de Riberos, for example, paid the cabildo twelve pesos annually for the use of the land on which his mill was located. In the same year that the ejido boundaries were defined, the cabildo granted a parcel of land on the Catuche stream north of the town to Manoel Figueredo, the owner of a small shop and a long-time vecino. The property was on the mountainside beyond the newly determined ejido boundary, near the road that climbed north and west out of the valley before descending to sea. Figueredo paid the required *composición* fee to have his titles confirmed by the crown, and the land was his, at least according to law. Then, in a cabildo session of August 1599, councilman (*regidor*) Garci González de Silva petitioned for a mill site and water from the Catuche as it came from the mill that belonged to Esteban Marmolejo. The location of the land in González de Silva's request seems to have been in the same place as Figueredo's holding, but the land was examined by the cabildo's alcaldes ordinarios and González de Silva's petition was granted in November, in disregard for Figueredo's title.[32]

Figueredo was not an encomendero and not a man of means. In 1598 he paid the royal fifth on 120 pesos of gold, an average sum and the only occasion he registered gold to be smelted by the royal treasury. He had been a member of González de Silva's company in the raids made against the Cumanagoto Indians of Nirgua in 1593, and the respect Figueredo held for his former chief was such that he claimed that he would "always feel as humble toward him as if I had been his own son." What was more, González de Silva had served as godfather at Figueredo's wedding in 1579.[33] This all mattered for little, however, because wheat farming and milling had become profitable and Figueredo's one-time patron was prepared to do whatever was necessary to secure Figueredo's Catuche land and water for himself.

Late in 1600, in preparation for the grinding that would be done following the spring harvest of 1601, González de Silva sent his sons and a carpenter to begin work on the new mill. When Figueredo turned them away from the site, González de Silva went to the Catuche himself, accompanied by five armed men, to warn Figueredo that the work would proceed in spite of any protest. Figueredo pled justice from Sebastián Díaz de Alfaro and Juan de Guevara, alcaldes ordinarios that year who held first jurisdiction over cases of this sort, but Sebastián Díaz was an important wheat farmer in his own right, and he had served as guarantor for the 1200 pesos González de Silva was obliged to pay for the office of provincial attorney (*depositor general*) which he had purchased in 1595. Juan de Guevara, for his part, was married to González de Silva's wife's niece, and he would soon be father-in-law to both of González de Silva's sons. He was also a frequent shipper of large quantities of wheat.[34] Perhaps the cabildo intended to compensate for this apparent conflict of interest by sending *regidores* Rodrigo de León, Nicolás de Peñalosa, and Martín de Gámez to examine Figueredo's claim again, but they too determined that the boundary should be set to suit González de Silva. To no avail, Figueredo complained about the disadvantages of disputing the will of a regidor and a rich man with the rest of the cabildo's officers as judges. With González de Silva's mill under construction the case disappears from the record, to emerge in a somewhat different context several years later.[35]

Sometime before April 1608 Leonardo Ferigo, a cleric, purchased Manoel Figueredo's town property and his disputed Catuche claim. Ferigo renewed litigation with the cabildo, noting that Figueredo, "a poor and miserable man," could not afford the appeal that he was now willing to make to the Audiencia in Santo Domingo. Although he had sold his mill to one Antonio Ortíz, Garci González de Silva responded to padre Ferigo with a series of legal arguments that would end the continuing conflict in a definitive manner. In a counterstatement to the cabildo he first disputed Ferigo's claim in a direct fashion, arguing that his grant had been legally made in 1599, that the mill had been built on land that, in the opinion of both alcaldes and regidores, did not belong to Figueredo. Then, to bring both municipal and royal interests into alignment with his own, and thus to block any appeal that might be presented by Ferigo to the Audiencia in Santo Domingo, González de Silva offered a new and effective proposal.

The Figueredo–Ferigo land was close to the town in a very favorable location "within a musket shot" of the place most of the mules used in haulage to and from the wharf at La Guaira were pastured. Mules and horses were dying from lack of pasture, he claimed, and the grant of this valuable land to Figueredo fifteen years earlier was an error and an injustice to the king who had been deceived about its value. He did not mention that he, as regidor, had signed the 1594 ejido act that failed to include the Figueredo property. But far from recognizing that the Figueredo claim included the mill which the new owner Ferigo insisted belong to him, González de Silva now argued that Ferigo should be denied all the property, which must be returned "to your majesty or to this city."[36] Royal cédulas of 1589 and 1591 ordered governors and viceroys to revoke cabildo grants if recipients did not pay fees, but there was neither legal provision nor precedent for the restructuring of the ejido on the simple initiative of the cabildo, and much less so when the action would cause legitimate titles to be vacated and land to be expropriated.[37]

In any event, in April 1608, some months after Ferigo made known his intention to take his cause to the Audiencia, members of the cabildo rode east from Caracas with the lieutenant governor to reclaim land for the town by evicting those whose property was located within the newly expanded ejido boundaries. On the second day the committee, which included González de Silva in his capacity as regidor, came to the Catuche land of padre Ferigo. Ignoring his pleas, the town attorney opened and closed the doors of his house, threw out some of his furniture, and pulled up handfuls of grass in execution of the symbols of eviction. The unfortunate cleric was able to afford litigation for a time, and the town attorney took favorable testimony on his behalf from a dozen vecinos, but his property had become too valuable to be left unworked and his claims threatened a powerful man who succeeded in defeating Ferigo by arranging for his land to be transferred to the public domain.[38]

Garci González de Silva was eager to plant wheat and grind flour in 1594 because the trade had become more profitable than in previous years. The force and legal chicanery he used to get his way in the Figueredo–Ferigo case was intended to maximize his gains in the context of the limited water resources in the Caracas Valley where wheat cultivation was possible. However, even the most powerful and ruthless vecinos could not dominate the weather or the increasingly strong competition from regions with climate and other natural conditions superior to those of Caracas for wheat farming. The Caracas wheat boom lasted long enough for trade patterns and partnerships to be formed and for commercial activity to change the identity of the town, but it was disappointingly short-lived.

Rainfall in the Caracas Valley could be harshly capricious. Cereal cultivation was always a gamble against rain that could not be counted on to fall when the grain needed it most. The first notice of the difficulties of farming wheat in a tropical rainfall system comes in 1592: Juan de Riberos lost his second consecutive harvest that year because, as he complained to the cabildo, "the weather in this province isn't natural for the harvesting of wheat because it is so variable [*mudable*]." Shortages in 1607 following the bad harvest of 1606 caused the local price of bread to go up by 200 percent. In 1609 the cabildo recorded that there had been but little rainfall for several years past, and 1610 brought new prohibitions against hoarding and a ban on all exports, with a guard placed on the La Guaira road to prevent clandestine night traffic. The year 1611 was described as sterile, and in 1619 the mills were idled by the lack of rainwater needed to turn the heavy millstones.[39]

In addition to the crop failures, revived and redoubled competition from the wheat producing towns of the northern Andes may have reduced more distant Caracas's share of the Cartagena market. Since the 1570s these highland settlements had sent their annual harvests by mule train to the village of Gibraltar on the southern shore of Lake Maracaibo, and from there the flour was ferried to the port town of Nueva Zamora de Maracaibo for shipment to Santo Domingo, Puerto Rico, and, especially, Cartagena. Only a few days by sea from this latter market, Maracaibo was recognized by contemporaries as the best harbor and most active port on the Venezuelan coast.[40] In 1608 a long hiatus in the Maracaibo wheat trade ended when more than fifteen years of intermittent Indian wars in the lake region were finally brought to an end by an expeditionary force assembled from neighboring towns, but not from

Caracas, as would have been customary thirty years earlier. The messages of gratitude sent to the king by the cabildos of the Andean towns of La Grita, Pamplona, Tunja, and Mérida, and by Cartagena, attest to the importance of Maracaibo as an essential point of embarkation for the Andean wheat trade with the Caribbean.[41] What is suggestive for the Caracas case is that it was precisely during the closure of the Maracaibo outlet that Caracas wheat began to enter the Caribbean market in unprecedented quantities. The first year of the Maracaibo Indian revolts, 1594, was also the year that Garci González de Silva began in earnest to expand his holdings in wheat farmland. Caracas enjoyed more than a decade as the principal wheat supplier on the Tierra Firme coast, but this fortunate situation had passed by the time González de Silva arranged for the Figueredo–Ferigo land to become part of the town ejido.

There is no direct proof that either the problems of growing grain in a tropical rainfall system or the reopening of the port at Maracaibo caused the collapse of the Caracas wheat trade. Of undoubtedly great importance is the leveling of wheat prices in Spain, which, in terms of the amount of wheat that could be purchased with a given quantity of silver, reached their highest point and began to decline in the 1590s. Presumably too, as the silver production at Potosí fell and the Atlantic trade of Seville leveled off, the demand for wheat at Cartagena was reduced.[42] Cultivation did not stop altogether. In 1684 there were some 500 fanegadas (about 800 acres) in the immediate vicinity of Caracas that were planted in wheat, but this was all consumed locally.[43]

Tobacco and cacao, crops more suited than wheat to the climate and water resources of the central Venezuelan coast and the interior valleys that run parallel to it, were much sought in seventeenth-century Indies and European markets, and it was not long before they became the region's primary exports. At the very beginning of this transition, however, before the substantial profits to be made from cacao had become evident and wheat had not yet disappeared as a trade item, the Caracas political elite demonstrated but little interest in the promotion of commerce in these tropical crops. In part this was because the cultivation of tobacco and cacao took place in distant regions far from the town, and the cabildo's zone of effective influence could not be stretched to include remote haciendas located along an expansive, difficult-to-patrol coastline. To a limited extent, wheat production and commerce could be influenced by the town council, but only the province-wide authority of the governor could apply adequately to the far-flung agriculture of tobacco and cacao. More importantly, the cabildo's members were personally committed to the wheat trade, they were among its principal beneficiaries, and the town council would not readily relinquish the influence it had over wheat in favor of some other product that could not be subjected to municipal authority. Not surprisingly from this perspective, the cabildo's initial reaction to tobacco, the first of the alternative crops to challenge wheat, was firmly negative.

Caracas tobacco exports began to surpass wheat exports just at the time when wheat exports began to decline. Suddenly, in a surprising move, the cabildo and the governor decided to prohibit not only tobacco exports but its cultivation as well. In December 1604, the cabildo sent its regidores to take account of the tobacco crop in the fields, and then it asked the governor to impose a general ban on tobacco agriculture. The following August, in response to the governor's request, the Audiencia in Santo Domingo prohibited the planting of tobacco in Venezuela for a period of ten years, except by license to be granted by the governor.[44]

The official explanation for this drastic action was given by the governor, Sancho de Alquiza, who claimed that all other attempts to keep the king's subjects from trading tobacco with smugglers had failed. Wheat did not attract pirates, but for tobacco these "enemies of our Catholic faith" offered goods that were "cheaper than if they had been bought in Spain," and given the poverty of the province it was understandable that otherwise loyal subjects would return to the illicit trade after the most severe punishment. Sancho de Alquiza had even hung a few pirates as a warning, but to no avail.[45] His reasoning may have been the authorities' only motivation behind the prohibition, yet the cure does seem to have been worse than the disease. Among Venezuelan historians, Tomás Polanco Martínez suggests that tobacco probably continued to be sent from Caracas and that the absolute ban was only an ultimatum needed to enforce compliance with the licensing aspect of the decree. Eduardo Arcila Farías views it as an attack on local Portuguese farmers, which, he argues, would have been consistent with prevailing prejudices and is plausible because Portuguese vecinos were not represented in the cabildo and their tobacco farms were often located beyond the easy vigilance of Caracas authorities.[46]

The tobacco ban, described as "disconcerting" and "mad" by these modern historians because it evidently offered no benefit to what was one of the poorest of Spain's colonies, is the more unusual for the full participation of the cabildo, in Caracas on other occasions and elsewhere usually the vociferous defender of local interests against restrictive royal economic policy. Cabildos could lead the residents of a region in armed rebellion when the crown sought to stop contraband by eliminating their only lucrative trade item, as happened in Tenerife in 1655.[47] That this reaction did not occur in Caracas suggests that the political elite of the town was either not trade-minded, as Pike had supposed, or was committed to the commercial exchange of some other product. In light of the importance of the wheat trade, which was still very active in 1606 and 1607, this latter possibility seems to be the more plausible.

An examination of the existing *almojarifazgo* (customs duty) records, which for the brief period 1603 to 1607 registered all of Caracas's legal trade,[48] allows a test of the hypothesis that a longstanding commitment to the wheat trade led the cabildo to seek to limit, perhaps even to eliminate, commerce in tobacco. The *almojarifazgo* registry lists every individual who imported and exported at La Guaira. To determine which of these traders were Caracas vecinos a variety of sources was most carefully surveyed. Of exceptional utility were the parish baptismal and marriage registries and a 1603 road-tax assessment made of all vecinos by the cabildo. Also invaluable was a document listing all non-Hispanic vecinos, including Portuguese, who were resident in Caracas in 1607.[49] So comprehensive are these sources for this short period of time that it is highly likely that every vecino who paid the *almojarifazgo* tax on his agricultural exports from 1603 to 1607 has been identified as a vecino, either Hispanic or foreign (including Portuguese in the foreigner category). Those traders who paid the tax but have not been located in the Caracas sources, with very little likelihood of error, are therefore considered *forasteros*, or non-vecinos.

Most of the wheat exported from Caracas, some 84 percent, was shipped during the months from May to August. Both vecinos and non-vecinos did most of their wheat business during this season (fig. 2). The major difference between the wheat commerce of

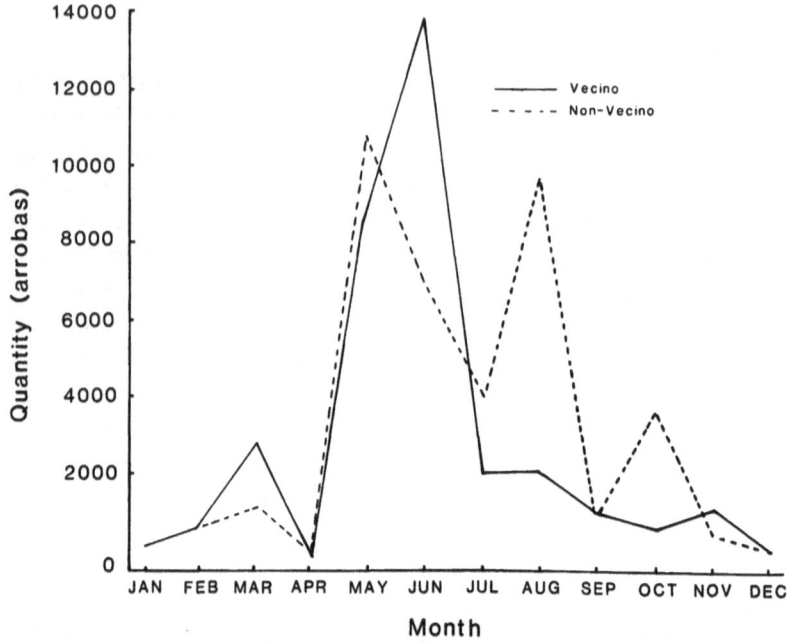

Fig 2. Caracas Wheat Flour to Indies Ports Vecinos and Non-Vecinos, 1603–1607

Vecinos and non-vecinos traded wheat during the same season, principally May to August, but they shipped to different destinations, vecinos preferring Cartagena and non-vecinos other ports (fig. 3).

vecinos and that of non-vecinos was the destinations of shipments. Vecinos preferred Cartagena, where they sent their grain in May and June, while non-vecinos did business in other Caribbean ports, returning to Cartagena in July and August after the vecinos had already made their sales there (fig. 3). The tobacco trade, like the flour trade, boomed in May and continued active for several months thereafter. Again like flour, once the season ended virtually nothing was traded until the following spring. For the four years for which complete data are available, 1604 through 1607, 88.8 percent of all Caracas tobacco exports (7954 arrobas) were made during the months from May to September (fig. 4a). Of this quantity, Caracas Hispanic vecinos shipped 51 percent (4062 arrobas), foreign vecinos 15 percent (1219 arrobas), and non-vecinos 34 percent (2673 arrobas). The August 1605 ban does not seem to have had much impact on the foreign vecinos of Caracas, most of

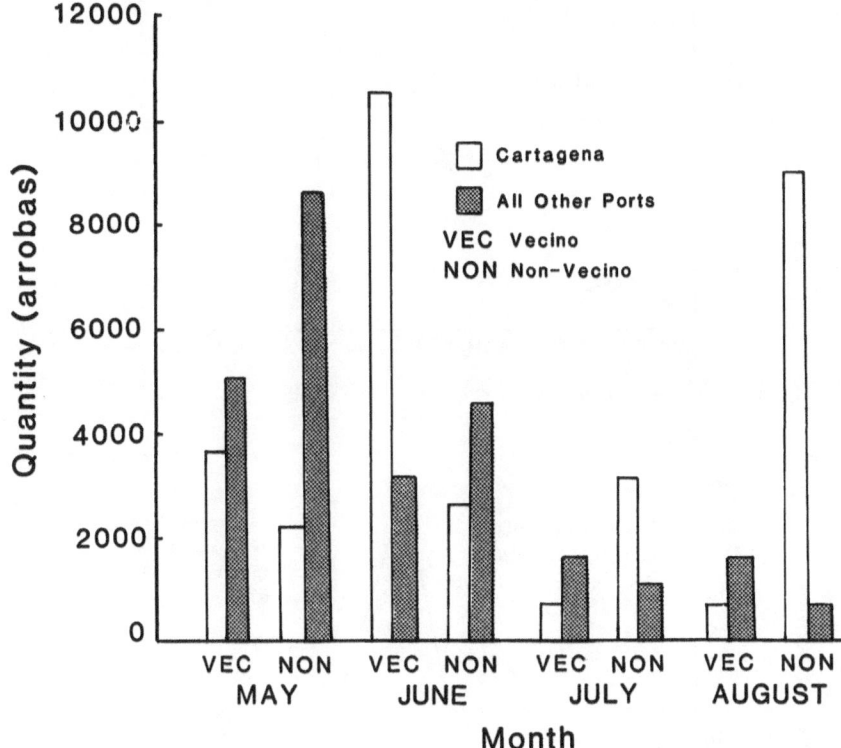

Fig. 3. Caracas Wheat to Indies Ports, May to August, 1603–1607
 May–August Totals: 57,618 arrobas, 84.4% of all wheat shipped 1603–1607; 26,066 arrobas by vecinos, 84.7% of all vecino wheat; 31,552 arrobas by non-vecinos, 84.2% of all non-vecino wheat.
 31,940 arrobas to Cartagena, 46.8% of all wheat shipped 1603–1607; 15,016 arrobas by vecinos to Cartagena, 48.8% of all vecino wheat; 16,924 arrobas by non-vecinos to Cartagena, 45.1% of all non-vecino wheat.

whom were Portuguese; they shipped 7 percent of the total quantity of tobacco exported in 1605, 18 percent of the 1606 exports (the first full year of the prohibition), and, in 1607, foreign vecinos again exported 18 percent of the total.[50] As with wheat, vecinos traded a month or so earlier than did outsiders, exporting substantial quantities of tobacco in June. Non-vecinos, who may have had to sell merchandise in Caracas before they could buy wheat or tobacco, exported twice as much tobacco in July as in any other month (fig. 4b).

Much the greater part of the tobacco exports from Caracas went

38   *The Seventeenth Century*

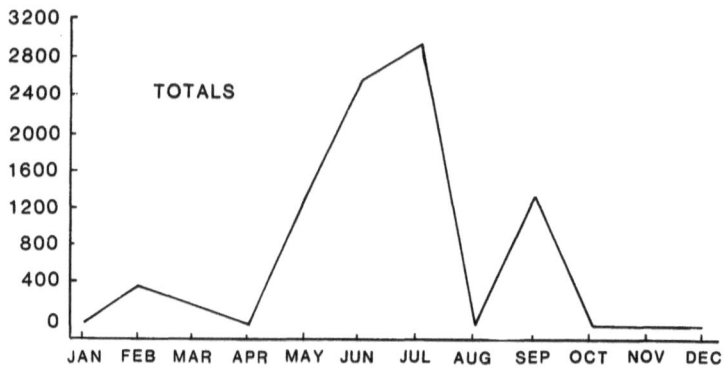

Fig. 4a   Caracas Tobacco Exports, 1604–1607, Totals

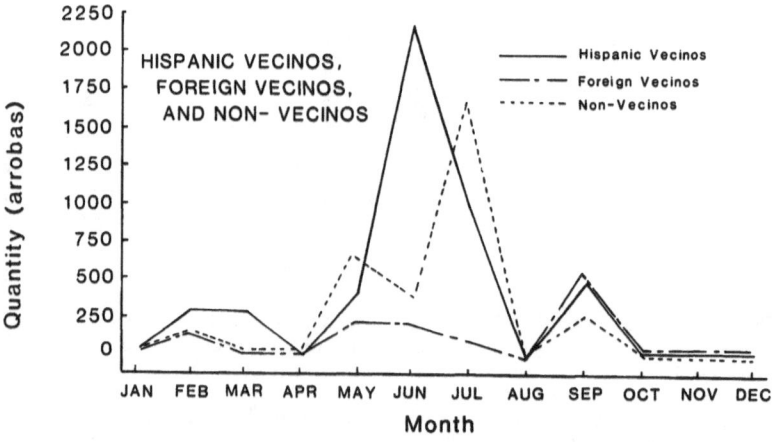

Fig. 4b   Caracas Tobacco Exports, 1604–1607, Hispanic Vecinos, Foreign Vecinos, and Non-Vecinos

to Seville—86 percent (6826 arrobas) of the May to September four-year total. The remainder was sent to Cartagena, and most of the Cartagena-bound tobacco was shipped by Hispanic vecinos. Indeed, foreign vecinos and non-vecinos only loaded tobacco for Cartagena in minimal quantities and only in June, usually to take advantage of the wheat boats that departed La Guaira then to meet the flota. Hispanic vecinos also preferred to sell tobacco in the Seville market, sending twice as much there as they did to Cartagena (fig. 5).

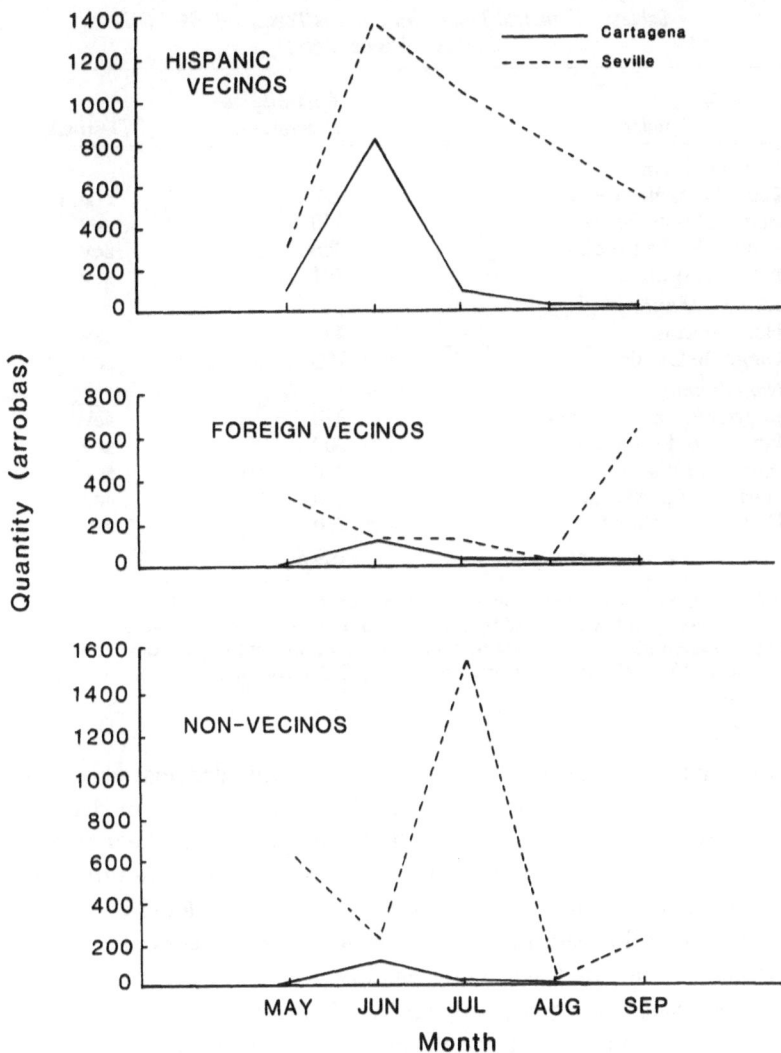

Fig. 5 Tobacco to Seville and to Cartagena, May to September

Identifying by name the principal tobacco traders (table 2) reveals that, of those who exported 200 arrobas or more, only one, Garci González de Silva, sent tobacco to ports other than Seville. The other three Hispanic vecinos who were major tobacco traders, Pedro Blanco de Ponte, Alonso Rodríguez Santos, and Juan de Aguirre, were newcomers in Caracas and they traded exclusively

Table 2 Principal Traders in Caracas Tobacco, 1604–1607
(200 Arrobas or More)

Traders	Quantity (in arrobas)	Destinations
Hispanic Vecinos		
Garci González de Silva	922	cna, pro
Pedro Blanco Ponte	540	sev
Alonso Rodríguez Santos	385	sev
Juan de Aguirre	294	sev
Foreign Vecinos		
Hernán Luis	495	sev
Diego de Ovalle	203	sev
Non-Vecinos		
Jorge Núñez de Acosta	320	sev
Francisco de Avotes	300	sev
Melchor Luis	270	sev
Hernán López de Acosta	240	sev
Diego de Colunga	200	sev
Total Quantity:	4169 arrobas	

Source: AGN, Real Hacienda, legs. 3, 5, 6. See chap. 1, nn. 14 and 49.

The total quantity exported by these eleven men, 4169 arrobas, represents 46.6% of all tobacco traded from 1604 to 1607. The amounts sent to each destination are: Seville (sev), 3247 arrobas; Cartagena (cna), 812 arrobas; Puerto Rico (pro), 110 arrobas.

with Spain. By contrast, most of the Hispanic vecinos who were principal wheat traders (table 3) had been in Caracas for decades prior to 1603–1607. As a group the Hispanic vecino wheat traders were, as their counterparts who exported tobacco were not, both closely aligned with the Cartagena market and holders of cabildo posts and other administrative positions in Caracas. Excepting Garci González de Silva, who was involved in nearly every available business enterprise, this Caracas political elite only dabbled in the tobacco trade in a marginal way, as a minor supplement to their wheat business in Cartagena.

Several of these principal wheat traders had more in common with one another than merely their political prominence and their Cartagena interests. Of the ten most active wheat traders who were also Caracas vecinos (Hispanic and foreign), six were aligned with one another by one or more social or kinship obligations. Nofre Carrasquer, Juan de Guevara, and Diego Vásquez de Escovedo were brothers-in-law. Two of Garci González de Silva's sons mar-

Table 3 Principal Traders in Caracas Wheat Flour, 1603–1607
(1000 Arrobas or More)

Traders	Quantity (in arrobas)	Destinations
Hispanic Vecinos		
Juan de Guevara	4150	cna, pro, sdo
Juan de Aguirre	3242	cna, pro, mta
Nofre Carrasquer	3154	cna, pro, sdo
Diego de Villanueva	2153	cna
Garci González de Silva	2060	cna, pro
Alonso Rodríguez Santos	1875	cna
Diego Vásquez de Escovedo	1300	cna, pro
Antonio Rodríguez Jaramillo	1000	cna
Foreign Vecinos		
Diego Díaz León	1450	cna, pro, sdo
Francisco de Caravajal	1250	pro, sdo
Non-Vecinos		
Sebastián de Bengoechea	8400	cna, mta
Francisco de Estrada	3292	cna, pro
Gonzalo Hernández	3020	cna, pro, sdo
Gaspar Martín	1500	cna
Francisco Hernández	1140	cna
Total Quantity:	38,986 arrobas	

Source: AGN, Real Hacienda, legs. 3, 5, 6. See chap. 1, nn. 14 and 49.

The total quantity exported by these fifteen men, 38,986 arrobas, was 57.1% of all flour traded 1603–1607. The amounts sent to each destination are: Cartagena (cna), 24, 454 arrobas; Puerto Rico (pro), 7465 arrobas; Santo Domingo (sdo), 4050 arrobas; Margarita (mta), 3017 arrobas.

ried two Guevara daughters. González de Silva was godfather to Diego de Villanueva's first child, born to fourteen-year-old Catalina Mejía some months after their marriage in 1602. Diego Vásquez de Escovedo accepted the same responsibility for the son of Antonio Rodríguez Jaramillo, master tailor and wheat trader. With the exception of Rodríguez Jaramillo, these men had all served as alcaldes ordinarios of the cabildo on at least one occasion; Diego de Villanueva, Diego Vásquez de Escovedo, Juan de Guevara, and Garci González de Silva were *regidores perpetuos*; and Juan de Guevara had served as lieutenant governor. Some members of this group also made exports of tobacco—Garci González de Silva (922 arrobas), Deigo de Villanueva (68 arrobas), Diego Vásquez de Escovedo (40 arrobas)—but they sent it exclusively with their wheat to the Cartagena market.

The remaining four of the ten most active vecino wheat traders had no visible relationship to one another, nor were they holders of prestigious and powerful office. Francisco de Caravajal and Diego León were Portuguese; Diaz León was the town's slave factor. Juan de Aguirre lived in a house in 1605 that was rented to traders who were in Caracas only for the season to secure cargoes, and Alonso Rodríguez Santos, a merchant from Extremadura who would become the patriarch of an important Caracas family, was first elected to political office and began to acquire community influence only after his marriage in 1607 to Melchora de Vera Ibargoyen, the daughter of a Caracas founder.[51]

The four unrelated Hispanic vecinos were more interested in the tobacco trade to Seville than they were in the wheat trade to Cartagena. Without local influence and authority, they were unable to prevent the restrictions placed on tobacco by men with more power and different commercial interests. However, as the next chapter makes clear, it will be these less-powerful tobacco traders, together with other vecinos of marginal status, such as the Portuguese encomendero Diego de Ovalle, and immigrants not yet resident in Caracas in 1607, who first discover the substantial profits to be realized from cacao and African slavery. For all their authority at the turn of the seventeenth century, few members of the interrelated wheat group successfully made the transition from encomienda labor, wheat, and the Cartagena market to slavery, cacao, and the Mexican market.

All this suggests the existence in Caracas during the first decade of the seventeenth century of what might be best called a faction, a group of men unified by possession of local political power and by kinship, who had little direct interest in the tobacco trade. They were therefore free to be rigorous about controlling this trade, even to the point of threatening to eliminate tobacco planting altogether. By securing the license policy and ban on exports they did not intend to permanently jeopardize the profits that might be realized from the cultivation of tobacco, in fact, to prevent competition the cabildo refused to allow tobacco seeds to be taken to Spain in 1605.[52] Rather, they sought to protect the established shipping on which they had come to depend. Committed as they had been for more than two decades to the Cartagena market and the outfitting of the flota there, it was in the interest of these individuals to control tobacco closely and to reduce the attraction to enemy corsairs that it represented. The eager participation in this of Sancho de Alquiza, governor of Venezuela from 1606 to 1611, lends credence to the idea that there was more to the 1606 ban than zeal to comply with royal directives against smuggling and a prevailing prejudice against Portuguese tobacco farmers. Alquiza had served as captain of ocean galleons, and he knew the Indies trade well. As son-in-law of Martín de las Alas, governor in Cartagena, he was no doubt familiar with the commercial interests in that port, and the fact that during his residence in Caracas he served as godfather only to officials of the crown and to Cartagena-faction families, the González de Silva, the Guevara, and the Carrasquer, may be taken as further proof that a preference for continued commercial relations with Cartagena, and the wheat business there in particular, shaped the strict tobacco policies of the Caracas elite.[53]

The effort of a few powerful men to gain a greater portion of the wheat and flour production in Caracas and to favor their established ties with Cartagena was to a large extent what determined the cabildo decisions to change the ejido boundaries in 1608 and to closely circumscribe tobacco cultivation and commerce after 1605. The institutional authority of the cabildo was a useful means to the achievement of these objectives, but only in a limited, short-term sense, for there was nothing to be done about the restricted land and water resources in the Caracas Valley or the resurgence of effective competition from Andean wheat farmers who traded from Maracaibo. In addition, Indian labor was always in short supply in Caracas, and only a few of the more successful vecinos, those like Nofre Carrasquer and Alonso Rodríguez Santos who were successful merchants first and encomenderos and wheat farmers afterwards, were able to purchase African slaves in quantity to augment their modest encomiendas. Wheat profits were sufficient to create a radical reorientation of the economic structure of Caracas, and in this context of change certain individuals collaborated and conspired to form policies that would assure them of an increasing share of such profits, but by the second decade of the seventeenth century wheat agriculture and trade had reached its natural and commercial limits in Caracas. Town politics could do nothing to extend these limits. Brought to importance by the wheat trade, the cabildo would not be able to control in any significant way the commercialization of the next export crop, cacao, whose dominance in the Caracas regional economy began, with most interesting consequences for the composition of the local society, at just the time when wheat could be developed no further.

2

Cacao in the Seventeenth Century: The First Boom

A report to the king by the royal treasurer don Diego de Villanueva indicates that by 1607 Caracas had developed a modest trade in a variety of agricultural items, hides, and crude cotton cloth (see table 4). For the most part, the hides went with the tobacco and sarsaparilla to Spain, while wheat and the other items found markets in Cartagena and other Caribbean ports. On the other side of the ledger, imports to Caracas consisted principally of Spanish dry goods, Canarian and Andalusian wines and olive oil, and a few African slaves. Only rarely were import duties paid on luxury merchandise, a bolt of Chinese silk or silver tableware for instance, and these goods were usually brought to the colony only by those few Caraqueños who exported tobacco, wheat, or hides in quantity. Equally rare in the royal tax register is the record of imported slaves. An occasional notation mentions several slaves bought in a lot from a supposed "forced entry" ship, and these were also purchased by men identified as major exporters.[1] By 1607 the more common of these imported goods had reached—in small amounts, to be sure—as far as the San Sebastián cattle district, thirty leagues south of Caracas. They were paid for there with hides, tobacco, cotton, and "some cacao," the only reference in the Villanueva report to the tropical plant that would shortly revolutionize the Caracas economy.[2]

The origins of cacao cultivation in this part of the New World are obscure. The plant is not mentioned in the *relaciones geográficas* of the sixteenth century or in any other official documents from the Caracas area before 1607. Most likely for this reason it is commonly assumed that the first cacao trees on the Venezuelan coast were planted there by native and African laborers at the command of Europeans. And yet, from only 0.5 percent of the total value of

Table 4 Caracas Exports, 1607

Product	Quantity		Unit Value (reales)	Total Value (reales)	Percentage Total Value
Tobacco	1,362	arrobas	25	34,050	42.9
Flour	7,127	arrobas	4	28,508	35.9
Hides	651		8	5,208	6.6
Sugar	139	arrobas	30	4,170	5.2
Sarsaparilla	75	quintales	50	3,750	4.7
Cotton Cloth	800	varas	3	2,400	3.0
Biscuit	45	arrobas	16	720	.9
Cacao	4.5	fanegas	96	432	.5
Cheese	25	arrobas	9	225	.3
				79,463	100.0

Source: AGN, Real Hacienda, legs. 3, 5, 6, passim, *almajarifazgo* tax. A similar table, with slightly different values, is to be found in Eduardo Arcila Farías, *Economía colonial de Venezuela* (Mexico City, 1946), 68. The year 1607 is the last for which we can be sure that all legal exports were recorded; see chap. 2, n. 5.

Caracas's exports in 1607, cacao became the region's foremost item of trade before 1650. It seems unlikely that this boom could have been created from newly planted trees, especially given the difficult labor situation of the colony. In fact, the earliest inventories of coastal cacao groves indicate that the first trees to be harvested were native to the region. Labeled *árboles viejos de la tierra*, or simply *de la tierra*, in the documents, these were almost certainly indigenous plants, both because the phrase itself, "of the land," virtually means as much, and because the estimated ages of the inventoried trees show that many of them were already standing when Hispanic commercialization of cacao began.

A family of Basque immigrants named Liendo was among the very first to ship Caracas cacao beans to Mexico; their first lot was sent to Veracruz in 1628. A quarter of a century later, in 1653, an inventory of the Liendo estate in the coastal valley of Cepi showed a total of 12,382 trees. Only 1165 had been planted during the previous twenty-five years, and the ages of these trees, labeled *árboles de Trujillo*, were known exactly. The remainder, 11,217 *árboles de la tierra*, were dated only as "more than twenty-five years old," which certainly means that the Liendo family found them standing in the valley when they arrived at Cepi in the late 1620s.

The best proof that cacao was native to the Caracas region, however, is a firsthand observation to that effect. In 1618, Juan de Ibarra, a Basque merchant, sent Portuguese encomendero Deigo de Ovalle cloth, wheat, wine, pepper, cinnamon, and copper worth 17,099 reales. According to their contract, these items were to be paid for with cacao gathered from the trees that grew wild on Ovalle's Choroní estate. Two years later, in a legal suit brought before the bishop, Ibarra complained that since no one had been much interested in the cacao trade in 1618, he had done Ovalle a favor by offering to take his cacao in exchange for merchandise and spices. But Ovalle, pointing out that the contract did not designate who should be responsible for shipping the cacao, had refused to pay to have Ibarra's beans taken to La Guaira. Months passed while the two men argued, and the market value of the beans fell by half. In his deposition, Ibarra gave evidence that leaves no doubt about the origins of cacao cultivation and commerce:

> Since I am a merchant, there will be no question [when I say] that in this city there was no cacao trade when the said *capitán* Diego de Ovalle bought my goods and sold me his cacao. [Only] because there came news that cacao was valuable did the vecinos get together and plant it; in other words, when the [Ovalle] sale was made, there was only wild cacao.[3]

Whether the first large quantities of cacao to be exported from Caracas were harvested from indigenous stands or from groves planted by laborers under the direction of Europeans is a question of more than academic importance. Murdo MacLeod is certain that the traditional source of cacao beans in the New Spain market, the Central American groves of Soconusco and Izalcos, were replaced in the 1620s by Caracas and Guayaquil.[4] Evidently the South American beans were preferred for their flavor, but even with taste in their favor, it is doubtful that in such a short time Caracas growers, located so much farther from Mexico than their Central American counterparts and with no important labor advantage, could have planted enough trees to capture a significant share of the New Spain cacao trade.

A related problem has to do with the very success of this commerce. Once begun, the export of cacao from Caracas expanded at a remarkable rate. The aggregate data compiled by Eduardo Arcila Farías, even though deficient because they do not include the exports of tax-exempt Caracas vecinos, still indicate a threefold increase in cacao shipped between the early 1630s and the late 1650s.[5] This expansion can be accounted for in part by new groves planted during these years; we know that much of the work of clearing and irrigating the land was done by African slaves who, in all probability, had been purchased with profits made in the 1620s and 1630s. These profits would have come as the result of very cheap encomienda labor at work in virgin cacao *arboledas*. That Caracas growers were able both to sell their beans at a competitive price in the Mexican market and purchase hundreds of slaves with the income from these sales would seem to have depended on the existence of substantial groves of indigenous cacao trees.

One clue to this process comes from the record of the Mexican Inquisition. Many of the prosperous Portuguese traders who were accused of being Jews by the Inquisition in the late 1630s and early 1640s had been active in the slave trade and the Caracas-to-Mexico cacao trade.[6] This fact suggests the following hypothesis: Caracas vecinos exchanged cacao for Africans at a rate that allowed the Portuguese slave traders–cacao merchants to undersell the Central American cacao dealers in New Spain. Eager to sell their fragile human cargoes as soon after the Atlantic crossing as possible, the slavers needed no large margin of profit in Caracas because they stood to make substantial gains in Mexico on the cacao that they took in return for slaves. In this way, Caraqueños both obtained slaves at a moderate price and found an outlet for their cacao.[7]

Concrete evidence shows that during the infant years of the cacao trade the initial advantage went to a small number of encomenderos with grants located along the Caribbean coast. Seventeenth-century Caracas encomiendas were of the archaic, *servicio personal* type. Rather than collect a fixed sum, or *tributo*, from their Indians, encomenderos expropriated their labor directly: that is, Indians were put to work gathering beans, planting new groves, or carrying on any other activity considered profitable or useful by the encomendero. Caracas encomenderos insisted that their Indians could not produce anything of value to be used as tribute, and by claiming abject poverty they resisted until the end of the century every attempt by the crown to eliminate *servicio personal*.[8] A royal order demanding conversion to tribute collection was received in Caracas in 1621, but it was not acted upon by

Governor Juan de Tribiño Guillamas. When his successor Gil de la Sierpe attempted to execute the king's will, he was arrested by order of the cabildo and sent under guard to Spain.[9] In 1633, in response to this act of lese majesty, the crown called for a new study of the Caracas encomiendas. The data compiled in compliance with this decree provide several clues to the relationship between encomienda labor and cacao cultivation at the very beginning of the trade with Mexico.

This document, written in about 1635, presents four series of facts: the names of the encomenderos and the titles of social distinction (*don* or *doña, maestre de campo, capitán,* and so forth) of those who were so identified; the geographical location of the encomiendas; the number of Indian tributaries in each grant; and a specific value in pesos defined only as the *renta* of each encomienda.[10] That this value represents the annual income of each grant is confirmed by an existing fragment of the church tithe record. *Diezmos* collected for the region described in treasury documents as *"costa del mar y caraballeda"* totaled 2600 pesos and 2979 pesos for the years 1632 and 1634 respectively.[11] These amounts correspond very closely to what would have been the Church's 10-percent share of the 27,450 pesos of total renta for the twenty-five encomiendas located along the *"costa del mar de la jurisdicción de Caracas,"* according to the 1635 list (Region 1 in table 5 and Map 2).

At that time, 3310 Indian tributaries were to be found divided unevenly among 100 encomiendas held by vecinos of three Spanish towns: Santiago de León de Caracas, Nueva Valencia del Rey, and San Sebastián de los Reyes. The surveyed area, comprising the legal jurisdictions of this triangle of towns, can be divided into four zones of agricultural production. Region 1, designated Coastal Caracas, includes all the narrow Venezuelan coastline from present-day Chuspa to Puerto Cabello. Here the conditions are good for cacao cultivation. Prevailing winds release moisture accumulated during the Atlantic crossing as they collide with coastal mountains, providing a moderate but constant supply of water to the hot, cloud-covered valleys that rise steeply from the edge of the sea. One-fourth of the encomiendas counted in 1635 were located in Region 1. In Region 2, Interior Caracas, a few Indians worked in isolated sugar trapiches on the banks of the Guarenas and Guaire Rivers, but the majority of native laborers in this region were second- and third-

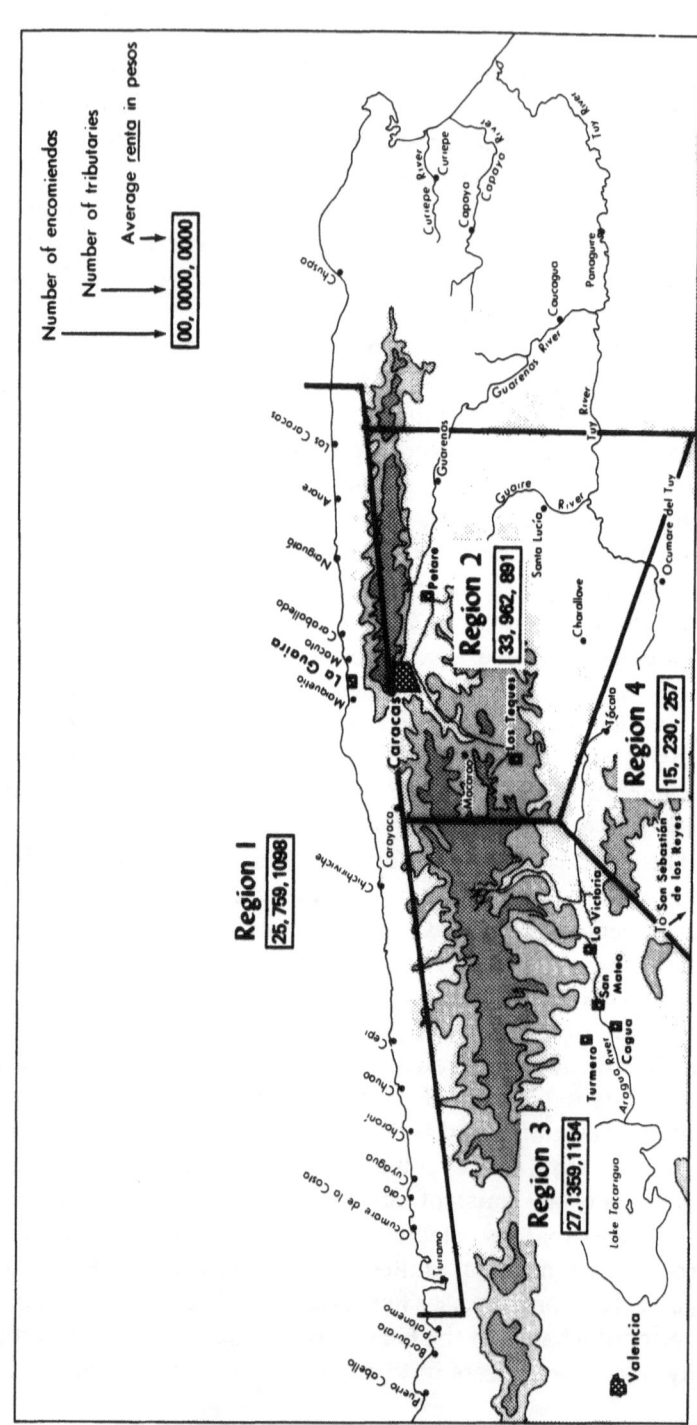

Map 2. Encomiendas, 1635

generation wheat farm and flour mill workers. Since the 1580s their toil had served a steady Spanish demand for bread, and in 1635 there were more encomiendas (thirty-three) in this temperate climate zone than in any other. Region 3, Interior Valencia, is the long, broad valley west of Caracas that forms at the inland base of the coastal mountains. In this area, described by archaeologist Cornelius Osgood as "probably the most hospitable site for a hungry population,"[12] the densest preconquest Indian population in central Venezuela had been divided into the province's largest encomiendas a decade before the foundation of Caracas. Thus concentrated, Valencia Indians survived as an ethnic group to become sharecroppers in that area in the nineteenth century.

By contrast, many of the Indians of the poor and distant San Sebastián district, Region 4, would be removed from their homeland during the early 1600s. Too few and too thinly scattered to be organized into encomiendas, in many cases the most profitable use of the San Sebastián natives was their capture and sale to Spaniards whose agricultural enterprises were more directly integrated with the marketplace. Slave raids were still formally organized and carried out in this frontier zone in the 1640s.[13] The few small encomiendas in San Sebastián in 1635 were employed exclusively in cattle ranching.

The most profitable encomiendas in 1635 were the large grants located in Region 3, the Valencia–Aragua Valley. Three hundred and fifty tributaries, the largest native labor force in the province, worked a sugar trapiche at Turmero and produced an annual renta of 4000 pesos for their encomendero, don Juan Martínez de Villegas. However, it was only because their grants held more tributaries that the Valencia encomenderos received relatively more income. Indians at labor on the coastal cacao haciendas and in the wheat fields north and east of Caracas returned a greater per-capita renta to their encomenderos. In terms of the value of each tributary's labor, average income from Region 3 encomiendas (23.1 pesos per tributary per annum) amounted to only two-thirds that of the coast (36.6 pesos) and three-fourths that of the immediate Caracas hinterland (30.7 pesos) (see table 5).

One of the several possible reasons for the lower labor profitability of these larger encomiendas was the high cost of transport from the fertile but landlocked Valencia–Aragua zone. Regular com-

Table 5 Encomiendas ca. 1635

Region:	(1) Coastal Caracas	(2) Interior Caracas	(3) Interior Valencia	(4) Interior San Sebastián	Province Overall
No. encomiendas	25	33	27	15	100
No. tributaries	759	962	1,359	230	3,310
Average no. of tributaries/encomienda	30	29	50	15	33
Total *renta* (pesos)	27,450	29,403	31,158	3,855	91,866
Average *renta*/encomienda (pesos)	1,098	891	1,154	257	908
Average *renta*/tributary (pesos)	36.6	30.7	23.1	16.7	27.6

Source: AGN, Fundación de Trujillo, leg. 10, fols. 335–346.

merce across the coastal mountains was difficult except at Caracas, where a break in the range provided relatively easy access to the sea. To reach Caracas from the west, agricultural produce was carried along the banks of first the Aragua and then the Guaire rivers. Except during the dry summer months from March to May, travel along these rivers was frequently interrupted by floods and was therefore difficult and expensive. Even as late as 1841, carriage costs from the Aragua River to port at La Guaira were equal to shipping charges paid to transport the same commodities from La Guaira to Liverpool.[14]

By 1635 encomienda labor was clearly most profitable in the coastal cacao zone. Coastal encomiendas produced an annual renta of about six pesos more per tributary than encomiendas in the traditionally profitable wheat-farming areas (36.6 pesos per annum in Region 1; 30.7 pesos in Region 2). With a similar population norm of twenty-nine or thirty tributaries, the annual income from a coastal grant was therefore about 200 pesos, or 20 percent, more than a year's earnings from a typical encomienda near Caracas. In itself, this difference, something less than the value of one African slave, does not adequately reflect the impact that the bonanza Mexican market for cacao had already had on Caracas society by the 1630s. More revealing is the cabildo's lament in 1626 that the lure of greater profits from coastal cacao arboledas was drawing Hispanic *labradores* from the wheat farms. Without their labradores—overseers who were willing to administer Indian labor in return for a share of the harvest—wheat farm encomenderos feared that they would be unable to bring a worthwhile crop to market.[15]

Cacao created fluidity at more than one level of early seventeenth-century Caracas society. Evidence from the 1635 document indicates that most of the richest coastal Indian grants were in the hands of recent immigrants to Caracas. Of twenty-three encomiendas with an annual *renta* of 1500 pesos or more, incomes comparable to those of the most profitable cacao encomiendas in Central America at the middle of the sixteenth century,[16] eight were located in the Valencia–Aragua region, eight near the town of Caracas, and seven on the coast. A measure of the local social standing of the holders of these high-income grants can be derived from the document compiler's recognition of some of them as "don" or "doña."[17] In the long-established regions of Valencia and Caracas, nearly two-thirds (ten of sixteen) of the encomiendas valued at 1500 pesos or more renta belonged to a "don" or "doña" in 1635, but only one of the seven holders of high-renta coastal encomiendas was distinguished by this suggestion of *hidalguía* (see table 6). Who were these seventeenth-century parvenus with profitable encomiendas on the inhospitable coastal fringe of Caracas society?

Enough biographical data can be gathered on four of the seven

Table 6 Encomiendas ca. 1635 With Renta of at least 1500 Pesos

Region:	(1) Coastal Caracas	(2) Interior Caracas	(3) Interior Valencia	(4) Interior San Sebastián	Province Overall
No. encomiendas with *renta* of at least 1500 pesos	7*	8	8	0	23
No. of these encomiendas held by dons and doñas	1	5	5	0	11

Source: AGN, Fundación de Trujillo, leg. 10, fols. 335–346.

*The seven coastal encomiendas of at least 1500-pesos *renta* in Region 1 may well have belonged to the eight unidentified vecinos described in 1628 as having "considerable wealth in *haciendas de cacao*." *Actas del Cabildo de Caracas*, 12 vols. (Caracas, 1943–1975), 6:266.

to allow for a composite rendering of these first important cacao producers, the very first of the *grandes cacaos*, as they would be called by subsequent generations. One was Portuguese. There were several Portuguese among the poorer encomenderos, but Diego de Ovalle was the only individual of this nationality whose grant was valued at 1500 pesos or more annual income. Alejandro Blanco Ponte was a Canary Islander: his father was from Tenerife, his mother from Flanders. His brother Pedro Blanco Ponte had been in Caracas since at least 1619 when he declared himself a vecino "without estancia or land" and asked the cabildo for a plot near the La Guaira road where he could pasture his pack mules. Alejandro did not leave Tenerife until after 1627, the year when the Casa de la Contratación formally prohibited direct trade between the Canaries and the Indies.[18] A third encomendero was Pedro de Liendo, a Vizcayan and the nephew of a retired admiral of the galleon fleet. Pedro and his brothers Santiago and Domingo de Liendo (they were not encomenderos) were perhaps Caracas's most ambitious cacao planters during the first half of the seventeenth century. The fourth grantholder for whom biographical information has been found, don José Rengifo Pimentel, was born in Santo Domingo, where his father was captain of the port and his grandfather had been a royal treasury accountant. The only encomendero on the coast whose rights to Indian labor earned him 1500 pesos or more annually and who was also classified as a "don" on the 1635 list, Rengifo Pimentel had in fact four encomiendas (which was illegal), three on the coast and one on the Guarenas River, east of Caracas. With a total of two hundred tributaries and an annual income from them of 6250 pesos, don José was Caracas's foremost encomendero.[19]

The first of these men to settle in Caracas was Diego de Ovalle. In 1602 he married the youngest daughter of don Juan Vásquez de Rojas, a descendant of Caracas conquistadors in both maternal and paternal lines, and received an encomienda at Choroní as part of his wife's dowry. Ovalle was born in the Vila do Mojadoiro on the upper Douro River in the Portuguese province of Tras-os-Montes. There his family had vineyards and fruit orchards, the produce of which had been sent traditionally to Medina del Campo and Valladolid. With central Spain in depression at the end of the sixteenth century, Tras-os-Montes became part of the burgeoning economic system of

Seville, and there Ovalle established commercial relations that he maintained throughout his life. These connections, and those he evidently had with the Portuguese slavers who monopolized the supply of African labor to the Caribbean, were no doubt of some interest in Caracas. In 1607, the slave factor and six of the town's encomenderos, including Ovalle, were from Portugal.[20]

He was also a shrewd trader. In 1618 Ovalle sold one of the first lots of cacao ever to leave the Caracas coast to the Basque merchant Juan de Ibarra. Ibarra sent wheat flour, spices, and dry goods to Choroní and waited for his cacao to arrive at the La Guaira wharf. These were the infant years of cacao commerce, however, and this was Ibarra's first purchase. In the future, contracts would specify the location of delivery, either *"puesto puerto La Guayra"* or *"puesto costa del mar,"* but on this occasion Ovalle, who had not made arrangements to do so, refused to ship the beans at his cost to La Guaira. Ibarra, having already given merchandise for the much-wanted cacao, had no choice but to send for it and to pay the transportation charges himself.[21]

Ovalle made a good deal of money selling cacao, and he used his wealth to protect himself from problems that might arise, both because he was Portuguese and because the cacao business was in its unsettled infancy. An appeal for funds by the crown or the cabildo would find him by far the most generous contributor.[22] However, unlike others of his economic position, he did not acquire municipal office, and neither he nor his wife owned town property. They were permanent residents at Choroní, and it was there that they made their principal investment: African slaves. This was an investment against any misfortune and one that those who survived the prolonged depression of the 1650s and 1660s seemed to have made freely while cacao sales were brisk and highly profitable. By 1626 Ovalle had added fifty slaves to his 1602 encomienda work force of thirty-six Indian tributaries. This number had risen to eighty-four African and creole bondsmen in 1644, and by 1650, the year of his death, Ovalle was master of ninety-four slaves.[23]

The inventory of Ovalle's Choroní estate provides a glimpse at the material life constructed from Indian and African labor and fifty years of vigorous trading. Although primitive by Mexico City or Cartagena standards, the principal house at Choroní was comparable to any Caracas dwelling at that time. It was a simply furnished, two-story stone structure with a tile roof. Two gilded mirrors, a cedar table and chairs, and a silver service for six were the items of greatest value. A dozen books, including Antonio de Herrera's *Historia de las Indias*, occupied a shelf.[24] The upstairs rooms contained just the touch of luxury in a style already common to Caracas cacao exporters: two carved cedar chests imported from New Spain and a four-poster bed covered with a Mexican quilt and pillows of Chinese silk reflected the importance of the market where Ovalle had made his modest fortune.[25]

Close by were the other buildings used for maintaining the estate and preparing cacao for shipment. A substantial wooden storehouse doubled in the upper loft as a drying shed. Carpentry tools and a forge, both used by African artisans, were kept in a second structure. The slaves' quarters, because they represented no value to Ovalle, were not included in the inventory of his holdings, but the livestock and agricultural implements used to produce the food to feed them were counted: seven milk cows, a hundred head of cattle, six teams of oxen with harnesses, several plows, hoes, and a variety of other tools filled out the list. The absence of expensive consumer goods may well have been the consequence of Ovalle's considerable investment in slaves. At 1650s prices, the Choroní blacks were worth no less than 24,000 pesos.[26]

Less is known about the agricultural estates and business activities of the three Spaniards who have been identified as being among the first of the Caracas cacao encomenderos. The last will and testament of Pedro de Liendo has survived. Like Ovalle, Liendo's principal expenditure was for African slaves. In 1635, his encomienda at Chuao was made up of thirty-five tributaries. In 1659, in addition to the estate house and tools, he owned a warehouse and two stores in La Guaira, a sloop to carry his cacao there, and 106 slaves.[27] For their part, the Blanco Ponte brothers participated directly in the slave trade; as buyers and brokers their credit was respected from Lisbon to Loanda to Cartagena. In May 1640, Pedro Blanco Ponte bought forty-eight slaves from Francisco Arias de Aquilena, a vecino of Cartagena and agent to don Francisco de Vasconcelos de Acuña, governor of Angola, on credit at the bargain price of 160 pesos each (the current Caracas price was about 250 pesos).[28] There is no will for don Rengifo Pimentel and no record of slaves held or sold by him.

The major significance for Caracas of this group of men, a Portuguese, a Basque, a Canary Islander, and a creole born in Santo Domingo, may lie in the fact that they were all men of seaborne and commercial experience. At the same time, they were not dependent on Seville or Cartagena and the traditional flota system, then in decline, which had provided a demand for Caracas wheat since the 1580s. Their entrepreneurial talents and their trading contracts in new regions, Africa, the Canaries, and Caribbean ports, made them first welcome in Caracas and then part of its propertied elite. They all married well in that soon after their marriages they obtained encomiendas on the basis of the station and merits of their Caracas-born wives' families.

Don Rengifo Pimentel married the Caracas cattle heiress doña Francisca Gámez and in her name and his held the four encomiendas already mentioned, including two on the coast worth 1000 and 3000 pesos per annum. Pedro de Liendo's wife was the wealthy doña Catalina Mexía. The granddaughter of Mérida (Venezuela) governor Suárez del Castillo, at her death—having outlived Liendo and two subsequent husbands—doña Catalina founded an *obra pía* on the encomienda and cacao groves at Chuao. While the encomienda was worth about 1600 pesos annually during the period of Liendo's possession, in time this estate became the most valuable ecclesiastical property in colonial Caracas. Alejandro Blanco Ponte's marriage to doña Francisca Infante, the granddaughter of town founders, brought him an encomienda at Caraballeda worth 1500 pesos per annum. In 1632, the year of his sister's wedding, don Francisco Infante transferred a debt to the royal treasury of 5403 pesos to his new brother-in-law, Alejandro Blanco Ponte, who immediately paid one-third of the outstanding amount in cash. In 1634, having already replaced Infante as encomendero at Caraballeda, Blanco Ponte received a 1000-peso loan in Caracas guaranteed by 5000 cacao trees in that coastal valley.[29] Perhaps entry into the Caracas elite in the 1630s required nothing more than one or two thousand pesos in gold coin. However, for the established families that provided these ambitious immigrants with wives, the major attraction of men like Ovalle, Liendo, and Blanco Ponte was undoubtedly their ability to convert cacao beans into large numbers of African slaves. As an investment that could very well multiply from one generation to the next regardless of the colonial economy, the acquisition of slaves made the future more certain for families whose wealth had been established on wheat, hides, and encomienda labor.

Cacao encomenderos were not alone in their desire to bring Africans to Caracas. From early in the century, before the cacao boom, some encomenderos had invested in slaves. Already in the 1620s the encomendero–merchant Alonso Rodríguez Santos had forty-seven slaves who farmed his wheat and herded his cattle. During the same decade, Francisco Castillo, encomendero and local tax collector for the Cartagena-based Inquisition court, directed a mixed-labor enterprise that was a variation on the common theme: the wheat grown by 50 African slaves in the Caracas Valley was shipped to Cartagena in cotton bags woven by the Indians of his Valencia encomienda.[30] In the 1630s and 1640s, cacao sales gave a significant boost to the quantity of slaves that Caraqueños could purchase, and although the cacao encomenderos' Indians afforded them the means to obtain the largest slave holdings, other ways were found to form a slave gang. A considerable variety of cases of non-encomenderos who acquired slaves could be cited, but two examples will suffice. Baltasar de Escovedo came from Granada to Caracas expecting to inherit his uncle's estate, but when the elder Escovedo decided that there was much to be gained by the marriage of his daughter to the powerful Juan Rodríguez Santos, what Baltasar had hoped would be his became his cousin's dowry instead. He turned to making bricks and tiles for the houses of those more directly favored by cacao, and in time he was able to accumulate, in addition to the brick works, a respectable town house, a dozen slaves, and considerable quantity of Mexican silver in coin. The Portuguese Agustín Pereira came to Caracas with a few slaves that he sold to buy two houses in the center of town. With this property as collateral, Pereira worked as a middleman, buying cacao with borrowed money guaranteed by Caracas real estate and selling it for a profit at La Guaira.[31]

The slave trade and these secondary economic activities depended increasingly on cacao sales that most often took place at the hacienda gate or wharf. Until about 1650 profits from these sales came easily, for the greater part of the beans was collected from the virgin (indigenous) trees known as *árboles de la tierra*. The difficult tasks of clearing the land, providing irrigation, and planting banana plants for shade for the young trees was not yet necessary, and there was no need to wait the five years or more after planting that it took for cacao trees to reach fruit-bearing maturity. A rather precise idea of the profitability of these groves is provided by accounts kept for the estate of Domingo de Liendo, brother of encomendero Pedro de Liendo.

More than 90 percent of Liendo's cacao in the coastal valley of Cepi was *de la tierra*. Since about 1640, his African slaves had planted some cacao trees in the valley, but in 1653 only 1165 trees of a total of more than 12,000 were not indigenous to the area. More than half of all the trees were then stricken with a blight known as *alhorra*, but the Cepi groves had an average annual yield of more than 200 fanegas (a fanega of cacao weighed about 110 pounds) for the seven years before 1653. Although harvests varied somewhat from one year to the next, and prices were falling steadily, Liendo's gross income averaged 3540 pesos per year during the period 1645–1652 (fig. 6).[32]

That fishhooks were imported to Cepi and small amounts of maize were exported from the valley suggests that food costs were low or nil and that the hacienda was largely self-sufficient. Since cacao beans were loaded directly from the groves onto ships that entered Cepi Bay, there were no freight or transportation costs. The value of the Cepi land in 1650 is unknown, but the half of the valley not owned by Liendo was sold for 1000 pesos in 1630 by someone who had no slaves to someone who did. The thirty-three slaves who formed the Cepi work force were worth a total of 8550 pesos in 1658.[33]

Thus the cacao groves and slaves at Cepi represented an investment of probably no more than 10,000 pesos, and, therefore, it seems reasonable that in an average year Liendo's gross income equaled about 35 percent of the value of his invested capital, with each adult slave annually earning, on the average, about 40 percent of his or her market value. Considering in addition that many groves were first harvested by "cheap" encomienda Indian labor and not by slaves, and that sales were made at high prices from the late 1620s until about 1650, the dynamic profitability of Caracas's first cacao bonanza becomes clear.[34]

At midcentury there coincided at Caracas several events that brought this period of remarkable prosperity to an abrupt end. The problems of supply at this critical juncture are much more evident

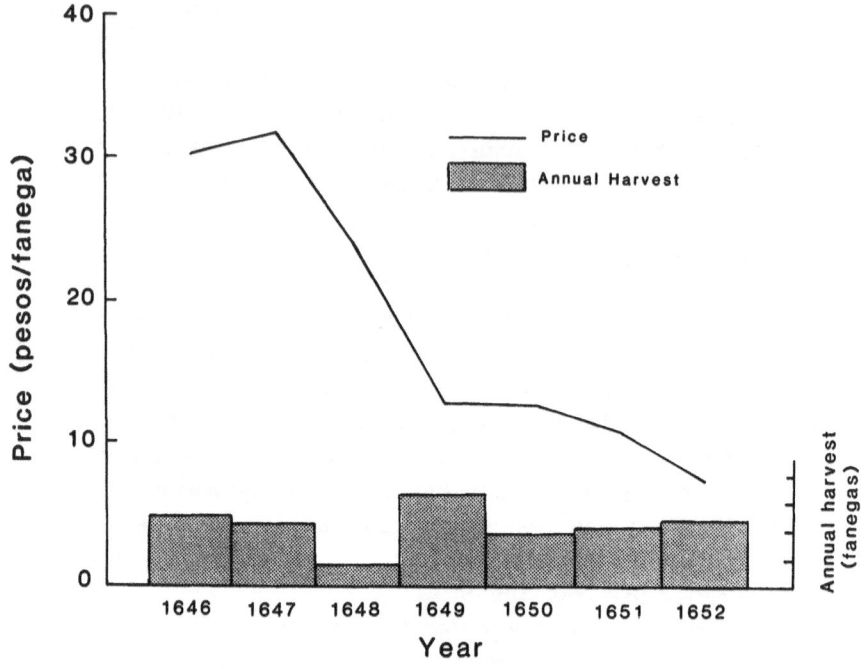
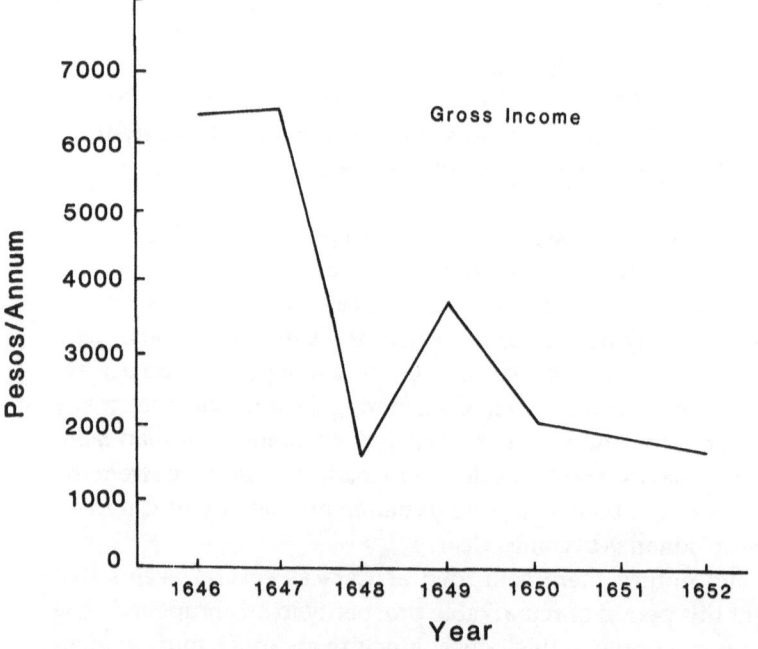

Fig. 6 Plantation Cepi: Cacao Prices, Harvests, and Income, 1646–1652

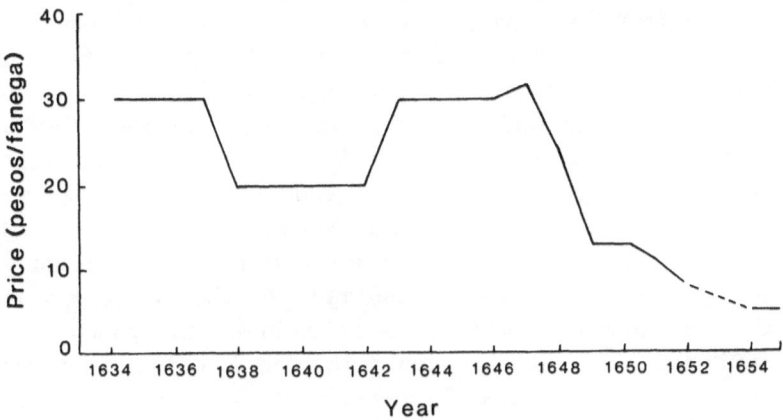

Fig. 7 Cacao Prices in Caracas, 1634–1655.

than those that caused the price paid for cacao in Caracas to drop to one-fifth of its customary level (fig. 7). A principal factor in the crisis was the alhorra blight. Beginning in the mid-1630s on the haciendas upwind of La Guaira, within a decade the alhorra had destroyed more than half of all the cacao trees on the coast, leaving many groves without a single fruit-bearing plant. Newly planted trees would begin to reach maturity by 1660, but the coastal groves would not recover their original productivity until the eighteenth century.[35] A second disaster took the form of a surprisingly destructive earthquake, which reduced modest Caracas to rubble in 1641. At one blow much of the urban property that had been used to finance purchases of slaves and cacao was eliminated. The ecclesiastical establishment, its temples and convents in ruins and the mortgages it held rendered worthless by the destruction, suffered the most. Exacerbated by the truculence of Bishop Mauro de Tovar, who refused the vecinos' request to move the town (his approval would have nullified all claims held by the Church against the owners of the destroyed property), these reverses initiated a rancorous epoch marked by spectacular quarrels between the bishop and many of Caracas's first citizens.[36]

The third and most important reason for the end of the first Caracas cacao boom is also the least understood. As yet there is no clear explanation why cacao prices, at twenty and thirty pesos the fanega until 1647, collapsed to five pesos by 1654. The answer will come from a fuller understanding of the Mexican market than is possible from the vantage point of Caracas. MacLeod documents falling prices for cacao in Santiago de Guatemala after 1651 and attributes the decline to successful competition in the New Spain market from Guayaquil and Venezuela: "In all the price history of cacao in Middle America, the main factor seems to have been the question of supply."[37] If this was indeed the case, the high prices paid for cacao in New Spain and elsewhere (including Caracas) until the late 1640s may have been due in part to the declining supply of beans because of the alhorra blight. The price collapse in Caracas at that time could then be linked to the rapidly increasing production of cacao in Guayaquil during the 1640s.[38] Thus it seems probable that the diseased Caracas industry, rather than contributing to the seventeenth-century crisis of the Central American cacao economy, was like it overwhelmed, if only temporarily, by competition from Guayaquil.

Undoubtedly much impressed by the combined disasters of earthquake and crop blight, Caraqueños appealed to divine providence for assistance. A festival with the Virgin Mary as patroness was held annually from 1638 to 1670 to plead for relief from the alhorra.[39] On the other hand, while the documents abound with laments about these acts of nature, a thorough search uncovered no comment whatsoever about the low prices paid for cacao. The little evidence pertaining to Caracas's commercial woes suggests that cacao growers did not understand their economic problems in terms of competition from other suppliers. A related problem had to do with a decrease in hard currency; with silver production in decline, and with trade exclusively dependent on the Mexican peso as a result of the crown's decision to devalue debased Peruvian coins, would-be buyers in New Spain may have preferred to hoard their sound coins or to keep them in local circulation rather than let them go out to distant markets such as Venezuela from whence they might not return. From 1650 to the 1670s a general crisis in the supply of currency choked trade in the Spanish Caribbean.[40]

To aggravate matters further, from 1620 to 1650 the Mexican Inquisition tried more than two hundred Portuguese for practicing Judaism, and many of the accused were cacao traders who had been the primary buyers of Caracas cacao.[41] By eliminating these middlemen and thereby restricting their opportunity to barter cacao for Africans, most Caracas growers were forced to depend on cash sales to Mexican merchants who were reluctant to make such purchases. There is evidence of the direct effect in Caracas of the currency shortage: Santiago de Liendo paid the priest at Cepi in 1649 in devalued copper coins, the unwanted *vellón*, because "there was nothing else." And there is evidence that at the same time few traders were interested in buying Caracas cacao beans: in 1654, even as the price dropped to five pesos the fanega, cacao had to be brought at Liendo's cost from Cepi to La Guaira, an unprecedented necessity, "to sell it and give it a market because there was none at Cepi and the cacao was about to be lost, rotting in the storehouse."[42] There is no indication, however, that Caracas planters recognized any relationship between the currency shortage and declining cacao sales.

At midcentury few Caracas vecinos owned cargo-carrying ships capable of making trans-Caribbean or Atlantic voyages, and this was one further reason why the cacao trade was severely restricted without Mexican cash and credit. The following case illustrates well the vital importance of both the African slave trade and the Mexican exchange for the Caracas economy. May, June, and July were the principal months for harvesting cacao on coastal haciendas, and in August of 1653 the frigate *Nuestra Señora de la Limpia Concepción*, owned by *capitán* Juan Rodríguez Quintanilla, stood loaded with cacao at La Guaira, its crew hired and ready to sail for Veracruz. However, it was then possible to depart only because Juan de Almeyda, a Canary Islander slave trader and cacao merchant who was on the occasion present in Caracas, had agreed in July to advance wages to the crew and to finance a new foremast for the ship. To make the needed repairs, Rodríguez Quintanilla, who was a vecino of San Antonio de Gibraltar on Lake Maracaibo, had been obliged to borrow in Caracas, and, "because he had no money in this town," he turned to Almeyda for credit. The loan, for 1820 pesos, did not introduce this same quantity of much-needed specie into Caracas circulation. In June and July, Almeyda sold five slaves for a total of 1870 pesos cash to Caracas vecinos, and he in turn loaned Rodríguez Quintanilla from this sum what was needed to pay the La Guaira shipwrights and sailors. Again, although this time in a rather round-about fashion, it was the slave trade that made it possible for Caracas cacao to reach the Mexican market. As it was already customary for loans made in Caracas to

64   *The Seventeenth Century*

be canceled in New Spain, Almeyda was to be paid in *"plata mexicana"* within twenty-four hours of the arrival of Rodríguez Quintanilla's ship at Veracruz.[43]

Hispanic traders such as Almeyda were infrequently present in Caracas after 1650, and it is reasonable to suppose that the opportunistic Dutch, then the Atlantic's leading merchants, provided planters with an alternative, if illicit, outlet for their cacao during these years of sluggish legal commerce. Caraqueños were evidently willing to overlook matters of religion and empire when it came to the Dutchmen. Indeed, fewer than half of all the men designated for the Caracas militia, encomenderos and planters among them, responded in 1639 when an expedition was formed to dislodge the Hollanders from the nearby island of Curaçao.[44] What took place along the miles of open coast is as difficult to account for now as it was to control then, but the Dutch were no doubt quite willing to replace the Portuguese in the lucrative slaves-for-cacao exchange. By 1671 the role of Curaçao in the supply of slaves was so commonplace that the Caracas cabildo issued a matter-of-fact warning that slaves afflicted with the "Dutch evil" (*mal 'olanda*) were entering from the island.[45] Yet it may be that Curaçao did not immediately become "little more than a gigantic slave pen" after the Dutch occupation of the island, as one historian recently suggested.[46]

Between 1659 and 1671, the slave population on the coastal hacienda at Chuao underwent changes in demographic composition that suggest that few, if any, African slaves had been introduced to that valley. The overall population declined from 110 to 100 individuals, and of those who can be identified by place of birth with certainty (76 percent in 1659; 79 percent in 1671), the number of African-born dropped from 36 to 26. A sharp decrease in the number of single men, from 30 to 11, and a significant rise in married or widowed men and women, from 20 to 27 men and from 26 to 34 women, are further indicators of adjustment to a reduced slave supply. More conjugal pairs and a greater sexual balance in 1671 occurred as single men found creole wives. At least in the Chuao case, the immediate presence of Dutch traders was unimportant and, from the point of view of the slave community, the stagnant African trade had beneficial social effects (see table 7) The evidence from Chuao suggests that even during these depressed decades a simple cacao-for-slaves exchange with the Dutch, without the

Table 7 Marriage Status and Regional Origins of Slaves at Chuao, 1659 and 1671

	1659		1671	
	Number	Percent Total	Number	Percent Total
Single Men				
West Africa	6		1	
Central Africa	5		0	
Creoles	12		7	
Unknown	7		3	
	30	27	11	11
Married/Widowed Men				
West Africa	4		4	
Central Africa	9		10	
Creoles	3		9	
Unknown	4		4	
	20	18	27	27
Single Women				
West Africa	0		1	
Central Africa	1		0	
Creoles	0		0	
Unknown	1		1	
	2	2	2	2
Married/Widowed Women				
West Africa	2		0	
Central Africa	9		10	
Creoles	3		9	
Unknown	4		4	
	26	24	34	34
Children under 12	32	29	26	26
Total Slaves	110	100	100	100

Source: *La obra pía de Chuao*, 191–193, 227–229. My thanks to Professors George Brooks and Phyllis Martin of Indiana University for their assistance in solving problems of nomenclature and establishing the ethnicity of these slaves.

added incentive of an eventual payoff in silver pesos that animated the trade with New Spain, could not replace the traditional (and legal) market for Caracas cacao in Mexico.

For the Hispanic population of the region, this combination of economic and natural events changed the focus and pace of social life. Urban functions and services came to a standstill as Caracas residents withdrew to the countryside; notaries closed their offices for lack of work, and for years the cabildo was without its full complement of *regidores*.⁴⁷ Finally, in the 1670s, with a revival of the cacao trade, concern for property and status reappeared and there was a renewed interest in urban life. Plans to construct a new seminary were presented and discussed in the cabildo. Of more dubious benefit, but a clear indication of the reemerging concern for social order, the jail, destroyed in the 1641 earthquake, was rebuilt in 1674. Frightened by marauding French corsairs and by raids on Maracaibo by the English buccaneer William Henry Morgan, townsmen expressed faith that Caracas was once again worth protecting and weighed the possibilities of persuading the crown to finance a new fort to be built on the road to La Guaira.⁴⁸

By the 1680s the Caracas economy was vigorous again. In 1684, the crown ordered a survey of rural property to determine whether noncollection of the alcabala, which had been suspended by royal favor since 1631, was still justified. Acknowledged by contemporaries as the first such census of the town's rural domain, the 1684 *padrón* is a crucial document for the history of seventeenth-century Caracas.⁴⁹ In 1684 Caraqueños owned 434,850 cacao trees distributed on 167 haciendas, 18 wheat farms, 26 sugar trapiches, and 28 cattle *hatos*. Comparison of the 1684 padrón with the list of encomenderos dated circa 1635 shows that wealth accumulated during the first years of booming cacao commerce made it possible for the families of many of the first encomendero–slaveholders to survive the decades of economic slump at midcentury. At least half of the 146 individuals who owned cacao haciendas in 1684 were descendants of encomenderos named in 1635, and of the 38 encomenderos who held grants in 1635 of 1000 pesos or more renta, the heirs of at least 28 were growing cacao in 1684.⁵⁰

The moderate size of many of the cacao groves belonging to children and grandchildren of the first planters, and the location of these haciendas in sites different from those of their ancestors' encomiendas, suggests that the majority of the 1684 groves had been planted since the 1640s. Started during the period of alhorra blight and low prices, this was expansion that already-purchased slaves could execute.⁵¹ More than 10 percent of the cacao trees counted in 1684 were new plants located at some distance from the coast along the banks of the Tuy River south and east of Caracas. This region was rapidly becoming the most important cacao farming zone in the Caracas province.

Once planted, a cacao arboleda required only a maintenance crew of waterers and weeders during most of the year, and this meant that the established planters could keep a gang of their younger and sturdier slaves at work bringing new land under cultivation. This is perhaps the most salient characteristic of the Caracas economy and society from the 1640s to the 1740s: the ready availability of irrigable cacao land and the mobility of the slave gang encouraged constant expansion. In 1720, before the establishment of the Guipuzcoana Company in Venezuela, there were more than 2 million cacao trees in the Caracas province, and by 1744 the number of trees had risen to over 5 million. In each case more than half the trees were located in the Tuy River region.

The multitude of haciendas of modest size that resulted, brought together and held in place by a complex system of carefully arranged marriages, kept elite status and profits in the hands of generations of select Caracas families. Even the more humble growers, indigent Canary Islanders for the most part, who came to Caracas in a steady stream after 1680,[52] could make a bid for gentry status with cacao and the few slaves they were able to buy. Before 1700 these hopeful immigrants had begun to harvest quantities of cacao in the valleys at the remote edge of the province. They also settled in Caracas itself, in the Candelaria parish on the settlement's eastern fringe, which in time became a *canario* barrio. This was a labor force of a somewhat different order, although as artisans, grocers, vegetable farmers, overseers, and, perhaps more than any other occupation, muleteers who brought the beans from increasingly distant arboledas, they were as closely dependent on the production and sale of cacao as the hacienda owners who bought their wares and hired their services.[53]

Before 1700 the population structure of the Caracas region had become a racial-class continuum, with white masters and black slaves at opposite poles and canarios, other poor Spaniards, and the mixed-blood *pardos* and mulattoes scattered in between. In this world that their forced labor had helped to create, Indians seem to have had no clearly defined place. At best, it was an uncertain and unstable order. With a growing slave population and at a time when several decades of economic hardship had ended and a new, poor white class had begun to fill the town and countryside, Caracas seems to have become quite race conscious. The marriage of a

Valencia favorite son to the daughter of an Aragua Valley Indian *cacique* provoked near hysteria in the Hispanic community.[54] In an effort to freeze melting social–racial distinctions, Caracas bishop González de Acuña declared that he would no longer ordain anyone who had as much as one-fourth Indian or African ancestry—an explicit challenge to the Church's evangelical mission that was subsequently disallowed by Pope Innocent XI.[55]

In this tense atmosphere, the crown's decision in 1691 to insist on the termination of the *servicio personal* encomienda and thereby put an end to more than 150 years of de facto defiance on the part of the Caracas encomenderos met surprisingly little resistance. Definitely not the outcome of easy *mestizaje* and racial toleration, the encomienda's demise was finally allowed because the immobile, legally circumscribed institution had little place in the dynamic cacao economy now based on African slavery. It was decided that once freed from encomienda service Indians would be required to pay a tax for the religious instruction that they were to continue to receive. Bishop Baños y Sotomayor's *Ynforme* of 1690, on which the tax was to be based, allows a glimpse at the remnant of Indian society that was then at the margin of Caracas's Hispano-African community.[56]

The bishop's agents found 7464 Indians divided among sixty-four encomiendas in the jurisdictions of Caracas, Valencia, and San Sebastián.[57] Of these, the majority, 5278 Indians and thirty-seven encomiendas, were in the possession of Caracas vecinos. Comparison with the agricultural property owned by the encomenderos who held these thirty-seven grants—as the 1684 padrón permits—makes it possible to account for the specific activities that employed Indian labor at the end of the century. More than three-fifths, 3262 Indians, were in nine encomiendas located near sugar mills owned by their encomenderos; 1085 Indians in eleven encomiendas were at work farming wheat; and only 931 were spread thinly among seventeen encomenderos whose grants were located near their coastal cacao groves. The same data is perhaps more revealing when viewed so as to see the portion of all agricultural estates that benefited from encomienda labor; while a third of sugar trapiches and fully two-thirds of the wheat farms were owned by encomenderos, only about one cacao planter in ten was also the holder of an Indian labor grant in 1690.

The bishop's *Ynforme* also indicates that for some time many encomenderos had allowed their grants to revert to the crown rather than pay fees for the confirmation of their titles. Twenty-four of the province's sixty-four encomiendas were already royal possessions in 1690. Legal rights had been allowed to lapse in both the case of the small coastal encomiendas, now of only minimal value, and in the case of the large, still important grants in the Valencia–Aragua sugar region. Only encomenderos with Indians in the wheat fields near Caracas, in Petare, Baruta, and La Vega, had uniformly paid their taxes and kept their titles in order. Why this was so can be inferred from the demographic composition of the encomiendas as recorded in the *Ynforme*.

By 1690, cacao cultivation and the forced immigration of black slaves had reduced the coastal Indian communities to fragments of their preconquest form. African men without African women were fortunate if, as occurred in Chuao, they were provided with creole black women; otherwise they found substitutes among the Indian women from the coastal villages. Many of the husbands of the women assigned to the coastal encomiendas at Maiquetía, Caraballeda, and Naiguatá were listed as anonymous *negros* in the *Ynforme*, and most of the coastal encomienda-born children were recognized as Afro-Indian *zambos*.[58] Since coastal encomienda women were often married to slaves, the wives of the Indian men from these encomiendas often lived elsewhere. Many coastal Indian men were married to women who belonged to populous inland encomiendas near the sugar trapiches at Turmero and Guarenas. These groups were still stable in 1690, sexually balanced, and headed by aged patriarchs, quite unlike the truncated, often caciqueless encomiendas on the coast.[59]

In the Aragua Valley, where the original population had been dense and indigenous culture was able to survive the seventeenth century more nearly intact than it had in the coast or in Caracas, it may have simply made good tactical sense to allow the encomiendas to return to the crown. In this area, eliminating the encomienda altogether assured access to Indian labor to those whose encomienda privileges had expired. In this way there would be no chance of one's competitors gaining exclusive control of a needed work force. As owners of two of the four trapiches located in the Aragua pueblo of Turmero, the powerful and wealthy Tovar family had no desire to part with the skilled Indian workers who had made sugar for them for decades. The end of the encomienda also put an end to this possibility, and the Tovar dominion in Aragua continued. In 1710, Turmero Indians complained that Tovar canefields were encroaching on their village, and in 1730 these same Indians were still identified as "the people of Don Antonio Tovar," their last encomendero—who had been dead for more than forty years.[60]

Finally, although now nearly insignificant as a source of income alongside slavery and cacao, the prestige value of the wheat farm encomienda had not diminished during the course of the seventeenth century. Mario Góngora has shown how the encomienda in agrarian Chile was absorbed by a "class of owners" who derived their power from various sources and who were therefore not dependent on Indian tribute for wealth and prestige.[61] This was all the more true in Caracas, where the monetary value of an encomienda frequently depended on the market skills of the encomendero, and where, especially after 1650, ownership of sizable, mobile gangs of slaves was the decisive factor in the maintenance of aristocratic status. In 1684, all eleven of the encomenderos whose Indians grew wheat near Caracas were also owners of either sugar or cacao properties. Born several generations after the time when wheat exports and Indian labor had determined membership in the local elite, these encomenderos could liken themselves to those earlier holders of Indian grants and thereby call attention to the tenure of their families' importance in Caracas. For a boom-and-bust society of slavers and smugglers, this was a useful symbol of stability and the nobility of their origins, and perhaps for this reason the titles of these encomiendas were nearly all still in order in 1690.

During the half century after 1630, Caracas completed its transformation from a minor supplier of a European food crop to Spanish sailors to a major supplier of a tropical quasi-drug to Indian and European consumers alike. In the process, African slavery rendered the encomienda a nonessential anachronism. The Mexican demand for cacao initiated this transformation, and it would appear that, once committed to cacao and slavery, Caracas continued to be very responsive to shifts in the economy of New Spain.

The Mexican market for cacao first surged in the late 1620s and lasted for about two decades thereafter. New Spain merchants offered considerably less for Caracas cacao from the late 1640s until the late 1660s, a period that corresponds closely to the general depression of Zacatecas silver mining. Silver production then reached new highs from 1675 to 1690 as the supply of mercury was made certain once again,[62] and it was at this time that cacao exports resumed and Caracas's prosperity returned. To what degree these trends are coincidental must await a study of the New Spain cacao market and its merchants, but such a study might well confirm that the rise of Caracas in the late seventeenth century was closely tied to the simultaneous development of a diversified capitalist economy in Mexico. Increasingly self-sufficient generally, New Spain found it profitable to depend on external suppliers for cacao, and when commercial capital was unavailable, as was the case from about 1650 until about 1670, Mexicans invested their money in local enterprise and probably did without imported cacao beans. For their part, Caracas growers might have taken Dutch slaves and merchandise in exchange for their harvests during these long years, but only after 1670, when "the discriminating customer"[63] from across the Caribbean was again willing to buy, did Caracas, permanently established as New Spain's cacao colony, enjoy a resurgence of wealth and well-being.

3

Wheat Farm and Cacao Hacienda: Agricultural Business and Elite Families

Black slavery was the overwhelmingly predominant labor form in the Caracas province from the early seventeenth century until at least the middle of the eighteenth century. The end of the English *asiento* in 1739 marked the beginning of an extended hiatus in the slave trade, with the result that owners of agricultural estates were increasingly obliged to turn to other sources of labor. Very little is known about this gradual transition, and there have been to date no studies of the reproductive rates of Venezuelan slaves which would give us an idea of how much the institution depended on the trans-Atlantic trade. For agricultural work slavery may well have been preferred over other labor options until emancipation in 1854; and we can be certain that there was no decline in the desirability of slaves for urban domestic service, even while they were in short supply in the countryside. At the beginning of the nineteenth century the resident French merchant Francois Depons, always a sensitive observer of Caracas society, noted that domestic slavery was a most important measure of status in Caracas: "the richness of a house is in proportion to the number of slaves in it." And in her statistical analysis of household censuses Waldron observes that the number of residental slaves proportionate to the rest of the population remained constant through the second half of the eighteenth century. More than one-third (35 percent) of Caracas households had slaves in 1759, with an average of 5.8 slaves per slaveholding household. As late as 1792 the proportion of slaveholding households had declined only slightly (29 percent), as had the mean number of slaves per household (5.5).[1]

The two case studies presented in this chapter allow us to see many of the particular characteristics of the Caracas slave labor system in formation. Given the rich detail of the two cases, it might be well to indicate beforehand in what ways the records of these estates help inform the general problem of the nature and significance of hacienda agriculture in colonial Caracas. In economic terms, both the wheat estancia and the cacao hacienda were tied directly to distant markets reached by seaborne commerce. They both generated a discernible profit, primarily from the intensive forced labor of slaves. The cacao hacienda was in fact several groves, *arboledas*, of trees, and the planting of new groves in different locations often distant from one another was seen, already in the 1650s, as an essential component of the successful cacao enterprise. The transition from wheat to cacao brought about significant economic and social changes. While wheat agriculture employed relatively expensive Spanish labor in several categories, the cacao hacienda needed only a single overseer, whose wages were typically no more than 100 pesos for a year's service. The rise of cacao simplified the colony's occupational hierarchy to include hacienda owners at the top and slaves at the bottom, with very few individuals besides overseers and muleteers in between. Cacao also greatly stretched the physical space of Caracas. The wheat farms all were located in the immediate vicinity of the town. Most cacao haciendas, on the other hand, were distant from Caracas, often requiring several days of travel to reach them. From their Caracas residences, absentee owners of cacao estates were able to convert agricultural profits into urban social status, spending for prestige items even as profits declined. In social terms, the impression of seigneurial status was created and maintained in the Caracas townhouse, and not in the distant and infrequently visited hacienda countryhouse. It would be in error to make too much of the social meaning of domestic slavery solely on the basis of the observed ratio of slaves to whites in Caracas homes (17.5 slaves on the average for less than 7 whites in each of eighty-five elite households in 1759), but by staffing their dwellings with a surfeit of domestic slaves, elites were no doubt able to live out at least some of the images of a seigneurial mentality without actually residing on the hacienda. This link was reinforced by bringing the kin of hacienda slaves to Caracas for domestic labor, and by the practice of bringing ill slaves to the city for treatment.

Although greatly appreciated for their prestige and symbolic value, the urban residences of many Caracas elites also functioned as administrative centers for the widespread activities of their owners. Beginning in the middle of the seventeenth century, successful cacao hacendados came to possess several groves located on separate sites (in the earliest pattern, the original hacienda of indigenous trees was located on the coast and new groves were planted to the south along the banks of the Tuy River). The expansion of cacao haciendas into the Tuy frontier had the effect of placing Caracas between the newer production zones and the port at La Guaira, and by the end of the seventeenth century even elite residences doubled as warehouses for cacao beans awaiting shipment. Thus, although each was a distinctive world different and quite distant in space from the other—the productive unit located on a hot and usually remote coast or river site, its population overwhelmingly African or creole black, and the unit of authority and consumption in cool and in many ways more Hispanic Caracas—the cacao hacienda and the townhouse were bound together as part of a single system. For the family that owned and operated it this system was economically capitalist yet socially seigneurial,[2] with the urban residence the place where the functions of profit, prestige, and patriarchalism were blended into a single mode of behavior, an elite lifestyle.

The purpose of this chapter is to illuminate the character of that lifestyle during its period of formation, before 1650. The method used is explained fully in due course, but at this point a comment is in order about the documentary material used in the analysis. In both the cases that follow, the sudden death of two sets of parents left the properties of minor children in the temporary custody of guardians; by custom they were charged with maintaining the agricultural estates (a wheat estancia and a cacao hacienda) and with providing for the orphaned wards. The ledgers kept by these custodians provide the raw material for this chapter. A far cry from neat and orderly bookkeeping practice, the accounts are jumbled chaotically in that the individuals who kept them tended to juxtapose without discrimination entries for harvests, sales, and hacienda expenditures with payments made for dancing lessons and new dresses. These data can be sorted into categories that seem logical and functional to the historian who would analyze them to determine, for example, the annual rate of return on the capital value of the estates, and this has been done in the pages that follow. Yet to do so is to risk distortion of the historical reality as it was understood by those who lived it, for what the modern eye sees as the chaos of disorganized accounting procedures may in fact be a manifestation of the thorough way in which Caraqueño minds combined the capitalist and the seigneurial elements of their lives. Recognizing this, although the measure of these properties as agricultural businesses is the primary objective here, an effort has been made to not lose sight of the likelihood that to the *mentalité* of the age the social significance of a wheat estancia or cacao hacienda was not always measured in terms of profits and losses.

The Rodríguez Santos wheat estancia and mill, as detailed in ledgers kept for a few years in the 1630s, represents a form of farming that by then no longer dominated the Caracas economy as it had since the 1580s. In contrast the Liendo cacao hacienda, as it operated for a somewhat longer period of time in the 1640s and 1650s, was one of the first large-scale Caracas cacao estates. The documents used are unusual and of a kind. They are ledgers of crop sales and expenditures for both the operation of the agricultural enterprise and the material needs and wants of the minor children of the estates' former owners. In each case these owners had recently died, and the person responsible for the property and for the care of the young heirs was obliged to keep close account of all goods and all expenditures made on behalf of these surviving children.[3]

Cash flow, both income and outgo, was recorded in the process, although in an almost incidental manner. It must be sorted out from lists of undifferentiated credits and debits that were made, not to facilitate ongoing business activity (the guardian was not obliged to show a profit), but only to allow for future reckoning of the use and whereabouts of the property of the minor children's inheritance. Expenditures made for the personal needs of the wards, such as clothing, were entered indiscriminately in these ledgers together with expenditures made as part of the operation and maintenance of the agricultural businesses, with amounts paid for tools, salaries, slave purchases, and so forth. Mixed with these items is an assortment of what might be best called social costs, such as expenditures for household needs, education, and religious services of all sorts. Analysis of the data recorded by such unselective bookkeeping techniques requires, as a minimum, some thoughtful categorization but, once they have been sorted systematically, these guardians' accounts permit a close look at the nature of estate management and the material culture of the families for whom the records were kept. If inventories of an estate with appraised property values are available, as they are in these cases, it is also possible to calculate the annual return on the capital value of the property held in custodianship.

The *tutela* ended when the wards came of age, married, or entered the convent, so the guardians' accounts encompass periods of only several years at best. Still, these documents do record a period of time equal to the better part of the childhood or adolescence of the individuals on whose behalf they were made, and they do reveal many things about the provisions made for children of the town's elite as they grew older, year by year. In addition, an interval of six or seven years is adequate for the purpose of observing how the estates operated.[4] The guardians were held accountable to the cabildo for every item of expense and income, and the detail of the entries suggests that every effort was made to give at least the appearance of faithfully reporting the fiscal history of the two estates examined here. For example, Bartolomé de Rivillapuerta, whose custodianship is examined below, declared that during his tutela he had replaced the worn and ragged bedsheets of his wife's younger brothers and sisters, but he had prudently used the old ones as burial shrouds for the slaves of the family's Chacao estancia.

Yet the guardianship was also a special situation. Since the function of the tutela was fundamentally to preserve the property until its rightful heirs could legally receive it, the guardian was circumscribed by law from taking full entrepreneurial advantage of the estate placed in his care. With the appropriate license from the cabildo, property held in tutela could be sold or mortgaged, and both grain and flour from the Rodríguez Santos estancia and cacao from the Liendo hacienda were sold for profit in the marketplace. However, all the wheat and cacao from these estates was sold in Caracas or La Guaira; none of it was merchandised in other ports, as had certainly been the customary practice of both families. Without direct evidence we can only conjecture that the risks of seaborne trade and the convoluted credit networks that characterized high-seas marketing made it difficult to maintain the strict accountability that the tutela required, and therefore such commerce was not allowed. We cannot know to what extent selling exclusively in the local market altered either production or the profits made from these estates.

It is also difficult to determine whether these cases were typical of agricultural business in the region as whole. In the first place there is a problem of scale. These enterprises were without doubt large by local standards but, without a census or similar document, just how large in comparison with other estates is impossible to know. In addition, the effect on the management of these properties of such highly variable factors as the exercise of entrepreneurial skill, the availability of investment capital, or the penchant to spend estate income on luxury goods cannot be calculated. Given these limitations, we must be content with the observation that the two families whose seventeenth-century estates are observed here were then in the process of establishing highly respected, powerful lineages that would last until the very end of the colonial period. These case studies are, then, best qualified as examples of successful estate operation, both in the short run as observed in the ledgers and in the long term in the sense that lasting family prestige would stem from these early agricultural ventures.

THE RODRÍGUEZ SANTOS WHEAT ESTANCIA AND MILL

Alonso Rodríguez Santos was one of Caracas's two or three most active merchants during the first decades of the seventeenth century. When he died in 1624 his Caracas estate was appraised at about 50,000 pesos, of which more than 14,000 pesos were in the form of outstanding debts owed him by the town's vecinos.[5] His worth in other Caribbean ports, which at his death could not be fixed exactly, was believed by his heirs to be considerable. As *alcalde ordinario*, encomendero, and owner of both cattle *hatos* and a wheat estancia, this merchant from Extremadura, like many other successful traders who immigrated to the Indies, converted his commercial profits into landed wealth with its accompanying social power and prestige.

Don Alonso had come to Caracas a widower, accompanied by his two adult sons, Juan Rodríguez Santos and Benito Arias

Montano. The eldest son, Juan Rodríguez Santos, like his father from Frenegal de la Sierra, Extremadura, evidently had little interest in the merchant profession. The Real Hacienda records show an occasional entry for shipment of hides to Spain in the name of Juan Rodríguez Santos, and he maintained small accounts with merchants in Seville, but he paid for the merchandise sent to him from Europe with the income from the rent of two houses in Spain, and not with agricultural products exported from Caracas.[6] He preferred to sell the wheat grain and flour produced on his Caracas estancia in the Caracas market, to other vecinos or to those merchants who would then resell the flour in other ports, especially Cartagena. When Juan died a few years after his father in 1628, he left a large estancia of ninety-two *fanegadas de sembradura*, about 140 acres, east of the town on the banks of the Chacao stream.[7] When the inventory and appraisal of this estate was made in 1631 the value of the estancia, including both farm and water-driven mill (but not its slaves, who were counted and evaluated separately), was placed at 6500 pesos.

Juan Rodríguez Santos's wife, Francisca de Escovedo, died in 1630, and the care of their orphaned children and the children's inheritance was briefly the responsibility of Benito Arias Montano, Juan's brother and Alonso Rodríguez Santos's second son from his Extremadura marriage. Arias remained in Caracas long enough to approve the marriage of his eldest niece, who was called María Arias Montano, to Bartolomé de Rivillapuerta. Arias then transferred the tutela to Rivillapuerta, who took charge of his wife's three brothers and two sisters in October 1631. Three of the five were his responsibility until November 1636, when his tutela ended: Juan de los Santos, Alonso Rodríguez Santos, and Paula Rodríguez Santos. These children were six, nine, and ten years old respectively in 1631. A third daughter orphaned by the deaths of Juan Rodríguez Santos and Francisca de Escovedo—called Germana de Rojas after her maternal grandmother—married Domingo de Liendo in April of 1633 and left Rivillapuerta's guardianship at that time. Finally, Diego Vásquez de Escovedo, Juan and Francisca's eldest son, who was named after his maternal grandfather, became eighteen in February of 1636 and left his brother-in-law's care in May of that year.[8]

Rivillapuerta was also responsible for a second, quite different group of individuals. The Rodríguez Santos–Escovedo children stood to inherit ninety-four slaves, including nineteen children nine years old and younger. Sixty-five of these slaves lived and worked at the Chacao wheat farm, fourteen provided domestic service in Caracas, and fifteen others labored on the family cattle hato east of the town. Of the ninety-four, thirty were adult women, and of these, fifteen lived at Chacao, each with a husband and most with children. Twelve single women, only one of whom had children, labored as domestics in the Rodríguez Santos townhouse. The remaining three women, one with a husband and all three with young children, were on the cattle hato. Of the forty-five adult men and boys, thirty-seven resided on the wheat estancia, and of these fourteen were married to female slaves belonging to the family (the fifteenth married woman, Phelipa Angola, was married to Antonico, "*mulato libre*") and the rest were single. None of the adult male slaves worked in domestic service in Caracas, and the remaining eight men, one who was married and seven who were not, herded cattle on the family hato (see table 8).

The appraised value of these slaves, set in 1631 by the cabildo's alcaldes ordinarios, makes it possible to estimate the total worth of the Rodríguez Santos wheat enterprise. The sixty-five slaves, both adults and children, on the Chacao estancia were appraised at 13,908 pesos (see appendix A). Added to the 6500 pesos given as the value of the farm land and mill, the total worth of the estancia and slaves was slightly more than 20,000 pesos when Rivillapuerta assumed responsibility for its management.

Table 8   Slaves of the Rodríguez Santos–Escovedo Heirs, 1631

	Townhouse	Estancia	Hato
Men and Boys			
Married	0	14	1
Unmarried	0	23	7
Women and Girls			
Married	0	15	1
Unmarried	12	0	2
Children			
(Under 9)	2	13	4
Totals	14	65	15

Source: ARPC, Testamentarías, 1638 R.

The Chacao estancia slaves brought two wheat crops to harvest every year. The "winter" crop was sown at the beginning of the rainy season in May or June and was grown without need for irrigation and in spite of often excessive rainfall. As a result of wet conditions, the winter grain was of limited quantity and perhaps inferior in quality, but it was evidently important, both to supply the town's needs and to provide seed for the planting of the more bountiful "summer" crop. Sown after the rains had stopped and irrigated during the dry months, summer wheat was the cash crop that first gave the Caracas Valley a role in Spain's commercial empire.

Winter wheat counted only for from 10 to 30 percent of the Rodríguez Santos annual harvest. This wheat was always sold in the grain, never as flour, and its buyers were most often Caracas vecinos. It was never designated by Rivillapuerta as delivered to La Guaira, either *"puesto La Guaira"* or *"puesto la mar,"* for export.

By contrast, summer wheat was always sold as flour, except, as happened in 1632 and 1633, when a shortage of cotton bags made it necessary to sell a part of the summer harvest in the grain. The shortage of flour sacks is fortunate: since wheat was sold both as grain and as flour in these two years, the difference in price can be taken as an indication of the added value created by milling wheat into flour. Summer wheat in the grain sold at 24 reales the *fanega* in 1632 and at an average price of 33.5 reales the fanega in 1633; ground into flour, a fanega of wheat sold for 42 reales in 1632 and for 48 reales in 1633 (see table 9). When he had them, Rivillapuerta supplied cotton sacks, at a cost to him of about 6 reales for every fanega of wheat flour he sold; discounting this, it seems that milled wheat was worth between 20 and 30 percent more than the unprocessed grain.[9] Besides the mill profits, under Rivillapuerta's direction earnings from the Rodríguez Santos estancia were increased by selling wheat and flour at higher prices to certain customers. Family, friends, and royal and ecclesiastical officials were favored with prices that were close to the cost of production, while out-of-town merchants, ship captains, and small retailers were charged more (see appendix B).

Cacao growers did not have the opportunity to increase the value of their harvests by processing their beans, nor did they have any influence over the price paid for them. Therefore, in order to compare the costs and income of wheat farming with the costs and

Table 9 Estancia Harvests, Prices, and Income, 1632–1636

	1632	1633	1634	1635	1636	Five-Year Total
Total Harvest	911.0 fs.[b]	1146.0 fs.	732.0 fs.	572.0 fs.	667.5 fs.	4028.5 fs.
Amount Sold[a]	682.0 fs.	863.5 fs.	517.0 fs.	374.0 fs	448.0 fs.	2884.5 fs.
Winter Wheat	137.0 fs.	171.0 fs.	177.0 fs.	125.0 fs.	57.0 fs.	667.0 fs. worth
Price (grain)[d]	32.0 rls.[c]	36.6 rls.	35.0 rls.	46.1 rls.	56.0 rls.	25,792 rls.
Summer Wheat	300.0 fs.	550.0 fs.	340.0 fs.	249.0 fs.	391.0 fs	1830.0 fs. worth
Price (flour)[d]	42.0 rls.	48.0 rls.	52.5 rls.	66.4 rls.	73.2 rls.	102,005 rls.
Summer Wheat	245.0 fs.	142.5 fs.	—	—	—	387.0 fs. worth
Price (grain)[d]	24.0 rls.	33.5 rls.				10,654 rls.
Total Income	22,864 rls.	37,432 rls.	27,147 rls.	22,250 rls.	31,813 rls.	138,451 rls. (17,306 pesos)

Source: ARPC, Testamentarías, 1638 R.
[a] Three deductions were made from the total harvest: the Church tithe or diezmo; a share given to Bartolomé Escudero, share-cropper and slave overseer; and a quantity of seed for the next season's planting. Flour consumed in the Rodríguez Santos household was entered in Rivillapuerta's ledger as a sale and is not discounted; see appendix B.
Price is average price for all wheat sold, either as grain or flour, during the given year.
[b] "fs." = fanegas.
[c] "rls." = reales.
[d] Price is reales per fanega.

income of cacao agriculture it is necessary to calculate the basic value of the wheat as it left the field, both before it was milled and before it was differentially marketed. To do this the value assigned in the Rivillapuerta ledger to the wheat consumed in the Rodríguez Santos household ("*gasté en casa*") is taken as a base price. To obtain a price for premilled summer wheat for the years 1634–1636, when all summer wheat was ground and only flour was sold, the value added by milling was estimated at 25 percent (based on the 1632–1633 data), and this percentage was discounted from the price of flour for these years.

Before milling and marketing, the estimated gross income of the wheat harvested on the Rodríguez Santos estancia from 1632 to 1636 is 14,118 pesos. This amount represents what would have been the income from all the winter and summer wheat sold in the grain at the favored-buyer or household price, plus 75 percent of the income from summer wheat flour for the five years, again estimating on the basis of the price given for flour consumed in the Rodríguez Santos household. Counting fifty-three working slaves (those nine years old and older) in the Chacao fields, the return to their masters from the labor of each can be estimated at about fifty pesos per year, only a fraction of what the average return from slaves working in the cacao groves produced per year, as we shall see. However, in the Rodríguez Santos case milling and selective pricing added more than 20 percent to the income on wheat taken from the fields: 17,306 pesos is the total gross income from the estancia reported by Rivillapuerta for the period from 1632 to 1636.

The net return was less. According to Rivillapuerta's ledgers, the cash outlay for wages and operating costs for the six years of his administration came to 4907 pesos (see appendix C). Wheat agriculture provided an income for a variety of Spanish laborers and professionals. The Rodríguez Santos labor bill was always paid in cash, with one exception. Bartolomé Escudero had served the family both as a sharecropper (*labrador*) and slave overseer for three decades prior to 1637. For his work he was given a fixed share of the harvest, the grain from 5.5 *fanegadas de sembradura* (about 6 percent of the estancia total of 92 fanegadas). Perhaps because of his advancing age and loyal service (he was sixty-five years old in 1637), perhaps because the booming market for cacao beans was drawing free labor (both labradores and overseers) from the wheat

Table 10 Estancia Earnings for Hispanic Labor, 1632–1636

	Bartolomé Escudero			Laborers	Total	Estancia	Labor Earnings as Percentage of Estancia
	Wheat	Price	Earnings	Wages	Wages	Income	Income
1632	55 ×	41.6 =	2288 +	136 =	2424	22,864	10.6
1633	71 ×	36.0 =	2556 +	608 =	3164	37,432	8.4
1634	48 ×	35.0 =	1680 +	304 =	1984	24,147	8.2
1635	38 ×	46.0 =	1748 +	560 =	2308	22,250	10.4
1636	51 ×	56.0 =	2856 +	288 =	3144	31,813	9.9

Source: ARPC. Testamentarías, 1638 R.
Note: Wheat is given in fanegas; Price, Earnings, Wages, and Income in reales. Bartolomé Escudero's share of the annual harvest and his earnings are given in columns 1 and 3. Estancia Income is gross income taken from table 9.

farms, Escudero had been given a one-half fanegada increase in 1627.[10] This arrangement was generous. Escudero's share of the annual harvest is given in table 10; calculated at the price charged by Rivillapuerta in each of these years, Escudero's income from 1632 to 1636 would have been about 280 pesos annually. By contrast, cacao hacienda *mayordomos* were seldom paid more than 100 pesos per year for their work. In addition, Escudero had the irregular assistance of one and sometimes two Spanish laborers during several months of the year. These men were paid in case by Rivillapuerta at an annual rate of about seventy pesos each. (Presumably they would have been drawn to the higher salaries and other opportunities, such as smuggling, available on coastal cacao haciendas.) The combined earnings of Escudero and his salaried assistants represents from 8 to 10 percent of the gross income of the estancia for the five years for which there are harvest data (see table 10). Thus it seems that while the return from slave labor was lower on this wheat estancia than it was on the Liendo cacao estate, at the same time the cost of overseers and other Hispanic labor on the wheat farm was also much higher. As is demonstrated below, the Liendo would pay only about 4 percent of their gross income for mayordomos' wages.

Other Spanish labor paid for by Rivillapuerta included retainers to lawyers to defend the interests of his wards. For example, don Tomás Gregorio de Mora was given 100 pesos on December 12,

1633, to tend to the family's legal business in the coming year. In all, 796 pesos were spent in six years for legal work. Thirty pesos a year went to physician don Juan Baptista Navarro as a retainer to care for "the sick who suffer in my house, me, my wife, and the remainder of the family." Navarro did not tend to the medical needs of the slave community; another 20 pesos every year were paid to Honorato de Aguillón, a medical practitioner of uncertain status, "to cure the *gente* of the household and the *negros* of the estancia." The labor of a surgeon, however, whose craft of bloodletting may have been regarded as less intimate than other aspects of medical practice, did not require the same attention to distinctions of race and class. A third retainer, also for 20 pesos, was given to Francisco Martín Pacheco, surgeon, for his services to both slaves and Spaniards alike. Carpenter Francisco de Medina and mason Diego Rodríguez Carrero were paid 30 and 12 pesos respectively for repair work on the mill in 1636 and 1637. Several different clergymen received a total of 70 pesos for burial masses for slaves said from January 1632 to September 1636. From time to time a mulatto muledriver earned a few pesos hauling merchandise to and from La Guaira. There was occasional need for the services of a blacksmith, who forged the iron tools, particularly plows and hoes, needed in the wheat fields. Finally, on rare occasions, certain Indians were paid from the Rodríguez Santos coffers for a particular task at which they specialized: successful slave catchers were rewarded with a bounty of 6 pesos for the return of the family's fugitive human property. Other expenditures for the slaves were minimal: a total of 220 pesos in six years went to merchants for cloth to be used by slaves, who evidently made their own clothing, and for medicine for their welfare. These costs, much the greater part of which were paid for Hispanic service and labor, came to 4907 pesos for the six years of Rivillapuerta's tutela.

There are no harvest data for 1631, and discounting the costs for that year leaves a total of 4739 pesos in operating expenditures for the five years for which we have calculated 14,118 pesos as the base market value (at prices charged family and friends) of the Rodríguez Santos wheat as it left the fields. Thus, the net income from agriculture for the years 1632 through 1636 would have been the difference between these amounts, or 9379 pesos. To this is added an additional 3198 pesos, the profit obtained by milling and marketing, for an overall net from the estancia of 12,577 pesos for the five-year period. This sum represents a mean annual net income of some 2515 pesos, and if the total appraised value in 1631 of the estancia land, mill, and slaves was 20,408 pesos (land and mill: 6500 pesos; slaves: 13,908 pesos), then we can estimate the average annual return on the capital value of the Rodríguez Santos estancia at about 12 percent.

This was not the total family income. When Rivillapuerta assumed the tutela in 1631 he took charge of 7077 pesos in outstanding loans made to eight Caracas vecinos, and from 1633 to 1636 he lent an additional 3525 pesos of his wards' cash to seven other town residents. At 5-percent interest, these loans brought the Rodríguez Santos heirs an additional annual income of 530 pesos. Added to the estancia income, this interest brought the total annual profit of the Rodríguez Santos estate to more than 3000 pesos. While not, by any means, on a par with the fabled fortunes of the Indies, this sum was sufficient to keep the young heirs of Juan Rodríguez Santos and Francisca de Escovedo from want.

The expenditures made by Rivillapuerta for the needs and comforts of his wife's brothers and sisters averaged about 1000 pesos per year, more than was spent on the operation of the wheat estancia and mill in four of the six years for which information is available. During this period, while estate operating costs totaled 6543 pesos, 6369 pesos were spent on clothing and education for the five heirs of Juan Rodríguez Santos and Francisca de Escovedo (see appendix C). The eldest child, doña Germana, received the largest share of these funds, some 2355 pesos, of which 300 were spent on her wedding trousseau in 1632. Thereafter her share consisted of dowry payments paid annually to her husband Domingo de Liendo. No other child received goods or services worth 300 pesos in any one year, but the eldest son, Diego Vásquez de Escovedo, who was thirteen years old in 1631, was favored with expenditures that were nearly twice that provided for each of the remaining children (165 pesos annually on the average compared to 89 pesos for Paula, 84 for Juan, and 67 for Alonso). This difference was due to the fact that in 1635 and during the first months of 1636, as the young *capitán* don Diego was about to turn eighteen and leave Rivillapuerta's tutelage, he was provided with the accouterments considered necessary for a young gentleman and slaveholder: a silk cape, a fine Castilian hat, a gilt-handled sword, and the saddlery befitting his station.

It is significant that while Rivillapuerta spent more on all of the children as they grew older, the wheat harvests of 1635 and 1636 were only slightly more than half as productive as those in 1632 and 1633. That Rivillapuerta continued to lend cash to the town's vecinos and to provide progressively more for his wards while the wheat harvests declined suggests that balancing the family's accounts, at least on an annual or seasonal basis, was not a predominating concern. Probably their numerous slaves offered the Rodríguez Santos a sense of long-term security that lessened their concern for short-term vacillations in grain production. With a substantial investment in slave labor already made, they could be sure that in any year they would be able to reap the maximum harvest the weather would allow. They also had the opportunity to make up for bad harvests by charging more for the wheat they sold. At 1632 prices, the 1635 and 1636 harvests would not have generated enough income to cover operating costs and expenditures for the children but, as the wheat yield declined, Rivillapuerta compensated by raising the sale price of grain and flour. On several occasions the cabildo had admonished the Rodríguez Santos clan for selling wheat bread at a higher price than that set by the municipal council,[11] but the price of wheat destined for export was not regulated by the council (although it had the authority to forbid exports altogether in times of local need), and the growers had a free hand to charge what they could get for their export crop. Bad harvests and the loss of Hispanic overseers and labradores to the better opportunities offered them on coastal cacao haciendas made wheat a scarce and expensive commodity,[12] and yet those who continued to grow it, although they may have had to pay a premium for Hispanic labor, were able to compensate by charging higher prices. Rivillapuerta raised the price of milled summer wheat from 42 reales the fanega in 1632 to an average of 66.4 reales in 1635, and then to 73.2 reales in 1636. As a result, the Rodríguez Santos estancia, had its manager cared to make the calculation, would have been able to show a reserve of cash on hand for these years after all costs had been paid (see appendix D).

THE LIENDO CACAO HACIENDA

The heyday of Caracas wheat had been over for some time by 1637. For at least a decade prior to that year a booming market for Caracas cacao in New Spain meant unprecedented profits for the owners of virgin groves of tropical cacao trees that dotted the coastal valleys. In 1637 Bartolomé de Rivillapuerta was pressured by his wife's brothers-in-law, his *concuñados*, for a division of the Rodríguez Santos estate among the surviving heirs. Domingo de Liendo, who had already received 1949 pesos of Germana de Rojas's (Rodríguez Santos) dowry, was eager for a division so that his wife could have her full share of the inheritance. He also doubted Rivillapuerta's ability to make good on new obligations to his brother, Santiago de Liendo, who married Paula Rodríguez Santos in February 1637. In April 1637, Santiago argued that, given the modest income from the wheat estancia, his wife could not expect the remainder of her dowry, 600 ducats (825 pesos), in the near future. It seems likely that Domingo and Santiago de Liendo were eager to claim the value of their wives' dowries in slaves, whose labor could at that time be put to more profitable use in cacao cultivation, and in fact a number of the same slaves who were listed in the inventory of the Rodríguez Santos estate in 1631 appear on the inventory list of Domingo de Liendo and Germana de Rojas's property taken in 1648. In any event, the cabildo honored the petitions of the Liendo brothers and in 1637 called for an inventory and division of property. At this time Rivillapuerta submitted the accounts he had kept since 1631, and in due course the property was divided among the heirs.[13]

The Liendo were Vizcayans. Three brothers, Pedro, Domingo, and Santiago, had come to Caracas in the late 1620s with their uncle, Pedro de Origüen. A former admiral in the New Spain flota, Origüen married doña Elena Suárez del Castillo in 1627 and in July 1628 he sent what was probably his first shipment of cacao to Veracruz as a Caracas vecino.[14] In 1630 doña Elena's niece Catalina Mejía married Origüen's eldest nephew Pedro, who became holder of the most important of the coastal encomiendas, the Chuao grant, in the process.[15] Domingo and Santiago de Liendo, together with their Rodríguez Santos wives, owned separate cacao haciendas in the neighboring coastal valley of Cepi. Without encomiendas, they depended for labor on black slaves, and in 1637 both Domingo and Santiago were in a hurry to see their wives take their due in inheritance from the abundant Rodríguez Santos pool of African laborers.

88   *The Seventeenth Century*

Domingo de Liendo and Germana de Rojas died suddenly in 1645. Their five minor children were then cared for in *tutela* by the childrens' uncles, first Santiago until his death in 1652, and then Pedro until 1657. From September 1645 until December 1657 these men carefully administered Domingo and Germana's heirs' property. As in the case of the Rodríguez Santos wheat estancia, these accounts provide an exact record of cacao harvests and sales and both hacienda and household expenditures.[16]

Two inventories, the first made in 1648 by Pedro Matute, then mayordomo at Cepi, and the second a decade later in 1658 by authorities of the cabildo, allow a close look at the slave population that by the middle of the seventeenth century had given the Liendo family wealth and status which they would retain until the very end of the colonial period. In 1658 the orphaned children of Domingo de Liendo and Germana de Rojas stood to inherit sixty-two slaves, of whom only six were children nine years old and younger. More than half (thirty-three) of these slaves lived and worked at the Cepi cacao hacienda (appendix E).

Seventeen of the sixty-two were women and girls ten years and older, and of these eight lived at Cepi, five with their husbands. Three married women and three teenaged girls were in domestic service in Caracas; the three women labored in the Liendo townhouse while the girls served three Liendo–Rodríguez Santos daughters as maids in the Immaculate Conception convent. Three other women, two with husbands and all three with young children, were at work on the new cacao hacienda then being planted at a site called Santa Lucía, south of Caracas on the Guaire River near where it enters the Tuy River. Of the thirty-nine adult men and boys, twenty-five lived on the established coastal cacao hacienda at Cepi, and of these six were married and the rest were single. Six others worked in domestic service in Caracas, and eight had been sent to the new hacienda at Santa Lucía (see table 11).

The thirty-three slaves at Cepi lived in sixteen houses. There were eight households of consanguineous kin, and eight of single, unrelated men. The kin households were of various sorts: four African couples, two with creole children; one creole couple; three old African men with their sons; and one African woman with her two creole children. The eight single, unrelated men at Cepi each lived in a separate dwelling; two of these men were creoles and six

Table 11 Slaves of the Liendo–Rodríguez Santos Heirs, 1658

	Townhouse	Cepi	Santa Lucía
Men and Boys			
Married	2	6	2
Unmarried	4	19	6
Women and Girls			
Married	3	5	2
Unmarried	3	3	1
Children			
(Under 9)	1	0	5
Totals	13	33	16

Source: ARPC, Testamentarías, 1653–1655 CL.

were African. Youthful strength was not a premium in the mature cacao groves at the Cepi hacienda. Many of the Cepi slaves were old and several were infirm. Two men were blind and Mauricio *criollo* was lame as well. Antón Fajero, at seventy the oldest slave of the Liendo–Rodríguez Santos group, lived at Cepi with his fifteen-year-old son Salvador. The mean age of Cepi slaves was thirty-nine for males and thirty-three for females, but the community was comprised of many older people and youngsters. Fifteen of the eighteen slaves aged forty-five or older owned by the heirs of Domingo de Liendo and Germana de Rojas lived at Cepi, and more than half of the slaves there were forty years old or older.

In the Caracas townhouse there were two slave couples, one widower with five creole children, three of whom were personal servants to the Liendo–Rodríguez Santos children, and two young creole slaves, the children of Cepi parents, one of whom served Francisca de Liendo in the Concepción convent. Mariela malemba, the wife of old Antón Fajero at Cepi, served the household as cook and *molendera*, grinder of corn. The oldest house slaves, Manuel Sacasaca and his wife Magdalena, had once belonged to Juan Rodríguez Santos and Francisca de Escovedo. On the average, however, the domestic slaves were younger than the other slaves owned by the Liendo–Rodríguez Santos heirs.

During most of the years of Santiago de Liendo's tutela a third group of slaves was at work clearing the land, digging irrigation ditches, and planting cacao at Santa Lucía. Youthful strength predominated here, where the Liendos were to learn the costly vagaries of cacao agriculture. Most of this planting crew was between the ages of twenty-five and thirty-five, and all the adults were African-born: Miguel *cacheo*, Antonio *carabali*, Sebastián *congo*, Nicolás *catoto*, and others.

The appraisal of the sixty-two slaves in 1658 was set at a total of 17,880 pesos, a mean value of 288 pesos for each man, woman, and child. The Cepi contingent, with a large number of older slaves, was valued at 267 pesos on the average, with the women worth some 30 pesos more than the men. The Caracas domestic slaves were more valuable than the Cepi blacks; their average appraised worth was 318 pesos, and in this case the men were given a cash value of about 50 pesos more than the women. The eleven adults who had been at work opening the ill-fated hacienda at Santa Lucía had a much higher mean assessment of 364 pesos, with men and women valued almost equally. In summary, the Cepi group was older and provided residence for a number of worn-out and infirm slaves, many of them men, who represented little or no market value to their Basque masters. Young, healthy, and very visible symbols of the Liendo's social importance, the Caracas domestic slaves ranked midway in value between the aged harvesters and weeders at Cepi and the younger and stronger field laborers who were engaged in the arduous tasks of clearing and irrigating the land at Santa Lucía (table 12).

Good data exist for cacao sales at the Cepi hacienda for the eighty-six months from October 1645 to November 1652 (table 13). During these years Santiago de Liendo kept a record of monthly harvests and sales from information sent to him by his mayordomo

Table 12 *Ages and Appraised Values of Liendo–Rodríguez Santos Slaves, 1658*

	Cepi			Caracas			Santa Lucía		
	Males	Females	All*	Males	Females	All	Males	Females	All
Mean Age	39	33	38	27	27	27	35	30	34
Mean Value (pesos)	258	294	267	343	293	318	369	350	364

Source: ARPC, Testamentarías, 1653–1655 CL.
* "All" excludes children nine years old and younger.

Table 13 Cepi Harvests, Prices, and Gross Income, 1645–1652

	1645	1646	1647	1648	1649	1650	1651	1652	Total	Monthly Mean
January		8/6	9	6	26	5/4	c	14/3	69/1	11/6
February		6/3	7/9	13/6	9	2/9	c	5/6	44/9	7/5
March		15	2	8	12/3	4	c	2/9	44	7/4
April		18	3/3	8/1	16/9	9/3	17	21	93/4	13/4
May		24	15/10	8	33/3	24/6	20	51/3	176/10	25/3
June		48	93/6	7/11	11/3	61/9	38	46/6	306/8	43/10
July		64	50	8/8	115	20/9	67	40/6	367/11	52/7
August		27	17/4	1/3	32/3	6/6	10	26	120/4	17/2
September		6	16	1/2	16/9	3/2	15/9	11	69/10	9/11
October	5	3/3	5	1/3	10/9	7	12/3	7/3	51/9	6/6
November	5/6[a]	5	1	5/6	11	16/3	9	10/3	63/6	7/11
December	10/1	11/6	5/1	12/1	34	15/3	9/3	—	97/3	12/2
Total Harvest	20/7	237	225/9	81/5	328/3	176/6	200/3	236/3	1505/3	
Price (pesos) per fanega	30	30	32	24	13	13	11	0		
Gross Income (pesos)	556[b]	6399	6502	1759	3841	2065	1983	1701	24,804	285[d]

Source: ARPC, Testamentarías, 1653–1655 CL.

[a] Harvests are given in fanegas and almudes, divided by a slash. Twelve almudes equal one fanega.
[b] Gross income does not include 10 percent deducted by the overseer for tithe payments. Income has been rounded to the nearest peso.
[c] Overseer Matute was sick and in Caracas during the first months of 1651. No cacao was shipped during this time, probably for this reason.
[d] Monthly gross income of 285 pesos was based on the total income divided by eighty-seven months.

Table 14 Cepi Sales, Prices, and Gross Income, 1654–1656

	1654	1655	1656	Total	Monthly Mean[c]
Sales[a]	289	172/3	193/10	655/1	18/3
Price (pesos per fanega)	10	10	10		
Gross Income (pesos)[b]	2709	1615	1817	6141	171

Source: ARPC, Testamentarías, 1653–1655 CL.

[a]Sales are given in fanegas and almudes; twelve almudes equal one fanega. Presumably, as was the case during the years from 1645 to 1652, the overseer deducted 10 percent of the harvest for payment of the diezmos. Thus sales represent 90 percent of the harvest.

[b]This data has been compiled from shipping receipts given in La Guaira. In order to compare this information with data given in table 13, which represents cacao as it was harvested at Cepi, it is necessary to deduct five reales for every fanega sold to account for the cost of shipment from Cepi to La Guaira. Thus, for example, in 1654, 289 fanegas were sold at 10 pesos, producing 2890 pesos income. From this, transport costs of 180.6 pesos (289 fanegas × 5 reales = 180.6 pesos) are subtracted to give 2709-pesos gross income. Income has been rounded to the nearest peso.

[c]Thirty-six months.

Pedro Matute. For the years after Matute left Cepi this information is not readily available; no data have been found for the year 1653, but a short series of cacao sales and prices for the years 1654 through 1656 have been assembled from receipts of sale signed by buyers who took delivery of Cepi cacao at the wharf in La Guaira[17] (see table 14).

The net annual income from Cepi during the Matute years, after the tithe had been discounted, was 3421 pesos. Counting thirty-one Cepi slaves who were neither blind nor lame, the annual income per slave laborer at Cepi was about 110 pesos. This was more than twice the income per slave on the Rodríguez Santos wheat estancia a decade earlier. However, after Matute's departure from service to the Liendo family, which coincided with the widespread currency crisis and the cacao blight (the alhorra, discussed in chapter 2), Cepi profits fell sharply. The blight had afflicted half the cacao trees at Cepi by 1653, but, surprisingly enough, production was not affected (18.25 fanegas/month were sold from 1654–1656, while 17.33 fanegas/month were harvested from 1645–1652). More important, the price of cacao fell steadily to 8 pesos the fanega in 1652 and 10 pesos in 1653, about one-third what it had been ten years earlier, and the gross income from the hacienda was reduced to an average of 171 pesos per month during the three years 1653–1655, down sharply from the 1645–1652 average of 285 pesos per month. During these last years for which data are available, the annual income per slave laborer was much closer to the Rodríguez Santos estancia average: 62 pesos per slave (2052 pesos per annum for thirty-three Cepi slaves) compared to 52 pesos for wheat laborers.

That cacao cultivation survived these difficulties was due in large part to the fact that, in terms of slave labor, cacao could be brought to market cheaply. Excepting the often strenuous work of planting new arboledas, the elderly and weaker slaves could carry on with all the labor of cacao agriculture and thus maintain the status quo of the haciendas during even extended periods of poor market conditions. This is what happened at the Cepi hacienda. And yet the specter of death, large families, and the obligation to divide the estate equally among all of one's heirs made expansion necessary if the family was to continue prosperous and to maintain its social station into the next generation. For the Liendo brothers, the exploitation of already-standing, virgin cacao groves and the high prices paid for cacao beans during the 1630s and the first years of the 1640s provided income for the purchase of enough slaves to permit them to continue to plant cacao during the several decades after 1650 when prices were very low. Operating costs for the established hacienda at Cepi were minimal, much lower than the costs associated with the Rodríguez Santos wheat farm, but the expenses, and the risks, of planting new groves could be quite high, as the Liendo case illustrates.

Hispanic labor at Cepi was limited to the overseer, and this was typical; in all the colonial documentation there is no evidence of labradores earning a share of the cacao harvest in exchange for directing and controlling the work force. Pedro Matute's annual salary was 128 pesos, only 3 or 4 percent of the gross income from cacao sales (based on the annual gross income from 1645–1652 of 3461 pesos), less than half the ratio of Hispanic labor earnings to gross income on the Rodríguez Santos estancia (table 10). The overseers who followed Matute were paid somewhat less. Clergy costs for religious instruction, marriage, and burial masses for the slaves came to about 50 pesos a year. Lawyers collected 75 to 100 pesos annually. Pruning knives, hoes, fishhooks, and salt were regular expenditures for the Cepi plantation, but they never amounted to more than 35 to 40 pesos in any one year. Similarly, about 30 pesos a year were spent on medicine, medical care, and midwives for the sick and pregnant slaves who belonged to Domingo and Germana's children. In this host of small payments, which did not differ significantly in amount or kind from those made by Bartolomé de Rivillapuerta on behalf of the Rodríguez Santos heirs, is revealed some of the more obscure threads in the social fabric of colonial Caracas society. In particular, the Liendo's treatment of their slaves when they were ill and of their slave women when they were pregnant, being fundamentally a matter of maintaining and extending the labor force, is especially illustrative of the social meaning of slavery in the Caracas setting.

Skin diseases were quite common among the slaves. Described as *gomas, bubas,* and *llagas,*[18] these were treated with ointments and infusions made of almond oil and with dietary supplements of honey, sugar, eggs, and chicken. Bloodletting was a common remedy for all sorts of internal ailments, and it was the single most costly slave expenditure made by the Liendo custodians. Town slaves were bled by a surgeon, Alonso de Heredia, who charged a peso each time he provided his services. At Cepi an itinerant barber did the same work for one-fourth the cost. Favored slave women were rewarded for becoming pregnant with a colorful woolen blanket imported from Mexico called a *frazada mestiza*. Magdalena, washerwoman and cook for the Liendo daughters in the Concepción convent, was given such a blanket in 1654. Pregnant slaves were tended to by Indian midwives who were also *curanderas,* healers and specialists in herbal medicines. These women were paid two or three pesos if they were able to restore to health a slave who had fallen ill.

Hispanic doctors and medicines were called upon and paid for in special instances. When Catalina returned to Cepi wrapped in a *frazada mestiza* to ward off her chills, Santiago de Liendo paid the town's doctors, who, after four months of observation, bleedings, and purges, were forced to declare her mysterious disease *"yncurable."* The Indian *curandera* Margarita was given a peso for her efforts to bring Catalina back to health, and the two women went together, otherwise unaccompanied, down to the coastal valley. When the house slave Juliana fell ill during her pregnancy, no cost was spared in the attempt to cure her. She was treated by the doctor Juan Bautista Osorio, who collected six pesos. Another peso went to the surgeon Heredia. Four pesos were paid for medicine, four reales for honey at the birthing, and two pesos to Bartola, the Indian midwife. All was for naught, however, as Juliana died while giving birth to twins. A creole, described as *ladina* in the records, she was buried in the cathedral cemetery at a cost of eight pesos, which included priests' charges and candles. The infants, who did not long survive their mother, were buried elsewhere at a total cost of five pesos. The sorry event was duly reported in the Liendo ledger as a total expense of twenty-six pesos.

Disease and death were not the only difficulties presented by the Liendo slaves to their masters. Many did not find that their bondage was much relieved by the woolen blanket and honey treatment, and the Liendo account book is dotted with payments to Indian slave-catchers who tracked down slaves who took advantage of the many opportunities to flee. Habitual runaways could expect special treatment of a different kind: four pesos went to a Caracas blacksmith for the manufacture of an iron bib (*braga*) for a slave who fled repeatedly from the planting gang at Santa Lucía. But, for all the trouble they presented, *cimarrones* were a minor problem and a minor expense compared to the difficulties associated with the new hacienda at Santa Lucía.

In 1647, with cacao selling at a remarkable thirty-two pesos the fanega and the Cepi harvests bountiful, Santiago de Liendo decided to plant cacao trees at Santa Lucía, fourteen leagues south of Caracas (about eighty miles distant) on the banks of the Guaire River. By August 1649, with the cabildo's permission, Santiago had purchased thirteen slaves with capital from his brother Domingo's estate. Francisco Sánchez, *compadre* to Liendo, agreed to oversee the planting for a salary of fifty pesos a year. From 1649 to 1653 Sánchez directed the planting of 15,000 *arboles de cacao* as well as maize, plantains, and yuca at the site.

Very few of the cacao trees at Santa Lucía ever bore fruit. First the water level in the Guaire dropped, leaving the newly dug irrigation ditches dry; then 6000 sapling trees succumbed to the alhorra blight; finally, most of the remaining trees were washed away in 1653 by the worst Guaire flood in contemporary memory. In this case it was not the slaves who ran away but rather the overseer Sánchez, and in an unusual reversal of loyalties the black *mandador*, or slave driver, a Carabali slave named Antonio, took it upon himself to save the last 3000 cacao trees. For his efforts Antonio was rewarded with a Mexican blanket for his pregnant wife. In 1656 the Caracas cabildo approved Pedro de Liendo's petition to transfer the slaves from Santa Lucía to Cepi, where he had already received permission in the name of his wards to purchase 1900 trees and a piece of land for them to work. The property sale was completed in September of that year, and by October the Santa Lucía slaves were in La Guaira en route down the coast to Cepi.[19]

In all, general operating costs for the Liendo estate totaled 14,424 pesos for the 141-month period from October 1645 to December 1656. Annual expenditures average 1228 pesos, about 400 pesos more than was spent by Rivillapuerta in order to maintain the Rodríguez Santos wheat estancia, but much of this difference can be attributed to the Liendo effort to expand cacao production. The Santa Lucía failure, at a cost of some 3500 pesos in slaves purchased and overseers' salaries, accounted for about 25 percent of these expenditures and produced almost no income (the only record of production from the ill-fated hacienda is an entry for 22 January 1656, which notes that 12 reales were spent to bring 3.5 fanegas of cacao beans from Santa Lucía to La Guaira). Totaling the returns from cacao sales for the same 141-month period gives an 11-year, 9-month estimated gross income of 30,871 pesos.[20] Less costs of 14,424 pesos, the net income for these years was 16,447 pesos, an annual average of 1400 pesos, or about 1100 pesos less per year than the Rodríguez Santos annual wheat farm earnings a decade earlier. Based on the appraised value of the Liendo field laborers, 13,130 pesos, plus the value of 6131 healthy cacao trees (at one peso each[21]), the annual return on the capital value of the Liendo cacao estate was about 7 percent. Without the costs of the Santa Lucía fiasco, these earnings would have been 10 percent or better.

The estimate of income for the Rodríguez Santos estancia, including profits from the milling of wheat and the sale of much of it at marked-up prices, was about 12 percent. Was cacao agriculture in the 1640s less profitable than wheat had been in the 1630s? It is important to recall that the Liendo accounts span a period of transition from highly profitable cacao cultivation to the beginnings of a general crisis. The years 1646 and 1647 mark the end of two decades of very high cacao prices. With more than 6000 pesos annual gross income, the net after costs in each of these years, and probably for many years prior to 1646, was at least 5000 pesos. For these years net income would have been about 25 percent on the appraised (1650s) value of slaves and cacao trees, or double that of the Rodríguez Santos wheat farm. These substantial returns, which were probably not unique to the Liendo cacao groves, were used to pay for the great many African slaves who were brought to the Caracas coast in the 1620s and 1630s. With this paid-for labor pool to rely upon, it is likely that the Basque Liendo brothers regarded nature's plagues and the low prices paid for cacao in the marketplace as only momentary problems that did not represent a serious menace to their favorable position in the Caracas community. Even as the alhorra claimed half the Cepi trees, as first drought and then floods ruined the infant Santa Lucía groves, and as the price of cacao fell from thirty to ten pesos the fanega, the comsumption patterns of the Liendo wards in Caracas continued apace, hardly reflecting economic events.

Domingo de Liendo and Germana de Rojas left five young children when they died, victims of an unidentified epidemic in 1645. Their eldest child and only son, Santiago, was then six years old; their youngest, Juana, had been baptized in October 1644. Personal expenditures for these children, including clothing, education, and food for themselves and the domestic slaves who served them, averaged 110 pesos a month for the eighty-seven month period of their uncle Santiago de Liendo's tutela (October 1645–December 1652) (see appendix F, "Children's Total"). Gross monthly income from the Cepi groves averaged 285 pesos during this time (table 13, "Gross Income"), with a net monthly income of 161 pesos after estate operating costs of 124 pesos (appendix F, "Estate Costs") were subtracted. During the years of Pedro de Liendo's tutela (from 1653 to 1657), as the children came of age and entered Caracas society, the cost of their maintenance increased considerably. Pedro de Liendo eliminated the one real per-day food allowance for his wards' seven domestic slaves (27 of the 110 pesos paid monthly by Santiago had been for food for these personal servants), but this did not compensate for the rising cost of providing for his nephew and nieces. In 1657 some 3300 pesos were paid out as eighteen-year-old Santiago was made alcalde of the Santa Hermandad, seventeen-year-old Francisca married the Vizcayan Francisco Aguirre Villela, and sixteen-year-old Germana took the vows of the Concepción convent.

While expenditures for these children rose from 110 pesos a month to 122, the monthly gross income from the Cepi hacienda declined from 258 pesos during Santiago's tutela to 171 pesos during Pedro de Liendo's wardship. After operating costs were discounted, the net income during the years 1653 to 1657 was only 103 pesos per month, which means that the heirs of Domingo de Liendo and Germana de Rojas consumed about 20 pesos a month more than they received in income from their hacienda during these years. Presumably, when it came to household expenditures, a substantial capital investment in slaves made it possible for families like the Liendo to ignore declining prices or bad harvests, at least in the short term.

In fact, it cost the Liendo children's uncles more than a hundred pesos a month, more than the annual salary of the Cepi overseer, to keep them at the standard of material culture considered appropriate for their social status. The dowry given for Germana's entry into the convent was the largest single nonagricultural debit made against the estate during the two uncles' custodianship, but the most frequent expenditures made on the heirs' behalf were for cloth, clothing, and shoes. The children received a new suit or dress on at least two occasions during the course of every year and a pair of new shoes every month. Santiago was given two or three pairs of new silk stockings every year and a new shirt made from imported cloth every month. During their younger years the expenditure for clothing seldom was more than 40 or 50 pesos a year each for Germana, Francisca, and Antonia, while purchases for Santiago totaled about 100 or 120 pesos annually. The greater part of this expense then went to the tailor who altered the clothing of the children's deceased parents. Later, when clothing costs for the four orphans were about 350 pesos a year, most of the expense was in the form of unworked cloth and only about 10 percent of the total was earned by tailors and shoemakers. Clothing for special occasions, when it would have the greatest visibility and social significance, accounted for something more than half the annual wardrobe expenditure. Francisca's wedding dress, which cost 120 pesos, was the most expensive clothing item, but when thirteen-year-old Santiago rode out to observe the cacao planting at Santa

Lucía, his first opportunity to act the part of lord of the domain and master of slaves, his uncle paid 318 pesos to outfit him completely: a new saddle, silver dagger, silk cape, and broad-brimmed hat complemented a suit trimmed in leather and velvet and knee-length boots.

The other form of personal expenditures for the Liendo children, which continued apace in bad times as well as good, was for education. High culture and learning were exceptional privileges in early colonial Caracas, and the Liendo wards were given what was available of them. Five pesos a year went to Pablo de Ojeda, Santiago's dance teacher, 6 pesos were paid to his grammar tutor, and 1 or 2 pesos were spent on school books. The girls' formal education began when they were five with a hired master who charged 6 pesos a year to teach each of them to read. Before their tenth birthdays the educational responsibility for Francisca, Germana, and Antonia had been transfered to the nuns at the Concepción convent. For 50 pesos a year they received academic and religious training there in the company of the daughters of Caracas's leading families. An additional 100 pesos per year on the average was spent for each girl for food and other incidental items. Some of these things may have served to set the Liendo sisters apart, as part of the new cacao planter elite, in the well-to-do female society of the convent. Mattresses and bordered coverlets brought from New Spain, painted ceramics from Puebla, and colorful, quality clothing woven on Mexican looms for the slave girls who lived with their mistresses behind the convent walls made the Liendo family's New Spain cacao connection evident for all to see.

Cacao would continue to serve them well. Beginning in 1628, when the uncle of Pedro, Santiago, and Domingo sent a small quantity of beans on consignment to Juan de Castro, vecino of Veracruz,[22] the Liendo family was able to fashion a slave-based agricultural enterprise that would survive the several depressed decades after 1650s to put it among the colony's foremost cacao planters in the eighteenth century. Pedro de Liendo died childless and the encomienda that had been his became the basis of the most important ecclesiastical benefice in Caracas, the *obra pía* of Chuao. The heirs of Santiago de Liendo, whose ambitions led to the Santa Lucía fiasco, emerged as the wealthier branch of the Liendo clan. In 1684 Santiago's son Juan de Liendo, regidor and maestre de campo, had 2000 cacao trees at a reestablished Santa Lucía hacienda, 3000 at the original Cepi estate, and 4000 trees as well as a sugar trapiche at San Matheo in the Aragua Valley.[23] By 1720 the grandchildren of Santiago de Liendo would own 40,000 cacao trees on the coast and in the Tuy River valleys. Finally, the orphaned children of Domingo de Liendo and Germana de Rojas, whose tutelas have provided the data for this analysis, did not fare as well as the cousins with whom they were raised.

Santiago de Liendo, alcalde of the Santa Hermandad, purchased three slaves and twenty-one fanegadas of irrigable land near Chuspa on the upwind coast in 1676. The sale price of 1833 pesos included the copper pans of an unworked trapiche there. In 1684 Santiago was dead, and this trapiche was the only agricultural property claimed by his widow, doña Isabel María Gedler. Their son, Juan Domingo de Liendo, would have 20,000 cacao trees at Chuspa in 1720. Francisca de Liendo, the only daughter of Domingo de Liendo and Germana de Rojas who did not remain in the Concepción convent, owned 3500 *árboles de cacao* at Cepi in 1684. There is no trace of her children (surname Aguirre Villela Liendo) among the province's cacao hacienda owners in 1720.[24]

The Liendo tutela accounts record only the last years of the first Caracas cacao boom. High prices from the 1620s through the 1640s, when most of the cacao harvested came from virgin groves, provided planters like the Liendo with annual income of perhaps 25 percent the capital value of their haciendas and slaves. Owners of wheat estancias and mills were able to add to their agricultural profits by raising the price of their grain and by grinding the grain to flour, while cacao profits were entirely dependent on prices set in the distant New Spain market. Nevertheless, the Liendo cacao hacienda during its best years earned for its owners about twice what was made from the Rodríguez Santos wheat estancia and mill, although during years of low prices its earnings were on a par with the wheat estate. In both of these cases the guardians were able to provide their young charges with spouses, a place in the convent, formal education, clothing, and the other material goods deemed appropriate for their social station. In both cases the cost of these things, which is to say the expenditure necessary to meet and maintain the elite standard of material wealth in seventeenth-century Caracas, was approximately equivalent to the net income from these properties. Probably this balancing of the books was the primary objective of the tutela, and we may suppose that other estates might have had a larger net income or a different ratio of expenditures to income. But these cases illustrate how an annual income of not less than 7 percent and probably often more than 20 percent of the capital value of these estates was spent by elite slaveholding agriculturalists in Caracas at midcentury. The Rodríguez Santos daughters married Liendo immigrants as wheat farming was eclipsed by cacao, and the substantial profits provided by the first cacao boom carried most of the expanding Liendo family through several difficult decades and into the eighteenth century with no significant loss of productive cacao property or social status. Like several other families that had acquired large numbers of slaves and had become well established in the cacao business before 1650, the Liendo emerged in the 1680s with the labor and land needed to take full advantage of the prolonged prosperity that would then continue unabated until the 1740s.

PART II

THE EIGHTEENTH CENTURY

4

The Tuy Valley Frontier

> These fruits [cacao] are not like those that emerge from the frightening fertility of the Nile, where nothing more is required than the diligence of the farmers who need only to plant their wheat once the flood waters have subsided in order to have a prodigious harvest. In this country, besides the initial cost of the land and the formation of the haciendas, it is necessary to have a gang of Blacks—what they cost is well known—who must be fed and clothed. It is necessary to buy for them the necessary tools for their labor, to pay for overseers, for chaplains, and they must plant, irrigate, weed, prune, and replant—most strenuous work—and then they must harvest, clean, dry, and bag the cacao beans. After these many tasks are done, it is necessary to pay for muleteams, which in some places cost four or five pesos the *carga*, and in others as much as eight pesos, to take the beans to port. And, after meeting so many other costs, it is only the most unusual hacienda owner who does not have a substantial mortgage on his land which also must be paid.
>
> —José Félix Valverde, Bishop of Caracas, to the King, 1745.
> AGI, Santo Domingo, leg. 786.

Only modest in size, subject to irregular rainfall, and without rich or resilient topsoil, most of the coastal valleys of the Caracas province had been planted in cacao to the limit of their productive capacity before the end of the seventeenth century. However, from at least the 1640s Caraqueños had also cleared land and cut irrigation canals for cacao haciendas on the banks of inland rivers, in particular the Tuy River and the lower portions of its several tributary streams. Coastal production still predominated in the 1680s, when enough Caracas cacao was grown to replace traditional Central American producers in the New Spain market,[1] but by the first years of the eighteenth century, after decades of steady planting, there were more cacao trees on the riverbank haciendas in the interior than there were on the coast. In addition, the newer riverine haciendas were significantly more bountiful. By the 1720s many coastal groves had been steadily worked for a century, with the result that the typical yield from these haciendas was no more than ten fanegas of beans from every 1000 mature trees. In the Tuy, by contrast, fertile soil, abundant rainfall, and the many stretches of low-lying river bank where irrigation systems could be dug meant that harvests of twenty-five and thirty fanegas of beans per 1000 trees were not uncommon. In 1720 some 60 percent of the cacao beans grown in the Caracas province came from new haciendas established along the Tuy and its tributaries, and by 1744 the Tuy share had risen to three-fourths of the total provincial harvest (see map 3).[2]

The Tuy cacao frontier was of major, and mostly overlooked, importance for the history of colonial Caracas. Had the cacao economy been limited to the coastal valleys, the colony would have no doubt faded to insignificance before the end of the seventeenth century. Instead, with a total of more than 5 million cacao trees in the province by 1744, a more than five-fold increase during the sixty years after 1684, the Tuy haciendas led a prolonged boom that had a profound effect on Caracas society. In the first place, such dynamic expansion attracted the attention of a group of Basque investors, who, using as a vehicle their royally chartered monopoly company, the *Real Compañía Guipuzcoana*, made a controversial effort to control the Caracas cacao trade for their own benefit.

The Tuy boom also drew many hundreds of migrants across the Atlantic to Venezuela. The great majority of these were African slaves, brought for immediate and involuntary labor in the new groves. Many others were Canary Islanders, known as *isleños* or *canarios*, most of them modest farmers in their homeland, who arrived with gentry ambitions of becoming slave holders and hacienda owners in their own right. The canarios' hopes would go largely unfulfilled however, and after the failure of the uprising of 1749 many of them would take a place alongside the slaves as wage laborers in the cacao groves of Caracas elites. Although they regarded the prospect of becoming a rural proletariat as tantamount to passing into the state of slavery, and were driven to rebellion to prevent it from happening, isleños shared an intertwined history

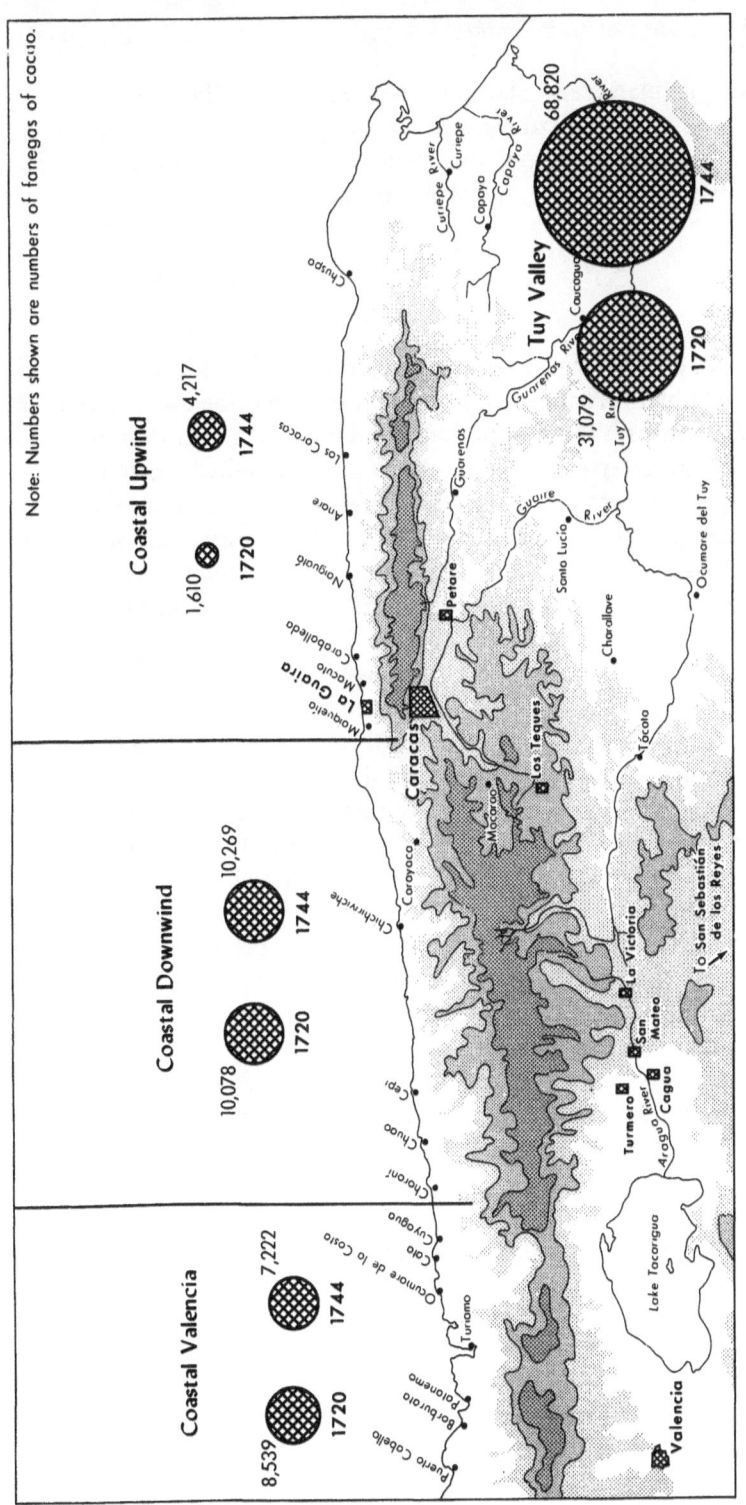

Map 3. Fanegas of Cacao in the Caracas Province, 1720 and 1744

with free blacks and slaves in the Tuy region. The example of the Curiepe Valley illustrates well the complex pattern of race, politics, and personal ambition that characterized settlement on the Tuy frontier early in the eighteenth century.

CONFLICT OVER SETTLEMENT: THE CASE OF CURIEPE

By the end of the seventeenth century, although some Caracas vecinos had forgotten who had first explored the lower Tuy River and environs, the value of the region had become evident to everyone. Controversies over land titles in the Tuy had created a boom in legal business in Caracas that paralleled the booming prosperity of the cacao business in the region. As the history of the settlement of Curiepe demonstrates, high station and influence were useful weapons in the competition for land. It is also evident that by the beginning of the century there was already a concern for the supply and cost of labor to work the new haciendas.

In March 1699, during his last month as governor of Venezuela, don Francisco de Berrotarán sent three dozen men to look for the gold mines of "Apa y Carapa" in the hills south of the Tuy. With Tomusa Indians as guides, these men spent six weeks looking for gold where they believed *"los antiguos"* had found it at the time of the conquest of Caracas. Struggling in torrential rains and opposed by resident Indians, they found nothing. Nevertheless, and there is good reason to suppose that this was the primary reason for the venture, as soon as his men returned Governor Berrotarán began to request title to the land in the area on the basis of the 7800 pesos he had invested in its exploration.

Berrotarán remained in Caracas after his administration of the colony ended, and in 1702, the same year that he was granted the title of first Marqués del Valle de Santiago, he received from the crown legal title to a vast region south of the lower Tuy called "Apacarapa." It turned out, however, that his title was in conflict with others held by Pedro de Ponte y Andrade, a Spanish immigrant from La Coruña, Galicia, who had come to Caracas before 1679. Ponte complained to the crown that the search for gold mines was part of a scheme to grab land from people, like himself, who had already planted cacao in the area. Over the course of several years Ponte had acquired 79 slaves from the Portuguese asiento, and these slaves had been at work on his Tuy Valley cacao hacienda for some time. Ponte acknowledged that it was possible for Berrotarán to buy 200 slaves, as he planned to do, because this quantity was occasionally available for sale in Caracas, but Ponte doubted that the new marqués had the money to make such a purchase. More importantly, even if Berrotarán bought 200 slaves, Ponte argued that it would be impossible for him to support them for the several years that would pass before the cacao trees matured and bore fruit. There were good profits to be made from cacao agriculture in the Tuy, Ponte acknowledged, but it was a very expensive business to begin from scratch on a large scale. With pointed irony, Ponte suggested that unless his adversary discovered the gold mines he had ostensibly set out to find, Berrotarán would not be able to feed his slaves while they brought his first cacao crop to harvest, "it being very expensive to keep slaves in the Tuy." As perhaps his best argument in defense of his property, Ponte reminded the king that if Berrotarán's titles were upheld and he lost his right to continue to grow cacao on his established hacienda, the monarchy would forfeit the revenues that were already being collected on the exports of Ponte's cacao beans.[3] Yet Ponte underestimated either his rival's wealth or the capacity of the Tuy to turn a quick profit. In the long run both men were successful there, and in 1720 their heirs were owners of the largest cacao haciendas in the Tuy: Miguel Berrotarán Tovar, the second Marqués del Valle, had a cacao estate of 30,000 trees in the Tuy in that year, and Pedro Ponte Marín, the eldest son of Pedro de Ponte y Andrade, had an even larger Tuy hacienda of some 50,000 trees.

Much of the land in the Tuy Valley had been claimed before the end of the seventeenth century by powerful recent immigrants like Berrotarán or by long-established Caracas residents like Ponte y Andrade. By the beginning of the next century the opportunities created by high cacao prices paid in the expanding New Spain market made the region very attractive to would-be cacao farmers who were neither politically powerful nor members of entrenched local families. The *mantuanos*, as members of the foremost Caracas families were called in the eighteenth century, fought legal and political battles with groups of these ambitious newcomers for Tuy cacao property. The newcomers, pioneers who were willing to settle on their frontier estates, fought among themselves as well. Illustrative of this conflict is the particularly well-documented struggle over the right to settle and plant cacao in the Curiepe Valley, located in the hills north of the lower Tuy some 20 leagues from Caracas, about halfway between the river and the Caribbean coast. More than a simple dispute at law over land on a remote frontier, the fight for Curiepe became part of some of the most important social and political issues of the day, including the new Bourbon regime's first efforts at centralizing its colonial authority and the challenge this presented to the traditional rights of the Caracas cabildo to govern the province in the absence of the governor.

Payment of a fee to the crown in 1663 had given the *mantuano* Juan Blanco de Villegas title to Curiepe land that was said to comprise an entire square league. In the early eighteenth century, two different groups challenged the exclusive rights of the Blanco de Villegas in Curiepe. Entirely without success in their effort was a large group of Canary Islanders, a total of 413 people in 73 families, who first petitioned the crown in 1728 for parcels of land drained by the Curiepe River. One of the leaders of the isleños then seeking land was Juan Francisco de León, who would, twenty years later, lead a large band of irate Tuy residents to Caracas to protest the policies of the Guipuzcoana Company. According to their petition in 1728, 60 of the Canary Islander families had been living in the immediate vicinity of Caracas and in the town proper for two decades. They had first gone out to Venezuela at the urging of the crown, but they had never been given land to plant as they had been promised, having been obliged instead, for all the ensuing years, to work as sharecroppers in the fields of others. The canarios recognized the legality of the Blanco de Villegas claim to Curiepe, but they argued that they should be given some of the property since nothing had ever been done by the family to put the land to productive use, and that it would be at best many more years before the Blanco family could acquire the slaves they needed to establish a profitable hacienda there.

To give their case the appearance of something more noble than their own self-interest, the petitioners concluded by depicting for the crown a dire scenario that could result if they were not given the opportunity to settle Curipe. They warned that their competitors in the region, a group of free blacks, *morenos libres*, who were also soliciting titles, had already illegally built houses and planted cacao at Curiepe. These blacks, the canarios argued, would multiply greatly in the sparsely populated zone. The petitioners believed that the danger inherent in this situation was obvious, but they recounted for the king rumors of English buccaneers who had raided the region in 1710, carrying off some cattle and a few slaves. The whole region could become a *"Nueva Jamayca,"* they warned, should the English return to find a large community of free people of color in Curiepe, people unsupervised and of uncertain loyalty, who would most certainly offer no resistance to the invaders. If the Blanco de Villegas titles were disallowed and they were given permission to settle, as trustworthy and hardworking subjects the canarios offered themselves as entirely suitable replacements for the morenos who were occupying Curiepe in violation of both the Blanco titles and the best interests of the empire.[4]

For their part, by the 1720s the morenos libres in Curiepe had earned a precarious right to their settlement after a fortuitous series of events punctuated by sharp turns of fortune.[5] Many of them had come to the Indies as Dutch slaves, and they had gained their liberty in a rather remarkable fashion. From 1702 to 1704 some thirty Africans, fleeing their Dutch masters on the island of Curaçao, crossed the narrow stretch of sea separating the island from the Venezuelan mainland. Carried westward by the prevailing winds and current, they arrived finally at the coastal town of Coro, where they were seized by the municipal authorities and put up for sale at public auction. This was probably not the first time that fugitive Dutch slaves in pursuit of their freedom had ended up as the bondsmen of Spaniards on the Venezuelan coast, but the destiny of these slaves was to be different, for in 1701, by means of some deft diplomacy, the French had replaced the Portuguese as holders of exclusive rights to supply Spain's colonies with African slaves.[6] The French factor of the *asiento de negros* in Coro claimed that the auction had been illegal, since by contract and by treaty he had the unique right to sell slaves entered into Spanish territory, including those who entered while fleeing from foreign masters. In 1703 the case was brought before the Audiencia of Santo Domingo, a venue with little sympathy for the French cause, since that island had been forcefully divided into French and Spanish portions only in 1697. Citing a *real cédula* dated November 1697, in which slaves fleeing from the French district of Santo Domingo to the Spanish zone were given their freedom, the Audiencia declared in 1704 that the Dutch slaves in Coro were also to be freed. As had been the case in Santo Domingo, the Coro *libres* were also to receive sufficient land so that they might support themselves. This totally unanticipated decision both denied the French factor his profits and the Coro vecinos the slaves they had expected. Word of the Audiencia's order spread quickly, but many Spaniards refused to comply with it. The order went largely unenforced until 1711, when another forty fugitives arrived from Curaçao. Most of these slaves were also seized and put to work for new masters, but some of them, together with a few of those who had been freed earlier, went to Caracas to petition the governor for their freedom and the land they were to be given by law.[7]

The governor in Caracas from 1711 to 1714 was José Francisco de Cañas y Merino, son of the sergeant major of the Spanish presidio at Orán, Africa. Cañas had been raised at Orán, and had risen in the ranks there to become captain of the infantry. As governor he supported the cause of the Curaçao refugees, and, perhaps as a gesture of defiance directed at the Caracas elite,[8] he instructed the freedmen to join the town's newly formed free black militia unit. The captain of this unit, the *Compañía de Morenos Libres*, was a mulatto, Juan del Rosario Blanco, who was named to the position by Cañas in 1711. He had been the slave, and was probably the illegitimate son, of don Alejandro Blanco de Villegas, heir to the Curiepe land. Juan del Rosario could read and write, and he was a popular leader of Caracas's free people of color. In 1715, the year after his patron Cañas had been forcibly removed from office, Juan del Rosario sent a memorial to the king in the name of his compañía, asking for land in compliance with the order given by the Audiencia of Santo Domingo in 1704. The memorial stated that the twenty-one freed Dutch slaves who belonged to his militia had not received land as the court had ordered, and that many other former slaves released by the Audiencia lived scattered about the countryside without legal means to sustain themselves and without the benefit of priest or religion.

Juan del Rosario provided the monarch with a brief description of the geography of the Venezuelan coastline east of the port at La Guaira. For a distance sixteen or eighteen leagues the valleys of this *barlovento* (windward) coast were filled with cacao haciendas; but beyond the valley of Chuspa, where the coastline falls away to the south, forming Cape Codera with its extensive bay known as Higuerote, there were no settlements or haciendas. Protected there from the prevailing westerly winds, ships of all kinds bound for La Guaira and beyond stopped at Higuerote to make sure of their bearings and to make sure that the coast was clear of pirates before continuing down the open Venezuelan coast. The strategic importance was twofold: first, unguarded, it was an attractive rendezvous for pirates, and second, it would be an ideal point of disembarkation for a land invasion of the colony. Juan del Rosario proposed that the morenos libres of his militia unit and others who had subscribed to his plan be allowed to settle in an area about five leagues west of the Higuerote coast called by him Sabana del Oro. This would comply with the Audiencia order to give the freed slaves land, and, since many of them were soldiers in the king's militia, their presence would control contraband and slow down any foreign army that might be put ashore there until aid could be sent from Caracas.

According to the proposal, once established the community would receive a priest named by the bishop in Caracas, and its inhabitants would recognize the local authority of a lieutenant named by the governor. To give their petition added respectability, the claimants reminded the king of a similar settlement of mulattos established by royal decree in New Spain; their community would be "an imitation of the one created in Vera Cruz, on the barlovento coast there, that they call San Miguel de la Antigua."[9]

The site referred to by Juan del Rosario as Sabana del Oro was in fact Curiepe, as he no doubt knew, and the mantuano family of Blanco de Villegas was quick to point out that fact in Caracas. The petition met with complete silence from the cabildo and the governor, and the cause of the morenos libres would most likely have advanced no further had it not been for the disjunctures and juridical confusion that befell the colony after 1719, when the word arrived in Caracas that the province of Venezuela had been transferred from Santo Domingo to the executive authority of the newly created viceroyalty of New Granada and the judicial authority of the Audiencia of Santa Fe de Bogotá.[10] As it turned out, the resulting disorder in Caracas allowed the morenos libres their chance to lay what proved to be a lasting claim to the Curiepe Valley.

The viceroy of New Granada took immediate interest in this new dominion, and in 1720 two of his agents, designated *jueces comisionarios*, arrived in Caracas. These men were charged with the responsibility of investigating the state of the royal treasury, making a census of the Indian population, and putting an end to contraband trade. An imbroglio quickly formed between these viceregal agents, Pedro Martín de Beato and Pedro José de Olavarriaga, who were Basques, and the Canary Islander governor, Marcos de Betancourt y Castro. From Bogotá the viceroy, Jorge de Villalonga, without having had time to receive Betancourt's defense of charges made against him by Beato and Olavarriaga, ordered the governor jailed for smuggling and other crimes. Licenciado Antonio José Alvarez y Abreu, who had come with Beato and Olavarriaga ostensibly as a legal advisor, was told to assume Betancourt's gubernatorial duties. This action violated the traditional privilege of the Caracas cabildo to act as interim governor, and the town council's regidores made an appeal to the viceroy. In no uncertain terms, threatening fines of 4000 pesos, arrest and transport to Bogotá, Villalonga ordered the cabildo to comply. Intimidated, the cabildo did comply, and from March until December 1721 Alvarez y Abreu exercised the governor's authority. During this time Juan del Rosario and the morenos libres would found a settlement at Curiepe.

In June 1721, governor pro tem Alvarez y Abreu granted Juan del Rosario a license to reconnoiter the Sabana del Oro site in preparation for the pueblo that he and his militiamen wanted to establish there. This license was understood by the morenos to be in fact permission to begin the settlement, and construction was begun. With sixteen houses and a church of wattle and daub clustered around a plaza, Juan del Rosario made clear to the governor the full range of his ambitious plans for Curiepe. In a letter he asked Alvarez y Abreu to order his lieutenants on the coast and the interior valleys to send to Caracas all the runaway slaves that they might capture. He asked that all these *cimarrones* then be "given to the Capitán and founder of Sabana del Oro, for the better establishment and increase of said Sabana."[11] Not surprisingly, this audacious relocation scheme never received serious consideration, but the settlement of morenos at Curiepe was established. In spite of subsequent efforts to remove them, they remained there, and, as it turned out, more than a few cimarrones would find their own way to the Curiepe region.

The decade of the 1720s was marked by a chaos of governance in Caracas which would, among its several major consequences, have a lasting effect on the way the Tuy was administered and on the attitudes of Tuy settlers toward royal and regional authority. Alvarez y Abreu was replaced in December 1721 by a new permanent governor, Diego Portales y Meneses, who immediately became involved in a serious controversy with both the viceroy in Bogotá and the Caracas cabildo. In the entire eighteenth century, the disorder created by the political struggles of the first years of the 1720s would be surpassed only by the open rebellion of 1749. Portales was as quick to take authority from the viceregal triumvirate of Beato, Olavarriaga, and Alvarez y Abreu as they had been to deny it to the previous governor Betancourt. Portales expelled Alvarez y Abreu and imprisoned Beato and Olavarriaga, acts that won him the approval of the Caracas elite. But the governor then lost his local support by curiously insisting that the bishop occupy his office rather than the cabildo while he made an obligatory tour of the province. The cabildo appealed this infringement to Spain, and in January 1723 a royal *cédula* was received in Caracas which reaffirmed the town council's right to replace the governor on an interim basis with its alcaldes ordinarios. Neither viceroys nor the governors themselves could abrogate this privilege.

Two months later an order for Portales's arrest arrived from Bogotá, citing his rough treatment of the viceroy's agents the previous year. This time local sensitivities were respected, and the order carefully stipulated that the cabildo would assume gubernatorial authority. From the Caracas jail, Portales complained to the king, and in response to his appeal a second cédula arrived from Spain late in 1723. Contradicting both tradition and the previous instructions, this order gave Portales his freedom and granted him permission to name the bishop, Escalona y Calatayud, as his temporary replacement. He was also told to disregard any challenge to his authority that might come from the viceroy of New Granada.

Armed with this support, Portales began a determined vendetta against certain prominent Caraqueños who had been responsible for his incarceration. In turn, these opponents turned for help to influential friends in the viceregal government, with the result that Portales was free for only a few months when, in February 1724, the Audiencia of Santa Fe demanded that the Caracas cabildo arrest him once again. Placed in chains and even in the stocks for a time,

Portales remained in jail for a month before he escaped and took refuge in the residence of his ally Escalona. The bishop tried to assume the governorship on the basis of the most recent royal missive, but the cabildo rejected the effort, claiming that the governor could not make appointments while under arrest in the Caracas jail. At this point, with the question of jurisdiction in complete confusion, and the practical matter of authority reduced to simple power, both sides took up arms. Bloodshed was averted because the cabildo faction had far greater support in the community than Portales and Escalona, and when Portales escaped to the coastal valley of Ocumare the confrontation ended, with no more immediate damage done than widespread anger. The bishop vented his feelings by excommunicating the alcaldes of the cabildo, but in time tempers cooled, the ecclesiastical dictate was removed, and a third royal cédula, sent in response to an appeal to the crown made by Escalona, brought Portales back to the governor's residence in June 1726. He remained in formal control of the colony until he was replaced in 1728.[12]

Central to an understanding of this controversy is the challenge that the viceroyalty of New Granada presented to the prerogatives of the Caracas governor. It was the responsibility and privilege of the governor, who in Venezuela was also chief military office as captain-general, to appoint officers who represented his authority in the rural districts of the province. This official, known by the title of *teniente de justicia mayor*, administered an often extensive jurisdiction. In the first decades of the eighteenth century there were three of these positions in the vicinity of Caracas: responsibility for the coast was given to a *castellano y justicia mayor* who also administered both the fort and the commercial activities of the port of La Guaira; a second lieutenant executed the king's justice in the Tuy region from the town of Ocumare del Tuy to the mouth of the river; while a third oversaw a jurisdiction that extended south of Caracas to Santa Lucía on the lower Guaire River. In addition to these regional officers, eight Hispanic *corregidores* were located in towns with Indian populations.[13] Tenientes could name assistants, or *cabos*, to patrol the more remote zones of their jurisdictions. As judges of first instance, these men had a variety of responsibilities, but principal among them were the duties of pursuing runaway slaves and preventing contraband trade. To supplement their modest salaries, all of these officials were entitled to retain a portion of the illegally transported cacao or other contraband merchandise which they seized.

The system of tenientes gave the governor at least nominal control over policing and the exercise of justice in the countryside, and also provided him with positions that he could use for patronage purposes. Until 1717, the names of men nominated for these positions were referred to the Audiencia of Santo Domingo for approval, and the Audiencia had always confirmed the governors' nominations as a matter of course.[14] But the transfer of administration to the viceroy of New Granada and the Audiencia of Santa Fe brought significant changes to Caracas. Enthusiastic about controlling Venezuelan smuggling, the viceroy sent his own agents, the *jueces de comiso* Beato and Olavarriaga, whose authority in the countryside superseded that of the governor-appointed tenientes. Resistance by Governor Betancourt to this challenge of his traditional prerogatives resulted in his imprisonment on the charge that he was himself a *contrabandista*. To enforce the effort to centralize control from Bogotá, Betancourt was removed from office altogether and replaced, not by the alcaldes of the Caracas cabildo, but by Alvarez y Abreu, who could then appoint tenientes to the liking of the viceroy, without any regard whatsoever for local sentiment. In a related matter, with blatant disregard for local opinion, Alvarez y Abreu granted Juan del Rosario permission to found a settlement of ex-slaves at Curiepe.

For the principal citizens of Caracas, who may or may not have benefited very much from smuggling, centralization from the distant viceregal capital meant that their influence in the rural hinterland of the Caracas province was diminished along with that of the governor. The vecinos' influence traditionally was dependent on their ability to persuade the governor to support their view—for instance, to be lax in his persecution of smugglers. In the case of Portales, his initial efforts to resist the viceroy's agents struck a blow in favor of regional autonomy that Caraqueños could applaud, but then, by denying the cabildo its right to replace him on a temporary basis, the governor demonstrated an unwillingness to share power. He then became an opponent of the colonists rather than their ally. To the relief of the Caracas elite, in 1726 the judicial responsibility for Venezuela was returned to the Audiencia of

Santo Domingo, and with it the authority of the governor was restored to the *status quo ante*.

The significance of these events went far beyond the particular case of the settlement of Curiepe, but the resolution of the controversy there demonstrates clearly the powerful impact on all claimants of the highly inconstant royal authority. The morenos continued to plant cacao while power struggles distracted Caracas, but the arrival of Portales and the eclipse of Alvarez y Abreu nearly brought to an end the Curiepe plans of Juan del Rosario. In 1722, while Portales was still on favorable terms with the Caracas mantuanos, Francisco de Monasterios presented the governor with the Blanco de Villegas titles to Curiepe and requested a ruling against the morenos who had no legal right to reside there. Monasterios's wife, Adriana Blanco Villegas, had died in 1721, and his interests in preventing Juan del Rosario from inhabiting the region were probably related to his wife's inheritance there. Portales responded to the Monasterios petition by ordering the destruction of the Curiepe settlement in September 1722. Although houses were burned and crops destroyed, the morenos remained in the vicinity of Curiepe, and in 1723, perhaps unsure to which jurisdiction his case belonged, Juan del Rosario sent appeals to both the Audiencia of Santo Domingo and the Audiencia of Sante Fe.

The final phase of the protracted conflict over Curiepe began in March 1724, with the death of Alejandro Blanco de Villegas. He had always been lukewarm in his resistance to the Curiepe efforts of Juan del Rosario Blanco, who was most likely his unrecognized son. Alejandro Blanco's widow, doña Luisa Catalina Martínez de Villegas, felt no similar compunctions, and in June 1724 she opened a vigorous campaign against "the violent pretensions of the *negro* Juan del Rosario, my *liberto*." In her petition to the Audiencia of Santa Fe, which would finally reach the Council of the Indies for judgment, she argued that there was no valid comparison to be made between the settlement of freed slaves in distant, isolated Curiepe and the land given to their counterparts in Santo Domingo, which was "within view" of the established colony on that Caribbean island. Her opponent's privileged relationship with her husband (she referred to the moreno militia captain disparagingly as her personal servant, or page: "*Juan Page, alias del Rosario*") had given rise to the whole problem. The morenos had never received actual permission from either governor or viceroy to settle Curiepe or any other place, and they had lied about the location of Sabana del Oro, which was in fact Curiepe, land that belonged to her and her children as heirs of her husband.[15]

While both parties waited for a decision from the institutions of higher justice, the cabildo took revenge on what it considered to be the pretensions of Juan del Rosario. Early in 1725, with Portales in hiding and the alcaldes ordinarios exercising gubernatorial authority, they relieved Juan del Rosario of the captaincy of the militia, using his advanced age as an excuse. However, Rosario and the moreno community had become pawns in the very serious play for power that dominated Caracas after 1722, and when Portales regained the governor's office in June 1726 he reversed the ruling of his opponents on the cabildo and restored Rosario to his militia command.[16]

In that year the Audiencia in Santo Domingo ordered the governor to send copies of all the documents pertaining to the Curiepe dispute, and to make no further changes in the status of the settlement until a final decision could be made. It was at this point that the landless Canary Islanders who had been working as laborers made their bid for land and a town in the Curiepe region of the Tuy Valley, ostensibly to protect the province from foreign invasion and the dubious loyalty of the morenos there. Gaining no support from Portales, the canarios were no doubt surprised to find that the morenos of Curiepe, their estwhile competitors, were willing to make common cause with them. A joint petition arguing that there was room for more than one settlement at Curipe was sent to Santo Domingo, and the response from the Audiencia appeared to reward this combined effort with a decisive victory. The decision of the Audiencia, issued in December 1728, was unequivocal:

> It is declared that the lands of the Valley of Curiepe, Sabana del Oro, Cabo de Codera, and the Ensenada de Higuerote belong to his Majesty, and the heirs of Don Juan Blanco de Villegas are to be returned the quantity of one hundred and seven and a half pesos, the value of the composition fee that they paid for titles to the Valley of Curiepe, but [since] the titles had never been confirmed and the Valley never settled by them, faculty and license is given so that two settlements can be established in that region, one by the Isleño families described in these Acts, and the other to the free Negros whose commander is Capitán Juan del Rosario Blanco.[17]

And yet the final resolution of the matter was to be quite different. Doña Luisa Martínez de Villegas made it known in Caracas that, due to the uncertainty and confusion caused by the involvement of both audiencias in the case, she had made a direct appeal to the Council of the Indies to resolve the dispute over Curiepe. The Council reviewed the entire issue and, in October 1731, nullified the decision of the Audiencia of Santo Domingo. In its wisdom the Council recognized two facts: one, that the moreno settlement at Curiepe, although without legal foundation, had become one of the most populous communities in the Tuy; and two, that the intimate link between Juan del Rosario Blanco and the family Blanco Villegas provided the best way out of the impasse. Doña Martínez de Villegas and the other heirs of Juan Blanco de Villegas were ordered to share in possession of Curiepe with the people of color led by Juan del Rosario. The decision of the council confirmed what had become a fait accompli, for the bishop José Félix Valverde, who had replaced Escalona y Calatayud in 1731, decided that since the nearest resident priest was five leagues distant a parish should be established at Curiepe. The first baptism in the new parish was celebrated in May 1732.[18] The Council of the Indies determined that the Canary Islanders were unnecessary interlopers in what had come to be seen as a Blanco family quarrel at Curiepe, and the council decreed that they be given land at a different site at least fifteen leagues from the coast. In 1733 they received permission from the governor, Martín de Lardizábal, to proceed with the foundation of the pueblo of Panaquire, on the distant bank of the lower Tuy, and by 1737, counting then thirty-two houses of canario residents, Panaquire was organized as a parish and granted a resident priest.[19] It was from Panaquire that Juan Francisco de León would march to Caracas in 1749 in what would become an armed rebellion against the authority of the king.

TUY CACAO HACIENDAS AND THE SLAVE TRADE

The gestation period of the Curiepe settlement was particularly long and difficult. Beneath the complex tangle of controversy in Caracas was a more simple cause for the Curiepe problems: the Blanco de Villegas family had clear titles, but they did not have

Table 15 Foundation Dates of Several Tuy Valley Parishes

Region	Parish	Foundation Date
Upper Tuy	Ocumare del Tuy	1693
	Tácata	1709
	Santa Lucía	1722
Caucagua	Caucagua	1727
Lower Tuy	Curiepe	1732
	Panaquire	1738

Source: Mariano Martí, *Documentos relativos a su visita pastoral de la diócesis de Caracas, 1771–1784*, 2:588–647.

enough slaves to work their land at the distant fringe of the province. The clamor for land from canario immigrants and morenos libres could not be ignored forever by royal officials who were charged with increasing revenues by promoting agriculture. Consequently, as it became evident that many of the elites who had prior claims did not have the labor resources necessary to plant there, these groups were given the opportunity to begin cacao groves in the valleys of the lower Tuy. Haciendas were established in generally successive fashion, the newest groves located always further from Caracas, downstream to the east. The dates for the foundation of Tuy Valley parishes reflect this pattern (see table 15).[20]

Comparison of censuses of cacao haciendas taken in 1684, 1720, and 1744 shows that the number of cacao trees in the Caracas province increased at a fairly steady rate of about 75,000 trees per year for the sixty-year period 1684 to 1744 (fig. 8).[21] A clearer idea of the social significance of the expansion of cacao cultivation into the Tuy can be had if data taken from the 1720 and 1744 censuses are arranged by region and by the social standing (elite or nonelite) of the hacienda owners. In the first place, expansion did not take place on the Caribbean coast. There were not many more cacao trees on coastal haciendas in 1744 than there had been in 1720. In valleys of the Costa Abajo (that is, downwind of La Guaira) the share of the trees belonging to elites declined, perhaps as a result of the sale of old haciendas to immigrants as mantuano planters shifted their interests and their slaves to the Tuy. In the Tuy growth was dynamic. Upper Tuy expansion continued for elites and nonelites alike, from about 1 million trees for both groups combined in 1720 to 1.5 million in 1744. But it was in the Lower Tuy

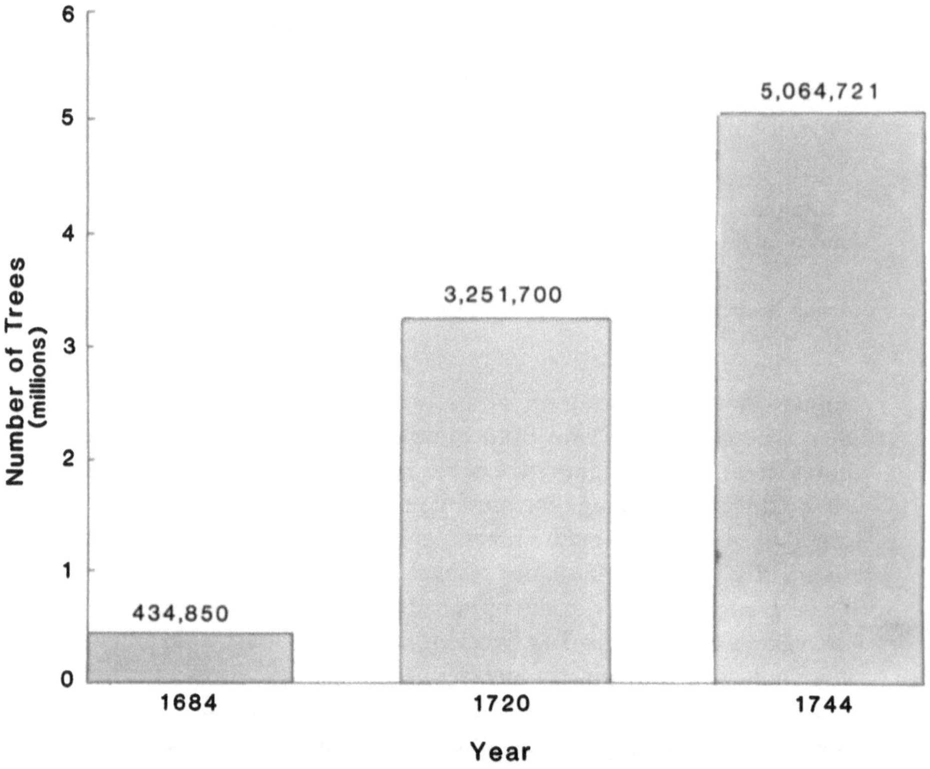

Fig. 8 Cacao Trees in the Caracas Province, 1684–1744

that planting was most dramatic, with a five-fold increase from about 300,000 trees in 1720 to 1.5 million trees in 1744. Much of this expansion was accomplished in this region by nonelite, first-time planters and settlers like the morenos of Curiepe and the canarios of Panaquire; the number of trees owned by nonelites in the Lower Tuy rose from 150,000 trees in 1720 to about 850,000 trees in 1744, an increase that represents almost half of all the new trees planted during the years from 1720 to 1744 (see figs. 9a and 9b).

Haciendas on the Lower Tuy operated at several disadvantages in comparison to those located closer to Caracas, and these disadvantages, which became more problematic as the eighteenth century progressed, were felt most acutely by nonelite hacendados. The Tuy was navigable in boats of minimal draft from its mouth to the point where the Caucagua River enters it (hence justification for dividing

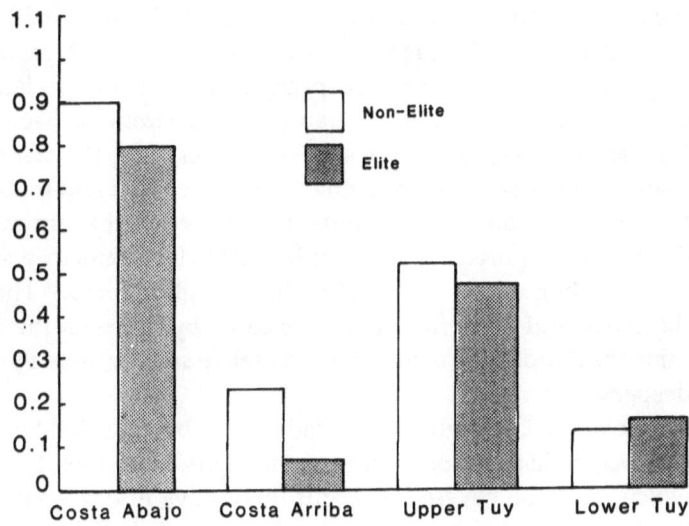

Fig. 9a Cacao Trees in 1720, by Region and Owner Status

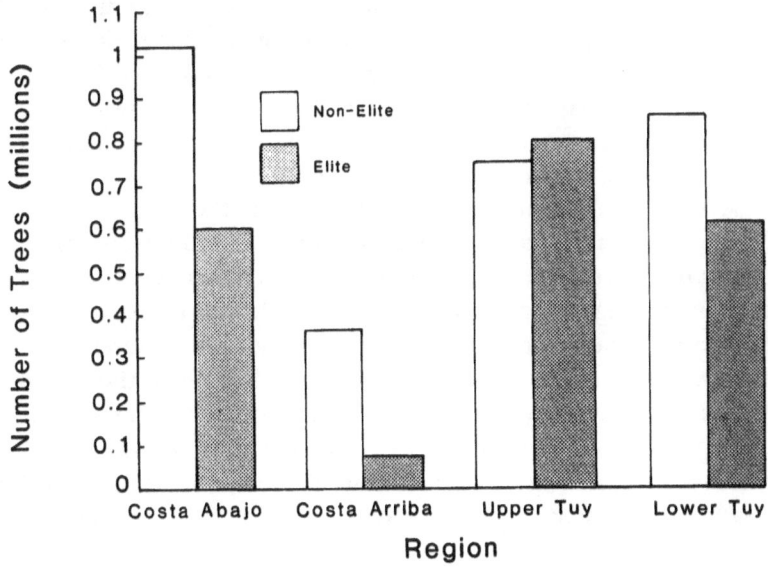

Fig. 9b Cacao Trees in 1744, by Region and Owner Status

the river into Upper and Lower Tuy at this confluence), a distance of about twenty-five leagues. For as long as it remained legal to do so, large canoes, with a carrying capacity of sixty or seventy fanegas of beans, were used regularly to transport cacao from the haciendas in the Caucagua vicinity to the sea.[22] However, a royal order of 1735, issued in the hope of eliminating the active contraband trading that took place all along the coast but especially where the Tuy enters the Caribbean, required that all cacao be sent to La Guaira by way of the more easily guarded overland route through Caracas.[23] Thereafter the cheap and efficient transport of cacao by canoe on the Tuy became the clandestine medium of smugglers and the more intrepid or desperate planters.

Above the Caucagua, cacao had always been carried by mule to Caracas, a distance of at most some eighteen to twenty leagues, which could be covered in about three days in dry weather. But this form of conveyance was expensive, especially if the cacao originated on haciendas downstream from Caucagua. In ordinary circumstances, mule transport from Caucagua to Caracas by way of the Guarenas River cost shippers 30 to 50 percent more than loads carried shorter distances from the Upper Tuy along the broad banks and less precipitous inclines of the Guaire River. But during the rainy season, while the prohibited (after 1735) travel by canoe became much easier, the swollen streams often made the mule trails altogether impassable. At best the overland trip then took much longer and was much more expensive.[24]

A second important distinction between the Upper and the Lower Tuy has to do with the declining availability of African slaves in the colony. Most of the Upper Tuy haciendas were first planted during the last years of the seventeenth century and the first three decades of the eighteenth, a period that corresponds to the first years of the English contract to sell slaves in the Spanish Indies. From 1715 to 1728 the South Sea Company sold a modest average of about 100 slaves in Caracas per year. Thereafter sales increased considerably, and for the eleven years 1729–1739 the yearly average was about 350 slaves sold. The first parish register for Caucagua is dated 1727, which means that much of the planting of cacao in this fertile valley coincided with the South Sea Company's best years in Caracas.

War between England and Spain ended the English asiento in

1739, and thereafter the Guipuzcoana Company proved singularly unable (or perhaps unwilling) to market African slaves in Venezuela. A total of only about 350 slaves were legally sold in the colony from 1739 to 1784, the year when the Company ceased operations.[25] The majority of haciendas in the Lower Tuy, such as those established by Canary Islanders in the vicinity of Panaquire, were begun in the late 1730s and after, and therefore they were developed for the most part after the trade in imported slaves had collapsed. As a result, from Caucagua upstream labor on Tuy cacao haciendas was predominantly slave labor, while downstream from that point many of the newer and smaller groves were commonly worked by their owners, who only occasionally had the assistance of a small gang of slaves.

Although the constraints of transportation costs and the much diminished supply of African slaves affected elite and nonelite alike, elites were in certain ways more able to take advantage of the natural bounty of the Tuy River valley. Elites were not usually newcomers to the Tuy during the boom years of the 1720s and 1730s. In most cases their families had established cacao haciendas there one or two generations earlier, and the estates belonging to them in 1744 were extensions of haciendas that had been in existence and were already harvesting cacao when the 1720 census was taken. With much of the difficult initial work already completed, such as the digging of the major irrigation networks and the construction of dwellings for overseers and storage facilities, before 1720, elite-owned haciendas were developed more rapidly during the interval of the two censuses than were the new groves planted on virgin soil by pioneers who settled in the Tuy after 1720. Elite haciendas were often located on the best sites, where the land was fertile and irrigation systems easier to set up, and in places located closer to Caracas on more easily traveled and less expensive mulepaths. Most importantly, the work of expanding elite haciendas could be accomplished with the labor of already acquired slaves.

These comparative advantages are reflected in the relative size of Tuy haciendas: on the average, elite-owned haciendas in both the Upper and Lower Tuy were larger by about 2000 cacao trees in 1744 than in 1720. Haciendas owned by nonelites, because many first-time planters had settled in the Tuy during the two decades before

1744, were about 1000 trees smaller on the average in 1744 than in 1720. Expressed somewhat differently, *mantuano* cacao estates were increasingly larger than nonelite cacao estates on the Tuy frontier; while elite haciendas typically had 20 to 40 percent more trees than nonelite haciendas in 1720, by 1744 this difference had increased to 50 to 70 percent more trees (see figs. 10a and 10b).

To have had producing haciendas in these decades gave elite planters other advantages as well. Founded in 1728, the Guipuzcoana Company opened up important new markets for Caracas cacao. Beginning in 1715 and ending in 1738, slaves were supplied to the province by the English asiento. Thus for the better part of an extraordinary decade, from 1730, when the first Basque ship arrived in the colony, to 1738, when the English factor stopped selling slaves, the presence in Caracas of these two commercial companies overlapped. Perhaps because they competed with one another to buy the fruits of the colony's haciendas, during this time the price paid for Caracas cacao was very high, about 30 percent above the average minimum price paid during the first half of the eighteenth century (see fig. 11). As cacao profits increased, so too did the number of slaves sold to Caracas buyers. During the late 1720s and early 1730s established cacao hacendados found themselves in the fortunate, if not exactly fortuitous, position of receiving more money for their beans just at the time when many more African slaves were made available for purchase by the South Sea Company (fig. 12).

A temporary cessation in the chronic hostilities between England and Spain in 1728 marked the beginning of the South Sea Company's best slave-trading years in Spain's American colonies. During the 1730s the English asiento sold more slaves in Caracas (3683) than it did in Havana (2874), Veracruz (1353), and Campeche (737). All of these ports, including Caracas, were only minor markets for the English slavers in comparison to Cartagena (5043 slaves sold from 1730 through 1736), Buenos Aires (6473 slaves sold from 1730 through 1738), and Portobelo/Panama (9168 slaves sold from 1730 through 1738),[26] but these major markets served as redistribution centers for the trade, providing slaves for the entire Pacific coast and the Andean highlands in addition to their more immediate hinterlands. From Caracas, by contrast, there was only one destination for the great majority of Africans imported during the

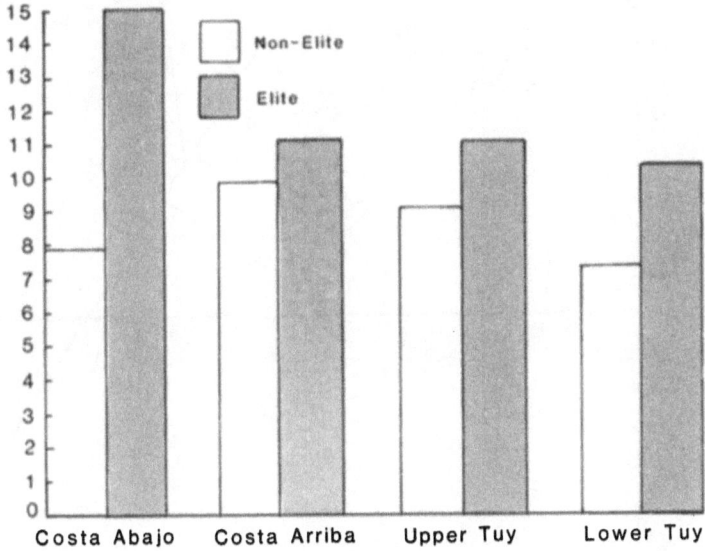

Fig. 10a Mean Hacienda Size in 1720, by Region and Owner Status

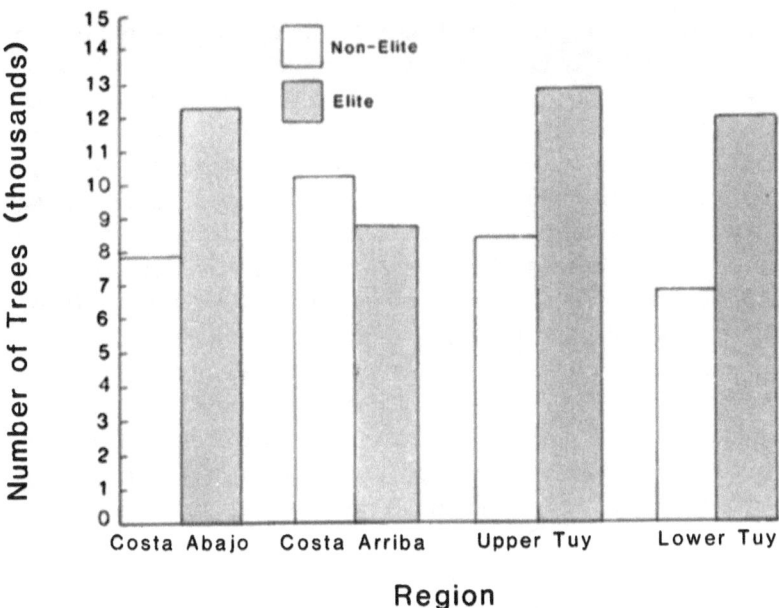

Fig. 10b Mean Hacienda Size in 1744, by Region and Owner Status

128   The Eighteenth Century

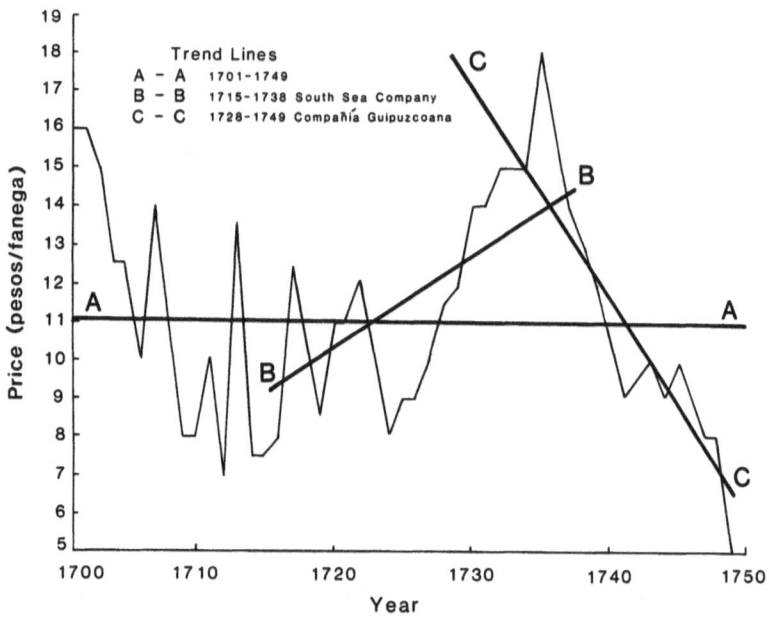

Fig. 11   Minimum Cacao Price, Caracas, 1700–1749

1730s: the burgeoning cacao haciendas then being planted on the banks of the Tuy River and its several tributaries.

In sum, *mantuano* hacienda owners of several generations' residence in Caracas were more likely to profit in the Tuy than were the ambitious newcomers to the province who settled there in hopes of making their first fortune. Although some families, like the Blanco de Villegas, had far too few slaves to work the extensive land to which they held title, possession of slave labor was an important difference between established elite planters and the aspiring pioneers. As in the case of the Liendo family in the 1650s, Caraqueños who already had slaves sent their overseers with a work gang of young and healthy men out to the Tuy to clear the land and plant cacao while their older and weaker slaves remained on the mature haciendas to carry out the easier tasks of weeding and harvesting. Most of the immigrants who actually settled in the Tuy, the canarios of Panaquire for instance, had few if any slaves and had to depend first on their own labor, and then on the English asiento and the Atlantic slave trade to provide them with African workers. After 1728 the supply of slaves to Caracas in-

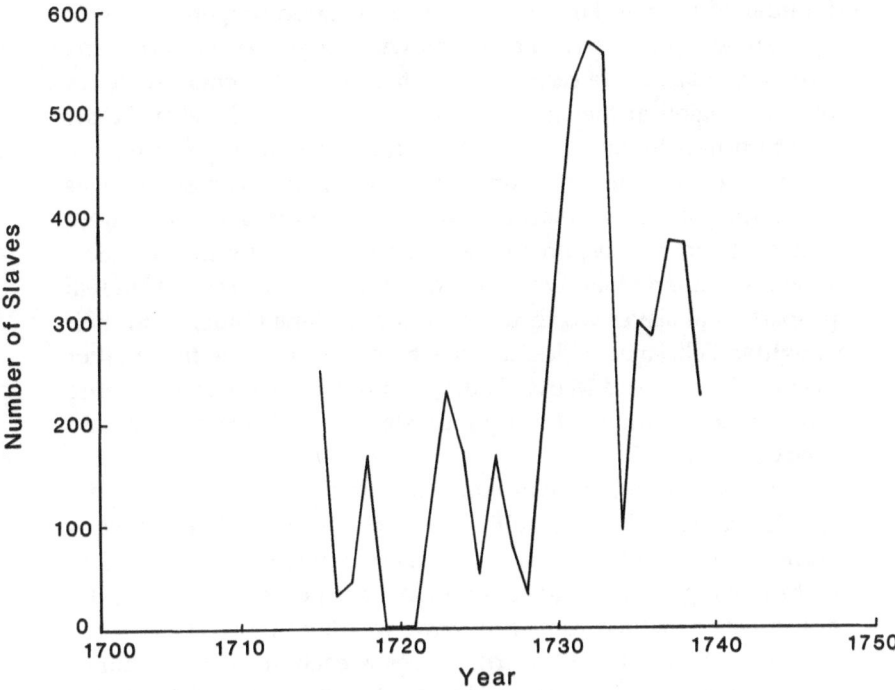

Fig. 12 Slaves Sold in Caracas, 1715–1739

creased as the price paid for cacao beans rose, but this conjuncture, which lasted less than a decade, really favored only growers who then owned fruit-bearing trees and had cacao beans in hand, ready to exchange them for slaves. High cacao prices were not much more than an incentive, although evidently a powerful one, to the Tuy River frontier-folk who could only hope that this concurrence of favorable conditions would continue until they had harvested a cacao crop and were able to buy a slave or two with their profits.

THE CALDERA–PIÑATE HACIENDAS: A CASE STUDY

The best extant record of an eighteenth-century Tuy Valley cacao estate is that of the haciendas of María Candelaria Caldera and her husband Simón Piñate. The case is not typical in that while the immigrant Piñate was neither a member of the Caracas elite nor the founder of an elite family, the census of cacao property taken in 1720 shows him to have been the owner of 56,000 cacao trees on two haciendas, more cacao trees in fact than any other grower in the Tuy region at that time. An Andalusian from Huelva, Piñate was fortunate to have come to Venezuela in time to participate in the best years of the Tuy boom, but his rapid rise to prosperity was due principally to his marriage to María Caldera, a widow whose first husband had begun to plant cacao in the Tuy in the 1680s. When the canario Juan Francisco de la Mar died in 1697, he left real property and slaves worth 18,250 pesos to María Caldera and their daughter Feliciana. Feliciana died a few years after her mother married Piñate, and María Caldera assumed her husband's entire inheritance, including twenty-four slaves worth 6750 pesos and 8800 cacao trees.[27]

There was nothing luxurious about de la Mar's hacienda. The simple wattle-and-daub, palmleaf-roofed dwelling that had been home to him and his family was valued at only 600 pesos in 1697. Its furnishings were set at an additional 222 pesos. Attached to the house was a kitchen roofed in straw worth 20 pesos. Eight slave huts were thought to be worth 10 pesos each, a stable for mules was appraised at 8 pesos, and a chicken coop was valued at 6 pesos. But from these rustic beginnings in the course of thirty years María Caldera and Simón Piñate developed the most extensive cacao enterprise on the Tuy frontier.

Piñate died in 1728, the year that the Guipuzcoana Company was founded. By that date he and his wife owned two flourishing cacao haciendas and had begun to plant a third. The original groves at San Joseph, planted by Juan de la Mar in the seventeenth century, then contained more than 36,000 trees that were tended by forty-six slaves. In three decades, the number of cacao trees at San Joseph had increased four-fold, and the number of slaves had almost doubled. The 1728 inventory of Piñate's estate reveals that most of the adult slaves at San Joseph (twenty-four of thirty-four adults) had been born in Africa (see appendix G). A newer hacienda at a site known as Cara had a kiln and a tile-roofed house used by the Piñate family. There were 27,229 cacao trees at all stages of maturity here, 15,891 of them were fruit-bearing. Forty-three adult slaves and their thirteen children worked and lived at Cara, and again the majority of adults (twenty-four of forty-three) were African-born. A third hacienda, located downstream on the Tuy from the first two at a place called Isnetta, was in the process of being planted under Piñate's personal supervision when he fell ill with an *achaque grave* in 1727. At Isnetta an unspecified number of slaves from the Cara groves labored together with a gang of Africans who had been bought from the English asiento for the specific purpose of peopling the new hacienda.²⁸

Sometime during the first decades of the eighteenth century María Caldera and Simón Piñate moved for a time from the banks of the Tuy to a substantial two-story brick house in Caracas. Here their growing family had many more comforts than they had known in the hot and humid Tuy Valley. Cedar chests and a long cedar table (three *varas* by one *vara*, nearly as long as the typical slave cabin at San Joseph was wide), a dozen chairs, a cedar desk, and two oak buffets filled the principal room of the house. Thirty-five paintings of religious themes, including one large (two *varas* by one-quarter *vara*) representation of the Virgin Mary, adorned the walls. Other furnishings included ten gilt mirrors imported from England and seven lacquered screens used as room dividers. Piñate did most of his cacao business with the English slavers, and for this reason Mexican merchandise, such as the Campeche mattresses, Puebla blankets, and pottery often listed in the inventories of other Caracas planters, were not to be found in his home. Also absent was the large retinue of domestic servants characteristic of elite Caraqueño households. Only three house servants were included in Piñate's 1728 testament: Manuel Congo ("old, lame, and half tame"), and a young couple on loan from the Tuy cacao estates.

By all appearances, Piñate and María Caldera preferred the rustic society of the Tuy Valley to the colonial sophistication of eighteenth-century Caracas. In October 1725 they returned to the Tuy and took up residence on the Cara hacienda. Piñate began planting the new groves at Isnetta. Their eldest son Joseph Silvestre Piñate remained in Caracas where he assumed responsibility for receiving the cacao sent from the Tuy groves, arranging its transport to La Guaira, and its sale there. First as his parents' agent and then, following his father's death in February 1728, as legal guardian of the estate on behalf of his younger siblings, Joseph Piñate kept close account of the family's cacao transactions. His ledgers, which cover the period from October 1725 to April 1733, offer valuable information about the operation and costs of operating this profitable Tuy estate.

The business of cacao agriculture as it was carried out by the Piñates in the 1720s and 1730s was generally similar to the coastal enterprises of a hundred years earlier. During the second and third decades of the eighteenth century the constraining commercial policies of the Guipuzcoana Company were not yet in effect, and prices were on the rise. Prices paid for cacao ranged from eight and a half pesos to twelve pesos per fanega of cacao beans during the last years of the 1720s to from between twelve and twenty pesos per fanega during the first years of the 1730s. Yet there were important differences between the early seventeenth century and this second period of cacao prosperity. While the first haciendas on the Caribbean coast enjoyed immediate access to what was the world's busiest commercial highway, by the eighteenth century most of Caracas's cacao was grown some distance from the coast, and transportation charges consumed a significant share of the income from sales. A second difference was that while in the seventeenth century African slaves had been in abundant supply and were easily acquired from Portuguese traders in exchange for cacao beans, in the early eighteenth century slaves were distributed by the English asiento and were not always available in numbers sufficient to meet planters' steadily increasing demands.

The Piñate estate paid more than 10 percent of its gross income on the transport of beans to market. The family kept a team of mules, but it was used only for carrying cacao from Caracas to La Guaira and for bringing goods up from the port to the city. A peon was hired for two pesos in wages and an additional half-peso for expenses, known as *matalotaje*, to make the round trip to the coast. To haul their cacao from the Tuy the Piñates paid salaries to professional teamsters who had their own mules. Two brothers, Andrés and Diego Báez, went back and forth to the San Joseph hacienda about twice each month. This was evidently full-time employment for these men. They charged fourteen reales for every full *carga*, which was something more than a fanega and a half of dried cacao beans. With eight or nine mules apiece, the Báez brothers were each paid about twenty pesos a month for transporting the Piñate cacao, and they were occasionally able to supplement this income by carrying on the return trip merchandise and iron bars that Tuy blacksmiths forged into hoes and pruning knives. Other muledrivers were paid at the same rate to carry the cacao from the Cara groves to Caracas. These wages were not collected after every trip. Perhaps to keep the muledrivers loyal and at his ready disposition, perhaps because he did not always have cash on hand with which to pay them, Joseph Piñate gave them their wages only at intervals of five or six months. In all, the cost of transporting cacao from the Tuy to Caracas amounted to 3231 pesos for the period October 1725 through November 1728. This amount represents almost 17 percent of the total operating expenditures for the same period (see table 16).

Some twenty years after Simón Piñate's death the Tuy would erupt in a bitter protest that would in turn become rebellion. As prosperous hacienda owners in a period of general expansion, the Piñates had no reason to think of revolt as a means to the ends that interested them. Preferred was the time-honored technique of giving gifts to those individuals who were in a position to favor the outcome of one's legal case or business dealings. From October 1725 to February 1728, at the instruction of his father, Joseph Piñate gave away 937 fanegas of cacao worth at least 7500 pesos, a rather remarkable sum for an enterprise of this size. Some of this cacao went to facilitate legal business in Santo Domingo, "as gifts to those who represent us there and to several judges of the court." A total of 311 fanegas of beans, about one-third of the amount given away, went to the factor of the English asiento in 1725 and 1726. Slaves were in short supply during the early years of the 1720s, and with few landless free blacks and Spaniards as yet willing to work for wages in the cacao groves, these payments were protection against labor shortages. Taking no chances, Piñate kept the English agent supplied with free cacao. Slave sales registered by the South Sea Company with the governor's secretary show that Piñate purchased a dozen slaves in 1724 and 1725, about 5 percent of all the slaves sold in Caracas by the British agent in those two years.[29]

The documentation for the Piñate estate is limited in such a way as to make impossible either a detailed analysis of expenditures or an estimate of the return on the capital value of the property. Expenditures are not itemized after November 1728, but the information for the period from October 1725 through November 1728 is summarized in table 16. Cacao sales for these thirty-seven months

Table 16 Piñate Expenditures, October 1725–November 1728

Category	Expenditure (pesos)	Percent of Total
Capital investments, slave and land purchases	4273	22.1
Ecclesiastical *censos* and *capellanía* payments	4152	21.5
Family and household consumption	3559	18.4
Cacao transportation	3231	16.7
Labor (not muleteers)	2909	15.1
Slave clothing, medicine, burials	850	4.4
Transportation (not cacao)	353	1.8
Total	19,327*	100.0

Source: ARPC, Testamentarías, 1735 P.
 *A substantial sum, 2873 pesos, was spent in 1728 for Simón Piñate's illness and funeral. This expenditure is not included in these calculations because it was not a customary cost of operating the estate; it is included in the expenditures for this period in table 17, however.

totaled 23,677 pesos, an annual mean from sales of 7679 pesos. That Piñate was a profit-conscious entrepreneur with but few social pretensions is reflected in the fact that he spent more on the purchase of slaves and land for the new Isnetta hacienda than he did on any other item, and made only modest outlays of cash for items of family and household consumption. These latter expenditures, which figured so prominently in the seventeenth-century accounts of the Rodríguez Santos and Liendo clans, were not very important to this Tuy pioneer who evidently preferred to live on his hacienda rather than in Caracas. In the ledger kept by his son such social expenditures total less than both capital investments and loan payments, and they are only slightly more than payments made for cacao cartage costs and for wages and salaries. The most striking feature of the financial management of this estate, however, is the fact that during the last three years of his life Simón Piñate gave away cacao roughly equivalent in value to the annual gross income of his properties. Although comprehensible behavior in a society economically capitalist and socially seigneurial, this extraordinary largesse is not easy to classify, falling as it does almost exactly between operating expenditures and payments for social and personal objectives.

Table 17 Piñate Estate Estimated Income, 1725–1733 (in pesos)

	October 1725–November 1728		January 1729–April 1733	
	Total	Annual Mean	Total	Annual Mean
Cacao Sales	23,677	7,679.0	55,927	12,906.2
Expenditures	22,200	7,200.0	23,528	5,429.5
Estimated Net Income	1,477	479.0	32,399	7,476.7

	October 1725–April 1733	
	Total	Annual Mean
Cacao Sales	79,604	10,733.1
Expenditures	45,728	6,165.6
Estimated Net Income	33,876	4,567.6

Source: ARPC, Testamentarías, 1735 P.

Discounting the value of the cacao that was given away, the income generated on this, the largest of the Tuy cacao properties, was considerable. As prices rose during the first years of the 1730s, the monthly income from cacao sales increased by some 75 percent, and the estimated net income from the Piñate haciendas for the period from January 1729 to April 1733 is 32,399 pesos, or 7477 pesos per year. This was considerably more than was earned by the estate during the previous three years, the last years of Piñate's life, when the income after expenditures totaled only 1477 pesos for thirty-seven months. For the entire period for which we have a record, the eighty-nine months from October 1725 to April 1733, the estimated net income is 45,728 pesos, or 4568 pesos per year (see table 17). This sum is about three or four times greater than the net income calculated for the Liendo coastal groves in the 1640s and 1650s, and we may therefore suppose that the eighteenth-century Tuy cacao boom was at least as profitable as the first bonanza a century earlier.[30]

THE CLOSING OF THE TUY FRONTIER

Evidently by choice very little of the Piñate income went for items of social significance, for material goods or prestigious community offices, but even a strict concentration of expenditures on hacienda expansion, for land, slaves, wages, and gifts of cacao to influential individuals, did not suffice to provide the Piñate family with a permanent place among Caracas's cacao-planter gentry. In contrast to their seventeenth-century predecessors, who, like the Liendo, established enduring family dynasties on the basis of similar or even smaller income, with the division of the estate in 1733 the Piñate family disappears from the Caracas record.

Piñate's failure to convert the substantial returns from his cacao haciendas into continuing gentry status for his family and heirs can be taken as a marker of the closing of the Tuy Valley frontier, and with it the end of the long formative phase of the Caracas elite. Rather than a Turnerian filling of the usable physical space, the end of bonanza cacao opportunities in the Tuy region was the direct consequence of two events: the radical commercial policies of the Guipuzcoana beginning in the 1730s, and the decline in the supply of slaves available for the Caracas market after the termination of the English asiento in 1738. From the early 1740s on, declining cacao income put increasing strain on established gentry families and virtually ruined the investment, comprised mostly of their own labor, of many modest migrants to the Tuy. Using the weight of their long tenure in Caracas and the authority of the town cabildo, which they dominated, to form their protest, many elites ran the risk of sedition in their opposition to the Guipuzcoana Company. At the other end of the Hispanic social scale, the vigorous reaction of many smallholder cacao farmers and other rural poor to the changing conditions led to armed rebellion in 1749.

The most important fact for an understanding of the tension that characterized political and social life in Caracas in the 1730s and 1740s, tension that resulted in the Tuy frontier rebellion in 1749, is that much of the expansion of the Caracas provinces cacao industry had been generated independent of the commercial and anti-smuggling activities of the Guipuzcoana Company.[31] Subsequent chapters will show how the Company's heavy-handed efforts to acquire an increasing portion of the colony's cacao had the effect of denying profits to planters and therefore, in contradiction to the image it projected, the Company in fact slowed expansion of cacao production. The provocative policies of the Company provided planters with a focus for their frustrations over the ending of the Tuy boom, but it is difficult to see how the customary growth of many decades could have continued after the end of the English slave contract. It seems probable that the most crucial immediate consequence of the cancellation of the asiento in 1739 was not so much the shortage of slaves that ensued, although this did indeed force a most significant shift to free labor in time, but rather the fall in price paid for cacao as the English no longer competed with the Basque monopolists for Caracas beans.

The *asientistas* were well informed about the market for cacao and they were especially interested in buying all they could from Caracas haciendas. An extraordinary document prepared by a South Sea Company accountant in 1733 demonstrates the substantial profit that could be expected from the sale in Mexico of Caracas cacao. The English company calculated that the cash sale of 600 slaves delivered at Caracas would produce a net profit, after transatlantic transportation and other charges had been discounted, of 24,003 pesos. If the proceeds of his sale were then used to buy cacao beans, which were priced at 23 pesos the fanega in Caracas, and if this cacao were to be sold in Veracruz at the current price there of 40 pesos the fanega, the South Sea Company could anticipate a much greater profit from its original 600 slaves of 51,356 pesos, even after duties and shipping costs between Caracas and Veracruz had been paid.[32] In other words, Caracas beans sold in the New Spain market in 1733 increased in value by more than 50 percent according to the South Sea Company estimate.

Therefore, the slave merchants were surely willing to bid up the price for cacao if they had to, knowing that substantial earnings were possible from subsequent sales in Mexico, a market that their Basque competitors could not enter. Probably because they were more interested in acquiring cacao beans than they were in selling slaves, the English *asientistas* were not willing to extend credit to Caraqueño buyers of their human commodity. In Caracas business with the asiento was done strictly on either an exchange-for-cacao or cash-and-carry basis; the total debt owed to the South Sea Company by Spanish American slaveholders was more than 750,000 pesos in 1736, but none of this debt was located in Caracas.[33]

Certain fortunate Caraqueños were not much affected by the price paid in Caracas by either the South Sea Company or the Guipuzcoana Company; some privileged elites traded directly with New Spain themselves, either in their own ships or in the vessels of other private shipowners. Their profits were therefore determined by the price paid for cacao in the Mexican market. The principal beneficiaries of the rising Caracas price were those more modest cacao producers, like the morenos and canarios of the Tuy, who had no choice but to sell their beans in the colony. For a few years in the 1730s, prices (fig. 11) and numbers of slaves sold (fig. 12) both reached record high levels. Prices had begun to fall before war put an end to the English slave business in Caracas, but for a time, while Tuy pioneers like Juan del Rosario and Juan Francisco de León struggled to start their haciendas, competition between the two commercial companies resulted in premium prices paid for their cacao harvests.

The end of the asiento thus had a double impact on the province of Caracas, and on the Tuy frontier in particular. First, left alone as the exclusive buyer of cacao for export, the Guipuzcoana Company could thereafter pay virtually what it cared to pay to hacienda owners who had no other way to get their beans to market. From a record high of eighteen pesos the fanega in 1735 and a respectable twelve pesos in 1739, cacao fell to nine pesos in 1741 and finally to five pesos in 1749, when protest against the Company erupted in rebellion. Second, the virtual end of slave imports reverberated throughout Caracas society. The immediate labor needs of *mantuano* hacendados were met by the slaves they already possessed, and such elites might well have supposed that their needs in the near future would be filled by the reproductive capacity of the same slaves. But the fact that after 1739 most of the newer Tuy hacienda owners were left with neither sufficient slaves nor the prospect of acquiring them was a cause for much concern.

The slaveholding ambitions of immigrants and other would-be hacendados evaporated, and in time many of them would themselves take the place of slaves as wage laborers on the haciendas of others. This would not begin to occur, however, until the failure of the rebellion of 1749 and the royal repression of the 1750s made it clear that there was no other alternative for most of those who had not solidly established themselves as slaveholding cacao planters by 1739.

5

León's Rebellion

Many Tuy settlers chose to defy royal law rather than accept the consequences of the end of the South Sea Company, the end of African slave imports, and the low prices paid for cacao by the Guipuzcoana Company. The sale of cacao to smugglers was a practice as old as the cacao trade itself, but after 1739 it took on new importance for many first-generation farmers who turned to the contrabandistas as the only alternative to losing their haciendas altogether. Since they were often not limited to the current Caracas price for cacao, but could sell their beans directly to New Spain, *mantuano* hacendados were much less likely to participate in the illicit trade. Yet the rise of smuggling in the countryside was of serious concern to them too. Many slaves were evidently willing to trade a portion of their masters' cacao for whatever merchandise an enterprising itinerant smuggler might have to offer. Since few mantuanos were willing to give up their permanent residence in Caracas, which was after all a basic privilege of their elite status, control of slaves and of trade in the hacienda districts was left to overseers and the police agents of the governor, who were not, by and large, able to stop the illegal exchanges.

This collusion, slaves who pilfered their absent owners' beans and sold them to Spaniards who peddled them, proved virtually impervious to efforts from Caracas to prevent it. The clearest comments on this subterranean trade were made in the 1770s and 1780s, but its origins as a serious problem date from the end of the English asiento a generation earlier. "Experience proves that a satisfactory overseer can never be found," wrote an absentee planter worried about the harvest from his Caucagua hacienda.[1] The bishop Mariano Martí visited the Tuy region in 1784, and he reported that "not the third part" of the cacao grown on estates in the Caucagua district ever reached the hacienda storehouses, let alone the point of legal embarkation at La Guaira. According to Martí this was because the owners rarely visited their estates and because few whites were willing to work as overseers. Free blacks and even slaves acted as estate supervisors, a fact that the bishop deplored because it allowed for rampant thievery of cacao by slaves and overseers alike. The beans were used by slaves to buy "rum, food, and clothing, especially rum," which was concocted in clandestine stills located all along the course of the Tuy.[2] In a report to the governor prepared in 1775, the *teniente de justicia* for Ocumare del Tuy gave three reasons why cacao smuggling continued unabated in his district:

> Sir: Desiring to fill in every way possible the obligations of the office that Your Lordship has kindly conferred upon me, and meriting among them particular attention to the frequent theft of cacao, I have made inquiry to the source of this crime which is so prejudicial in this district, and the result, Sir, of some careful observation is that I now understand the interesting reasons that we so wanted to learn [as to why and how cacao is stolen].
>
> There are three sources of the vice: the first is the abandoned state in which many hacendados keep their slaves, which keeps them in great poverty and extreme need, from which they redeem themselves with the property of their masters and others who do not watch them carefully; the second, the malice of the peddlers commonly called saddlebag salesmen [*vendedores de alforja*]. Finding in the apparent laxness of government sustenance for their avarice, these men sell their goods from hacienda to hacienda, advancing clothing and other merchandise on credit to the slaves with payments arranged to coincide with the harvests. When the harvests are gathered the salesmen appear to collect, and the slaves, who have no property of their own, make payment with that which belongs to others, most obviously, the fruit of the cacao which they cultivate. The third is *aguardiente de caña*, because, the propensity of the slaves for this beverage being great, they give the mentioned cacao in exchange for it, taking the beans from the haciendas in great excess.[3]

Elite cacao planters were reluctant to live on their haciendas and they were unwilling or unable to provide efficient estate administration that would have kept the illegal cacao trade at a minimum. They preferred to rely on the rural agents of royal authority, the *tenientes de justicia mayor*, to keep peace and order on their behalf, to pursue runaway slaves, and to stop smuggling. A teniente held extensive formal authority. His jurisdiction always covered more territory than he could administer effectively alone, and he usually relied on several subordinates, his *cabos*. The teniente granted operating licenses to all the retail stores, the *pulperías*, and to all the muleteers who worked in his district. In the countryside a governor's lieutenant was obliged to provide police service and to act as a judge of first instance in civil and criminal cases, much in the same way that the cabildo's alcaldes ordinarios did in the towns. However, unlike the town alcalde, who was elected annually, the teniente was appointed by the governor from distant Caracas and for an indeterminate period.[4] In lieu of a salary, the lieutenants and the small band of men they recruited to assist them were allowed a part of the contraband they confiscated, which may have increased the diligence with which they carried out their duties.

As both police officer and justice of the peace, the position of rural sheriff carried both abundant authority and also considerable opportunity for corruption. From the point of view of the colony's administrators the *tenientazgo* was often difficult to monitor effectively. This was so because, even though the post could be and occasionally was filled by the governor with his own friends and minions, in the time-honored tradition of Habsburg administrative thought it was believed that the best way to keep the teniente from becoming a petty tyrant in his bailiwick was to appoint the most prominent resident in the district. It was assumed that the self-interest of such men would move them to maintain the public order and to protect the legal cacao trade. Further, such men could be counted upon to utilize their extensive networks of kin and clients to help them administer the royal justice. Consistent with this idea, in the Tuy it was customary, before the arrival of the Guipuzcoana Company and the centralizing spirit of the Bourbon regime, for the founders and first planters to be named *teniente de justicia mayor*.

In the Caracas context, although the tenientes were by law assistants to the governor and subject to his authority, in fact they enjoyed a valued measure of autonomy. In the first place, supervision was complicated by the distance and difficult terrain which separated the governor in Caracas from his subalterns. In addition, in theory the influence of the governor over these rural officials was limited traditionally by the superior authority of the Audiencia in Santo Domingo, where matters pertaining to the execution of law were sent on appeal. The names of tenientes nominated by the governor had to be sent to the audiencia for confirmation, and lieutenants could appeal directly to Santo Domingo in any controversy they might have with the Caracas governors. As with his appointment, the dismissal of a teniente was subject to approval by audiencia judges.

This tradition was altered in 1738, in the midst of many important changes then taking place in Caracas, when by royal cédula several of the governor's prerogatives were enhanced, including the right to appoint or to dismiss tenientes without approval of the audiencia. This autonomy of appointment was first granted to don Gabriel José de Zuloaga, governor from 1737 to 1747 and a Basque with strong sympathy for the Guipuzcoana Company. Zuloaga requested greater independence in the matter of these appointments, arguing that closer control over the naming and replacement of lieutenants would give the governor greater control over smuggling. In 1739, when the province was transferred for a second time to the jurisdiction of the reestablished viceroyalty of New Granada, Zuloaga petitioned to defend his newly acquired privilege to name or replace tenientes without judicial review, citing the four hundred leagues of very poor roads between Caracas and Bogotá as a major obstacle to the swift execution of justice. He argued that the inevitable delays due to this distance and the war with England would reverse the recent progress made by gubernatorial diligence and the Guipuzcoana Company's coast guard in the effort to halt illegal cacao trading. Smugglers would be encouraged in their activities if they knew that an ineffective or corrupt teniente would remain in office until his replacement were approved by the viceroy in New Granada. With the assistance of pressure brought on the Council of the Indies by the Guipuzcoana Company, its agents agreeing that prosperity in Venezuela depended on the ability of the governor to react swiftly and decisively to contraband, the crown approved Zuloaga's request in 1742. To this end, although in other respects Venezuela remained subordinate to the viceroyalty of New Granada, the Caracas governor was to retain complete authority to "name the *tenientes de justicia mayor* for the towns and villas and places where they are needed, without requiring confirmation for those named."[5]

REBELLION

The governor's right to appoint or remove a teniente from his post became the catalyst for revolt in 1749. Before that date colonists suspected collusion between Basque governors and Basque Guipuzcoana monopolists, and in the 1740s they came to believe that royal justice was being subverted so that Company ships would have full cargoes of cheaply purchased cacao beans. Tensions peaked as prices dropped to record low levels. As early as 1745 governor Zuloaga was certain that a conspiracy had been formed to demand the expulsion of the Guipuzcoana Company;

> I was told secretly by several different ecclesiastics, both seculars and regulars, that a plot has been formed here by the Conde [de San Javier] and Don Alejandro [Blanco Uribe] and their partisans, and as a part of it they have made an alliance with the majority of the many Isleños from the Canary Islands who live in this city and in the different areas adjacent to it. Although the Conde and Don Francisco de Ponte, his cousin, plan to travel to the Court to present their case, they and many others intend to begin something here; to be better able to do it they have elected Alcaldes and a Procurador General favorable to the thoughts of the Conde and Don Alejandro Blanco, and they have gone so far as to propose violence. If I do not agree with them or defer to them they will rebel against me, arrest me if necessary, and arrest the agents of the Guipuzcoana Company so that they can do away with it altogether.[6]

But no uprising took place in 1745, and, although it is unlikely that Juan Francisco de León would have led a march on the city without the support of some influential mantuanos, when he and the isleños and other Tuy settlers did take their protest to Caracas there would be very little concrete proof to link them and the colony's elites.[7]

In any event, the occurrence which precipitated León's rebellion had nothing to do with the Caracas elite. Governor Luis Castellanos decided to favor the request of Company factor Juan Manuel Goizueta and send an employee of the Company to control the cacao trade leaving the valleys of Panaquire and Caucagua. Martín de Echeverría, Vizcayan, first met with Juan Francisco de León in Panaquire on March 27, 1749. Together with his patrol of a dozen men, Echeverría, who was mistakenly thought to be León's replacement as *teniente de justicia mayor*, was immediately forced to leave Panaquire, because, as León wrote to governor Castellanos a week later, "the Vecinos in this Valley refused to allow me to recognize a Vizcayan *Teniente* or Vizcayan soldiers, afraid as they are of the hostilities that are suffered in the places where there are such

Tenientes and patrols."⁸ Castellanos held León in enough respect to write him a letter of explanation, in which he insisted that Echeverría had a legitimate commission in the Tuy, and that it was within the rights of the Guipuzcoana Company to place officers and soldiers wherever they saw a need in order to stop smuggling and to keep cacao from being shipped to La Guaira by sea. As governor, Castellanos was obliged to assist the Company in this effort and he claimed that he could not overrule the Company if its agent was qualified. What was more, León misunderstood the nature of Echeverría's mission, for he had been sent only as a *cabo de guerra y juez de comisos,* with authority only to halt contraband, and not as a replacement *teniente de justicia.*

Under the circumstances, the difference between *cabo* and *teniente* was too fine a point for León and his followers, who, to profit from their cacao, had come to depend on the illegal sea trade by way of the Tuy. They were fed up with the Company, its low prices and other policies. Particularly aggravating to them was the complete prohibition, ordered by governor Martín de Lardizábal in 1735, of all commercial activity along the coast east of La Guaira. Only the owners of a handful of haciendas that were located along this coast were allowed to bring their harvests by sea to La Guaira, and this was permitted because, blocked by the mountains that rose steeply from behind their estates, there was no other way for them to get their beans to market. Otherwise, even off-shore fishing was prohibited, as the crown supported the view of local royal authorities that such activity attracted and served as a cover for smuggling.

Therefore, since the only authorized route to La Guaira for cacao from Tuy Valley haciendas was overland by way of Caracas, when the price of cacao fell sharply in the 1740s, the cost of transport over as many as forty leagues of difficult mulepath made the cacao business unprofitable in the Tuy. Despite many appeals to rescind the prohibition, Zuloaga remained steadfast in support of the policy of his predecessor Lardizábal, rejecting in 1744 and 1745 requests to allow the owners of haciendas in the remote valleys of Curiepe, Caucagua, Panaquire, Mamporal, Capaya, and others to ship their cacao to La Guaira by way of the Tuy River and the Caribbean. We may suppose that the policy probably provoked as much smuggling as it prevented, and when the Basque *cabo*

Echeverría was named for the Panaquire post no cacao had reached Caracas by the legal routes from some of the lower Tuy haciendas for more than two years.[9]

To protest general conditions and Echeverría's appointment, a march to Caracas was decided upon during the first weeks of April 1749. Several years later, as he was about to surrender to the royal authorities, an anxious Juan Francisco de León claimed that he had not been alone in the organization of the march. They had planned only a simple protest, which the government, not León, had turned into a rebellion. The canario leader emphasized that while those who accompanied him on the march were bold enough to openly challenge the royally licensed Company to the beat of drums with flags flying and arms in hand, there had been many others, in particular several Caracas mantuanos, who had given their encouragement but were careful to protect their anonymity. León later remembered that during this time he had "received a great many letters from all over the Province, but none of them signed."[10]

Much to the disgust of the king's investigators, the matter of clandestine support would never be made clear, primarily because León refused to name those elites who had called on him to lead the protest. But in 1749 there was no doubt about who actually marched on Caracas. Those who came from the Tuy with León to manifest their opposition to the Company were modest and even humble men from the middling and lower ranks of rural provincial society. Many were isleños, others were free blacks, a few were runaway slaves, and yet others Indians. Most joined the band as it passed by the large cacao haciendas located along the the Caucagua stream, but others had traveled a considerable distance, from the Aragua Valley sixty leagues to the west and from San Sebastián to the south, to participate.

On April 19, several hundred armed men made camp with León at Tócome, about an hour east of Caracas. Upon hearing of the arrival of León there, Manuel de Goizueta, the principal factor of the Guipuzcoana Company, and a number of other Company employees, including the would-be cabo Martín de Echeverría, fled the city straightaway for the safety of the fortress at La Guaira, taking with them only what they could carry. That afternoon the Caracas cabildo met in hurried session and resolved to go as a body to meet with León, bringing with them don Lorenzo de Ponte y Villegas and the Marqués de Mijares, respectively the oldest and the most prestigious of the town's mantuano men. At the request of governor Castellanos a delegation of leading churchmen was organized to accompany the councilmen, and two officials of the Real Hacienda were sent as the governor's personal delegates with a letter for León.[11]

As they reached the Tócome encampment this contingent of elites was greeted with shouts of "Long live the King and Death to the Vizcayans." León refused to read the governor's letter, insisting that he was interested only in the departure of the "Vizcayans." He told the emissaries that, although he had no intention of harming anyone, he was determined to accomplish his objective and more than 3000 men were on their way to join him in Caracas. The councilmen informed León that they had never heard rumors calling for the expulsion of the Company, that not even the Conde de San Javier, their spokesman at court, had asked for the removal of the Company. León replied that they were wrong, that the Conde had gone to court exactly for that purpose, but, once in Madrid the king's agents "had tricked him, taking him to dances and parties so that he might enjoy himself."[12]

Once they determined that there was to be no break in León's resolve to go to Caracas in order to bring a halt to the operations of the Guipuzcoana Company and to force its agents to leave the province, the negotiators returned to the city. The next morning the governor sent Manuel de Sosa Betancourt, archdeacon of the cathedral and an isleño, who succeeded in persuading León not to enter the city with all of his men. León agreed to bring them only as far as the plaza of the Candelaria church in the canario barrio on the eastern fringe of Caracas, but he reiterated to Sosa that his reason for coming to Caracas was to insist on the total destruction of the Guipuzcoana Company. More than that, he told Sosa that he was determined to see that "in all of this Province there does not remain even one person of that [Basque] race; all of them must leave on the first vessel or ship in the bay."[13]

The arrangement with the archdeacon called for the protesters to arrive at Candelaria the next day, April 21, but when word reached Tócome that Castellanos was about to flee Caracas for La Guaira, León and his men left immediately for the town, and they arrived in the Candelaria barrio at about three o'clock in the afternoon on April 20, 1749. As events were to prove, this haste was of singular importance. Castellanos's fear for his own safety may have been his primary reason for wanting to go to La Guaira, but as a strategic matter such a move was particularly significant because if it appeared that he, as governor, had been forced to leave Caracas under pressure from León's mob, then the protest against the Guipuzcoana Company could be understood in a much more serious light as an insurrection against the constituted authority of the crown. It was one thing to disobey the governor's orders to detain his march or to keep his men out of Caracas, but it was quite another to be responsible for forcing the king's representative from his post, and, perhaps with this in mind, León had left immediately for Caracas when he heard that Castellanos was preparing to flee.

Ignoring the agreement he had made with Sosa, León entered Caracas with all of his men. To the accompaniment of drumbeats and with banners flying, in a great commotion the band of protesters advanced through the streets of Candelaria and the cathedral parish, stopping only when they reached the Plaza Mayor. Once guards had been placed at the office and warehouse of the Guipuzcoana Company and sentinels stationed at the street corners, a mounted Juan Francisco de León confronted Castellanos, who stood above him on the balcony of the governor's residence. The exchange was strained but polite. Castellanos spoke first: "Your Honor is very welcome *señor capitán* León. I did not expect Your Honor until tomorrow at noon." León: "That was my intention, but I received three letters today which advised me that Your Highness wanted to go to La Guaira, and for that reason I came more quickly." Castellanos: "I did not have such a plan, and I am here to serve you, Sir."[14] León then demanded the immediate expulsion of the Company.

With no choice but violence should he refuse, Castellanos issued an order to the purpose. However, unknown to León and those who witnessed the event, earlier Castellanos had signed a secret document discounting anything that he might subsequently agree to do or be coerced into doing.[15] Believing that they had obtained their initial objective, León and some two thousand men set up camp in the plaza to await the execution of the governor's order. Three-fourths of them were isleños or other Spaniards, and the rest were Indians, mulattos, and zambos. On the march they had divided themselves into three companies: *españoles blancos*, blacks and mulattos, and Indians; now the first two groups pitched their tents inside the plaza, the *españoles* against the walls of the cathedral and the men of color against the royal jail, while the Indian company was divided and placed in appropriate locations on the streets leading into the plaza. León, with permission of the governor, spent the night in the vacant bishop's residence. The poor among the protesters were fed by the vecinos of Caracas, many of whom openly expressed their support for León and his movement.[16]

The next day León asked Castellanos for an attorney, and a legal counselor was assigned to him.[17] León also began to receive the advice of elites who were opposed to the Company. It was determined that the governor should give license for an open cabildo, termed by them a *junta general*, to decide whether the Company had been beneficial or prejudicial to the province during its tenure of nearly two decades. This meeting was of major importance to León and his followers, for a vote against the Company by the town's foremost citizenry meant that they would share responsibility for its expulsion. The procedure would also give much-wanted additional legality to their movement. With alacrity the people of prominence in Caracas came together to denounce the Guipuzcoana Company. Castellanos would write to the king that in the past,

> for some Juntas that have taken place, even when the issue was to their advantage, not in two days has it been possible to bring together 20 men, while for this one requested by Juan Francisco de León in less than a half hour 97 people gathered, all of them *principales* and people of distinction in this town, and in this it is evident that they were involved with León in the planning of the said Junta.[18]

The decision taken by the assembled town was overwhelmingly in opposition to the Basque monopoly. Among the principal complaints were that it had failed in its obligation to supply the province with clothing and food, it had seriously hindered the cacao trade, it had forced the price of cacao beans down to record low levels, and in these and other particulars it had failed to comply both with many of the terms of its original contract and subsequent royal orders governing its management.[19]

The Company factor and many of its employees had already disembarked from La Guaira on April 21 when the open cabildo issued its support for expulsion the following day. Not yet satisfied, on April 23 León asked for further guarantees. Among them were two that reflect the perception which the demonstrators had of their own precarious position. First was a request for complete assurance that Castellanos would not leave Caracas, and second was a guarantee of indemnity for León and those who had marched with him. Castellanos agreed to these things as he had to everything else that had been asked of him. To become law these terms had to be announced to the community at large, and for the next three nights on different street corners town criers made the termination of the Company and the indemnity public knowledge. On the third night, beating their drums and firing their arquebuses and shotguns into the air, León led most of his men from the Plaza Mayor down the Calle Real to the Candelaria plaza. Their victory parade was made to the accompaniment of the shouts of thankful Caraqueños. Only a few men were left to guard the governor's residence and to patrol the streets at night, and the anti-Company campaign appeared to have come to a quite successful end.

The character of the León protest changed completely a week later. During the night of May 3, Governor Castellanos, disguised as a priest, repudiated his promise to remain in Caracas and fled to La Guaira. No effort by anyone in Caracas could persuade him to return, and by the end of the month a total collapse of authority, and with it social order, seemed likely. Word of an uprising of slaves in Ocumare del Tuy further frightened an already agitated citizenry, and arrests, torture, and confessions, culminating in the execution of a supposed ringleader, were the result. Some members of the Caracas elite began to try to distance themselves from the León movement by blaming Castellanos for giving in to the protesters and ordering the Guipuzcoana Company out of the province entirely on his own volition, without consulting the municipal authority or anyone else. The cabildo also blamed the governor for the rumored slave uprising, saying that his precipitous flight from the city and his failure to replace the tenientes removed by León from their Tuy Valley posts during the march to Caracas had caused a breakdown of authority and order in the countryside, which in turn had given slaves the courage to try to claim their freedom.

Anxious that their declared support for León's protest now made them accomplices in rebellion, the town's councilmen told Castellanos that he could not accuse the city of disloyalty, for he had not called on either the cabildo or the militia for assitance before he determined to take refuge in the fortress at La Guaira. For his part León understood perfectly well that the governor's action made him and his mean "traitors and rebels." In frustration and perhaps in an effort to force a direction on events that he felt were carrying him toward open rebellion, he closed the Caracas-La Guaira road in June and refused to allow supplies to be sent to Castellano and the troops in the fortress there. Advised by mantuanos that this would likely lead first to an armed confrontation with the royal and Guipuzcoana Company soldiers stationed at La Guaira and then to a general war when reinforcements arrived from Santo Domingo or Spain, León responded, "then in such case they will kill all of us, for there is no reason why I alone should die in defense of this province."[20]

The initial support given León by the Caracas elite began to evaporate before the spectre of violence. The possibility of a slave uprising, to come either in direct support of the rebels or simply with the collapse of royal authority in the wake of the flight of the governor, was particularly troubling. Even if it was nothing more than a rumor, this fear was genuinely felt. What had taken place was well understood by the lieutenant governor, Domingo Aguirre y Castillos, a frequent friend of the elite and occasional opponent of Governor Castellanos. In a letter to the king, Aguirre argued that the policies of the Basque governors and the Guipuzcoana Company had created considerable tension in the province. Although his fears of the eventual outcome of the uprising might have clouded his view of León's objectives, he knew very well that the isleño chief had broad popular support:

> Juan Francisco de León, until now your Majesty's faithful vassal, has been made over by the Government into a renegade of justice addicted to disobedience; . . . he will be a rebel powerful enough to establish a principality here, a principality whose main strength will consist in the liberty of black slaves and Indians who will come here from the surrounding provinces and from the nearby islands, and even religion and the Catholic faith will be shaken.[21]

For his part, León decided that his original objective, the expulsion of the Guipuzcoana Company, could now be accomplished only by accepting the role of rebel that Castellanos had cast upon him by leaving Caracas. The intense antagonism felt by León and those who followed him can be seen in a statement made by the reluctant rebel leader in response to the warning that he and his men were about to commit a serious crime of lese majesty by attacking La Guaira. As the lieutenant governor Aguirre recalled in his letter to the king, León had said:

> All that was lacking was for us to be accused of treason and rebellion, for His Majesty is ruining the settlers of this Province by giving it over to the Vizcayans [i.e., the Basque Guipuzcoana Company, the Basque governors and their subalterns] as if they were its conquistadors, although in truth there is nothing left to give them but our very wives, for everything else is already theirs, the settlers of the province now work and cultivate the provincial lands for them, lands that we had cleared at our own expense and with our own sweat.[22]

In late July 1749 León issued a call to his supporters throughout the province to assemble in Caracas in preparation for an attack on La Guaira, which was set for August 1.[23] In response to this summons to arms at least 5000 isleños and other rural residents of the province converged on Caracas, then a town of about 18,000 people.[24] Many of the elite traveled the same roads but in the opposite direction, taking refuge on their haciendas in the countryside, while others of similar social station sought sanctuary in the cathedral from what they believed was imminent war. The rebels were deployed on the La Guaira road on August 2, and on the night of August 3 artillery stationed in the plaza of the La Guaira fortress and in the Guipuzcoana Company factory exchanged fire with León's advance troops, which had reached the outskirts of the port town. Neither side suffered casualties however. La Guaira was well defended by several hundred royal and Company troops, who had as reinforcements militiamen from coastal towns and loyal Indians from coastal villages. Although the tension of a seige would have made life difficult there, without a blockade of port, which was probably beyond the military capacity of the rebels, the town could have been supplied by sea for an indefinite period. Rather than attempt a certainly costly assault of uncertain outcome on the fortress, after several days of posturing on the perimeter of

La Guaira and having proved that he was fully committed to his cause, León began negotiations with Castellanos.

The governor made several promises, most of them similar to those he had made earlier in Caracas, and all of them subject to the secret disclaimer he had signed the day before his encounter with León in the Plaza Mayor. The administrative personnel of the Guipuzcoana Company, who had been quietly allowed to return to La Guaira, were again banned from the province and the monopoly was suspended until the king and his ministers heard the colonists' complaints and had resolved the problems surrounding its operation. In the meantime, debts owed by colonists to the Company were recognized as payable and due. For his part, Castellanos promised to return to Caracas in as short a time as possible.

In exchange, León opened the road to Caracas and disbanded his men. Claiming victory, he returned to the isleño barrio of Candelaria to await further developments. The show of force in La Guaira was the limit of the violence exercised against the state by León and his followers. They had given over their protest in favor of armed insurrection, their attack on La Guaira was indeed a serious crime, most certainly an act of treason. Still, no one had died, and both the objective and the general tenor of the event remained one of protest, not rebellion. Perhaps León believed at this point that his behavior would be vindicated now that his complaints about the Guipuzcoana Company and the Basque governors were sure to be heard.

ROYAL REACTION

The gravity of the situation as it was perceived by royal authorities is reflected in the immediate response it evoked from administrative centers in the Indies and in Spain. The Caracas cabildo had informed the Audiencia of Santo Domingo of events in July 1749, after Castellanos had left the city and the threat of hostilities by León raised the protest to the point of open rebellion. On August 21, three ships arrived at La Guaira with troops sent by the governor and captain-general of Santo Domingo. Accompanying them was don Francisco Galindo Quiñones y Barrientos, oidor of the audiencia, who had been charged by the court to pacify Caracas and then to hear the complaints of the cabildo and Juan Francisco de León. The actions of León and his compatriots, encouraged and supported as they had been in secret by the Caracas elite, would now be answered by the king's justice. Although this is exactly what they sought in what had become a desperate struggle with the Company, the severe judgment they received offered nothing to the Leonist rebels, and very little satisfaction for the local elite.

The atmosphere in Caracas was one of relief, as the judge Galindo demonstrated both concerned and impartial royal justice. A formal inquiry was begun, and the complaints of all parties were heard. It was not immediately evident, however, that the fundamental purpose of Galindo's mission was to secure the peace while a lasting solution to the problems could be decided upon in Spain. Word of the impending trouble had been dispatched to the Council of the Indies as soon as the frightened Company factor appeared in La Guaira, while León was still camped at Tócome. Months later, when the Council heard that rebels had taken the road to La Guaira and armed confrontation appeared unavoidable, it was decided that a substantial royal force should be sent to the colony, and in late October two warships with twelve hundred men departed Cádiz for the Venezuelan coast. These men were under the command of don Julián de Arriaga, former Chief of Squadron of the Real Armada, whose military mission to return the province to order was coupled with a commission to replace Castellanos as governor.

On November 28 Arriaga's troops disembarked at La Guaira. Galindo left the colony to return to Santo Domingo. In Caracas, rumors ran rampant: the soldiers had been sent by the Guipuzcoana Company without the knowledge of the king; they were royal troops, but they had been sent to forcibly reestablish the Company; they had come to punish, not only León and his mob for rebellion, but the entire Caracas community for disobedience to the royal will. Further, some believed that León intended to use force if necessary to stop the new governor on his way to Caracas. As it turned out, to inspire confidence and to impress the colonists with his valor, Arriaga made the trip from the port to the capital with only a few soldiers of his personal guard, and he reached Caracas without incident on December 6. He called on León to present his case on December 10, and, after hearing him out, Arriaga generously pardoned the isleño leader and his followers for all that had taken place.

Then, in groups of six and eight, royal soldiers began to arrive in Caracas, ordered there from La Guaira by the new governor. Arriaga addressed an anxious cabildo, informing the elites on the town council that he did not intend to restore the Guipuzcoana Company by force of arms as they feared. But he emphasized the point that continued existence or extermination of the Company was a royal prerogative, and that he was in the province both to restore order and gather information about the Company so that its abuses could be corrected in the event that the crown decided it should be reinstated. Its own worst fears resolved, the cabildo carried its protest of the military presence no further, and Arriaga brought most of his remaining soldiers to Caracas. As they patrolled the streets, the governor's troops had an occasional encounter with small groups of protesters, and they were greeted with shouts of *"Viva el Rey y fuera la Compañía"* wherever they went, but the peace was maintained.[25] In the countryside, however, the presence of the royal army in Caracas was understood to mean only one thing—the imminent reestablishment of the Guipuzcoana Company and the Basque domination of both society and economy. Believing that Arriaga's military strength had caused the urban mantuanos to lose their nerve, fearing that Arriaga had tricked them and was waiting for the right moment to invite the Company back, Juan Francisco de León and his lieutenants once again called on their supporters to demonstrate their implacable opposition to the Basque monopoly.

In response to this call, two different groups converged on Caracas in late December 1749. The first to arrive were León and his compatriots from the Tuy region. They met Arriaga's troops on the outskirts of the Candelaria barrio on Christmas eve. They had come to demonstrate, not to fight, but the governor threatened to order his men to fire unless León came forward alone to present his complaints. After prevailing in a heated discussion with his lieutenants, who urged him to withdraw if they could not make their show of strength, León and only his closest aides went to the governor's palace to denounce the Company and to make their appeal for its continued removal from the colony. Face to face with a disciplined armed force, León had in fact backed down. Standing in the central plaza, surrounded by royal soldiers and the Caracas elite, he claimed that he and his men had come in opposition to the Guipuzcoana Company, not to the crown, and he asked Arriaga to forgive the threatening nature of their demonstration. Arriaga was quick to offer a pardon to everyone involved, but a humiliated León was obliged to kneel before him and ask for it, and to remain on his knees for half an hour while the pardon was read from the four corners of the plaza around him.

The next day a second band of more than three thousand men, residents of the haciendas and settlements along the banks of the Aragua River to the west and south of Caracas, halted its march on the city when word was received that León had conceded to Arriaga and had disbanded his followers after asking forgiveness for the rudeness of their protest. On January 2, 1750, the subdued Aragua men, having also abandoned the idea of a show of force, asked and received permission from the governor to send their representatives to Caracas with written complaints about the Company's misdeeds in the Aragua Valley.

Julián de Arriaga had accomplished the pacification portion of his instructions by the first months of 1750. But it was evident to everyone that peace was possible only as long as the Company remained suspended from exercising its monopoly privileges, and the fear that these privileges would be forcibly restored meant that the potential for renewed insurrection was always present. The suspension remained in effect, and months passed while memorials denouncing the Company and position papers in defense of the actions already taken were prepared by the Caracas cabildo and by the Tuy and Aragua Valley dissidents. These documents lacked the stridence and determination of the petitions and letters sent to Castellanos the previous spring. In place of the demands to dismantle the Company and put its employees aboard the first available ship at the La Guaira wharf there were now requests for reforms of specific Company policies. León studiously addressed problems such as the low price paid for cacao and the harmful impact of the *alternativa* (see chap. 6) on the Veracruz trade. He denounced Company administrators for failure to comply with the conditions of their royal charter, but no longer did he question the legitimacy of the monopoly itself. His protest made, León turned his attention to Panaquire and his neglected *arboledas de cacao*.

The Caracas cabildo repeated the view that the Company had caused great damage and discomfort, adding that the many just complaints that had been duly registered with the king's representative in the colony were never heard in Spain because the recent governors of the province, in particular the Basques Lardizábal and Zuloaga, had exercised a despotic rule, suppressing all criticism. But the cabildo was mostly concerned with assuring Arriaga that the council and the town's elite had been consistently loyal, despite the vociferous support they had given León when he first demanded the expulsion of the Company. They were sure that the protest they had supported was in harmony with the royal will in such circumstances, and a royal decree issued by Philip V in 1715 was quoted to the governor to prove their point:

> It is my will that . . . the Governments in my Kingdoms not only support me in what is convenient and necessary to maintain complete Christian liberty, but also that they object to my resolutions, that they do so always when (because I have not taken them under consideration with full knowledge of the facts) it is judged that they are contradictory in any way, protesting to me before God that it is not in my best interest to use the authority that God has been served to place in me.[26]

Arriaga's policy of entertaining the petitions of the Caracas cacao growers successfully diverted the widespread antagonism toward the Company from direct confrontation to a paper war waged by scribes and copyists. In this temporizing, however, the planters remained firm in their insistence that the Company not be restored to its previous status. A stalemate had been reached, at the expense of the Guipuzcoana Company. During the tumultuous year 1749, four Company ships arrived in Spain with more than 22,000 fanegas of cacao, a typical quantity for a single year. Much of this cacao, like the 8302 fanegas brought on the *San Joseph* to Cádiz in December, were beans that were already in warehouse storage at La Guaira when the troubles began. Thereafter, Company business came to a standstill.[27] This was a situation that the king could not allow to continue indefinitely, particularly after reports were received from a royal agent in Holland which provided evidence that smuggling between Caracas and the Dutch island of Curaçao had become suddenly vigorous as *contrabandistas* effectively replaced the Guipuzcoana Company as the colony's primary commercial carrier.[28]

The first reports from Governor Arriaga in Caracas to the Marqués de la Ensenada, then foremost minister in the government of Ferdinand VI,[29] were written in January 1750, just after the protests of Tuy and Aragua planters had ended short of armed confrontation. Arriaga classified the rebels' view that they had not challenged the sovereignty of the king in their protests as ignorance or sophistry, but he reported that he had found no proof that the elite of the region had participated directly or indirectly in the December marches on Caracas or in the action against the fortress at La Guaira the previous August. The governor also informed the Council of the Indies that in his opinion many of the complaints of both elites and rebels were justified. In a copy of a letter he had sent to the Company, Arriaga showed the Council that he had pointed out to the directors of the Basque enterprise that the abuse of their monopoly privilege to set prices and their insistence on the *alternativa* rule (see chap. 6), which meant that every second ship loaded at La Guaira could be a Company ship, had resulted in a critical disruption of the cacao trade. Arriaga believed that planters were understandably reluctant to give up their traditional right to ship on their own account to New Spain and accept the low prices offered by the Company. The logical result was that the Company ship at the head of the *alternativa* line was loaded very slowly, while other, privately owned, ships were forced to wait until more desperate sellers came forward to do business with the Guipuzcoana agents. This policy constricted trade so much that planters whose storehouses were overflowing with cacao beans "found it necessary to sell their cacao while it was still in flower," for no profit at ruinous low prices. Arriaga tried to make it clear to the directors that, while of great immediate benefit to the Company, by 1749 this squeeze on the cacao producers had reached the point where the province was at the point of being "so ruined that no one would be able to buy from them even a sombrero."[30]

REPRESSION

From his vantage point in Madrid the Marqués de la Ensenada saw no reason to share Arriaga's balanced view. It is likely that his response to the events in Caracas was colored by his concern with important changes that were taking place in the empire as a whole.

Ten years of war with England, the War of Jenkin's Ear, had come to an end with the peace of Aix-la-Chapelle in 1748. During the first months of 1750, at the same time as the Arriaga reports from Caracas were placed before him, Ensenada was meeting in the Council of the Indies with ex-colonial ministers, economists, and merchants with experience in the Atlantic trade. Deeply concerned about European competition for the products of their American colonies, these men favored a conservative commercial policy directed from the Council of the Indies, and they argued in support of a return to the traditional fleet system. Firmly opposed to independent trade of the sort carried between Caracas and Veracruz, they were eager to see the resumption of the Guipuzcoana Company. They also favored the permanent elimination of the contract with the English South Sea Company, especially the slave asiento, which had been a source of controversy between Spain and England for decades.[31] In October 1750, a commercial treaty between the two countries formally terminated the contract.[32]

For most of Spanish America the end of the agreement with the South Sea Company had exclusively commercial importance. It meant, to the great relief of major export and import merchants, both in Spain and in the colonies, that the "annual ship" that the English had been allowed to send to the Indies would no longer sail.[33] For Caracas, where the slaving aspect of the contract was more important than its commercial features, the abrogation of the asiento had a profound impact, heretofore entirely overlooked by historians, because there were no Spanish suppliers of slaves able to take the place of the English. More than two hundred slaves were sold by the asiento in Caracas in 1739, the last year before hostilities interrupted the trade, but it would be almost fifty years thereafter, when the English would again be allowed to trade in human cargoes with Spain's dominions, before that many slaves would enter the colony in a single year. The decision to eliminate the English contract meant, in effect, that cacao agriculture would increasingly depend on colony-born slaves and, when slavery proved insufficient, on free labor.

In their high-level deliberations in 1750 the Council of the Indies and the king's ministers most likely did not anticipate the difficulties Spanish traders would have in supplying slaves to the few colonies, like Caracas, which depended on them. Although several of Ensenada's advisors were familiar with Caracas, there is no evidence that they foresaw the major transformation of the colony's labor base which an end to the English asiento implied.[34] Similarly, there is nothing in the correspondence between the marqués and his counselors which suggests that they decided to take severe measures against the rebels of Caracas for any reason other than the most obvious one, that the Leonists had presented an armed challenge to the authority of the monarch. Yet it was known in Spain that in the Caracas province there was an abundance, for some an excess, of Canary Islanders, a people often seen as both contentious and lazy when viewed through the distorting filter of ethnic bias common to many peninsular Spaniards. Although it was not an articulated objective of the policies adopted for Caracas in 1750, it is plausible that Ensenada believed that any shortages of African slaves in the Caracas cacao groves caused by the end of the English asiento would be made up by free, especially free isleño, labor. Such an idea would have been doubly appealing, for by ending dependency on trade with the English for slaves, gainful employment would be provided for the colony's abundant Canary Islander immigrant population.

Whether or not this fundamental change in the nature of cacao labor was a conscious goal of the king's ministers in Spain, many of the Canary Islanders in Caracas did indeed view events there as purposefully directed at them. Beginning with the low prices of the 1740s, isleños like Juan Francisco de León and his sons could see their hopes of becoming slaveholders and hacienda owners in their own right diminishing, and they could begin to imagine a future in which they would labor, not on their own cacao arboledas, but as wage earners on the haciendas of the established Caracas elite instead. It was in opposition to this disturbing prospect that they had become willing to carry their protest to the edge of insurrection and beyond. In a letter written in 1751 to convince a canario compatriot of the need to join his father's cause, Nicolás de León wrote that the Basques were "trying to make slaves of all of us." He most likely meant "slaves" quite literally.[35]

Several of Ensenada's advisors recommended a policy for Caracas that continued the attitude of clemency begun by Arriaga, but in the end those whose counsels he followed argued for a much more forceful course of action.[36] This hard-line position favored restoration of the Guipuzcoana Company as well as the arrest and punishment of the rebels and those who had encouraged them in secret. Three of Ensenada's advisors who favored repression had previous administrative experience with Caracas. One was Gabriel de Zuloaga, governor in Caracas from 1737 to 1747. Zuloaga was no friend of the Tuy Valley cacao planters, and during much of his term as governor he had carried on a determined legal battle with the isleños of Panaquire, questioning the legitimacy of their right to establish a church and permanent settlement on the site where they had planted their haciendas. Zuloaga angered mantuano and more modest immigrant hacendados alike with his firm resolve that to prevent seaborne smuggling all cacao harvested in the Tuy had to reach La Guaira by way of Caracas, that is, by muleback over the expensive and sometimes impassable overland routes.

So disliked was this Basque governor that lively rumors circulated early in 1745 to the effect that a conspiracy had been formed to rid the province of both him and the Guipuzcoana Company. After León's rebellion, Zuloaga could see no reason not to use force to put Caracas in its place, and he argued that a temporizing policy would only encourage future uprisings. He suggested that a demonstration of royal authority would impress and subdue his former charges, for the typical Caraqueño, he derisively claimed, was timid and cowardly. Referring to the rumored plot to kill him in 1745, Zuloaga reported that he had taken up the challenge and gone to a designated spot "alone, with a friend and lackey, and never did they dare it." He thought that two hundred soldiers would be enough to control the entire province.[37]

The second voice in favor of major reforms for Caracas was that of don Sebastián de Eslava, first viceroy of the viceroyalty of New Granada after its resurrection in 1739, and a contemporary of Zuloaga in the Indies service. Eslava, who had served as viceroy for nearly a decade, had been Zuloaga's immediate superior from 1739 to 1742, when Venezuela was part of the New Grandad viceroyalty. During those years Governor Zuloaga had struggled successfully to separate Venezuela from the administrative authority of Santa Fe de Bogotá. In his arguments at the time Zuloaga gave free rein to his limited opinion of the people he governed: given "the genius for intrigue of the natives of the Province of Venezuela," he wrote to the king, if their governor were to have his authority and freedom of action limited by the distant viceroy, it would "encourage them to carry on with even greater freedom their impossible notions."[38] Whether Eslava accepted Zuloaga's evaluation of Caraqueño attitudes is not known, and he did not have Zuloaga's direct experience with Caracas, but in 1750 Eslava was both a war hero and the most senior colonial administrator with experience on the Spanish Main,[39] and his opinions therefore held considerable weight with the Marqués de la Ensenada, who solicited them on behalf of the Council of the Indies.

Eslava believed that a demonstration of the king's military strength was needed in Caracas, but his lack of firsthand knowledge of the province spared him the animosity that recent governors held for the Caracas elite, and the objectivity this afforded him may have been the source of Eslava's original and most important contribution to the high-level debate over the problems in the colony. He believed that there was no natural or lasting bond between the first-family planters of the colony and the low-class and contentious isleños, and he argued that it would be possible to gain the loyalty of the elite if the Guipuzcoana Company were made more Caraqueño and less Basque. To a certain extent this could be accomplished by a change in the Company's image, and Eslava suggested that the name of the enterprise be changed from the *Real Compañía Guipuzcoana de Caracas* to simply the *Compañía de Caracas*. It would also be necessary to alter the structure of the monopoly somewhat, and Eslava proposed to Ensenada that, once the province had been pacified, the principal hacienda owners among the Caracas elite be encouraged to become shareholders and even members of the board of directors of a reformed Company. As a model he suggested the Havana Company, founded in 1740 to handle the export of Cuban tobacco, which had been organized to allow for the investment of Cuban capital, and he noted that Havana planters were satisfied with the commercial profits they received from their tobacco. In due course Eslava's proposal proved to be a successful strategy for Caracas as well.[40]

The last of Ensenada's advisors who was both personally familiar with Caracas and in favor of a strong royal response to the turmoil there was Antonio José Alvarez y Abreu, Marqués de la Regalia. His first career assignment as a young man brought him to Caracas in 1715, and his activities in 1721 to help enforce the authority of the viceroy of New Granada involved him in Caracas's most important political struggle of the early eighteenth century. Although he was born in Santa Cruz de la Palma, *Islas Canarias*, in 1688, Alvarez y Abreu was no canario commoner. From the convent of San Agustin in Tenerife he went on to graduate as *bachiller* from Salamanca in 1707, and in 1711 he received the licentiate in Madrid. In 1714, the young *letrado* was given a commission in a post newly created by order of Philip V, the *Alcalde Visitador de la Veeduria General del Comercio entre Castilla y las Indias*. The primary responsibilities of this office were to uncover individuals involved in contraband trade and to observe in secret the behavior of royal officials, including the governors. Associated with these duties Alvarez y Abreu was given broad powers to investigate and to arrest those he suspected of smuggling, fraud, or disoyalty to the new Bourbon regime. His authority was superior to that of the governors, and viceroys were required to give him their assistance. He was also commissioned to recommend goods and produce that would be best traded to and from the colonies, and to make suggestions for policy both for the better execution of royal justice and for the increased benefit of the royal treasury.[41]

Alvarez y Abreu arrived at Caracas in February 1715. Ostensibly there by appointment of the bishop to serve as professor of law in the Colegio Seminario de Santa Rosa de Lima, a post that gave him the distinction of being the first law professor in Caracas (the Colegio de Santa Rosa would become the Universidad de Caracas in 1725), in fact the position was primarily a cover for Alvarez y Abreu's secret mission to observe commerce and the king's administrators. In April 1716 he married a widow, doña Teresa de Bertodano, daughter of the governor of the province, don Alberto Bertodano y Navarra, a decision that no doubt limited Alvarez y Abreu's impartiality as much as it served to protect the interests of his new father-in-law.[42]

The events of the next several years would thoroughly enmesh the alcalde visitador in local politics and society. Bertodano became governor of Puerto Rico in June 1716 and was replaced in Caracas by don Marcos de Betancourt y Castro, like Alvarez y Abreu a native of the Canary Islands. In 1718, the province of Venezuela was transferred from the executive authority of Santo Domingo to the new viceroyalty of New Granada, and in 1720 two agents of the viceroy arrived in Caracas from Santa Fe de Bogotá to carry on the war against contraband commerce. These *jueces comisionarios*, the Basques Pedro Martín de Beato and Pedro José de Olavarriaga, accused governor Betancourt of abetting the smuggling, and in quick response to their recommendation the viceroy in Santa Fe, don Jorge de Villalonga, ordered that Betancourt be imprisoned in the Caracas jail. Alvarez y Abreu was named his temporary replacement, but this caused much resentment among the local elite, for it violated the traditional preogatives of alcaldes ordinarios of the Caracas cabildo to execute the responsibilities of the governor in his absence. Threats of fines and military intervention forced the Caraqueños's compliance, and from March to December 1721 Alvarez y Abreu served a short term as interim governor. He was then replaced by a new, permanent magistrate, Diego Portales y Meneses, who, as was seen earlier, began with the support of most of the Caracas citizenry in what would be a bitter struggle with viceroy Villalonga by jailing Beato and Olavarriaga and expelling the alcalde visitador, Alvarez y Abreu, from the colony.

Upon his return to Spain, Alvarez y Abreu continued what would be an impressive administrative career. In recognition of his legal talent and his efforts in the area of commerce and commercial revenue, he was granted the title of Marqués de la Regalía in 1726. Before the end of the decade he was oidor in the Casa de Contratación in Cádiz. By 1730 he was a minister of the Council of the Indies, and in 1732 he assumed responsibility for the *asiento de negros*, held by the English, which he had witnessed personally during its initial years in Caracas. At the time of the outbreak of rebellion in Caracas he had risen to the position of dean of the Council of the Indies, and it was in this capacity that he responded to the request of the Marqués de la Ensenada for information about the Guipuzcoana Company and the Caracas tumult: "In all centuries and all nations experience has shown that no insurrection . . . has been pacified by suave means," he wrote. The Caracas cabildo was following a strategy common to insurrectionists, namely to conceal their rebellious objectives with the argument that their just complaints had been kept from the king by corrupt and deceitful ministers. The Prince of Orange had used this tactic until he launched the Revolt of the Netherlands against Philip II in 1581.

The Marqués de la Regalía also argued that it was common for nobles to urge the plebeians of their dominions to take up arms for causes that were of principal benefit to the nobility. To illustrate this point Alvarez y Abreu used an example from contemporary history, one that was no doubt fresh in the minds of his fellow councilors and their king. The war in Italy had been the major diplomatic interest of Philip V during his last years, and Ensenada himself, as secretary to the king's son the Infante Felipe, had played an active part in the campaigns, especially the conquest of the Duchy of Savoy, which he directed in 1743. In December 1746 the Republic of Genoa, allied with Spain but then occupied by the Austro-Sardinian enemy, rose up against its foreign oppressors in a popular struggle that was understood to have begun when a boy threw a rock at an Austrian soldier. It was also understood that the battle that liberated the Italian republic was inspired by the Genoese elite, but carried out, with considerable loss of life, by the commoners. This was a comparison that Alvarez y Abreu knew Ensenada would appreciate, and he arrogantly wrote that were the Caracas elite "better educated people," he would accuse them of consciously following the example of the Genoese gentry by inciting León and his followers among the provincial rabble to revolt.[43]

The marquis Ensenada, ex-governor Zuloaga, ex-viceroy Eslava, and ex-governor and minister Alvarez y Abreu were all in agreement on two points: first, force should be used to bring Juan Francisco de León and the visible rebels to obedience, and second, in order to punish the elites who were the surreptitious authors of the uprising, the institutions and symbols of Caracas's prestige and authority, the officer of governor, the bishopric, and the university, should be transferred to Valencia, a much smaller town of markedly inferior status.[44] There would be second thoughts about stripping Caracas of its provincial importance, but the decision to use force against León was ordered by the Marqués de la Ensenada to proceed without reservation. Precise instructions were written for the man selected by Ensenada to replace Arriaga as governor and to finish the pacification of Caracas, Brigadier General Felipe Ricardos.

Ricardos had served in the Italian dynastic wars of Philip V and had been promoted to brigadier in 1741. His promotion may have been related to his marriage to the daughter of the Duke of Montemar, who led Spain's armies in the reconquest of Orán from the Moors in 1732, and who became military commander of Spain's Italian army from 1733 until 1742. So brilliant was Montemar's performance that he was given the Order of the Golden Fleece for his actions in North Africa and the title of duke, the status of grandee, and a large pension for his successes in Italy. The accession of Ferdinand VI in 1746 had marked the end of dynastic adventurism abroad, and two years later the nations of Europe sought to resolve their differences in the Treaty of Aix-la-Chapelle. In 1748 the young officer Ricardos was named military governor of the island of Málaga. It was from this post, which must have seemed excessively quiet to him, that this veteran of the recent Italian wars, the son-in-law of Spain's most illustrious soldier, was called in 1750 to restore order and the Guipuzcoana Company to Caracas.[45] His arrival in May 1751 meant the beginning of a royal military presence without precedent in the history of the town and province.

Ricardos was given precise instructions from Ensenada and he carried them out exactly. With regard to the Company, he was to see that it resumed operations in accord with its original charter. In effect this meant that the *alternativa* system was abandoned and several ships could take on cargo at the same time, which in turn meant that the colony's cacao planters were free to ship all of their beans to Veracruz on ships other than those of the Company. The only limit to the open trade to Mexico was the responsibility given to Ricardos to guarantee that a sufficient quantity of cacao was sent annually to Spain to meet the demand there. The very controversial matter of the price paid for beans was resolved by arranging for the price to be set every year by a committee comprised of the governor, a regidor of the cabildo, and the Guipuzcoana Company factor.

With regard to the rebels and architects of the rebellion, Ricardos was ordered to arrest Juan Francisco de León and his sons and to send them to Spain. This was to take place even if León offered no new resistance to the reestablishment of the Company. Several members of the Caracas gentry who were known to have encouraged the insurrection, Juan Félix Blanco, Miguel Blanco Uribe, and Juan Nicolás Ponte, were arrested and transported to Spain. Other elites to be deported for the same reason, but to no specified location, were the Maestre del Campo Luis Arias Altamirano, his brother Francisco Arias, Pedro Blanco de Ponte, Francisco de Paula

Toro y Istúriz (the second Marqués del Toro), and Francisco Nicolás Mijares y Tovar (the third Marqués de Mijares). Domingo Aguirre del Castillo, lieutenant to governors Castellanos and Arriaga, and Manuel de Sosa Betancourt, isleño archdeacon of the cathedral, were also to be arrested for their support of León. These men were to be apprehended and judgments were to be made against them without any delay or impediment. Finally, the general pardons issued by former governors to everyone involved in the tumult of 1749 were declared to be without effect.[46]

The easiest part of Ricardos's mission was to secure the submission of Caracas. His troops numbered 600 soldiers and officers, half as many as had come with Arriaga, but many of Arriaga's soldiers had deserted, some of them subsequently joining León's movement.[47] In contrast, Ricardos's men were experienced veterans of the Italian wars, they were better disciplined and, importantly, better paid. While most of this force was sent in pursuit of León and the other rebels in the valleys of Aragua and the Tuy, Ricardos moved against the elite of Caracas. Within days of his arrival in the town in June 1751 he informed the cabildo that the Guipuzcoana Company was again in operation by royal order.

Charged with fomenting rebellion in Caracas, the Conde de San Javier and Francisco de Ponte, representatives of the town at the royal court, were arrested in Madrid. Then followed the arrests of some of Caracas's foremost citizens. Lieutenant governor Domingo de Aguirre y Castillo, Juan Nicolás de Ponte, and Juan Félix Blanco de Villegas were seized and sent straightaway to Spain. In July Ricardos ordered other heads of gentry households confined to their haciendas in the countryside, a moderate move intended to avoid the backlash that might have occurred had more severe treatment been given them.[48] As he wrote to Ensenada, Ricardos felt that "by applying themselves to field labor for a time they will improve their estates, help pay for the expenses of the Republic, and forget about the Company and the Province. And then, when things are more stable, there will be no problem in allowing them to return, thus by this prudent means we will prevent complaints and rumors from the younger people (*para evitar conversaciones de la juventud*)."[49]

Temporary deportation and imprisonment were the limits of the physical punishment suffered by the Caracas elite. The measures taken were sufficient for the purpose of reestablishing order, and Ricardos did not want to give the elite further cause to resist the royal authority that he represented. More severe sanctions might have been forthcoming were it not for the fact that it proved impossible to demonstrate direct involvement of prominent individuals in the León protest. Luis Arias Altamirano was the only member of Caracas elite society who was named by witnesses as an active supporter of the insurgency. After his capture Nicolás de León testified that in 1749, when the Vizcayan Martín de Echeverría arrived in Panaquire and challenged his father's authority, Juan Francisco de León had sent him to ask for advice from maestre de campo Arias. On that occasion Arias had counseled Nicolás to tell his father that he should expel Echeverría "and all the Vizcayans who were dominating this land," and that he should march to Caracas and call for the suspension of the Guipuzcoana Company with all the armed men he could gather together.[50] But Arias, who had been allowed to leave his hacienda and return to his home in Caracas because of a serious illness, died in July 1752, after a year's confinement, and his case was closed by Ricardos, "because he is now being judged by the All Powerful, and in honor of his widow, a *señora principal* in this city, his many children of tender age, and the honor of his family, which has served the King."

Within a month of the death of Luis Arias Altamirano all of the other elites held under house arrest in Caracas or on their haciendas were freed, for reasons like those given by Ricardos for the release of regidor Pedro Blanco de Ponte: "because no evidence of guilt has been found in his case, . . . and having served a long term in confinement he is in need of rest and recuperation." Those who had been held in Spain were released later, Juan Nicolás de Ponte in September 1752 and the Conde de San Javier and his cousin Francisco de Ponte early in 1753.[51]

With those of lesser social status Ricardos had no need to use the same moderation. His soldiers hunted Juan Francisco de León for more than six months without success before León and his son, abandoned by supporters both noble and humble and exhausted by the constant pursuit of royal patrols and colonial militiamen, surrendered in January 1752. While León remained a fugitive, Ricardos laid the heavy hand of royal justice on the rebellious province. A dozen men were condemned to death before Ricardos had been two months in Caracas. The first to die was José Morillo, deserter from the Victoria Regiment of Governor Arriaga and an active León sympathizer, who was captured in Caucagua and summarily executed there by Ricardos's order.

Much more effective for the impression made on public opinion were the executions carried out in Caracas on 3 September 1751. The first sweep through the Tuy in search of León resulted in the arrest of several isleños, blacks, and Indians who had marched with him to Caracas and to La Guaira in 1749. Sent to Ricardos in Caracas, the governor first ordered them to be shot or hanged, and then, deciding that the Indians were "easy to seduce and subject to great imbecility," he reduced their sentence to whipping and eight years of prison. No clemency, however, was shown to Juan "Muchingo," free mulatto; Raimundo Romero, zambo; and Andrés Rodríguez Betancourt, isleño. The Canary Islander met a relatively privileged death before a firing squad and was given an immediate burial, but the two men of color were hung and their severed heads, "as an example and for the embarrassment of the population," were placed on public view, one nailed to the door of the fugitive León's house in the Candelaria barrio, and the other placed on a post along the side of the *camino real* leading from Caracas to the Tuy.[52]

Governor Ricardos brought the will of the king before the province's residents with unmistakable clarity. The executions had a shuddering impact on Caracas society; for all the violence that was threatened by the Leonist rebels, no one had died in the demonstrations against the Guipuzcoana Company or in the military action taken against Castellanos and the soldiers of the La Guaira fort. In addition to the house arrest of a dozen elites, scores of other men who had carried arms with León were jailed during 1751. The will to resist the Guipuzcoana, or to protest its presence or even its policies, disappeared from Caracas. Ricardos's only difficulty proved to be the capture of Juan Francisco de León, and this was because, forced to flee with his son and only a few men after a final, desperate attempt to challenge Ricardos and the Company failed, León proved impossible to find in the Tuy region he knew so well. Before he became a fugitive, however, León was obliged to be a rebel one last time.

When Ricardos arrived at La Guaira, León was in Panaquire,

tending his cacao groves. He heard of the arrests and learned that the general pardon given by Arriaga had no validity. He was advised that Ricardos had sent troops from La Guaira by sea to enter the Tuy at its mouth, to proceed upriver, and to take him prisoner. A decision was made to march, as before, to Caracas, and in mid-August about 80 men went from Panaquire to Caucagua, the most populous settlement in the region. Gathering recruits en route from the largest haciendas in the province, some 200 men took possession of Caucagua, disarming the few soldiers stationed there and wounding the *teniente de justicia* in the process.[53] In the meantime, the royalist plan to take León by surprise resulted in a surprise for the Spanish force instead. At Boca del Tuy they encountered a Dutch fleet of some seventeen ships which had gathered there to trade in contraband cacao. The Dutch smugglers were operating in close collaboration with Tuy planters and were fully informed about the events in Caracas. Although Holland and Spain were not at war, the Dutch seized and disarmed the Spaniards. Later Ricardos was told that the attitude of the Dutch had gone from hostile to furious (insulting the Spaniards as "Vizcayan dogs" and threatening to throw them into the sea) when it became known that they had come to capture Juan Francisco de León.[54]

Ricardo's reaction to the news of the Caucagua uprising and the Dutch presence at Boca del Tuy was to prepare for war. All the milita units at his command were ordered to mobilize, all boys and men aged fourteen to sixty were ordered into militia service, requests for additional troops were sent to Havana and Cumaná, and would-be collaborators and accomplices were threatened with capital punishment. The population at large was forbidden "to say or write anything, in either public or private conversation, nor to make any sign or even the most remote form of demonstration against the Royal resolution of His Majesty with regard to the permanence and subsistence of the Company."[55] When Ricardos's troops reached Caucagua several prisoners were taken, including the isleño González Betancourt and the zambo Raimundo Romero, later executed in Caracas, but León and the other rebels had fled the village before the governor's men arrived.

León's flight took him downriver to the Dutch ships. He stopped first at Panaquire where he gathered money and several of his slaves. All the residents of Panaquire, except one old man and the priest, fled with León in seven or eight large *canoas*, arriving at Boca del Tuy on August 24, four days after the rebels had been forced from Caucagua.[56] One of the Spanish soldiers held captive at Boca del Tuy, a Vizcayan named Martín de Sansinenea, observed the arrival of the flotilla of canoes from Panaquire. He also watched more than thirty canoes move back and forth from the beach to the Dutch ships with hides and cacao, and on August 27 he witnessed six ships with León and his company on board weigh anchor and sail out to sea. Once the insurgents had left, their escape from the Tuy successfully executed according to what he believed was a prearranged plan, Sansinenea and the other Spanish soldiers were released by their Dutch captors and allowed to return to Caracas. Sansinenea told Ricardos that one of the vessels, armed with twelve cannon, was referred to as "León's ship" by the Hollanders because it had been armed and its crew paid for by León.[57]

León's destination was believed to be Curaçao, the Caribbean island off the coast of Venezuela which, together with Bonaire and Aruba, had been held by Holland since the 1630s. Ricardos sent a spy to Curaçao in September, both to look for León and to report on the results of the efforts he was making to stop contraband trading between the Dutch islands and the mainland. Shortly after his arrival in Caracas Ricardos had ordered the destruction of the settlement at the Bay of Chuao, the removal of the huts that had served as homes and a church for the residents, all of whom were believed to be active smugglers. Ricardo's secret agent, one Manuel de Agreda, reported that in Curaçao "the loss of Chuao was sorely felt, because its commerce had been worth thirty to forty thousand pesos in silver a month, [the Dutch] saying that they have lost their Potosí." The agent informed Ricardos that smuggling continued to be active on the islands, that many single- and some double-masted Dutch ships (*balanderas* and *goletas*) manned almost exclusively by Spanish sailors could be observed arriving with Venezuelan cacao, that more than two hundred Spaniards were resident on Bonaire Island, and a similar number made a living by smuggling on Curaçao.[58] Clearly the suspension of Guipuzcoana Company activities forced by the rebellion of 1749 had not suspended cacao trading altogether, and it is probable that the contraband activity had flourished on the Dutch islands for some time, at least since the early 1740s when the Company began to pay record low prices.

With regard to León, Agreda learned that he had not gone to Curaçao, but rather he had sailed east along the coast from Boca del Tuy and had been put ashore near Píritu, a village near the mouth of the Unare River about seventy-five miles distant from the Tuy.

For the next four months, León and a small band of about thirty men wandered about in the savanna and plains of the Unare Basin, a region designated Píritu by the Franciscan fathers, who had developed a strong presence there. Unlike the Franciscans near Caracas, most of whom were Venezuelan-born creoles who might have had some sympathy for the León cause, the Píritu missionaries were peninsular-born and they rejected the fugitives' request for sustenance, informing instead the authorities who were pursuing them of their whereabouts.[59] Since Píritu was beyond the jurisdiction of Caracas authorities, belonging to the district of Barcelona, the westernmost part of the Province of Cumaná, Ricardos requested help from the *teniente de justicia* of Barcelona. Permission was granted by the governor of Cumaná on September 17 and, until the end of 1751, the teniente of Barcelona, Martín de Coronado, searched from hacienda to hacienda and from mission to mission in his district. The trail was always warm. Several rebels and suspected accomplices were arrested, but León was never sighted.[60]

Three other contingents of soldiers sent on Ricardos's order were equally unsuccessful. Each of the two sent from Caracas, the veteran royal soldiers led by *capitán* Antonio González and a combined force of Caracas and Aragua militia headed by Sergeant-Major José de Bolívar, was eager to better the other by capturing León, but neither was successful. Equally without result was the effort of Martín de Tovar Blanco, a member of a distinguished Caracas family (he would become the first Conde de Tovar in 1771) and the owner of substantial cattle herds in the region, who was asked by Governor Ricardos to participate in the search.[61] Then, in December 1751, the manhunt ended as Juan Francisco de León and his son Nicolás decided to surrender and to seek royal clemency.

In a long letter to Ricardos, which he left nailed to the door of the house of the new *teniente* in Panaquire,[62] León defended his actions at the same time that he asked the governor to pardon him for them. Nearly everyone in the colony had opposed the Company, he wrote. The people of Panaquire refused to allow him to accept the Company's agent as *teniente de justicia* there, and he had received letters from the entire province asking him to lead the protest against the Guipuzcoana monopoly. In Caracas he had not made any attempt to drive Governor Castellanos from office, and although he had led 8500 men to La Guaira to bring him back, his men had not so much as wounded anyone in the effort. Like everyone else, he had received a general pardon from governor Arriaga, a pardon that was not honored by Ricardos, who arrested even prominent citizens of Caracas. He had determined to march once again in protest to the city when he and his followers were forced from Caucagua by royal soldiers, and he had been running for his life ever since. There was simply no reason, he wrote, "to pursue me like I have been pursued, to have dishonored me, to have taken from me all the fruit of my personal labor, that of my children and my wife, and that of the rest of the poor people of this valley of Panaquire."

He asked Ricardos how he should have attempted to gain redress for the gross injustices of the Basques, "being the Governor vizcayan and tenientes vizcayans and [Guipuzcoana Company] factors vizcayans." León declared that his actions were in resistance to the total and immoral domination that the Basques exercised in Caracas, and he had decided to surrender because he believed Ricardos would not find him guilty of unpardonable crimes. Finally, he declared that he no longer believed that the monopoly had to be removed from the province, it was in fact a good thing, but only if it had no direct hand in the administration of justice in the colony: "And if the Real Compañía is not what they say it is, Your Lordship could reform it, because, if the Company would comply with what it offered our King to do, it would be of benefit to the Province, [but only as long as] none of them are Judges."[63]

Ricardos had planned to execute León, his son Nicolás, and the other fugitives, "to make the most frightening example of their crimes by hanging them in the public plaza, a punishment and spectacle which would serve as an example to others and reduce everyone to docile obedience." But their voluntary surrender and appeal for mercy made such a demonstration unnecessary.[64] The governor knew that a public hanging of the repentant isleño caudillo in the plaza had the potentiality of igniting the pacified province into rebellion once again. It may be that León counted on this and saw in surrender a chance to save his life. Regardless,

Ricardos placed León and his son aboard a Guipuzcoana Company ship, the *Santa Bárbara*, in complete secrecy. The Caracas public had been led to believe that the vessel would sail for Veracruz with a simple shipment of cacao, but in fact it was bound for Spain, its cargo of accused insurrectionaries destined for judgment before the president of the Council of the Indies in Cádiz.[65]

Governor Ricardos was not content to merely rid the colony of León. He very much wanted to make an example of the popular rebel. On February 5, only days after León turned himself over to the authorities, Ricardos declared that he had requested the king's permission to tear down León's house on the Candelaria plaza, to spread the ruins with salt, and to place a metal plaque denouncing him and his crimes on a post in front of where the house had stood. Permission was granted in July, some months after León had been deported, but the destruction was not carried out until September, after word had reached Caracas of the caudillo's death, reportedly of smallpox, which occurred in August 1752.[66] A copper placard bearing the following inscription was erected where the house had stood:

> This is the Justice of the King our *Señor*, ordered to be done by the Excellent *señor* Don Phelipe Ricardos Lieutenant General of the Armies of His Majesty his Governor and Captain General in this Province of Caracas, to Francisco León, owner of this house, for obstinacy, a rebel and traitor to the Royal Crown, and therefore a Criminal. May the destruction and spreading of salt stand to the perpetual memory of his Infamy.[67]

During the course of the year 1752 Ricardos and Ensenada also determined the fate of the settlement and haciendas at Panaquire. The slaves and cacao property of León, his sons, and others of his followers had been confiscated in August and September of 1751, while the rebels were in Píritu. In his desire to punish and make indelible examples of the potency of the royal will, Ricardos was sympathetic to the king's order, which Ensenada sent to him in September 1752, to destroy Panaquire and to resettle its inhabitants elsewhere in the province. Ricardos waited for more than a year with this order in hand before, in April 1754, he sent the *teniente de justicia* of Caucagua and a contingent of soldiers to Panaquire to notify the inhabitants that they had to leave the valley. Having gained his basic objective of submission to the royal will, however, the governor preferred not to enforce execution of the king's command. By 1754 Ricardos had probably decided not to drive the isleños from Panaquire, for at the same time he ordered them to move he also wrote to Ensenada that the destruction of the cacao haciendas would be a serious loss to the royal treasury. In September 1754, on the basis of Ricardos's recommendation, the Council of the Indies advised the king that, except for the payment by landowners of a new *composición* fee to confirm or reconfirm the titles to their property, Panaquire should be left as it was.[68]

POSTSCRIPT

The significance of the León rebellion transcends the events of that insurrection. In the first place, the memory of León's deed remained in the Caraqueño consciousness during the second half of the eighteenth century, and it was still potent enough to be brought forward in revolutionary Caracas as an inspirational symbol of resistance. Independence was declared on July 5, 1811, and in the *La Gazeta de Caracas* of September, 20, 1811, Rodulfo Vasallo, director of public works in the revolutionary town, issued this executive order:

> [T]o demolish with all solemnity the post of ignominy that the system of tyranny and oppression raised a half century ago on the plot where the magnanimous Juan Francisco de León had his house, and which has unjustly stained the memory of this caudillo of those valiant men who at that time tried to shake off the hard mercantile yoke which the avaricious and despotic kings of Spain had used to constrain the commerce of these provinces, using for the purpose the swindling Guipuzcoana Company, whose exclusive privileges made Venezuelans groan for more than forty years.[69]

Obviously the memory had been sustained by the agents of royal authority who had maintained the "post of ignominy" at the site of León's Caracas residence for more than half-century after the 1749 uprising.

From the perspective of the colonists the warning in the Candelaria plaza had several meanings. It was a constant and probably frightening reminder of the personal grief that an angry monarch could cause his disobedient subjects to suffer. The salt spread on the lot where his house had stood gave León's actions the symbolic quality of sin; and the destruction of his home meant more than simply the removal of his family from the Caracas community. The post and its plaque evoked another, no less disturbing memory: the nailing of a mulatto's head to the door of León's house in 1751. In this case the meaning of the message was double. A gruesome death awaited people of color who would follow whites in insurrection, and to lead such people would result in the most public humiliation imaginable. The black man's head hanging on the door of León's home made it horrifyingly clear that black obedience to white authority could not be misused to challenge the authority of the king. To people of color this symbol must have had the additional effect of making them question the allegiance owed to lower-class whites. For Canary Islanders and other such whites, the racial consequence of León's error was the burden of having their authority over blacks placed in doubt by the crown.

The most significant result of León's rebellion was not manifest in the message of the Candelaria post. But with no less clarity the events of 1749 exposed the limits of the social bonds between elites and countryfolk like León. Those who knew the internal history of the uprising knew that it was rooted in the frustrated ambitions of immigrant isleño cacao farmers who had hoped to follow the Caracas tradition and become owners of prosperous haciendas and many slaves. They knew also that in its initial phase the rebellion had received the support of many of those elites whose success as cacao planters in the seventeenth century had established this tradition, and they knew that the same elites had abandoned the movement when it became more than a demonstration of discontent.

They could also recall that the repression engineered by Ricardos had been more harsh for members of the lower orders, who were executed and exiled, than it was for the elite, who were merely confined to their estates. Finally, people knew that during the years following the uprising the foremost families of Caracas established a modus vivendi with the crown and the Guipuzcoana Company that allowed them to maintain their accustomed wealth and status. At the same time, the middle stratum of the colony saw its lifestyle decline from that of having the chance to become hacienda owners on the Tuy frontier to that of choosing between vagabondage or wage labor on the haciendas of others. Those whose social station was similar to that of León before 1749 most likely looked upon the Caracas elite with some resentment or anger during the subsequent decades. That the split between the mantuanos and these folk had become permanent was reflected in the fact that many isleños and the rural proletariat in general fought on the royalist side in the Caracas insurrection of 1810. From this perspective, the decision of the mantuano revolutionaries in 1811 to destroy the marker at León's residence was indeed designed to evoke the memory of the rebel in the name of independence, but it may have also been a gesture calculated to close the gap between the elite and those of the lower orders which had first become evident half a century earlier. For many of the decendants of León the gesture was a hollow one, and they chose to remain loyal to the king.

6

The Protest of the Caracas Elite

Not all Caracas mantuanos were vociferously opposed to the Guipuzcoana Company. This observation stands against the standard view of a monolithic planter class united in opposition to the Company, a view which may have originated in the community-wide support given to León upon his first arrival in Caracas in 1749. Such an image was certainly the one projected by those who wrote protest memorials to the king and the Council of the Indies during the years immediately preceding 1749, and to the indiscriminating eighteenth-century counselor or twentieth-century historian the long list of elite signatures appended to these documents could be taken to mean that virtually everyone of social distinction had spoken out against the Company. The authorities made an effort to identify the leadership of the protest, and the governors identified certain influential individuals with close ties to the New Spain trade as instigators of the agitation. The extent of these leaders' influence, although it was generally taken to be considerable, was never determined precisely. From Madrid, Eslava and other administrators simply perceived a largely undifferentiated elite directorship behind the activities of the Leonist protesters. In the aftermath of the uprising, the preferred treatment given elite activists, so different from the harsh punishments given León and those of more modest social standing, probably reinforced the view in the popular mind of a single, cohesive elite planter class that had first shouted down the Company and surreptitiously supported the plebeian armed protest and then reached a convenient accord with crown and Company. With the exception of certain references given to Ricardos naming individual colonials he might trust,[1] those mantuanos who might have been Company supporters or sympathizers were not singled out in the eighteenth century, and historians have continued to suppose that all elite Caracas planters worked actively in opposition to the Guipuzcoana Company.

In fact, only certain mantuanos had strong reasons to protest in earnest against the Company, to the point of promoting rebellion if necessary. To distinguish the protesters from the remainder of foremost Caracas citizenry, and then to understand better why they might have been moved to act as they did, is to see that the policies of the Guipuzcoana Company aggravated and accelerated but did not create the critical juncture that these elite planters had reached before 1750. Once the midcentury crisis of the Caracas elite has been identified, both the determined nature of the mantuanos' opposition to the Company and the significance of the benefits they received in the outcome of León's rebellion will become clear.

This chapter is comprised of three sections. The first examines the ways in which the commercial strategies of the Guipuzcoana Company upset the colonials' traditional trade practices. Although there is new material presented here, this perspective reinforces the customary way of seeing these events in that it sets a greedy Company against an oppressed and therefore presumably unified colonial population.[2] The second section seeks to modify this view and thereby to better understand the complexities of the social setting in which opposition to the Company was formed. To do this it is necessary to distinguish those mantuanos who made visible protest against the Company from those who left no record of their opposition. Protest memorials written during the years immediately preceding the León uprising were signed by only a portion of those who could claim elite status. Identified by their signatures, elite signatories are compared to prominent Caraqueños who did not sign according to the following criteria: size of cacao holdings, length of family tenure in Caracas, Basque parentage, family history of political activism, endebtedness to the Company, and possession of sugar trapiches as an alternative to dependency on cacao. These comparisons lead to the conclusion, illustrated by case studies in the third section, that certain large and expanding, cacao-dependent elite families had reached a critical point in the 1740s. In fact the last years of the decade represent a time of serious crisis for these families, inasmuch as the continuation of their status as elites came to depend on the successful outcome of a desperate, direct confrontation with the Guipuzcoana Company.

THE COMPANY AND CACAO COMMERCE

For many years the business of shipping Caracas cacao to Mexico was a simple affair. Anyone with beans could sell them at the current local price to a merchant or directly to a ship's captain or supercargo. An alternative method, preferred by those who could forgo cash payments for their cacao in Caracas, was a practice of shipping by way of what was known as the *tercio buque* (one-third of the ship's hold). By custom, one-third of the cargo space in every vessel that departed the colony was reserved for the produce of hacienda owners, *cosecheros* as they are referred to in eighteenth-century documents. A second third was allocated to Caracas merchants for the cacao that they had acquired, and a final component or *tercio* was reserved for the ship's captain in the name of the owners of the vessel. Once the third part of the hold reserved for them had been filled with cosechero cacao, hacienda owners who still had cacao to ship could sell their beans at current market prices to local merchants or the ship's captain or supercargo. Sales in Caracas provided immediate cash or credit and freed the seller from the risk of losses that could take place on the high seas. But such sales, while more secure, were not nearly as profitable as those made by way of the tercio buque. Caracas cosecheros and merchants shipping by tercio buque had to pay freight charges to the ship's owner or captain and they renounced the right to collect for damages or losses that might occur in transit, but they retained ownership of their cacao until it was sold in Mexico, and this, despite the risks, often meant substantial income.

Within twenty-four hours of the ship's arrival in Veracruz the captain of the vessel was obliged to transfer Caracas-owned cacao to an agent in that port named by the cosechero or merchant. Those who shipped cacao in this fashion had to depend on the reliability of this associate, and often they had to wait for extended periods before the profits from the sale of their beans were returned to them. Frequently, such profits took the form of credits to be drawn on merchants in Mexico or Spain, which meant that many of the elite Caracas cosecheros who utilized the tercio-buque provision functioned much like merchants in that their assets were not always liquid and they were often located outside Caracas. But the great advantage of shipping cacao in the tercio buque was, of course, that Caraqueños who sold in New Spain could profit from the much higher prices paid for cacao there.[3]

Until 1721, those who had cacao for export or sale could do business with the agent of any ship that happened to be taking on cargo at La Guaira. In that tumultuous year, to the great disgust of the Caracas citizenry, Antonio José Alvarez y Abreu was named governor pro tem in Caracas by the viceroy of New Granada.[4] During his short tenure Alvarez y Abreu introduced the *alternativa* to La Guaira shipping, a system which required that the first ship entering port had to be loaded to capacity before any subsequent vessel could open its hold for cargo. Influential Caraqueños resisted the alternativa, and Andrés de Urbina, owner of more than 50,000 cacao trees and recognized as the *mayor cosechero* in Caracas, went to Spain to obtain the repeal of the plan. He won his case, and the *real cédula* issued in favor of his appeal, dated 25 May 1722, would be known to a generation of Caraqueños as the *cédula de Urbina*.[5]

The alternativa was intended to attract ships to the *carrera de Veracruz* by guaranteeing a full cacao cargo for every vessel that might arrive at La Guaira. Although it is not entirely clear what was troublesome about this policy, it could be that it had the effect of retarding rather than expediting shipping. If, for example, Caracas cosecheros wanted to choose their carrier, favoring for instance the Caracas-owned ships of their associates or kinsmen, the alternativa would have obliged them to wait to load their cacao until all ships in line at the La Guaira wharf ahead of the one they preferred had been filled and had cleared port. In any event, thanks to Urbina's efforts, the alternativa was inoperative from 1722 until 1731, when it was reinstated as the rule—but this time it was to serve as a tool in the hands of the powerful Guipuzcoana Company, which was then striving to dominate the colony's cacao trade.

In 1728 a royal license was given to a group of Basque merchants which granted them exclusive rights to bring Caracas cacao to Spain. The *Real Compañía Guipuzcoana de Caracas*, Spain's first royally chartered commercial monopoly company, was created only to provide Spanish markets with cacao, which was to be done by stimulating production and stopping illegal commerce with foreign merchants. In no way whatsoever was the Company to inferfere or compete with the traditional trade between Caracas and New Spain. This trade therefore remained open as before to anyone who could secure a ship and a cargo. Until 1731 Caracas cosecheros, independent merchants, and shipowners who were not associated with the Guipuzcoana Company continued to ship their own cacao to Veracruz on the basis of direct sales and the traditional tercio buque in vessels that did not belong to the Company. In addition, shortly after the Company's creation, Caraqueños sought to limit its monopoly by arguing that their traditional rights to a third part of the hold of any ship departing La Guaira also included those belonging to the Company. No royal cédula could be found to provide a legal basis for the tercio buque practice, however, and the Company was exempted from granting the customary tercio buque. Caracas residents continued to protest the exception to their traditional right, but as long as there was no infringement on their customary trade with New Spain, most planters and merchants were evidently not much harmed by their exclusion from the transatlantic cacao commerce with Spain.

A serious problem did arise, however, after the alternativa policy was reinstated in 1731. In Caracas the alternativa meant that once a Guipuzcoana Company ship had reached the head of the queue and had opened its hold to take on cargo, cosecheros with beans for market had to either sell their cacao to the monopoly at current prices or wait until others had sold their harvests to the Basques and the Company ship had loaded and departed. Hacienda owners who had traditionally exercised their tercio buque right to transport their harvests to the lucrative New Spain market had no interest in selling to the Company, for by doing so they would forfeit the considerable profit they stood to gain if they sold their beans on their own account in Mexico. As the flow of cacao to New Spain slowed and the resulting shortages in that colony caused Mexican buyers to offer more for Caracas beans,[6] cosecheros became even less willing to do business with the Guipuzcoana Company. While Company ships stood at the La Guaira wharf taking on but little cargo, with other ships waiting empty behind them, Caracas mantuanos vented their frustration and discontent by making formal objection to royal officials in Madrid. The Caracas cabildo wrote to the crown in 1745 that the time spent waiting to load in La Guaira so slowed the cacao trade to New

Spain that it had become common for a year and a half to pass before a ship could complete the cycle of loading, sailing to Veracruz and back, and passing to the head of the line at La Guaira to be ready to load again. This was true even though the process of loading and unloading could be done in a matter of days and the sailing time from La Guaira to Veracruz was typically less than a month. While the quantity of cacao grown on their haciendas steadily increased, the alternativa very effectively kept the Veracruz trade bottled up in the colony.

A further aggravation came as a result of a policy initiated in 1744 by the Basque governor Zuloaga. In that year a survey was made of all the cacao haciendas in the Caracas province. From this census a checklist was prepared in which each estate was recorded by the name of its owner and by the number of fruit-bearing trees it contained. Zuloaga then determined that each cosechero's portion of all the cacao grown in the province would also be the maximum portion of any (non-Company) ship's tercio buque that the cosechero could fill with cacao. In other words, for example, the Panaquire hacienda of Juan Francisco de León consisted of 15,000 cacao trees in 1744. León thus owned about three-tenths of one percent of the more than 5 million trees counted that year. By Zuloaga's decree León could not load more cacao than three-tenths of one percent of the tercio buque capacity of any ship bound for New Spain. Similarly, the Marqués de Toro, whose 90,000 trees on seven haciendas made him the province's foremost cacao hacendado in 1744, could send a maximum of one and a quarter percent of the tercio buque of any ship carrying cacao to New Spain.[7]

This policy of allocation, known as the *repartimiento por padrón*, probably appeared fair on paper, since its ostensible objectives were to give all cosecheros a chance to ship in the tercio buque and to make it impossible for mantuano planters or merchants to buy up all the cacao available, in direct competition with the Guipuzcoana Company, and transport it as their own to New Spain. Yet since in practice the policy made it virtually certain that planters would not be able to ship all of their own cacao in the tercio buque, it was most likely designed to force them to sell some of their beans to interested buyers, in particular to the factors of the Guipuzcoana Company. Since the portions allocated by the repartimiento applied exclusively to the cargo space of each individual vessel, a cosechero who enjoyed a bountiful harvest might have beans on hand for shipment in La Guaira which exceeded his predetermined share of the tercio buque of any given ship bound for Veracruz. Similarly, if a ship had substantial cargo capacity it could happen that there would be available space remaining in its hold after all interested cosecheros had loaded their portions, but the hacienda owner with beans in excess of his allotment would not be allowed to put them in that vessel's still unfilled tercio buque, and the ship would have to sail only partially loaded. In addition, since the assigned portions could not be accumulated or carried over from one vessel to the next, if a cosechero had too little cacao on hand in La Guaira to fill his portion of the tercio buque on one occasion, he could not expect to make up the difference by receiving an expanded share in a future sailing.

Caraqueños claimed that the repartimiento benefited only the Guipuzcoana Company, and that it was in fact a strategem designed for that purpose by the Basque governor Zuloaga. In 1750 Juan Francisco de León, then in the midst of the full-scale popular movement that had succeeded in temporarily driving the Company from the colony, included the repartimiento in the list of injurious practices that had forced him and his followers to take up arms in protest:

> The *repartimiento por Padrón*, although at first glance it seems to treat all the cosecheros equally, distributing to each one of them a diminutive proportion according to the number of trees that he owns, is actually unfair, because it is certain that there are many [cosecheros] in the province who miss the opportunity to ship cacao [in the tercio buque], either because they are unaware of the opportunity or because they cannot quickly cover the great distance [from their haciendas to La Guaira]. And even those who do ship are not treated fairly by this *Padrón*, for not everyone is able to send a shipment every time [a vessel is available], and if an opportunity is missed it is impossible to compensate with the next vessel, because on each occasion no one is allowed to load more cacao than his allotted share.[8]

In the late 1730s and 1740s, the principal opponents of the Guipuzcoana Company and advocates of the customary privileges of the cosecheros were three Caracas noblemen, the Marqués del Toro until his death in 1742, the Conde de San Javier (Juan Jacinto Pacheco y Mijares), and don Francisco de Ponte y Mijares, cousin to the Conde. These men took their case to Spain, residing at court for several years at a time while they carried on a paper war of major importance for Caracas. Dismissed by attorneys for the Guipuzcoana Company as the self-interested managers of the traditional trade, they nevertheless presented dispassionate arguments that demonstrated for the Council of the Indies the damage done to commerce and cacao agriculture by the Company and the Basque governors who, as its allies, established and enforced the alternativa and the repartimiento por padrón.

The published remonstrances of these mantuanos contain criticisms of the alternativa, the repartimiento, and a third policy that they believed was also designed to redirect the cacao trade away from New Spain and into the hands of the Guipuzcoana Company. They criticized a system of quotas begun in 1734 by governor Martín de Lardizábal in what the governor claimed was an effort to eliminate conflict while retaining the alternativa. Based on an estimated 60,000 fanegas annual cacao production in the province, Lardizábal had determined that 10,000 fanegas should be discounted for local consumption, 20,000 fanegas were then allocated for New Spain and 30,000 fanegas for Spain proper. Once the quota for one destination had been reached, exports were to be directed exclusively to the other market until its quota was achieved. The representatives of the Caracas planters claimed that the quota system was illegal since it in effect deprived them of their right to trade freely with New Spain. Since the Guipuzcoana Company's exclusive right to trade with Spain was always in effect, in practice the quota system meant that once 20,000 fanegas were sent to Mexico, no more cacao could be shipped there until the Company had purchased 30,000 fanegas for shipment to Spain, at whatever price the Company chose to pay. As a further benefit for the Basque monopolists, once both quotas had been filled Lardizábal's system gave the Company permission to sell in the lucrative New Spain market—a direct violation of the Company's charter.

The Conde de San Javier and Francisco de Ponte made their objections to the quota policy in a *memorial* presented to the Council in January 1746. Rather than accept the quotas and relinquish the benefits of their traditional trade to New Spain, cosecheros simply refused to sell their beans to anyone, preferring to keep them in their warehouses. Far from advancing the productivity and commerce of the colony, the Company and the Basque governors who favored it had in fact forced stagnation upon the colony. As evidence of this, San Javier and Ponte argued that it was widely accepted in Caracas that annual production had been underestimated at 60,000 fanegas in 1734, and that by 1740 a more accurate figure would have been 90,000 fanegas. Since Lardizábal made his allotments, many new cacao haciendas had been brought to harvest. The entire valleys of Curiepe, Panaquire, and Araguita had begun to produce in the interim, and there had been great expansion in other Tuy valleys such as Capaya, Mamporal, and Caucagua. Yet not once since 1740 had the quota of 20,000 fanegas been sent to New Spain; about 9000 fanegas were sent in 1741, and not even 7000 fanegas went in 1743. Nor had the Atlantic trade to Spain benefited from the system. San Javier and Ponte pointed out that in the decade that had passed since the quotas were established, the Company had been able to fill its allotment only once, in 1740, when 40,000 fanegas were sent to Spain.

According to San Javier and Ponte, the reason why the quotas were not filled, even when there was more cacao in the colony than Lardizábal had estimated, was due directly to the low prices offered by the Guipuzcoana monopoly. San Javier and Ponte offered the council an argument that placed blame entirely on the Company for creating the surfeit of cacao that had accumulated in Caracas, an oversupply of beans that in turn drove prices to record low levels.[9] Since many cosecheros were unwilling to sell their beans to the Company, the Company ships were filled only very slowly, other ships stood empty at the wharf waiting to load, and the legal export of cacao from the provice came to a virtual standstill. The bottleneck created by the quotas and the alternativa caused a dramatic increase in cacao beans planters had stored in their Caracas and La Guaira warehouses, as cosecheros waited for the chance to ship to New Spain. With such an abundance of beans available for sale the local price paid for cacao fell to unprecedented low levels.

There was so much cacao available that many planters had no choice but to sell to the Guipuzcoana Company at ruinous prices. Desperate planters who needed immediate cash for their crop "found themselves obliged to sell their cacao while it was still in flower"[10] at whatever price they could get for it, which was often as little as seven or eight pesos. This was made all the more disturbing because in Veracruz, where the demand for beans had come to far exceed the restricted supply coming from Caracas, would-be buyers were offering fifty pesos and more per fanega. In the graphic metaphor of the frustrated cabildo, these constrictive policies had made the legal cacao trade "a throat too small for the vomit of the great stomach that is this province."[11]

In what was perhaps their most serious criticism, surely designed to attract royal attention to their complaints, San Javier and Ponte hinted that for many colonists in the Caracas province smuggling had become the only viable alternative to this situation. They suggested that it was an ironic, but very disturbing, circumstance that by its avarice the Company had in fact come to foment the illegal trade that it had been created to eliminate. How else except by smuggling, they asked rhetorically, could the great discrepancy between production and exports be explained?

The reduced flow of cacao to New Spain brought other serious problems in its train. New Spain had always been Venezuela's principal source of circulating specie, but with fewer ships arriving with cacao at Veracruz, very little silver coin came back across the Caribbean on their return voyages. Mexican merchants, who had traditionally advanced cash for the purchase of Caracas cacao,[12] were now reluctant to tie up their investments for as long as two years in a market brought to stagnation. Together the abundance of cacao for sale and the shortage of coin caused prices to come crashing down. San Javier and Ponte pointed out that low prices were ruinous to many other people in addition to cacao planters, especially in Caracas, where the lack of cash made business of all kinds difficult. Even artisans were forced to leave their crafts and take up subsistence agriculture in the countryside. On the haciendas, slaves who ran away or died could not be replaced, and there was no cash to pay wage labor as a substitute. The best that could be done, under the circumstances of torpid trade and low prices, was to "keep the slaves busy, without expecting to get any benefit from them or from one's *árboles de cacao.*"[13]

The Guipuzcoana Company made no great effort to counter the specific criticisms directed at it by Toro, San Javier, Ponte, and others. Some resistance to its establishment in Venezuela no doubt had been expected, and perhaps the Company's directors were secure that their royal license guaranteed support. Rather than answer the colonists' charges directly, Company spokesmen and influential friends of the Company tried to discredit Toro and the other Caraqueño critics by claiming that they argued only on the basis of self-interest. In 1739, an attorney for the Company claimed that the Marqués de Toro and the Conde de San Javier were "the only, or at least the principal merchants, who for themselves, and for their commission agents in Vera Cruz, resist the Company." It was said that these men had dominated the cacao trade for many years and that they denounced the Company for no motive other than the desire to return to a condition in which they had no competitors. In February 1745, the Basque governor Zuloaga questioned the disinterestedness of the Caracas cabildo, which a month earlier had described commerce under the Company and the alternativa as a "throat too small" for the great productivity of the province. Most of the officers elected to the town council in 1745, Zuloaga claimed, were members "of the family Solórzano, which is the family of the Conde [de San Javier]."[14]

In fact, however, opposition was widespread. Caraqueños of diverse social standing expressed their objections to the alternativa and low prices. The Company's policies and the results of those policies created immediate hardships for many hacienda owners and others whose livelihoods depended on the exchange of cacao for silver coin. These immediate difficulties were all the more intolerable for certain of the colony's oldest and most prestigious families because they threatened to dislodge them from their accustomed positions of privilege in Caracas society.

THE MANTUANOS' PROTEST

For several successive generations, in some cases as many as four generations by the 1740s, steadily expanding cacao production had given similarly steadily expanding elite families the means to sustain the level of material wealth and social standing which their ancestors had enjoyed. For these Caraqueños the Tuy River boom of the 1720s and 1730s was only the continuation of a remarkable process of expansion that had gone on without much variation since the 1670s. But there are indications that by the 1740s, especially after the importation of African slaves came to a virtual stop in 1738, the cacao economy could no longer support the expanding number of people who could claim elite status in the Caracas community by virtue of their illustrious lineage and family name. The fear of downward social mobility does not appear stated explicitly in any of the available sources, but a conspicuous theme in the literature of protest is that the Guipuzcoana Company's policies were harmful to families, and to elite families in particular, especially those that were headed by elderly parents soon to be succeeded by a new generation. The prominent place given to elite widows on many of the petitions drawn up to protest the Company manifests this concern. As bulwarks of the social order, there were no individuals who were more vulnerable or more worthy of royal attention and protection than these women.

In January 1741 the Council of the Indies received a petition protesting the policies of the Guipuzcoana Company signed by "eleven widows, *vecinas* of Caracas and *cosecheras de cacao*." The memorial claimed that the households of these women had haciendas that together produced more than 4000 fanegas of cacao per year, but that they had very little else besides cacao to sell, and that because of the low prices offered by the Company for cacao they had become "indebted and subjugated" to the Basque monopolists. The widows informed the council that the previous years had been ones of great agricultural expansion for the province, that many new haciendas had been created, some of them with credit provided by the ecclesiastical establishment, and that many of these haciendas were now in danger of foreclosure because the price paid for cacao, even at ten pesos the fanega, was not enough to pay what was owed. The Caracas diocese stood to suffer if prices did not rise, for the tithes were reduced and the people had nothing with which to make gifts (*limosna*) to the church.

The sale of imported African slaves, so essential to the expansion of cacao agriculture, had become part of the Company monopoly as a result of the war with England and the collapse of the English asiento, but in 1741 there were very few slaves offered for sale and the Company collected "20, 25 and more" fanegas of cacao for each one. Twenty years earlier, the women complained, the same amount of cacao would have purchased as many as three slaves. What was especially galling to the widows was the very different image of itself that the Company projected: "They would make you believe that the Company is the cause of the progress in the Province, because the people of this city can take advantage of the fact that the Company will buy at a reasonable price all the cacao we can grow, but it is certain that for the most part they do not pay even ten pesos." At this price, the widows' haciendas, despite their productive potential, had become nearly "useless," which was "a great misfortune."[15]

The price paid for cacao stood at nine pesos the fanega in 1744, and, because it was widely known that the same cacao would bring fifty-two pesos on the Mexican market, the ire of most Caracas hacienda owners reached a critical point. They were angry because they were sure that the alternativa, *repartimiento por padrón*, and quota policies were designed to allow the Guipuzcoana Company to make excessive profits by keeping the purchase price for cacao far below what it would have been in a free market. In November 1744 many of Caracas's most influential townspeople, describing themselves as "Interested Citizens, both Merchants and Planters," prepared a petition to the king, begging for royal clemency and relief from the Company's exploitative practices. Beginning once more with the town's prominent widows, this memorial bore the signatures of ninety-three people, representatives of most but, significantly, not all of the elite families of Caracas.[16]

The 1744 memorial is a most useful document, both for the names it provides of those mantuanos who were willing to protest the Company, and for the names of similarly prominent individuals who are conspicuous by their absence from the list (appendix H). Comparison of elite townspeople who protested in 1744 with other mantuanos who did not sign the memorial on the basis of certain pertinent characteristics provides a rather clear idea of the Guipuzcoana Company's impact in Caracas. In the following pages the signatories are first identified by family and the quantity of cacao owned by them is determined. Then three possible reasons for their opposition to the Company, none directly related to the economy or cacao agriculture, are considered: they were members of families with longer tenure in the colony than those who did not sign; their origins were not identifiably Basque; and they were members of families with considerable political influence in Caracas, measured by town council activism, while those who did not sign did not have this activist tradition in their family backgrounds. Next, two factors of an economic sort, debts owed the Company and the possession of sugar trapiches (sugar sold in the local market was an alternative to the cacao export trade), are used as a test of the financial vulnerability of the memorial signatories. Finally, all of these circumstances are examined in the specific cases of three families, one, the Blanco, who were firmly opposed to the Company, and two, the Bolívar and the Palacios, who either made no complaint or supported the Basque monopolists.

Who Signed

Of the ninety-three who signed, seventy-six (twenty-one women and fifty-five men) can be identified and linked to a reconstituted elite family whose genealogy for several generations is known. These linkages make it possible to construct age and marriage profiles for these people. All of the elite women who signed were unmarried in 1744, eleven were widows, eight others would never marry, and the remaining two would marry after 1744. It is significant that no married woman whose husband was then alive signed the memorial. In clear contrast, most of the men who signed were husbands and fathers; only eight of the fifty-five identified elite men were not then married and would never marry. Of the remaining forty-seven, twenty-four were married and their spouses were also living in 1744, and twenty-three were either widowers in 1744 or single men who had not yet married but would do so subsequently. Although the data is not complete in every case, it is evident that the elite protesters were mature individuals, with an average age in 1744 of 39.0 years for the men (number of cases with known birth date is forty-two of the fifty-five) and 45.6 years for the women (number of known birth dates, nineteen of twenty-one).[17]

The census of cacao haciendas also taken in 1744 (for the purpose of allocating tercio buque space on the repartimiento basis) makes it possible to determine how much cacao was owned by elite protesters and elite nonprotesters alike. Only half of the seventy-six identified elite signatories were actually owners of cacao haciendas in 1744; in all, thirty-eight individuals, seven of them women, held a total of 781,500 cacao trees on 64 haciendas, or 15.3 percent of the total number of cacao trees (5,102,221) on 11.5 percent of the total number of Caracas-province haciendas (556) according to the

1744 census of cacao estates. The cacao properties owned by these thirty-eight signatories comprised slightly more than one-third of the cacao holdings of all elites. The thirty-eight owned 37.7 percent of all the trees held by elite hacendados in 1744 (781,500 of 2,071,392 elite-owned trees), and virtually the same percentage, 36.8 percent, of the haciendas owned by elites (64 of 174). In general then, the thirty-eight elite cacao hacendados who made formal protest against the Guipuzcoana Company in 1744 owned about 15 percent of all the cacao trees then grown in the Caracas province, and they owned about one-third of the cacao trees that belonged to people who were members of established elite families.[18] It would be in error, however, to suppose that the owners of the remaining two-thirds of elite-owned trees who did not sign the 1744 document were supporters of the Guipuzcoana Company.

Social conventions kept some elite cacao hacendados from signing. Evidently it was deemed inappropriate or unnecessary for women or adult children to put their names on the memorial if they were married or if their fathers were alive in 1744. For example, one woman who did not sign was Ana Josefa Ibarra y Ibarra, owner of 36,000 cacao trees on two haciendas in the coastal valley of Borburata. Her mother, María Petronila Ibarra, who had 14,000 trees in the coastal valley of Patanemo, was one of the widows whose signatures headed the list. Two of doña Ana's brothers signed, one had a small hacienda of 5000 trees in Patanemo, the other owned no cacao. At first glance it is curious that Ana's sister Antonia, who likewise owned no cacao in 1744, did sign, but closer examination reveals that Antonia was also a widow in 1744, and her signature follows her mother's on the list. It turns out that Ana Josefa Ibarra, who held more cacao in her own name than her mother and all of her siblings together, did not protest against the Guipuzcoana Company in her own name, probably because she was married. Her husband, her first-cousin Diego Ibarra y Herrera, owner of 13,000 trees on one hacienda in Borburata, was one of the memorial's signatories. Presumably, even though his wife's cacao holdings were three times greater than his, the signature of Diego Ibarra represented Ana Josefa Ibarra as well.

There were other women whose protests were made by their men. Noblewoman doña María Teresa Rodríguez del Toro Istúriz owned 10,000 cacao trees on the banks of the Capaya River in the flood plain of the lower Tuy River. Her brother, the Marqués de Toro, with 90,000 trees on seven haciendas, the owner of more cacao than any other individual in 1744, was among the first men to sign the memorial. Her husband, the second Conde de San Javier, was the principal organizer of the campaign against the Guipuzcoana monopoly. The Caracas elite gathered in the house of doña María to put their names on the appeal for help that they would send to Spain, but the *condesa* did not sign it. José Rada Arias and Isabel Soto Ibarra had married in 1717. He signed the memorial but did not have a cacao hacienda; she had an estate of 8000 trees in 1744 but did not sign. Fernando Rada Liendo married his cousin Josefa Clara Liendo Blanco in 1738. He signed the memorial but did not own a cacao hacienda; she did not sign but was holder of 10,000 trees on the coast upwind of La Guaira. In 1737 Pedro Gedler Ponte also married his cousin, María Jacinta Bolívar Ponte. In 1744 each of them was owner of a cacao estate in the Tuy Valley; he had 10,000 trees and she had 12,000. But while his signature appears on the protest document, hers does not.

This patriarchy of protest was extended to the children of the signatories. In only four cases did representatives of two generations of the same family sign the memorial. In three of these cases the younger signers were the adult children of elderly widows. There was only one man whose name was accompanied by the signatures of his children: don Lorenzo Ponte Villegas, sixty-two years old in 1744, allowed his three eldest sons to sign the memorial. Ponte Villegas was a major cacao hacendado, with 79,000 trees on six haciendas, but none of his children, including the adult sons who signed in 1744, owned cacao haciendas in that year. This was not exceptional. The fact that, with the exception of Ponte Villegas and his sons, adult sons and daughters did not sign the document if their fathers signed reflects the status of these sons and daughters as cacao hacienda owners: in general they had no cacao in 1744. A total of twenty-seven of the fifty-five identified elite men who signed the 1744 document were married or widowed men with living children in that year. Two-thirds of these men had married in the mid-1730s or later and therefore their children were still adolescents in 1744, but nine men had married during the period 1699 to 1728, and most of their children were adults in 1744. Not one of these adult offspring signed the protest statement, however, and none of them owned cacao property in that year. Unlike their mothers, who did not sign but may have possessed haciendas in their own right, these adult sons and daughters of elite cacao hacendados had neither political voice nor cacao estates of their own while their fathers were still alive.

This all means that the signatures on the 1744 memorial signified determined opposition to the Company, not only on the part of those who actually signed, but also on behalf of the signatories' wives and their offspring, both children and adults. Yet, few of these represented kin had cacao haciendas; only the five wives mentioned above, who held a total of 76,000 trees, can be added with certainty to the names of hacienda owners who spoke out against the Company. There were many other mantuanos in 1744 who did not sign the document and were neither the wives nor the children of those who did. Is it probable that they opposed the Guipuzcoana Company, or should we suppose that they were either its supporters or had simply chosen to maintain a neutral position in the struggle?

An additional six individuals, owners of 187,000 cacao trees on ten haciendas, were most likely allies of those who signed, although they did not themselves sign the protest memorial. Doña Ana Carrasquer Rada was one of the "eleven widows" who wrote to the Council of the Indies in 1741, and her three cacao estates were inventoried in her name during the course of 1744. She died in September, however, before she could sign the memorial, which was written in November of that year. Fernando Aguado Lovera and Miguel Aristeguieta Lovera were hacendados who did not sign in 1744, but when the rebellion began in 1749 they made surreptitious cash contributions to the cause against the Guipuzcoana Company.[19] Three other hacienda owners might be considered allies because of their close familial relationship with signatories: the widow doña María Ponte Marín, because her brother-in-law signed, as did her son, Pedro Francisco Gedler, a principal organizer of the movement against the Company; Antonio Liendo Blanco, because his brother and sister signed, as did his mother's sister and several of his maternal cousins; and finally, Juan Lovera Bolívar, because his brother signed, may have opposed the Company as well.

Altogether the identified and presumed opponents of the Guipuzcoana Company held more than a million cacao trees, about 20 percent of all the trees bearing fruit in the Caracas province in 1744.[20] No other person of elite status can be directly or indirectly linked to the protest, which is surprising in light of the fact that historians heretofore have assumed that the local elite was united in its desire to limit or end the Basque monopoly.[21] Several score planters, many of them much like the outspoken opponents of the Company in terms of their prestige and many generations' presence in Caracas, made no discernible effort to have the Company's control over the colony's economy limited or removed. A total of fifty-eight planters, owners of 722,924 trees on seventy-eight haciendas, have been identified as elite Caraqueños who neither signed the protest letter nor expressed their dissatisfaction with the monopoly in any other form. What were the differences between these two groups of mantuanos which might elucidate why some protested the Company and others did not?

Why They Signed

Deeper Roots?

In respect to the possibility that protesters were from older and therefore more venerable families, perhaps with more at stake therefore in the colony, there was only the slightest difference between those who did or did not sign the 1744 memorial. For the most part all elite cosecheros, consistent with the definition of their elite status, belonged to families that had been resident in Caracas since the seventeenth century. By definition—except in the very unusual case of immigrants who had married into an elite family—all elite hacendados, both signatories and nonsigners, were colony-born creoles. As a rule the parents of both factions had been born in Caracas as well. At the level of grandparents a modest difference emerges: while fully three-fourths (twenty-nine of thirty-eight) of the elite hacendado signatories knew that all four of their grandparents had been native Caraqueños, a somewhat smaller proportion, two-thirds (thirty-six of fifty-eight) of the elite hacendados who did not sign shared this status of having four Caracas-born grandparents. At the level of great-grandparents the signatories' roots continued strong, since many (sixteen of thirty-eight; 42 percent) of the signatories could find in their family trees that all eight of their great-grandparents had been resident in Caracas, while those who made no overt protest did not have quite the same long family tenure in the colony. Less than a quarter (thirteen of fifty-eight; 22 percent) of elite planters who did not sign were descendants of eight native-Caraqueño great-grandparents.

The depth of these family roots, when viewed from the perspective of the mid-eighteenth century, meant that for signatories the most recent ancestor to immigrate had typically come to Caracas at least two, and typically three or more, generations before they were born, which meant that in 1744 the last family member to immigrate to Caracas was only a historical figure, never known to them in person. They and their families were truly part of the permanent elite of the town. For those elites who did not sign, although they were all locally born *criollos*, and although a few of them were members of families such as Bolívar and Tovar that had been in Caracas since the late sixteenth and early seventeenth centuries, it was somewhat more likely that a grandfather or, rarely, even a father had been an immigrant to the colony. And yet, as conscious as these provincial aristocrats might have been of the tenure of their families' residence in Caracas, the difference in *antigüedad* between those who signed the protest memorial in 1744 and those who did not sign was slight, not more than a generation on the average.

A Basque Connection?

A second possible distinction between signatories and nonsignatories is that of an affinity for the Guipuzcoana Company based on the Basque origins of some of them. A number of the elite hacendados who did not oppose the Guipuzcoana Company in 1744 were of Basque parentage. Three examples will suffice: the father of Feliciano Sojo Palacios Gedler had come to Caracas from Burgos in the 1670s and died in the town in 1703. Don Feliciano had served as alcalde ordinario in 1719, in 1735, 1736, and again in 1744; his son, José de Sojo Palacios Lovera, was born in 1705 and was elected alcalde in 1743. Together father and son owned 57,000 cacao trees on four haciendas; neither of them signed the 1744 memorial. Domingo Rodríguez de la Madrid, born in Santander, immigrated to Caracas and married there in 1664. His son, Andrés Rodríguez de la Madrid

Vásquez, married Germana Liendo Gedler, the granddaughter of Basque immigrants, in 1693. In 1744 don Andrés and his sons, Santiago and Salvador Rodríguez de la Madrid y Liendo, owned 18,824 cacao trees on three haciendas. They did not sign the memorial. Finally, the grandfather of Sebastián de Arechederra Tovar, a Vizcayan, had come to Caracas as royal treasurer late in the seventeenth century. Arechederra's father married Luisa Catalina de Tovar y Mijares, a daughter of perhaps the wealthiest Caracas family, in 1682. In 1729 and 1730, with the cabildo locked in a bitter struggle with Governor Lope Carrillo y Andrade, no elections for alcalde were held and in both years Sebastián de Arechederra was named to the position by the king's representative. In June 1730 the replacement for Carrillo y Andrade arrived at La Guaira aboard the first of the Guipuzcoana Company's ships to sail to Venezuela, and as the new governor disembarked he was received by the alcalde Arechederra.[22] In 1744 Sebastián de Arechederra and his sister María were owners of 37,000 cacao trees on three haciendas. They did not sign the 1744 memorial.

In general, then, elite hacienda owners whose families were of slightly more recent residence in Caracas, some of whom were of Basque ancestry, did not protest the policies and activities of the Guipuzcoana Company in the years just prior to the 1749 rebellion. And yet, some individuals with deep criollo roots in the colony and no immediate Basque connection did not come forward in outspoken opposition to the Company. Cacao hacendados from several of the colony's oldest families remained silent in 1744: José Bolívar Aguirre, owner of 20,000 trees on two haciendas; sisters Josefa and Teresa Bolívar Arias, with 17,000 trees on two haciendas; the brothers José Domingo, José Manuel, and Fernando Tovar Galindo, owners of 62,500 trees on six haciendas; their cousin Martín Tovar Galindo, whose large hacienda in the coastal valley of Cuyagua contained 24,000 trees; and the brothers Mauro and Antonio Tovar Mijares, who held 27,000 trees on three haciendas. A criollo presence of many generations and no Basque ancestors describes many of the elite who wanted the crown to rescind the Company monopoly; but the fact that there were more than a few mantuanos who fit these criteria yet did not sign the 1744 memorial suggests that other factors may more adequately explain why some mantuanos protested against the Company while others did not.

Political Activists?

One such factor may be a tradition of political activism possibly more characteristic of the families of those who protested the Company than of the families of those who did not. The political history of Caracas during the half-century prior to the rebellion of 1749 was marked by a series of confrontations over the right of the cabildo's annually elected alcaldes ordinarios to administer the province in the absence of the governor. This privilege applied both to short-term absences, for example when the governor left Caracas to inspect the other towns in the province, and also in the event that the governor died while in office, in which case the alcaldes would occupy the post until a successor arrived from Spain. Originally granted by royal cédula to the Venezuelan town of Coro in 1560 and reaffirmed for Caracas in 1676 and again in 1723, cabildo alcaldes exercised the authority of the governor for more than six months in no fewer than eight years during the period 1700 to 1730, the year in which the first ships and employees of the Guipuzcoana Company reached Caracas.[23] On only one occasion did the cabildo assume the obligations of governor because the holder of the office was physically unable to carry on with his duties: in 1704 it became evident that Governor Nicolás Ponte y Hoyo was mentally unbalanced and the alcaldes replaced him. It was far more common for governors to be removed for political reasons: three of the four governors appointed to the Caracas post after Ponte y Hoyo were charged with malfeasance and forced from office by order of higher royal authority (Cañas y Merino in 1714 by the Audiencia of Santo Domingo; Betancourt y Castro in 1719 by the viceroy of New Granada; and Portales y Meneses in 1723 and again in 1724, also by the viceroy of New Granada).[24]

In most of these instances, the cabildo's alcaldes did not simply take possession of the governor's office, but rather they were obliged to struggle for the gubernatorial authority against aggressive viceroys and other agents of the centralizing Bourbon monarchy who probably regarded the Caracas cabildo's traditional privilege as excessive. Conflict was especially bitter in the 1720s. Supported by the Caracas bishop, and with backing from influential friends at court in Spain, Governor Diego de Portales y Meneses fought openly with the Caracas mantuanos, who were in turn usually sup-

ported in their opposition to the governor by the colony's new vicere‑
gal administrators in Santa Fe de Bogotá.[25] Tensions generated dur‑
ing this bitter political struggle, discussed in detail in chapter 4,
carried into the governorship of don Lope Carrillo y Andrade, who
succeeded Portales in 1728. Under Carrillo, the issue was one of red
damask parasols, which the cathedral clerics used in formal proces‑
sions out-of-doors to protect themselves from the tropical sun. The
governor found the practice to be excessively vain and lacking dig‑
nity, and threatened the churchmen with physical violence when
they refused to give up their umbrellas. The regidores of the cabildo
made common cause with the clerics, and in protest they refused to
attend the New Year's session of the municipal council, with the
result that elections for alcaldes ordinarios were not held for the
years 1729 and 1730. Governor Carrillo was obliged to appoint
alcaldes for these years.[26]

On the surface these fights may be viewed simply as the petty
posturing of provincial aristocrats who were starved for symbols of
status, but the rights to act as governor pro tem and to use red
parasols were in fact issues of deeper meaning. At stake was noth‑
ing less than royal usurpation of customary local authority in the
Caracas polity, authority that in the minds of many Caraqueños
was naturally theirs to exercise. Jealous of privileges embodied in
their town government, the town's political elite showed little pa‑
tience in matters that seemed to threaten the traditional balance of
power in their relationship with the monarch and state. In fact, at
the turn of the century, some elites had even been bold enough to
question whether the Bourbon Philip of Anjou, victor in the War of
Spanish Succession, had sovereignty over the Caracas province.[27]

Local political sensitivities were directly challenged in a more
serious and threatening fashion after 1730 by the activities of two
Basque governors. That the first years of the Guipuzcoana Com‑
pany's residence in the province coincided with a long period of
Basque governorship, the administrations of Martín de Lardizábal
(1732 to 1737) and Gabriel José de Zuloaga (1737 to 1747) caused
many Caraqueños to believe that the governors and the monopo‑
lists were conspiring to deny them their traditional authority for
the economic benefit of the Company. The long-standing belief of
the Caracas elite that the Bourbon state was eager to reclaim local
administrative privileges thus merged with a widespread popular

antagonism toward the Company. As a result, the political tradition of protest against royal encroachment provided a rationale for the participation of many mantuanos in the popular uprising in 1749 when Juan Francisco de León and his followers from Panaquire and other settlements in the Tuy Valley occupied the Caracas plaza. There was little doubt about the collaboration of the Caracas elite in this armed protest; the view of Juan Manuel Goyzueta, the Guipuzcoana Company factor who fled for his safety to La Guaira in 1749, was widely held if difficult to prove:

> Juan Francisco de León is the head of this uprising, but there is no doubt that all the citizens of Caracas have agitated for it, for it is said that this infamy originated on the 25th of August, 1744, first put into motion by a woman, and this is obviously true because since the time of his arrival in this port, no gentleman, neither military nor civil nor cleric, has come down to give support to the Governor, not even for the sake of appearances.[28]

With events out of hand, the cabildo defended itself and placed the blame on the governor, who had fled to La Guaira, abandoning the city and his authority. The cabildo's struggle for interim authority was an old game in 1749; on other occasions the town council had fought with official decrees and jail terms for the right to govern in the absence of the royal representative. But with an armed mob in the plaza and accusations of conspiracy and treason in the air, the old debate took dramatic new meaning. By leaving the cabildo to resolve the problem of the rebellion, the governor in fact forced the town's principal citizens to either give up their support for León's protest, which had now become a rebellion because the king's representative had been forced from his office, or leave themselves open to charges that they were part of the conspiracy.

Castellanos's flight proved to be an effective tactic, and on this occasion, for the first time in the history of the town council, the alcaldes ordinarios were not eager to assume the governor's authority. The cabildo's claim of innocence in 1749 does not specifically mention the nature of the responsibility placed upon it by the governor's departure, but its self-image as long suffering was made perfectly clear:

> [F]or eighteen years this Province has begged Your Majesty to release it from the yoke and tyranny of the Company, and just as we have been loyal while we made such efforts (even though our ap-

peals were not heard), so will we remain loyal as long as we are able to serve Your Majesty; but for the Governor, because the citizens of Panaquire have forced the Company to abandon Caracas, out of fear and because of other things that took place here in Your Dominion, to pass the blame to this city, treating it as a town of traitors and provoking the townspeople in any way possible, is a hardship never before dealt against a loyalty maintained in the face of so much suffering.[29]

As the list of signatures on the protest memorials reveals, the Guipuzcoana Company factor exaggerated when he claimed that "all the citizens of Caracas" had been actively seeking an end to the Company since "the 25th of August, 1744," a date that refers to no event that has yet been identified.[30] But there was a sharply contentious political tradition in Caracas that antedated the creation of the Guipuzcoana Company. Rather than a homogeneous elite, united in opposition to the Company (as the Company stated for its own purposes in 1749 and historians have accepted since), perhaps only the most politically active portion of the Caracas elite, those whose families had participated in the cabildo's struggles to administer the province in the absence of the governor during the first decades of the eighteenth century, made their opposition manifest by signing the 1744 letter. Those of the elite who wrote to the king claiming that the Company was openly abetted in its activities by the Basque governors Lardizábal and Zuloaga might have been following in an activist tradition begun by their fathers in the decades before the establishment of the Guipuzcoana Company. Is it possible that the opposition of certain prominent Caraqueños to the Company in 1744 was still primarily political, the most recent of a series of jurisdictional struggles between local and royal agencies?

Two men were elected by the cabildo regidores on the first day of every year to be alcaldes ordinarios for a one-year term. This means that from 1700 to 1749, the half-century prior to the rebellion, a hundred different men could have been selected for the position; in fact, seventy-one men actually served, many of them on more than one occasion.[31] Of the seventy-one, sixty-six have been identified as men who were born to elite Caracas families or were immigrants who had married into such families. If the relationship of these sixty-six men to the mantuanos who signed and did not sign the 1744 protest memorial is determined, it appears that the signatories did in fact have a stronger history of cabildo participation than those who did not sign, although this is not immediately evident. Of all adult elite men who were alive in 1744, both signers and nonsigners had cabildo experience, and elite men who signed the 1744 document were only slightly more likely to have been alcaldes ordinarios before León's rebellion in 1749 (thirteen of fifty-five signatories; 24 percent) than were elite men who did not sign (nine of forty-eight nonsignatories; 19 percent). However, the somewhat deeper generational roots of the signer group contributed to the fact that they were twice as likely as the nonsigners to have had fathers who had been alcaldes ordinarios. There were seventy-six elite men and women who signed the 1744 memorial, and forty-five of them (59 percent) were the children of men who had served at least one term as alcalde. Of the fifty-eight elite cacao hacienda owners who did not sign, only seventeen (29 percent) were the children of fathers who had been selected for the alcalde position.

Only a few of all those men who became alcaldes ordinarios ever governed the Caracas province in the absence of the governor, and very few of them were still alive in 1744. During the twenty years of the Guipuzcoana Company presence in Caracas prior to the events of 1749, the Basque governors remained healthy and dutifully at their post, and consequently the cabildo alcaldes did not have occasion to act as governor as their predecessors had done with such frequency during the first thirty years of the eighteenth century. Most of those men who, decades earlier, as alcaldes ordinarios had served as governor pro tem (eight men on six occasions), were either protesters themselves in 1744 or the fathers of individuals who signed the 1744 letter. Conversely, although the mantuano cacao hacendados who did not speak against the Company in 1744 were more numerous than those of their class who did sign the memorial that year (fifty-eight in contrast to thirty-eight), they and their fathers were only half as likely to have governed the province in the absence of the royal executive (four men on three occasions).[32]

Comparison of those elites who protested against the Guipuzcoana Company in 1744 and those elites who made no written remonstrance indicates that the protesters were for the most part members of families that had been Caracas residents in both the paternal and maternal lines for three and four generations. The protesters' families had been well represented on the town council during the first half of the eighteenth century and, what is more significant for the protest against the Basque monopoly, members of these families had participated directly in a rough-and-tumble political tradition in which the violent quarrels between cabildo and governor were frequently decided by distant higher authority, both viceroy and king. Mantuanos who did not protest in 1744 had local roots that were somewhat less deep, and their involvement in cabildo politics was both more recent (their fathers had not often served as alcaldes ordinarios) and had not been directed at the royal governors (they rarely served as alcaldes—governors pro tem). Yet the difference between the two elite groups on these social and political points is still less than striking. Were there other differences that might better distinguish them from one another, and in the process provide us with a clearer idea of the impact of the Guipuzcoana Company on the Caracas planter elite?

Debt with the Company?

Within a few weeks of the creation of the 1744 protest memorial, officials of the Guipuzcoana Company prepared a most interesting document of their own. A complete list of all the debts owed it by hacienda owners and merchants, both Caracas vecinos and non-vecinos, showed that the Company had provided a substantial sum in loans and merchandise on credit in the Caracas region, most of it since 1740, and much of it to those same individuals who were most vociferous in their opposition to the Company. By the reckoning of accountant Nicolás de Aizpurua, as of December 1744, at its Caracas *factoría*, the Company was owed 299,444 pesos. About 12 percent of this amount (37,195 pesos) were loans made to unnamed individuals in Spain to be paid in Caracas; the remainder was loaned out in Caracas and registered by name of the debtor in two categories: cosecheros and merchants. Cosecheros had been given cash and goods in credit to the value of 200,618 pesos, and *mercaderes* had received 61,631 pesos.[33]

The individual with by far the largest debt owed to the Basque monopoly was don Juan Javier Pacheco Mijares, the second Conde de San Javier,[34] who was also the principal activist among the elites who opposed the Company. The 1744 protest memorial was signed in his house. In 1740, the year his father the first Conde de San

Javier died, don Juan Pacheco borrowed 20,671 pesos from the Company factor, Nicolás de Francia. The Conde made but one small payment, and the loan had not been paid when its term expired in March 1743. In December 1744, he still owed 19,365 pesos, 6 reales. This sum amounted to 7.4 percent of all the loans made by the Company in Caracas. There were three other debtors with obligations of more than 10,000 pesos, and two of them, Antonio Gregorio Landaeta and Fernando de Aguado Lovera, were also signers of the 1744 protest. Doña Ana Juana de Tovar, Marquesa del Valle de Santiago, who did not sign, owed 11,911 pesos. These four owed a total of 55,806 pesos, 21.3 percent of the total debt, but in all, 154 individuals and 3 convents owed money to the Guipuzcoana Company in 1744. Of these, 56 have been identified as members of Caracas elite families, 28 of whom signed the 1744 memorial, and 28 who did not. The signatories' total debt was 87,141 pesos, more than twice the 42,922 pesos owed by those who did not sign. But in both cases this was mostly new endebtedness, contracted since 1740, and on the average the sums were not particularly large. Excluding the four debts of more than 10,000 pesos (three belonging to signers, one to a nonsigner), the average amount owed by 25 elite signatories was 1730 pesos, while 27 mantuanos who did not sign owed an average of 1149 pesos.

The large debts held by the Conde de San Javier, Antonio Landaeta, and Fernando de Aguado may go far toward explaining their personal interest in reforming or suspending the monopoly's operations, but since the typical amount owed was less than 2000 pesos, and since there was but little difference in the debt of those who protested versus those who did not, it does not seem likely that endebtedness by itself was a strong motive for protest against the Company. Yet it may have been the case that, as cacao prices sharply declined and few ships departed La Guaira loaded for Veracruz—circumstances both related to one another and directly caused by Company policies in the minds of many—there were those who feared that the Company was purposefully seeking to keep them in its debt indefinitely. The 1744 protesters had more reason to be concerned because they were, as a group, more dependent on cacao sales to repay their loans than were other elite Caraqueños, some of whom had sugar as an alternative cash crop.

Sugar Trapiche Ownership?

Sugar was an agricultural commodity that was sold exclusively within the Caracas region, and it was therefore isolated to a degree from the crisis in cacao exports. A census taken in 1752 estimated the annual *renta*, or gross income, of all the sugar trapiches throughout Venezuela.[35] Of the 135 trapiches located in Caracas, the Tuy Valley, Valencia, and the coastal regions, 41 belonged to elite citizens of Caracas. The total renta from these 41 sugar estates amounted to 91,400 pesos, of which 36,100 pesos came from the 17 trapiches that belonged to the protest group; another 55,300 pesos were generated on 24 trapiches that belonged to mantuanos who did not sign the 1744 memorial. The sugar earnings of the protesters represented less than half of the 87,141 pesos that they owed the Company, but the nonprotesters, with a total debt of 42,922 pesos, could have paid their obligation to the Guipuzcoana Company with the income from one year's sugar sales. Thus protesters had no choice but to export or sell cacao in exchange for the cash they borrowed and the merchandise that they bought from the Basque monopolists, who held the exclusive license for the sale of imported goods of all kinds, including food and clothing. In 1744, with the price paid for cacao at only 8 pesos the fanega, this had become an intolerable situation for those Caraqueños whose income came mostly or entirely from cacao.

PROFITS AND PROTEST: THE FORTUNES OF THREE MANTUANO FAMILIES

There is perhaps one more reason why certain Caracas elites were adamant in their opposition to the Guipuzcoana Company, and this may have been the most important. Both the number of cacao trees and the number of haciendas in the Caracas province increased significantly during the sixty-year period from 1684 to 1744 (from 434,850 trees in 1684 to 3,251,700 trees in 1720 and 5,102,221 trees in 1744; and from 167 haciendas in 1684 to 326 haciendas in 1720 and 556 haciendas in 1744).[36] The Guipuzcoana Company claimed credit for the dramatic expansion in cacao planting and production which its directors argued took place after the monopoly began operations in 1728. But these figures make clear that the elite widows who complained in 1741 were right: the Company did no more than take direct advantage of expansion that had begun more than forty years before 1728. This was substantial growth, even if the monopoly was not responsible for it, but was it enough growth to keep pace with the ever-greater number of individuals in Caracas with claims to elite status? On a per capita basis, did mantuanos possess as many cacao trees in 1744 as their parents had owned in 1720 and their grandparents in 1684?

In fact, the Guipuzcoana Company's creation coincided with that point in time when the Caracas cacao boom began to fail to keep pace with the surging increase in numbers of many of the town's foremost families. The Company monopoly grew increasingly more threatening, first as Basque governors worked to further the objectives of the Company at the expense of the traditional cacao trade to New Spain, and then as the price paid for cacao dropped to record low levels. That this all resulted in crisis for some elite families in the 1740s is surely related to the fact that for them, after many decades of adequate expansion, per capita cacao wealth had then begun to decline. This trend cannot be illustrated effectively for the elite in aggregate but must be analyzed on a family-by-family basis. For this purpose three cases have been selected: (1) the Blanco Uribe, a family of many generations' residence with strong grievances against the Guipuzcoana Company; (2) the Bolívar, a family of equal generational depth in Caracas but without strong grievances; and (3) the Palacios, a family of more recent vintage in Caracas with no recorded complaint against the Company. The data presented in the following pages are summarized in table 18.

From Blanco Ochoa to Blanco Uribe

Alejandro Antonio Blanco Uribe was the eldest child of Antonio Blanco Ochoa, regidor and *alférez mayor* of the Caracas cabildo, and Isabel de Uribe y Gaviola. His parents were married in May 1696 and Alejandro was born in June of 1697. His father died in 1736; his mother, a widow before she married Blanco Ochoa, had three children by her first husband and thirteen, including Alejandro, by Blanco Ochoa.[37] The elder Blanco had been one of the region's largest cacao owners in 1720; in the coastal valleys of Aroa,

Table 18 Three Families: Per Capita Cacao Income, Family Sugar Income, and Guipuzcoana Company Debt, 1720–1744

	Blanco		Bolívar		Palacios	
	1720	1744	1720	1744	1720	1744
Number of Family Members	16	36	6	10	7	12
Cacao Trees (per capita)	3,875	2,639	2,167	2,500	857	3,250
Fanegas of Beans (per capita)	41.3	43.8	53.3	76.0	34.2	130.0
Cacao Income* (per capita)	495	394	640	684	411	1,170
Total Annual Sugar Income*	2,000		1,000		11,000	
Total Debt to Guipuzcoana Co.*	3,117		654		7,108	

Source:
See chap. 6, nn. 31 and 33–40.
 *Amounts are given in pesos.

Guaiguaza, Ocumare, and Cata he owned four haciendas with a total of 62,000 cacao trees. He had thirteen living children in 1720, but only the eldest son, Alejandro, then aged twenty-three, was a cacao hacendado in his own right that year: he owned 10,000 trees in the expanding Tuy Valley. In 1744 Alejandro Blanco Uribe would have 18,000 trees at Caucagua on the lower Tuy, 80 percent more trees than he personally had owned twenty-four years earlier. However, in 1744 Alejandro Blanco, at forty-seven years of age, was owner of only one-third the cacao trees that his father had owned at age forty-four in 1720. In fact, all the cacao owned by Alejandro Blanco Uribe and his brothers and sisters in 1744 amounted to 95,000 trees (on eight haciendas). Together these siblings held just 50 percent more trees than their father alone had owned in 1720; on an estimated per capita basis, the cacao tree wealth in 1744 of the Blanco Uribe siblings and their dependents was much less than the wealth in trees that had provided for them when they were their father's dependents in 1720.

A look at this matter in detail reveals that in 1720 the benefits from the income of regidor Antonio Blanco Ochoa's 62,000 cacao trees probably went to fourteen people: the regidor, his wife, and twelve of their thirteen children (not counting eldest son Alejandro, who already had 10,000 trees of his own). Possibly Isabel de Uribe's two daughters by her first marriage, Juana and María Bolívar Uribe, who were unmarried and in their late twenties in 1720, were also dependent on their stepfather's cacao haciendas. If sixteen individuals took their sustenance and their social standing from these four haciendas and 62,000 cacao trees, the average benefit to each one of them would have come from the annual production of 3875 trees. In 1744, the descendants of Antonio Blanco Ochoa and Isabel de Uribe numbered thirty-five individuals, the thirteen Blanco Uribe siblings and the twenty-two children who belonged to the five of them who had married. Leaving aside, for the sake of simplicity, the five spouses of the Blanco Uribe—who may have shared in the benefits from trees owned by their own consanguineous kin, but adding mother and grandmother Isabel de Uribe to the list (the date of her death is unknown), then the best estimate is that in 1744 thirty-six people derived their needs and status from these eight haciendas and 95,000 trees. Thus the average per capita portion of the overall Blanco Uribe family cacao holdings was 2639 trees, down 1236 trees, or about 30 percent fewer trees per capita than a generation earlier.

That the Blanco Uribe kin experienced declining cacao wealth during the first two decades of the Guipuzcoana Company presence in Caracas can be made clearer if cacao prices and the probable yield from their haciendas in fanegas of cacao beans are considered. First, the lower number of trees per capita is misleading, because many of the 1744 trees were located in the high-yield Tuy Valley. Tuy Valley haciendas typically produced 40 fanegas of cacao per 1000 trees, compared to 10 fanegas per 1000 trees on coastal estates.[38] In 1720 the annual yield from regidor Antonio Blanco Ochoa's 62,000 trees would have been 620 fanegas, or about 41.3 fanegas per year for each of the fifteen people who shared in the benefit from his haciendas. Twenty-four years later, the Caucagua hacienda of Alejandro Blanco Uribe contained 18,000 trees, his brother Miguel had a new grove of 1000 trees in Curiepe, and at the high-yield rate of 40 fanegas these two haciendas produced some 760 fanegas of cacao annually. The other 76,000 trees that belonged to Blanco Uribe siblings were on six coastal haciendas, the same haciendas in most cases that had belonged to their father, and these trees, at the ratio of 10 fanegas per 1000 trees, produced an equal amount, 760 fanegas of cacao, every year. The per capita share of the thirty-six people who benefited from this quantity of cacao, 1580 fanegas, was about 43.8 fanegas, slightly more in fact than the 1720 per capita figure. Without Alejandro Blanco's Caucagua hacienda, however, the cacao wealth of the Blanco Uribe kin and their children would have fallen far behind that of the previous generation; a widower without children, Alejandro was only one of thirty-six individuals in 1744, but the other thirty-five, without his 720 fanegas of annual production, would have each received the benefit from only 22.8 fanegas of cacao annually, about 48 percent less than the Blanco Uribe siblings had received as children in 1720.

Even with the Caucagua hacienda, the declining price paid for cacao left the Blanco Uribe siblings poorer as adults with children than their parents had been a generation earlier. The 1720 price paid in Caracas for cacao was about 12 pesos per fanega, a sum that had risen from a low of about 7 pesos in 1710 and would continue to fluctuate upward until 1735, when it would reach a high of 18 pesos. In 1744 the cacao price stood at 9 pesos, having fallen steadily from the 1735 peak. At the 1720 price of 12 pesos per fanega the per capita gross income of regidor Blanco Ochoa, his wife, and their children was about 495 pesos (12 pesos times 41.3 fanegas); at the 1744 price of 9 pesos, the Blanco Uribe siblings and their children would have received a per capita gross income of about 394 pesos (9 pesos times 43.8 fanegas), a decrease of about 20 percent over the course of the lifetimes of the Blanco Uribe siblings. Without the Caucagua hacienda earnings, the per capita income of this family would have stood at only about 205 persos, a decline of about 59 percent during the previous quarter century. For the Blanco Uribes new cacao planting in the fertile Tuy region had not been enough to keep pace with both a flourishing family and declining prices. The individual wealth of Alejandro Blanco Uribe improved by 70 percent from 1720 to 1744, but the modest expansion of the coastal haciendas inherited by his siblings from their father did not keep up with falling cacao prices. As eldest son and brother, holder of the hacienda that earned about 50 percent of his extended family's declining income in 1744, and as a bachelor with no immediate family to make him cautious, Alejandro Blanco Uribe became a leader in the cause against the Guipuzcoana Company.

From Bolívar Martínez to Bolívar Aguirre

It is curious, in light of the enormous fame that history would bestow on Simón Bolívar, to discover that the Bolívars were never significant owners of cacao haciendas. This fact may help explain why José Bolívar Aguirre, the uncle of the Liberator, was ready to take an active part in opposition to the rebellion that many other prominent citizens supported, at least surreptitiously. José Bolívar owned 8000 trees in the lower Tuy Valley district of Taguasa in 1720, and 12,000 trees in the same place in 1744. By that year he had also begun to harvest cacao for the benefit of two of his daughters, young women who would marry in 1747 and 1749, from a new hacienda of 5000 trees also located on the banks of the lower Tuy. In addition, he was owner of 8000 trees on the Costa Abajo, in the Cepi Valley. The Cepi hacienda may have come to him as his inheritance from his father, Juan Bolívar Martínez, who had 5000 trees there in 1720 and who died in 1729.[39]

José Bolívar Aguirre was the first of the Bolívars to own cacao in the Tuy; the small haciendas of his father and grandfather were all located on the coast. His father's 5000-tree Cepi estate was modest, but in 1720 this hacienda had provided income for only five people: the elder Bolívar, his second wife, María Petronila Ponte Marín, and their three young daughters (they would have two more children, including Simón Bolívar's father, Juan, who was born in 1727). On a per capita basis, the 5000 trees belonging to Juan Bolívar Martínez provided the benefit from 1000 trees to him, his wife, and to each one of their three children. However, the measure of the total cacao tree wealth of this family in 1720 should include the 8000 trees at Taguasa of José Bolívar Aguirre, who was twenty years older than his half-siblings and holder of his own cacao groves in that year. With these additional trees the estimate of the number of trees per capita for José Bolívar, his father and stepmother, and his three stepsisters comes to 2,167 (13,000 trees divided by six people). Twenty-four years later, José Bolívar had married and he and his wife María Arias were the parents of eight children. This was a young family in 1744; none of the Bolívar Arias offspring was yet married and none of them owned a cacao hacienda. Therefore, the 25,000 trees that belonged to José Bolívar Aguirre in 1744 represent per capita cacao wealth of 2,500 trees for each of the ten members of his immediate family. Don José may not have noticed the modest increase in his family's cacao wealth that had taken place during the generation after 1720, but it was no doubt evident in 1744 that size of Bolívar's family had not yet begun to surpass the productive capacity of his haciendas.

In fact, José Bolívar Aguirre had reason to be satisfied in 1744 with the progress that his family had made in its cacao enterprise since 1720. The 5000 trees of his father were all located on a low-yield (10 fanegas per 1000 trees) coastal estate, returning probably a total of 50 fanegas of cacao annually. At 12 pesos per fanega, the total annual gross income from his father's hacienda could be estimated at a modest 600 pesos in that year. Adding José Bolívar's 8000 trees, which presumably produced at the high-yield Tuy Valley ratio of 40 fanegas per 1000 trees, the total family cacao harvest in 1720 was likely to have been about 320 fanegas of beans, worth 3840 pesos. In per capita terms (divided by six), this would have amounted to 640 pesos of gross income for each member of the family in 1720. In 1744, although cacao prices had fallen to 9 pesos, José Bolívar's holdings included 17,000 trees in the Tuy and 8000 on the coast, which would have given an estimated total yield of 760 fanegas, worth 6840 pesos. In per capita terms (divided by ten), this was about 684 pesos for the ten members of Bolívar's immediate family. With almost twice the number of dependents as his father, his cacao earnings had nearly doubled since he had married, and he was providing for his family better than he and his father together had done twenty-four years earlier when prices were 25 percent higher.

It is also curious to discover that the uncle of Venezuela's foremost patriot was, of all the old-family Caracas elites, one of the most visible supporters of the royal effort to suppress the colonial opposition to the Guipuzcoana Company. José Bolívar Aguirre was named *sargento mayor* of the Caracas militia in 1722, and in 1751 he was named principal accountant, *contador mayor*, of the royal treasury. The latter appointment was made by Governor Felipe Ricardos, who was then about to begin his offensive against Juan Francisco de León and the other rebels of 1749. Ricardos was eager to enlist the help of the militia in his search for León, and Bolívar was willing. He led the militia on an extensive march through the Aragua and Tuy Valleys during the last months of 1751 but failed to find León. For his collaboration he was rewarded by Ricardos with the contador position and a recommendation for knighthood in one of the three military orders, Santiago, Alcántara, or Calatrava.[40] This favor did not result in membership in one of the honored orders for José Bolívar, perhaps because he died, at age sixty-five, in 1758. His sons would also become militia officers, and his eldest son, Juan Bolívar y Arias (b. 1723, d. 1789) held his father's post of contador on an interim basis in the 1760s but was denied permanent, formal possession of it for interesting reasons.

The governor and captain-general in Caracas from 1763 to 1771 was don José Solano y Bote, a naval officer, the fourth active military officer to govern the province since the rebellion of Juan Francisco de León in 1749. Juan Bolívar petitioned the crown for the position of contador mayor, and in a letter to the Council of the Indies in 1768 Solano noted that "Bolívar [the father] . . . acted with much disinterestedness [in the conflict with the Guipuzcoana Company], and he [the son] is without doubt efficient and of sufficient ability to fulfill the obligations of the position. . . ." Solano, however, preferred to advance the career of one of his own retinue, a peninsular Spaniard named Joseph de la Guardia. The previous service and tenure of the Bolívar family in this royal post made the situation difficult for Solano, who recommended that there be "two *contadores mayores*," which would make it possible to "accommodate Bolívar for the good work he has done," but at the same time he would not be the exclusive occupant of a royal office that, it had been determined, "was not convenient for Viscayans, Isleños or Criollos to hold."[41]

From Palacios Gedler to Palacios Lovera

Whereas the Blanco and the Bolívar were among Caracas's oldest families, the first of the Palacios came to the town in the middle of the seventeenth century, some decades after cacao agriculture had become the region's primary economic activity. Don Bernabé de Palacios y Sojo, royal treasurer in Caracas from 1653 to 1675, native of the Basque province of Alava, came to the Indies accompanied by his niece, doña Juana Teresa Palacios. Doña Juana married, in 1678, her cousin don José Palacios, who had come in turn to Caracas from Alava to inherit the estate of their uncle, don Bernabé. Doña Juana died in childbirth in 1684, and in that year José Palacios owned 5000 cacao trees in the coastal valley of Chuspa.[42]

In 1686 widower José Palacios married widow Isabel María Gedler, and in 1689 Feliciano de Palacios y Gedler was born. He was to be their only child. In 1720 Feliciano Palacios lived with his wife, Juana Josefa de Lovera y Bolívar, whom he had married in

1707, and their four children. Their eldest child, José, was then twelve. Don Feliciano's only living half-sibling, Ana Juana de Palacios y Palacios, was a nun in the Concepción convent. Counting the *monja* Ana Juana, in 1720 these seven people received the benefit from 6000 cacao trees (857 trees each) belonging to don Feliciano in the burgeoning Tuy tributary valley of Caucagua. In 1725 Juana de Lovera died, and in July of 1727 Feliciano Palacios married Isabel Gil de Aguirre. By 1744 don Feliciano and doña Isabel were the parents of ten living children.

Feliciano Palacios was owner of 39,000 trees on three cacao estates in 1744. In that year the only surviving offspring of Feliciano Palacios's first marriage was José Palacios Lovera, who had married a cousin of his deceased mother's family (Lovera) in June of 1727, a month before his father remarried. José Palacios had children and a substantial cacao hacienda of his own in 1744. Not counting his son José, in that year don Feliciano probably provided for himself and eleven other people with the cacao from his 39,000 trees. This was a per capita holding of 3250 trees, 279 percent more trees per capita than had been available to the members of Palacios's "first" family in 1720. Unlike many other Caracas mantuanos, Feliciano Palacios did very well in the cacao business during the 1730s and 1740s. Even with cacao prices at 9 pesos the fanega, with holdings of 39,000 trees in 1744 the gross per capita income of his three haciendas (all located in the high-yield Tuy Valley) was 1170 pesos annually for twelve people. This was more than twice the per capita income from 6000 trees for seven people in 1720 (411 pesos), even though prices then had been 12 pesos the fanega of cacao. Feliciano's son José, with six children and his wife, would have received a gross per capita income of about 810 pesos from his Caucagua hacienda of 18,000 trees in 1744. This was more than twice the gross per capita income gotten from his father's hacienda in 1720 when José Palacios was a youngster. It was also more than twice the gross per capita income estimated for the Blanco Uribe siblings and their children in 1744.

Company Debts and Sugar Income

The period 1720 to 1744 marks a significant phase of generational change in each of the three families: individuals who were children or young adults in 1720 had married and were parents of children of their own by 1744. In each case there is a discernible and different pattern of gross per capita income from cacao agriculture, estimated on the basis of the number of people in each family at each date, the number of trees owned by family members, and the current price of cacao in 1720 and 1744. The Blanco Uribe experienced declining per capita cacao income, the Bolívar Aguirre remained relatively steady, and the Palacios benefited from their increased holdings. For the Blanco Uribe the worsening situation was made more difficult because the numerous family was largely dependent on cacao. In 1752 Alejandro Blanco Uribe earned 1000 pesos annual renta from a sugar trapiche in the Caracas region; a second mill, also valued at 1000 pesos, belonging to *"los Blanco Uribe"* was located in the Tuy. José Bolívar Aguirre, his large family matched by a proportionate increase in cacao property from 1720 to 1744, had a 1000-pesos-renta trapiche in the Aragua Valley.[43] Neither of these sugar properties produced significant income, but the Palacios, who had prospered in cacao during the 1720s and 1730s, were also protected from the vagaries of cacao exports and prices by their several trapiches, which produced sugar exclusively for the local Caracas market. They owned three profitable mills in the hinterland of the town: Feliciano Palacios with one of 5000 pesos annual renta; his son José Palacios Lovera, whose trapiche produced 4000 pesos annually; and his eldest son by his second marriage, Feliciano Palacios Gil, with a mill of 2000 pesos renta.

Together with more than 20,000 pesos of gross cacao income, these 11,000 pesos of sugar income brought the per capita income, at midcentury, of Feliciano Palacios and his children and grandchildren to about 1500 pesos per year. By comparison, the 2000 pesos renta received from the two trapiches that belonged to the Blanco Uribe did not go far toward raising the per capita income of the thirty-six individuals who would have stood to take some benefit from them. The combined cacao and sugar per capita income for the Blanco Uribe siblings and their children can be estimated at about 450 pesos. For the Bolívar Aguirre kin the additional income from sugar was similarly slight; 1000 pesos per annum from the Aragua sugar trapiche, divided among eleven immediate kin, would have brought the per capita gross income up from the cacao estimate of 622 pesos to about 710 pesos.

Counting all individuals, adults and children alike, in families at comparable stages in the generational cycle, the 1500 pesos per capita gross annual income of the Palacios and the 450 pesos income of the Blanco Uribe kin would probably have placed them at the upper and lower ends, respectively, of the elite income spectrum in midcentury Caracas. More important for the protest written against the Guipuzcoana Company in 1744 and the much more serious uprising that took place beginning in 1749, is the observation that such income was, in the Palacios case, significantly more than had been gotten in 1720, and, in the Blanco Uribe case, much less. This difference was critical because wealth and social status of the kin group depended on the expansion of their cacao estates, which required acquisition of both land and slaves at a rate at least equal to the generational increase in number of family members. The evidence is that by the 1740s their large families had taken some of the well-established Caracas elite beyond a critical conjuncture, at which they were no longer able to plant enough cacao to keep their per capita income at levels attained a generation earlier.

The evidence also suggests that at midcentury families in straitened circumstances such as the Blanco Uribe had acquired debts that were substantial when considered in light of their declining income and dependency on cacao. In isolation, information about an individual's indebtedness, such as one finds in a last will and testament, cannot be taken as a measure of the economic health of that individual's estate. If income is also known, however, the proportion of debt to income does offer a means to take the pulse of productive property.

One mantuano whose family was definitely not in economic difficulty was Feliciano Palacios, and he had more debt with the Guipuzcoana Company than most other Caracas residents. In 1740 he received several slaves from the Company factor on credit, and in 1744 his obligation to the monopoly was 6218 pesos. His son José had also borrowed, and together they owed 7108 pesos. Four of the Blanco Uribe siblings, all of whom signed the 1744 protest, had gotten credit against future payment in cacao beans from the Company: Alejandro Antonio owed 468 pesos in 1744, Miguel owed 501, Cornelio Blanco was the major debtor of the family with an obligation of 2124 pesos, and María Josefa owed 24 pesos for merchandise she had received. The total Blanco Uribe debt to the

Guipuzcoana Company was 3117 pesos. Of the members of the third kin group considered, only José Bolívar had contracted a debt with the Company, and he owed a modest sum, 654 pesos.

What is most significant about this indebtedness is that although the Palacios owed almost one-quarter of their estimated gross annual income (7108 of 31,000 pesos), the Blanco Uribe owed about one-fifth of their collective annual income (3117 of 16,200 pesos), and the Bolívar Aguirre owed less than one-tenth of theirs (654 of 7810 pesos), both the Palacios and the Bolívar Aguirre could have easily paid their Guipuzcoana loans with one year's sugar income (Palacios: 11,000 pesos of sugar income and 7108 pesos of debt; Bolívar Aguirre: 1000 pesos of sugar income and 654 pesos of debt), while the Blanco Uribe (2000 pesos of sugar income and 3117 pesos of debt) could not. Unless they could ship in the tercio buque to New Spain, the Blanco Uribe were, in the last analysis, directly dependent on the declining price paid by the Company for their cacao beans, both to pay for standing obligations and to finance expansion of cacao haciendas that were already unable to match the cacao earnings of the previous generation. Perhaps understandably then, while the Palacios and the Bolívar Aguirre remained quiet, the Blanco Uribe and dozens of Caracas mantuanos in similar circumstances, their present well-being and several generations of elite social status at risk, first made formal and legal protest to the king. When that brought no relief, they offered their clandestine support to men of lesser status with even more at stake who were willing to risk their lives in order to rid the colony of the Guipuzcoana monopoly.

7

First Families

The rebellion of 1749 ended in pain and punishment for those identified as having taken up arms against the royal order; a few were executed in the uprising's aftermath, and many were imprisoned or exiled from the colony. No member of the elite would be found guilty of treason, however, and the most severely punished spent only two years in a Madrid jail. This was because even those elites who were most desperate for a change in the Guipuzcoana Company's policies quickly abandoned their overt support for the movement when it suddenly shifted from protest to rebellion. Judging from the ease with which a royal army brigade restored the rebellious colony to order, it was probably apparent to many that an armed confrontation with the king's forces was at best foolhardy. In the first place mantuanos had more to lose, in that they had several generations of accumulated wealth and social prestige to protect and preserve. They also had other means with which to fight the Company. After more than a century of often bitter dealings between the cabildo and the administrators of empire, elites' knowledge of law and their experience at using it gave them confidence that their quarrel with the Basque monopoly could be resolved without resort to violence. Perhaps they put some trust in the belief that royal justice would eventually recognize the legitimacy of their complaints. Finally, as this chapter illustrates, in several other ways many of the elite families were closely bound to one another, and in their cohesiveness the gentry cacao planters may have found the strength for political, nonviolent resistance that was not available to those who chose instead to take up arms against the king's Company.

RESIDENCE AND MARRIAGE PATTERNS OF THE CARACAS ELITE

From one perspective, the following inquiry is a kind of interlude that examines the nature of the Caracas elite in the eighteenth century. It departs from the political and economic analysis that has been central up to this point to consider questions of residence, marriage, and demography. And it necessarily transcends the temporal focus of the rest of this study to include most of the eighteenth century. Although limited to the elites, the analysis of demographic data is in certain ways more detailed than any done to date for Latin America, and in its own right it will be of interest to population and family historians.

At the same time, however, the central interest in this data is in the light that they can shed on the internal processes that distinguished early Caracas, and the effort is made at every point to relate the changing web of elite kindred to the changes in the larger colonial society and economy. We begin with a discussion of elite residence using as a source a household census taken in 1759, a decade after León's rebellion.

PATTERNS OF ELITE RESIDENCE IN 1759

This census, probably the first in the history of the town, is the earliest complete count that exists. Not a direct result of the uprising ten years earlier, the house-to-house canvas nevertheless followed logically the desire of the military governor, Brigadier General Felipe Ricardos, and the reforming ministers in Spain, to more efficiently control the Caracas population. The total population of the four parishes of Caracas in 1759 was 21,683 individuals who lived in 2628 households.[1] Of interest here is just the elite portion of the whole, 2059 people, 574 hispanic whites, and the other residents in their households—1485 black slaves or free servants. Taken together these people comprised about 9 percent of the total population. They lived in 85 households, about 3 percent of all households, of which 73 were located in the Cathedral parish and the remaining 12 in Altagracia, the contiguous parish to the north of Cathedral. The definition of *elite* used here is the one outlined in the introduction to this book, namely, those individuals whose paternal and maternal ancestors in most cases had been in Caracas since the middle of the seventeenth century, whose male relatives and ancestors had served as regidores or alcaldes ordinarios on the town cabildo, and whose family members appear on the lists of cacao haciendas taken in 1684, 1720, and 1744.[2] These *mantuanos*, as they were called by their contemporaries, will be viewed from two perspectives. The first is frozen in time and strictly empirical in that the characteristics of elite residence taken from the 1759 census are studied. The second is dynamic and more conjectural as it seeks to link the patterns of mantuano marriage to the economic history of Caracas during the course of the eighteenth century.

At first glance, except for the large number of either slave or free domestic laborers, 17.5 per household on the average, many of the residences that were home to the Caracas elite in 1759 seem quite modern in their composition. More than half, forty-seven of the eighty-five, were headed by married couples, and of the forty-seven, all but two were single-family households, comprised of 2 parents, 3.7 children on the average, and an occasional cousin, uncle, or niece. This high proportion of nuclear-family mantuano households (plus slaves and servants) may seem surprising, given the traditional assumptions about extended families in colonial Latin America. However, recent research has begun to show that elite households were not always complex, multifamily and multigenerational in composition.[3] That many elites lived in simple, single-family households at midcentury is not without significance, yet it would be erroneous to suppose that these households functioned essentially as independent units. Of course the census tells us nothing about day-to-day relationships within these homes, and the nature of domestic life, child-rearing practices for example, remains virtually unknown. But at a minimum we can sure that in spatial terms the mantuano society of urban Caracas was a small, highly concentrated world in 1759, where people, especially kin, associated with one another both frequently and intimately.

The town as a whole was a physically small community, reaching at its longest extension (north to south) about fourteen blocks, or *cuadras*, and about twelve or thirteen cuadras from east to west. No member of the elite lived in a house that was more than six blocks from the *plaza mayor* and the cathedral (see map 4). More importantly, in the typical case only two blocks separated the dwelling of one elite head of household from the residences of all the rest of his or her siblings.[4] With most of the kindred so close at hand, individual households may have lacked autonomy, and the numerous single-family, few-children households may have functioned essentially as so many knots in the several nets of clan residence. In this restricted environment neither the physical distance between houses of kin nor the precise location of residence probably mattered for very much. A sample of six sets of kin households in 1759 shows a pattern of elite residences concentrated generally north of the plaza, which may, more than any other factor, reflect an advantage of the terrain. Since Caracas was built on a hillside that slopes notably downward from north to south, water flowing in the tile-lined canals, or *acequias*, would have reached the northernmost houses first, while houses downhill to the south would have run the risk of receiving the discharge water from those above them (see map 5 and appendix I). But by and large, the fact that the Herrera households were to be found on the blocks east of the cathedral or the Pacheco Mijares and Tovar households were clustered north and west of the plaza mayor probably did not make these families different in any significant way from other elite families, such as the Blanco, whose several households were scattered about the Cathedral parish.[5] The best measure of the limited spatial context of elite residence in the town may well be the case of Juan Antonio Mijares, the illegitimate son of Francisco Felipe Mijares Tovar and the half-brother of Francisco Nicolás Mijares, the third Marqués de Mijares. This man married his cousin, the fully legitimate doña Melchora Tovar Mijares, in 1756, the year after her father died, and the location of their residence in 1759, on the fringe of the parish seven blocks from the nearest house belonging to kin of either of them, was more isolated in this sense than any other elite dwelling in Caracas.[6] Perhaps outcasts for his birth and their marriage, in terms of time and space this couple lived at the outer physical margin of mantuano society, but they were just minutes from the plaza and the homes of their siblings and other relatives.

PATTERNS OF ELITE MARRIAGE

As close as the Caracas elite lived to one another in physical space, many were even more closely knit by kinship and marriage. Of the forty-seven elite households headed by both living husband and wife in 1759, in eighteen households the spouses were consanguineous kin. In twelve of these eighteen cases the spouses were first cousins. More than one-fourth (twelve of forty-seven) of all

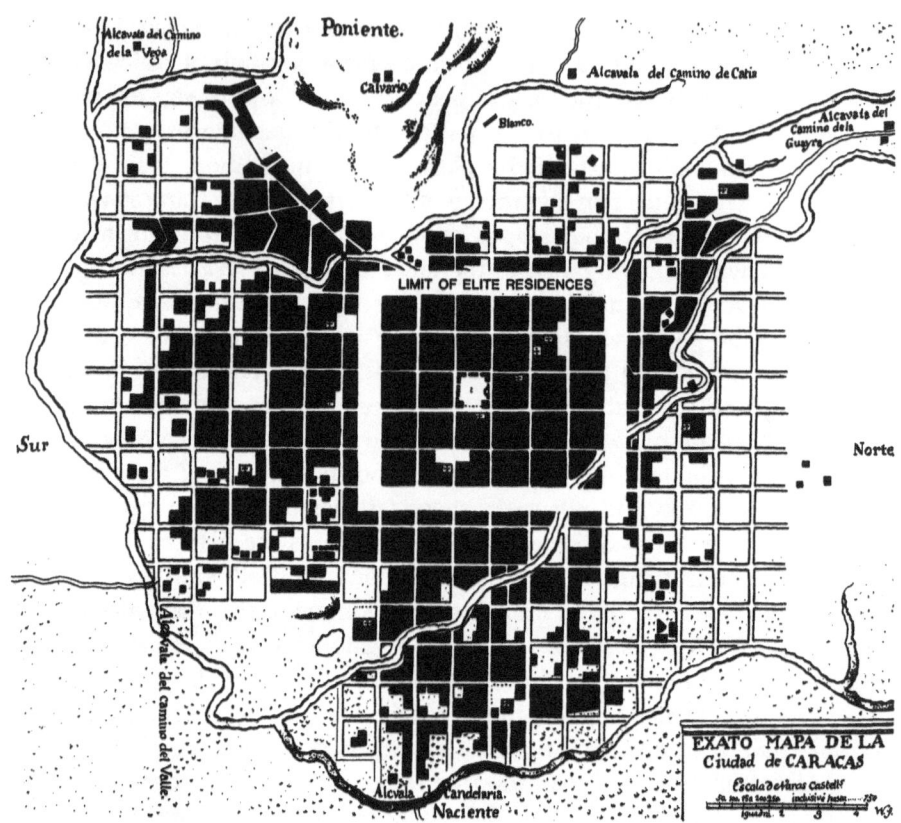

Map 4 *Exacto Mapa de la Cuedad de Caracas* (1772). AGI, Caracas, leg. 81.

elite couples who were heads of household in 1759 were first cousins. What does it mean that such endogamous unions were so common in eighteenth-century Caracas? More basically, why was first-cousin marriage so common among Caracas elites? To examine these and other patterns of elite marriage over the long run of the eighteenth century a data set was compiled of 262 elite individuals, 128 men and 134 women, for whom age at first marriage can be determined. They are all of those elites who married in the eighteenth century for whom date of birth and date of marriage are known. While they represent less than 5 percent of the total 5778 people who were married in the Cathedral parish from 1700 to 1799, they are almost 40 percent of the 656 men and women who belonged to the families identified as elite who married in the parish during that century.[7]

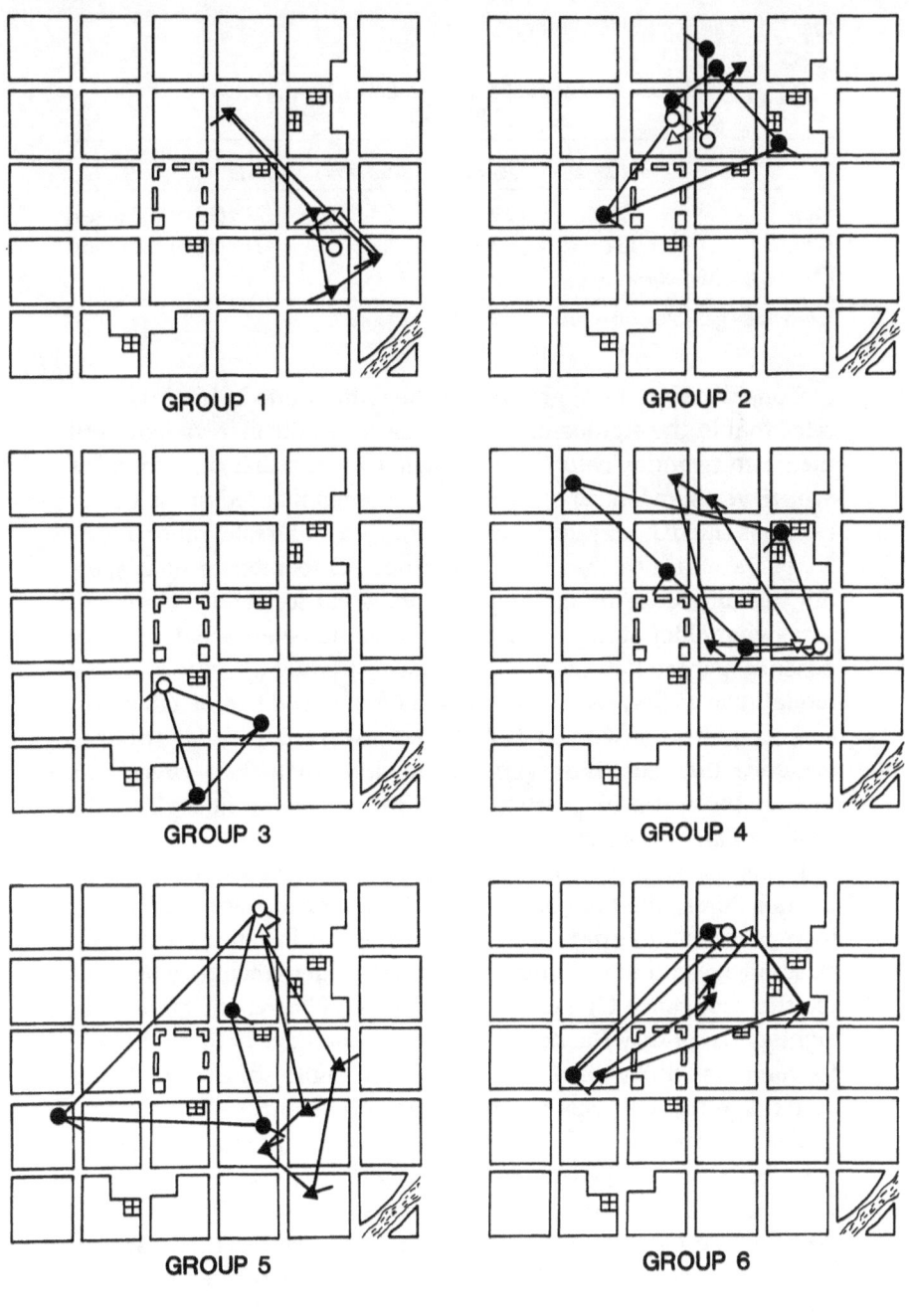

Map 5 Spatial Distribution of the Households of Six Sets of Elite Kin, 1759. See Appendix I.

Table 19 Age at First Marriage, Elite Men and Women, 1700–1799

	No. Cases	Mean	Median	Mode
Men	128	29.0	28.4	23 (10 of 128 cases)
Women	134	23.9	22.3	22 (14 of 134 cases)
Difference (in years)		5.1	6.1	1

Source: See genealogical sources in chap 7., nn. 4 and 7.

Considered in the aggregate for the entire period, this data indicates that in the eighteenth century Caracas elite men waited until their late twenties before they married for the first time (median age: 28 years; mean: 29.0), while elite women married in their early twenties (median age: 22 years; mean: 23.9). The interval of five or six years indicates that these were not companionate marriages, but the difference in age may be somewhat less and the women somewhat older at first marriage than would be expected in a supposedly patriarchal society. The most frequently occurring, or modal, age at first marriage, 23 years for men (in 10 of 128 cases) and 22 years for women (14 of 134 cases) offers even stronger evidence that husbands very much older than their wives was neither the norm in practice nor a desired value in eighteenth-century Caracas (see table 19).

In comparison with their contemporaries and social equals in Buenos Aires, the only other Spanish American colony for which there is comparable data, Caracas elite men and women were much closer in age and the women several years older when they married for the first time. Of 142 first marriages of merchant families in eighteenth-century Buenos Aires, the median age at first marriage for men was thirty years and for women eighteen, and while the modal age for men was twenty-seven, it was fifteen for women.[8]

The median age at first marriage in Caracas increased modestly over the course of the century, very slightly for women and somewhat more significantly for men, especially toward the end of the century (see fig. 13). Elite men typically married in their early to middle twenties in the early decades, in their late twenties and early thirties by the 1770s and thereafter. Women married for the first time at about age twenty or twenty-one early in the century and at about age twenty-two or twenty-three from the 1740s on. The major impor-

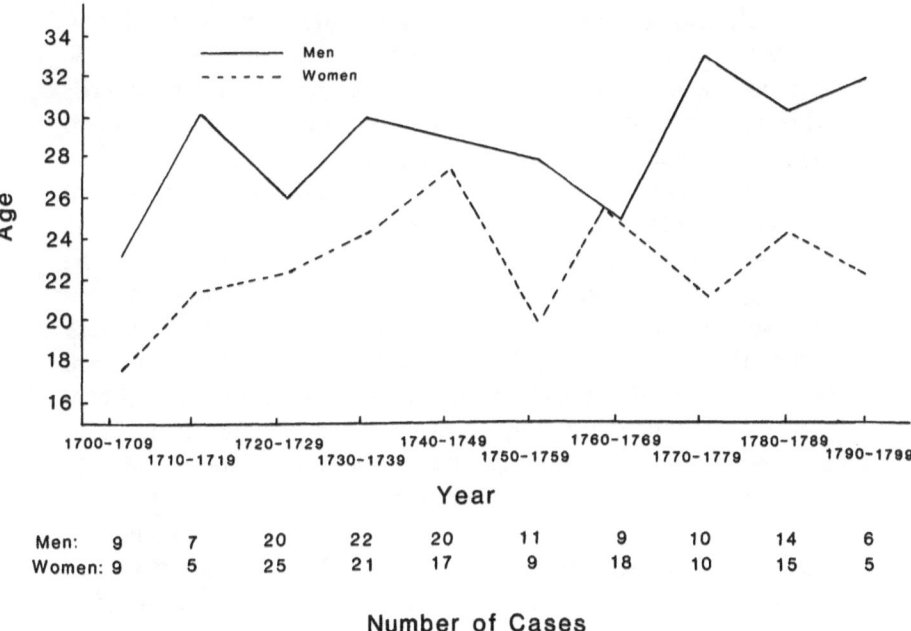

Fig. 13   Median Age at First Marriage, Elite Men and Women, 1700–1799

tance of this moderate trend only becomes clear when it is combined with a second trend derived from the known information about date of death for the Caracas elite. The death date is known for many of the parents of the 262 individuals in the data set, and a factor of some significance becomes apparent if, in the cases where it is possible to do so, the death date of the parents is compared with the marriage date of their children. By studying the relationship between paternal death and the timing of marriage a most interesting pattern emerges: as elites married at an older age during the course of the eighteenth century, it was increasingly likely, particularly in the case of men, that they would marry after the death of their parents, especially their fathers. This pattern, which coincides with slowing of the cacao economy, the problems presented by the Guipuzcoana Company, and the hiatus in the slave trade after 1739, may reflect the decision of many mantuanos to marry only after they had received their inheritance portion.

With few exceptions, the death date of parents is unknown for individuals whose first marriages took place before 1720, and, strangely enough, for those who married after 1789 as well. Limiting the temporal focus to the seventy years from 1720 to 1789 reduces the size of the data base from 262 to 221 elite individuals whose age at first marriage is known. For this subset of 221 cases (33 percent of all elites who married in Cathedral parish from 1700 to 1799), the death date can be established for more than 75 percent of their parents (342 of 442 possible cases). The interval in years between the year of the death of the parent and the year of the marriage of the child can then be calculated, a positive interval representing the years that had passed after the death of a parent before the year of the child's first marriage, a negative interval being the years after the child's marriage before the parent's death.

The arithmetic mean of these intervals can then be calculated for the seventy-year period 1720–1789 on the basis of the sex of both parent and child. The interval between the marriage date of daughters and the death date of their mothers indicates that mothers typically survived the marriage of their daughters by several years (−2.32 years; 76 cases). Fathers of daughters lived to the wedding date, but died shortly thereafter (−.36 years; 102 cases). In the average case mothers of sons died a few years before their son's first marriage (2.12 years; 77 cases), while the fathers of elite sons were least likely to be alive when their sons married, having died about four years on the average before the event (3.88 years; 87 cases). When plotted by decade, the intervals between the parent's death and the child's marriage indicate that a dramatic transition may have taken place in the decade of the 1730s (see fig. 14). Before this time elite sons and daughters went to the altar usually accompanied by their father and mother; afterwards, especially in the case of sons, they went without their parents, who had died earlier.[9]

It is possible that Caraqueño elites married with increasing frequency after the death of their parents not so much because they were themselves older when they married later in the century, but rather because their parents died somewhat younger. There is no evidence, however, to suggest that longevity declined over the course of the eighteenth century. The available data, 145 cases of men and 151 cases of women from elite families for whom age at death can be calculated, is not entirely satisfactory for the purpose of determining a trend because only 20 percent of the cases are for deaths that occurred prior to 1750.[10] Nevertheless, with the excep-

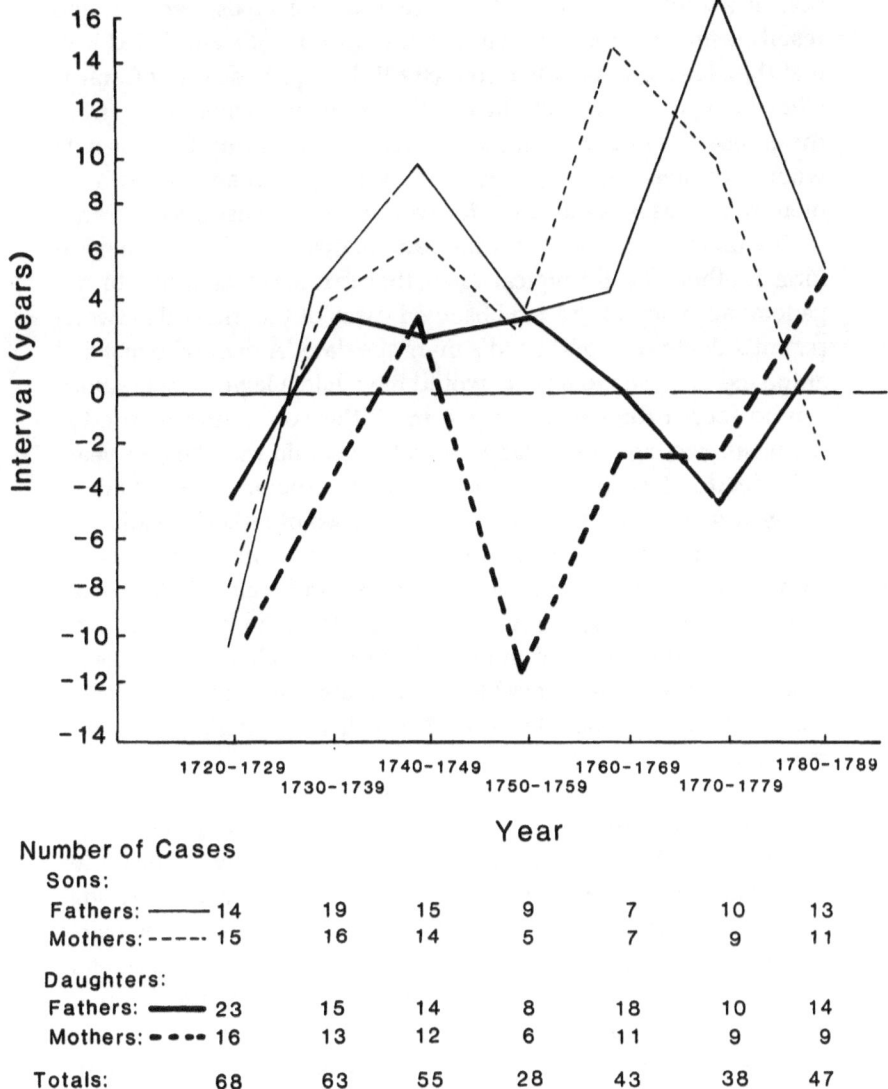

Fig. 14 Interval Between Death Date of Parents and Date of First Marriage of Their Children, 1720–1789

tion of a slight decline for the decade of the 1760s, certainly the result of the smallpox epidemic that began in 1761 and killed several thousand inhabitants of the city,[11] the age at death of Caracas elites remained constant during the century. Generalizing from these cases, it would seem that in eighteenth-century Caracas elite women outlived men by only a few years (mean age at death for men in 145 cases: 53.2 years; for women in 151 cases: 55.1 years).

The mean ages at first marriage and at death can be combined to form mathematically typical cases that can serve as a test of the general accuracy of the 342 observed cases of the interval between parent's death date and child's marriage date. A man who married at the mean age of 29.0 years would have had a legitimate firstborn son no sooner than at age 29.7 years. If this son in turn married at the mean age, 29.0 years later, his father would then be 58.7 years old—dead in fact for 5.5 years, if he died at the mean death age of 53.2 years. The interval of 87 observed cases of father's death date and son's marriage date for the period 1720–1789 is 3.88 years. Although the difference between these intervals is slight, we should expect the typical mathematical interval to be smaller than the mean of the observed intervals, because while the test interval is based on the earliest possible case of a firstborn son, the mean of observed intervals includes second and all subsequent sons as well as firstborn.

In the case of fathers and daughters, the marriage of a firstborn daughter at the mean age of 23.9 years would occur when her father was 53.6 years old, 0.4 years after the mean age of death for men. The mean interval of 102 observed cases, −.36 years, suggests that fathers typically died within several months following their daughters' marriage date. These two intervals are also similar, but, again, since the test interval is calculated for the firstborn daughter we should expect it to be somewhat smaller, not larger, than the mean of the observed intervals, which consider all daughters, not just the firstborn. This discrepancy could mean that the mean age at death for men should be somewhat higher than 53.2 years, or that the fathers in the observed cases lived somewhat longer than the average, but in any event the fact is clear that there was but a small likelihood that an elite father in eighteenth-century Caracas would survive to attend even his firstborn son's wedding, and that the chance was about equal that he would be alive for even his firstborn daughter's *matrimonio*.

To consider mothers, a woman who married at the mean age of 23.9 years would have a legitimate firstborn daughter no sooner than age 24.6 years. If this daughter in turn married at the mean age, 23.9 years later, her mother would then be 48.5 years old, not to die for another 6.5 years if she were to die at the mean death age for women of 55.1 years. The average interval for seventy-six observed cases of mother's death and daughter's marriage is −2.3, a difference from the test interval of 4 years, but in this case the discrepancy is as it should be, since a mother who outlived her firstborn daughter's wedding by 6.5 years might well live beyond the marriage date of all of her daughters by an average 2.3 years.

In the instance of the final possibility, that of mothers and sons, a woman who married at the mean age for first marriage and whose firstborn child was a son would be 52.9 years old in the year of his wedding if the son married at the mean age of 29.0 years. If the woman survived to the mean age of female death she would live 2.2 years beyond the date of her son's wedding, a period similar to the average observed interval in 77 cases of mothers and sons, 2.1 years. The difference in this case is again too small, given that the interval derived from the arithmetic means is based on the firstborn son, while the observed cases include all sons born to mothers. But the general similarity of the two sets of intervals supports the results obtained from the 342 observed cases: for the period 1720 to 1789 as a whole, elite men, who typically married in their late twenties and died in their early fifties, were rarely still alive when their sons married, and alive to attend the weddings of their daughters in only about half the observed cases. Elite women, who married in their middle twenties and died in their middle fifties, might not witness their sons' weddings, but they would almost certainly be alive when their daughters were married. The eighteenth-century trend was toward increasing age at first marriage, and therefore toward greater frequency of marriages made in the absence of the parents of the nuptial pair, especially the father of the groom, who was almost always missing after 1730.

With some minor variations these patterns are replicated among the elite heads of household in Caracas in 1759. The age at death can be determined for 91 percent (107 of 118 cases) of the parents of 29 elite men and 30 women who were either a married or widowed head of household or the spouse of a household head in 1759, and for whom age at first marriage has been established. Of these parents, 61 percent (65 of 107 cases) had died before the year in which their children were married.

The fathers of fifteen of the twenty-five men for whom data is available had died before their son's marriage, and twenty of the fathers of thirty women had similarly died before their daughter's wedding day. With good reason the survey of mantuano households in 1759 reveals but two grandfathers, one of whom, Lorenzo Antonio Ponte, was head of the only three-generation elite household in Caracas at that time. In two-thirds of the fifty-five known cases, fathers had already died before even their own children were even married, and very few indeed ever knew their grandchildren. Ponte, a man who lived to see not only the wedding of most of his children but also the birth of many of his grandchildren and two great-grandchildren, would have been a rarity in mid–eighteenth-century Caracas even if he had not lived in the same house with some of these married children and grandchildren. Elite grandmothers were more common, there were ten grandmothers who were heads of household in 1759, but even in the case of women a majority of mothers, thirty of the fifty-two known cases, did not live to see the weddings of their sons and daughters. The mothers of elite household heads in 1759 varied somewhat from the seventy-year norm in that a majority of both mothers of sons (fourteen of twenty-six cases) and mothers of daughters (sixteen of twenty-six cases) had died before their children were married.

Finally, the observation that it was less common after the 1730s for parents to be alive at the time of their children's marriage is supported by the 1759 population. Alive in Caracas in 1759 were some twenty elites, married or widowed heads of household and their spouses, who had been married before 1729. In about half of the cases for which the necessary parent's death date and child's marriage date are known (nineteen of thirty-nine cases), the parents of these elites had been alive in the year of their marriage. On the other hand, of those elites who had married in the subsequent thirty years, from 1730 to 1759, in less than one-third of the known cases (twenty-two of sixty-eight) had the parent been alive in the

Table 20 Interval Between Date of First Marriage of Elite
Household Heads and Death Date of Their Parents, in years
(N = 107)

	Date of Marriage of Head		
	1711–1729	1730–1759	1711–1759
Fathers and Sons	−2.4 (10)*	4.9 (15)	1.9 (25)
Mothers and Sons	−4.9 (11)	1.3 (15)	−1.3 (26)
Fathers and Daughters	0.5 (10)	6.4 (20)	4.7 (30)
Mothers and Daughters	−6.5 (8)	3.4 (18)	0.3 (26)
	1711–1729	1730–1759	
Fathers and both Sons and Daughters	−0.9 (20)	5.8 (35)	
Mothers and both Sons and Daughters	−5.6 (19)	2.5 (32)	

Source: See genealogical sources in chap. 7, nn. 4 and 7.
*Number of cases is in parentheses. A negative interval indicates that the parent survived the marriage of the child by the given number of years; a positive interval indicates that the parent had died the given number of years before the marriage of the child.

marriage year of his or her son or daughter. The average interval between the date of marriage for elite household heads in 1759 and the death date of their parents is given in table 20.

Two major points remain to be made with the information derived from the long-term marriage patterns of the Caracas elite and from the nature of elite residence as it is revealed in the 1759 household census. The first has to do with the patriarchal character of Caracas elite society, which is placed in some doubt by these data. The second, necessarily rather hypothetical in nature, tries to relate the boom (from the 1650s to the late 1730s) and bust (in the 1740s) of the Tuy River cacao economy to the changes in elite marriage behavior and the changing role of patriarchs which may have occurred at the time.

Beginning in the 1730s, because they typically died before their sons married, fathers had no direct influence over their sons as they reached adulthood and formed families of their own. They did not participate either in the selection of a bride or in the domestic life of these sons once they had married. Thus what might be called the direct psychological generational transmission of male authority, that which a father might convey as a role model and "father figure," came to young adult sons only in retrospect, as they remembered the behavior and recalled the image of their deceased fathers. For the rest, paternal authority reached a son only indirectly, through his father's property, his lasting reputation and social standing, and perhaps also indirectly through his uncles, his father's surviving younger brothers. Therefore, because they did not often survive to influence their children as adults, much of the authority of the father's lineage that was felt and exercised by Caracas mantuano men in the eighteenth century had to be resurrected or recreated in every generation, using the symbols and inherited wealth of the deceased fathers. In Caracas, where noble titles and entailed estates were rare, the force of personality of each new husband and father must have counted for a great deal in the establishment of his stature as *padre de familia* and holder of community power and prestige.

By contrast, the generational transfer of the valued qualities of the mother's family, either the groom's mother's family or the bride's mother's family, often came directly from the mother herself. This was particularly true for the mother of the bride, who usually lived long enough after the wedding to have had a continuing influence on a newly married couple. The exact nature of this influence is for the most part a matter of conjecture, but it was no doubt enhanced by the mother's presence in the household of the couple or by their residence in her household, both practices being common. In addition, it was not unusual for daughters to receive houses, household goods, and domestic slaves as their inheritance portion, while their brothers were assigned haciendas, field slaves, and other agricultural property. For these three reasons, because women customarily lived beyond the marriage date of their daughters and were the only parent to do so, because these women then shared a household with their married daughters, and because it was common for women to possess urban real estate, elite residence was strongly matrifocal in Caracas.

Expressed in a different way, the absence of fathers in lives of their married children meant that the authority of the male lineage was likely to be diffused at marriage. As meaningful or cherished as it might have been, without primogeniture, and with few titles of nobility or entails, the lineage of the father was a difficult concept to perpetuate. Marriage, the link between generations as well as between families, could have served the purpose of reinforcing the patrilineage if an appropriate match were made. In the absence of the fathers, and often mothers as well, influence in determining suitable partners fell to other kin, aunts and uncles who were, in many cases, the younger siblings of the deceased parents of the marriage-age children. With remarkable frequency, these kin approved of marriages in which the nuptial pair were consanguineously related, usually as cousins, often as first cousins. In the seventeenth century cousin marriage among the elite was rare, but, beginning in the 1720s and continuing until the end of the century, there were, on the average, three elite weddings celebrated in the Caracas cathedral every year, and in one of the three the bride and groom were first cousins. Although the death of fathers typically took place some years before elite marriages were realized, emphasis could have been given to the father's lineage in these increasingly common cousin unions if the bride and groom were related through their fathers, or at least through the father of the groom. However, despite the potential present in cousin marriage for the generational transfer of patriarchal influence, in Caracas the many elite cousins who married were more often linked through their mothers than through their fathers.

Marriage has many meanings, but marriage between cousins has the distinctive function of retaining for the next generation a double portion of those things that are transferred from one generation to the next, especially wealth, but also such social attributes as status and authority. For example, in cousin marriage a dowry is given by a woman's father to the son of his own brother or sister, but the source of wealth that comprised that dowry, a cacao hacienda for instance, might have been created in the first place by a man who was the grandfather of both the bride and groom. A society or a segment of society may practice cousin marriage when wealth or status are in short supply, as was increasingly the case of the Caracas elite after the creation of the Guipuzcoana Company and the end of the South Sea Company asiento. Cousin marriages did become more common just at that time when, while the number of living people of elite ancestry continued to increase, the cacao boom that had lasted for several generations came to an end. Yet it is difficult to demonstrate an incontrovertible link between the function and frequency of cousin marriage and the mantuanos' economic problems. It is more readily evident that these marriages, although they could have fortified the patrilineages of the usually deceased fathers, most often served the very different purpose of strengthening the ties between sons and the families of their mothers.

A total of seventy-seven first-cousin marriages of the Caracas elite have been identified for the period 1700–1799, all but three of which occurred after 1720. Of this number, five were matches in which not only were the bride and groom cousins to one another, but they were also the children of parents who were also first cousins. The multiple kinship links that result in these five cases make them difficult to classify, but each of the remaining seventy-two cases can be sorted into one of four categories. For cousins who marry, a man's wife will be either his father's brother's daughter, his father's sister's daughter, his mother's brother's daughter, or his mother's sister's daughter. First-cousin marriage in a society governed by patriarchal rules of authority, even if the inheritance of wealth was bipartible and not patrilineal, might be expected to be most often of the sort where brothers arrange for the son of one of them to marry the daughter of the other. In eighteenth-century Caracas this form of cousin marriage did not predominate, however, occurring in precisely one-quarter of the cases (eighteen of seventy-two). The most matrilineal link, the one in which the groom's mother and the bride's mother were sisters, was equally likely; Caracas elite men who married their cousins married their mother's sister's daughter 25 percent of the time (eighteen of seventy-two). The rarest kind of cousin marriage, occurring in less than 10 percent of the observed cases (seven of seventy-two), was that in which a man married his father's sister's daughter. The most common form of this most endogamous kind of marriage was that in which the man married his mother's brother's daughter, which took place in 40 percent of the cases (twenty-nine of seventy-two) (see table 21).

In two-thirds (forty-seven of seventy-two) of the instances in which first cousins of elite status married, the man was related to his cousin–wife through his mother. Given the observed fact that mothers were more likely than fathers to be alive for the weddings of their children, the matrimonial politics that influenced these unions probably operated on a principal of proximity. In other words, an elite mother, often a widow, considering acceptable

Table 21 The Structure of First-Cousin Marriage Among Caracas Elites, 1700–1799 (N = 72)

Number of cases in which a woman's relationship to her first-cousin husband was his:			
FATHER'S BROTHER'S DAUGHTER:	18	MOTHER'S BROTHER'S DAUGHTER:	29
FATHER'S SISTER'S DAUGHTER:	7	MOTHER'S SISTER'S DAUGHTER:	18

wives for her son, turned first to her own brothers, then to her sisters, and only infrequently to the family of her deceased husband. The least appealing cousin match for her son was the daughter of her husband's sister, the daughter of a man to whom she was not in any way related herself, and this kind of union did not often occur. The daughter of her husband's brother was also not consanguineous kin to the mother of an elite son, but the daughter of her brother-in-law did belong to her husband's patrilineage, and this sort of marriage regularly met with acceptance. But the daughter of her own brother or sister was the most attractive choice, and if the opportunity to select between these two was present, her brother's daughter was preferred.[12]

These patterns are also replicated in the eighty-five elite households culled from the 1759 census. Of the forty-seven single-family households in which both husband and wife were alive in 1759, twelve of these spouse pairs were first cousins, and in two-thirds of the twelve cases the male heads were related to their wives through their mothers. Of the remaining thirty-eight (of the eighty-five total) elite households that were not headed by a spouse pair, five were headed by widowers, of whom four had been married to their first cousins, and twenty were headed by widows, of whom three had been married to their first cousins as well.[13] Including these seven cases of cousin spouses which had been truncated by the death of one of them, nineteen of the eighty-five elite households in Caracas in 1759 was or recently had been headed by a husband and wife who were first cousins. True to the observed pattern, in almost two-thirds of these cases, twelve of nineteen, husbands were or had been related to wives through their mothers.[14]

This evidence suggests that at midcentury, elite women were more influential than men in the strategies of family formation and in matters of residence. Both the predominance of mother-linked first-cousin marriages and the fact that in cousin and noncousin marriages alike only the mothers, and particularly the mother of the bride, were likely to be alive for the wedding and for some years thereafter indicate that the elite women of one generation had a strong and lasting influence on the next generation that elite men did not have. It was common, especially after 1730, for elite men to marry after their fathers had died, and in the absence of fathers the influence of mothers' families in the marriage choices of elite men was significant. In two-thirds of the observed cases of first-cousin marriages, elite men married the daughters of their mothers' brothers and sisters. It may also be supposed that women's influence was great in their homes, and this would be especially true in the case of widows. Almost one-fourth of the elite households in 1759 was headed by a widow (twenty of eighty-five). Of the ten elite grandmothers alive in that year, two, Josefa Mijares Tovar and her niece Melchora Ana Mijares Ascanio, lived with their husbands, but the other eight were widows and heads of household in their own right. All of them lived with their unmarried children, three lived in the same household with their married daughters and the spouses and children of those daughters, and one lived with a married son and his children. These widowed grandmothers were true matriarchs in their homes: the only males in these households were their sons, sons-in-law, grandsons, and great-grandsons. No brothers or nephews of their deceased spouses were present to represent his lineage, the patrilineage of the children they had had together. The strong influence of mantuano women, which might be called matriarchy both in the synchronic sense of their influence in their homes and in the diachronic sense that their predominant influence in the selection of marriage partners for their children allowed them to exercise authority into the next generation, was most likely on the increase in eighteenth-century Caracas.

At any given moment, the decisive role of a mantuano woman in the past, present, and future lives of her family was made manifest in the visible qualities of her residence. The continuation of prestige and status associated with a household was more in the domain of women than it was of men, and not only in the narrow sense that it was a woman's duty to manage the domestic business of the home during her lifetime. Just as an adolescent girl learned of the influence of her grandmothers in decisions that had determined the marriages of her parents and aunts and uncles, decisions that had resulted in the makeup of the world of kin in which she was reared, so too did a young woman experience a similar influence firsthand, with considerable interest and anxiety no doubt, as her mother's will made its impact on the matter of marriage in her own life. In her turn, an adult mantuano woman knew that she would be influential in such decisions as they affected her own children and her nieces and nephews, decisions that would determine the future composition of the dwelling in which she resided, and often that of other households occupied by her kin as well. That women received houses, household goods, and domestic slaves in the wills of their parents, while their brothers were typically given agricultural property, means something more than the commonplace observation that a woman's place was in the home. The home was a locus of the lineages of the people who lived in it as well as their residence, and because domestic material wealth played an important part in the continuing prestige and status of those who lived in the household, the furniture of the house, its slaves, and often the house itself appropriately belonged to eighteenth-century elite women, the foremost arbiters of the future shape of these lineages.

MIDCENTURY: A CRITICAL CONJUNCTURE FOR SOME MANTUANO FAMILIES

Occasionally, the society-wide significance of elite women was manifest in an arena outside the related realms of marriage and household. The prominence of widow signatories in the memorials written in 1741 and 1744 to protest the excesses of the Guipuzcoana Company is illustrative of this. However, the arena of their major social influence, the household, was more visible than the women themselves in the tumultuous political life of midcentury Caracas. As will be seen in the following chapter, the household, as the physical manifestation of the family contained within it, was the principal target of much of the repression and many of the reforms of Governor Ricardos in the 1750s: candles and lamps were to be placed in windows and doorways, a household census was taken, and mantuano men were removed from their town homes and forced to remain under arrest on their haciendas. The most graphic and threatening expressions of the royal power in the hands of the reforming governor struck directly at the central place of the household in the social life of Caracas. First the door of the house of Juan Francisco de León was hung with the head of a black man who had joined him in protest, and then, after the canario rebel was himself dead in Spain, his family was turned out of their house, it was torn down and its ruins covered with salt. This brutal lesson, the example of household and family destroyed, was probably not lost on the elite, even though the immediate victims were not of their same social rank.

In the decades before León's rebellion many elite families experienced economic difficulties that directly threatened their collective wealth and established prestige in the Caracas community, and their protest against the Guipuzcoana Company was based on this sense that Company policies challenged them collectively, more as kin than as individuals. But the protest went too far, became a rebellion in the eyes of the authorities, and in response the action taken by Ricardos was to threaten the destruction of families and homes as he had destroyed the León family by in effect executing the father and in fact pulling down their dwelling and covering the ruins with salt. Indeed, the considerable success of the royal reaction to the events of 1749 may have been due as much to the threat presented to family and household as it was to the large contingent of king's troops at Ricardos's command. The fact that Ricardos's object lesson was not lost on the community may be one major reason why the newly permanent military presence in Caracas and the new taxes created to support the soldiers met with virtually none of the resistance that royal officials anticipated.

The reform decade of the 1750s confirmed as permanent a process of changes in the character of the Caracas elite which had begun prior to the creation of the Guipuzcoana Company in 1728. For elites the protest against the Company stemmed in part from anxiety that accompanied a fundamental restructuring of the nature of family authority, nothing less than the erosion of patriarchy. Similarly, the forceful expression of royal authority, the Bourbon reforms as they were meted out to Caracas by a vindictive Governor Ricardos, were received by Caraqueños whose traditional base of power, that of the patriarchs of elite families, had weakened noticeably in the previous generation. Cousin marriage and the mother-linked structure of cousin marriage are measures of this process drawn exclusively from family reconstitution data. The same data combined with surveys of cacao haciendas made in 1720 and in 1744 reveal the decline of patriarchal influence in another context: the ownership of the agricultural estates that had always been the basis of elite wealth and status.

The birth date is known for forty-seven mantuanos who owned cacao haciendas in 1720, hence their ages in that year can be calculated. These elite hacendados held 906,600 cacao trees on sixty-seven haciendas, which was 27.8 percent of all the trees in the province in that year, and 61.3 percent of all the trees owned by elites. Their mean age in 1720 was 37.8 years, the median age 38. For most of the forty-seven hacienda owners (thirty-nine of forty-seven cases) it is also possible to know whether the owners' fathers were still alive in 1720, and in nine of thirty-nine cases (23 percent) the father was in fact still alive in that year.

A similar portion of elite owners with a known birth date can be taken from the 1744 census. The sixty-four elite hacendados for whom age can be calculated in 1744 owned 1,266,724 cacao trees on 100 haciendas, 24.8 percent of all the trees in the province in 1744, and 61.3 percent of all the cacao trees owned by mantuanos. The mean age of these sixty-four owners was 43.8 years, the median age 43. They were, therefore, on the average 5 years older than their counterparts a quarter of a century earlier. However, the most significant difference in cacao hacienda ownership between 1720 and 1744 is revealed in the much smaller proportion of fathers of the 1744 owners who were still alive at that time. Again, the death date for the fathers of most of the sixty-seven owners is known (fifty-six of sixty-seven cases), but while the father of one mantuano hacienda owner in four was still alive in 1720 and such a circumstance was therefore common if not typical, in 1744 mantuanos who owned cacao haciendas had almost always outlived their fathers. The fathers of only three of the fifty-six elite owners for whom this fact can be determined were alive in 1744.

Thus it would seem that in 1720 it was not unusual for young elites to marry and to begin their own *haciendas de cacao*, usually in the Tuy Valley, while their fathers were still alive. But by 1744 the era of the rapidly expanding cacao frontier had passed, and in response elite marriages were ever more frequently postponed until after the death of the fathers, when the slaves and cacao groves that had belonged to these men became the property of their heirs. For many of Caracas's foremost families even this inheritance was not enough to compensate for the economic difficulties caused by shortages of slaves, and, in the 1740s, the low price paid for cacao beans by the Guipuzcoana Company. To minimize the dispersion of wealth from one generation to the next, those elites most affected by the end of almost a century of booming cacao prosperity made active use of the most endogamous form of marriage available to them, the marriage between first cousins. In the twenty-year period from 1700 to 1719, only 4 of 41 weddings celebrated in the Caracas cathedral in which at least one of the spouses was a mantuano brought first cousins together as husband and wife. But during the next thirty years, of 128 Cathedral parish weddings involving elites, 31 nuptial pairs were first cousins. One family far surpassed the others in these conservative unions. In one-fourth of the first-cousin marriages that took place from 1720 to 1749 (8 of 31), the celebrants were related to one another either paternally or maternally through the large and expanding family Blanco. The second-most frequent link, although it occurred only half as often as the Blanco tie, was through the family Mijares (4 of 31 cases). The probability that first-cousin marriage was indeed a strategy used by elites faced with declining cacao profits in the decades leading up to León's rebellion is strengthened by the fact that these same families, the Blanco and the Mijares, were also the most vocal and visible of the Caracas elite in their opposition to the Guipuzcoana Company.[15] As early as 1739, the royalist perspective held that the colony's troubles originated with a self-seeking faction that was determined to force the Guipuzcoana Company out of Caracas. In 1745 Governor Zuloaga described this faction as "the Conde de San Javier, Don Alejandro Blanco y Uribe, and the rest of the [Mijares de] Solórzano family, which is that of the conde, and his relatives and allies."[16]

The surname Blanco was as venerable as any other in eighteenth-century Caracas. The first Blanco immigrant had arrived in the colony from the Canary Islands in 1603 and, although they never acquired a noble title or married into a noble family,[17] the Blanco had always been alcaldes ordinarios, regidores, and the holders of other prestigious positions in the community. In 1744 members of many of the first families of Caracas gathered to sign a statement of protest against the Guipuzcoana Company in the house identified as belonging to "doña Luisa de Villegas, widow of the Provincial of the Santa Hermandad, don Alejandro Blanco," the same woman who had carried on a legal fight with the morenos libres and the canarios over land at Curiepe. Of the names of the ninety-four vecinos who signed the document, none appears more often than Blanco. A total of eighteen carried Blanco as a first surname, and seven others were sons and daughters of Blanco mothers. They were closely involved in the León uprising. A majority of the mantuano men arrested by Felipe Ricardos in 1751 were named Blanco: Juan Félix Blanco de Villegas, the son of doña Luisa de Villegas and don Alejandro Blanco, was identified as a covert ringleader and sent to Spain. Among those forced to spend the next year on their haciendas were his brothers Miguel Blanco de Villegas and Alejandro Blanco de Villegas, and several of their cousins: the regidor Pedro Blanco de Ponte, Pío Blanco de Ponte, Alejandro Blanco Uribe, and Miguel Blanco Uribe.[18] After Blanco, the next-most-frequent name on the 1744 memorial was the more prestigious one of Mijares, which was father's surname to four signatories, including the third Marqués de Mijares, and mother's surname to six others, including the second Conde de San Javier, Juan Jacinto Pacheco Mijares. It was the Conde de San Javier who, in the company of Alejandro Blanco Uribe, took the signatures gathered in November 1744 to Madrid early in 1745 to plead the Caracas case against the Guipuzcoana Company.[19] He was still there in May 1751, when he was arrested for his assumed part in the rebellion.[20]

By way of contrast, before he set sail from Spain with orders to crush the Caracas rebellion, Ricardos was given a list of principal citizens of the town whom he could count on as "peaceful and loyal to the King": named were Domingo Galindo y Sayas, Pedro Ruiz Arquinzones, José Bolívar, Feliciano Sojo Palacios, Agustín Piñango, Miguel de Aristeguieta, Antolín de Liendo, Mateo de Monasterios, and Miguel de Rengifo.[21] None of these men had signed the 1744 protest statement and, except for the family of Antolín de Liendo, cousin marriage was rare in their families;

before 1749 a first-cousin match had taken place only in the families Bolívar and Rengifo, and there was only one instance of such a marriage in each case.[22] Neither cousin marriage nor active opposition to the Company were characteristic of these families at midcentury, probably because they had not yet reached a critical juncture between family expansion and cacao profits, as had the Blanco, Mijares, and others.

8

The King in Caracas: The Bourbon Reforms

The English capture of Havana in the Seven Years War has always been regarded as the most important catalyst for change in eighteenth-century Spanish America. Once Cuba was recovered, a shocked Charles III introduced major military, administrative, and fiscal reforms on the island that were then extended to the other American colonies. In subsequent decades these so-called Bourbon reforms would have a virtually unprecedented impact in the Indies, considered by some second in importance only to the original Conquest.[1] But now it is clear that Caracas, not Cuba, was the initial arena for royal colonial reform. More than a decade before the loss of Havana, the 1749 rebellion in Caracas presented Spanish ministers with a serious problem and provided a laboratory where many of the new policies were given their first practical application in the Indies.

By coincidence, León's uprising occurred soon after the accession of Ferdinand VI to the Spanish throne in 1746, an event that marked both the end of several decades of dedicated Spanish military activity in Italy and the beginnings of renewed interest by Spain's Bourbon monarchs in their American empire. Reflecting this interest, in 1754, the responsibilities of the secretary of the Navy and Indies in the monarch's cabinet were limited exclusively to the Atlantic trade and New World colonies. The first occupant of this reformed post was also the first colonial minister of this rank to have had administrative experience in America. Julián de Arriaga y Rivera[2] had been governor of Caracas from December 1749 until the arrival of Felipe Ricardos in June 1751. Sent to put down the disturbance there, Arriaga's objective in Caracas was to reestablish royal authority, and his understanding of events had been largely impartial. He witnessed how the self-interestedness of the Guipuzcoana

Company had hurt commerce and deprived the royal treasury of income, and he wrote to the king in 1750 that the controversial *alternativa* system of loading was prejudicial to the most important branch of the cacao trade, the trade with New Spain.[3] He had no sympathy for the rebellion that had broken out, but he understood the resentment felt by cacao planters who had no choice but to take their complaints against the Basque monopolists to hostile Basque governors. His attitude toward Basques as colonial administrators remained fixed thereafter.

As Ferdinand's minister, Julián de Arriaga was dedicated to the goal of bringing the colonies more completely under the dominion of the crown, and he initiated an effort to restrict the number of American-born Spaniards, or creoles, in colonial administrative and juridical positions, a cornerstone of Bourbon reform policy.[4] At the same time, however, perhaps on the basis of his Caracas experience, Arriaga made a point of excepting Basques from his preference for Europeans as administrators and judges. This was especially true in Caracas, where, although the reformed Guipuzcoana Company would continue to play a dominant role in the economy for several decades, it would be many years before Basques were again allowed to occupy positions of administrative authority. Arriaga's evenhanded rejection of both creoles and Basques in Caracas was made clear when Juan Bolívar, first cousin of Simón Bolívar, was denied the minor post of *contador mayor* in the 1760s. None of the Caracas elites had collaborated more closely with the royal effort to suppress the León rebellion than Juan Bolívar's father, José Bolívar Aguirre, who led the militia in a futile search for the fugitives in 1751. Ricardos had rewarded José Bolívar by recommending him for knighthood in one of the military orders, although the honor was not confirmed, and by naming him principal accountant of the royal treasury in Caracas.[5] After Bolívar's death in 1758 his eldest son Juan held the *contador* position on an interim basis. In 1768 the younger Bolívar received the support of the governor, José Solano y Bote, when he requested permanent possession of the post. Solano wrote to Minister Arriaga that Bolívar was "without doubt efficient and of sufficient ability to fulfill the obligations of the position, . . . and if you want to accommodate Bolívar for the good work he has done, and want to make an exception for him [from the policy] that it is not convenient for Vizcayans, Isleños or

Criollos to hold royal offices, it seems to me that he will fulfill the obligations of the position." Arriaga's note in the margin of Solano's letter indicates that his attitude toward Basques remained unchanged two decades after the Caracas rebellion: "It is understood what he says to me about the *contador mayor*, and I have always been persuaded that in royal offices it is best to have a European, but not a Vizcayan."[6]

León's rebellion freed Caracas from excesssive Basque authority. The Basque governors disappeared and the reformed Guipuzcoana Company offered capital stock to Caraqueños. The alternativa system of loading ships was ended and cacao prices were set by a regidor of the cabildo and the Company factor, with the governor to adjudicate when they could not agree. In 1752 the hated prohibition against bringing cacao to La Guaira by sea was lifted and, at the meeting of the Company's Junta General in May 1753, it was decided that one-sixth of the cargo capacity of Company ships would be reserved for colonials who wanted to ship cacao to Spain on their own account.[7] But these welcome changes were accompanied by a much resented increase in royal government in Caracas. Established during the 1750s by Governor Felipe Ricardos, who justified his actions with the argument that Caracas was a disloyal city and its citizens were prone to revolt, the expanded presence of the crown was received with anger by Caraqueños who insisted that they had been constant in their respect for the king and his authority. These protests of innocence and fidelity had no effect, however. Ricardos was certain that León had enjoyed the encouragement and direct support of many of the colony's first citizens, and although there was no evidence to prove his conviction, he determined that the town's populace should be punished collectively for its crime of rebellion. And yet the royal response was more than a set of punitive measures designed exclusively for Caracas. Ricardos worked closely with his superiors, first Ensenada and then his successor Arriaga, principal architects of reforms for the colonies as a whole, and therefore it is not surprising that policies applied in Caracas in the 1750s closely resemble the general reform policies that would be widely applied in Spanish America in the 1760s and after.

The Bourbon reforms in Caracas did not begin with Arriaga. Within a month of his arrival in the colony he wrote to the king that his mission was completed. He had pardoned almost everyone, things were quiet, and although everyone spoke against the Company, he did not think that anyone was then secretly fomenting unrest. His role had been to reestablish order, and, that done, he believed that a governor "of other firmness" was needed to carry out the more difficult tasks of returning the Company to operation and preventing future crises. To his mind, however, Caraqueños were loyal vassals at heart, and he recommended that more royal troops not be sent, both because they were not needed and because it was expensive to transport them and to quarter them in the colony.[8]

Brigadier Felipe Ricardos, a man of decidedly different "firmness," replaced Arriaga in June 1751. He brought with him instructions from the king, some of which would be quickly implemented, such as the order providing that a "just price" for cacao would be established annually by a junta comprised of the regidor of the Caracas cabildo and the Guipuzcoana Company factor. Others, in particular an order to move "the ecclesiastical and secular tribunals, the reverend bishop, the cathedral dean and cabildo, the administration of the the Royal Company [Guipuzcoana], and the residence of the governor" from Caracas to Valencia, would be held in abeyance and used instead as a threat to force compliance with the remainder of the instructions. Arriaga's suggestion that additional troops were not needed was ignored, and the six hundred soldiers who arrived with Ricardos brought the total number of men in the royal service in Caracas to about eighteen hundred.[9]

During his first six months in Caracas, while royal troops and an expanded militia swept the Tuy and Píritu in search of Juan Francisco de León, Ricardos took measures to bring royal order and a new discipline to the population of the town. At the crier's nine o'clock call on dark nights all householders were to place candles in a window and a lamp outside in the doorway of their houses. Ricardos was serious about this, failure to comply meant a fine of twenty-five pesos for elites (*personas de calidad*) or eight days in jail for others (*plebeyos*), and soon the king's presence shown from every window on every moonless night. In the town were many married men, most of them canarios according to Ricardos, who had left their wives on the far side of the Atlantic. The governor attacked this problem, which was as old as Spanish America, by ordering out of Caracas men who had been away from their wives for three or more years. All foreigners were obliged to leave, and all individuals aged twelve to sixty without satisfactory employment were classified as vagabonds and given ten days to find work. Men who failed to do as the governor ordered were sent to Spain as criminals to work for the king. Orphans were assigned to masters to learn trades, and women without work were placed in "virtuous houses" where they would learn "good customs." The comportment of women troubled Ricardos. The soldiers in his command expanded the population of Caracas by about 10 percent,[10] they created a problem of prostitution, and to curb it Ricardos prohibited women from going to the barracks or even the plaza after nightfall (as they did, he said, under the pretext of selling chickens and fruit). Those who violated this dictum as well as any woman of less than elite "quality" discovered talking to a soldier after dusk would be sent to the town's hospice.[11]

The impression created by these orders was surely insignificant in comparison with the persecutions of deserters, rebels, and suspected rebels which were carried out at the same time. Beginning in June 1751, immediately after Ricardos's arrival in Caracas, these actions ranged from house arrest to deportment and, in a few cases designed as a warning and graphic expression of the king's wrath,[12] to execution. Yet, as chillingly effective as these harsh measures were in extinguishing the spirit of protest in Caracas, a series of more mundane institutional changes had greater result in the long run in gaining for Ricardos his primary goal of establishing an enduring royal presence in the town.

Two fundamental functions of civic life, town government and taxation, were altered in substantial ways by the governor. In these repressive circumstances, with some of its alcaldes and regidores in jail, a cowed cabildo did nothing but approve Ricardos's policies. From 1752 to 1754, the same men were elected alcaldes ordinarios by their peers on the council. This was completely without precedent in the history of the Caracas cabildo. Traditionally the bastion of local authority, the council had been taken over by the governor, who made certain that men suited to his purposes were elected.[13] The governor's cabildo created a number of new offices to help it execute the new rules he had promulgated. These officials included a public defender to serve the incarcerated poor, a director of public works, an inspector of city streets, an assessor of real property, an auditor of estates of the deceased, a recorder of mortgages, an officer who evaluated the worth of slaves, and a supervisor of food stores. In addition, Ricardos continued the practice, begun by Arriaga in 1750, of having a representative of the cabildo read to the public on New Year's day a list of town ordinances with an exhortation to comply with them.[14]

The creation of public offices was an important part of the effort to make Caracas modern, self-conscious, and loyal. But Ricardo's greatest talent as a colonial governor was in his ability to manipulate the visual, tangible, and symbolic. The head hung on the door of Juan Francisco de León's house and the spreading of salt on its ruins were messages powerfully conveyed to a largely illiterate population. In a similar style, the centerpiece of Ricardos's reforms was both symbolic and distinctly utilitarian. The central plaza, formerly an open quadrangle that functioned as the main market of the town, became an impressive enclosed emporium where retail activities could be closely controlled and, more importantly, efficiently taxed. Work was begun in 1753 and finished in 1755. Excavation allowed the floor of the plaza to be lowered six feet and brick walls were constructed on three sides, leaving open only the east side, facing the cathedral. Built into the inner side of the walls were small shops, known as *paquetes* or *canastillas*, which were rented by the city. A variety of dry goods and other merchandise were sold from most of these cells, while the offices of notaries and a market supervisor occupied others. Food items were sold in the center of the plaza from tent-covered wooden stalls called *ranchos*. Entrance to the plaza was by way of three elaborate arches, of "first-quality construction" according to the merchant Joseph Luis de Cisneros, who saw them in 1764.[15]

Cisneros made no mention of the reason for the reconstruction of the plaza, and Ricardos's aims in having it rebuilt have been lost to the historical record. Twentieth-century historians and chroniclers, who describe the work in neutral or positive terms as "an adornment," "enhancement," "improvement," and "modernization" of the city, have missed the meaning of Ricardos's structural reform.[16] One clue to the essentially repressive nature of the new plaza comes from the fact that the cabildo paid for its construction.

Characteristically reluctant to make even modest expenditures, and with only 1285 pesos in its treasury in July 1752, it seems most likely that coercion was used six months later to force the council to contract a debt of 4000 pesos at a high rate of interest to pay for the plaza project.[17] In fact this debt was just a very small part of the many thousands of pesos that Ricardos determined were owed to the king by the province of Caracas for its rebelliousness.

In January 1752 the treasurer of the royal exchequer in Caracas informed the governor that the cost of putting down the uprising of 1749, from the time Governor Castellanos had fled the city through the last day of January 1752, including the transport of supplies and troops to the colony, the cost of sustaining the soldiers in Caracas and in the field, and the expenditures made to outfit an expanded militia, was 366,573 pesos.[18] Ricardos determined that this sum should be repaid over a period of years in annual installments of never less than 50,000 pesos. In addition, the province was to bear the cost of supporting a major contingent of regular army troops, to be permanently stationed in Caracas, at an estimated cost of 100,000 pesos a year. The governor spent the first months of 1752 analyzing possible ways for the colony to pay this substantial sum. By May he had rejected the idea of placing a special tax on exports, and had decided that the funds could be raised by reforming the alcabala tax.[19]

The alcabala duty was a percentage of the value of all items entering or passing through Caracas, including both merchandise for local consumption that came from outside the colony and items grown or raised in the colony for either local consumption or export. Ricardos calculated that more than 100,000 pesos could be collected every year by increasing the alcabala charge from 2 to 5 percent on the market price of certain export items, primarily cacao, tobacco, sugar, and hides. This was the modified *alcabala de mar*. The remaining 50,000 pesos would come from the *alcabala de tierra*, a tax collected on every sale throughout the province of all food items, and a few other essential commodities, such as firewood, mules, and horses. For example, an arroba of cheese was taxed half a real, a fanega of cacao, an arroba of sugar, or an entire head of beef were assessed a real, and a fanega of rice or beans was charged two reales. The tax on horses was also two reales, while mules, perhaps because of their greater utility as overland carriers, were taxed at the much higher rate of eight reales. Items usually sold in smaller quantities, such as firewood, salt, and salted fish, were included in the annual license fee of twenty pesos paid to the crown by the owners of the small stores, the *pulperías*, where such goods were retailed.[20] That colonials would pay for the costs of León's rebellion with the food they ate was particularly pleasing to Ricardos, who remained eager to punish the province as a whole for the uprising. He wrote to Ensenada in 1752 regarding the justice that would be served by the increased alcabala: "for it is undeniable that meat and bread are eaten by the rich, the middling, and the poor, the noble and the plebeian, free and slave, stranger and native, these things they all have to eat, and consequently they all have to pay the new *contribución*, those who are guilty and those who are not guilty alike."[21]

Goods moving in, out, and through Caracas would be registered with agents in the five roadside alcabala posts located on the outskirts of town. Sales made in town had to take place in the new plaza, where they could be closely scrutinized. Ricardos's estimates indicate that he assumed that about 25 percent of the beef, maize, cacao, and other food items consumed in the province were sold in Caracas, which meant that more than 10,000 pesos of the revised *alcabala de tierra* would be collected in the town every year. Some of this revenue would be collected in the town's slaughterhouses, the *carnicerías*,[22] some in the *pulperías*, but much of it would come from sales made in the renovated central plaza. The marketplace was enclosed, therefore, not to improve the city in some abstract sense or to make it more attractive, but rather to make certain that taxes were paid to the royal treasurer for every arroba of cheese or quantity of fish sold there. Ricardos could not control the illegal trade with foreigners who entered the province by way of the many isolated beaches and sheltered coves along its extensive coast,[23] but he was able to encircle the immediate Caracas economy with a walled market accessible only by way of elaborate portals. As such, the reformed plaza was an effective expression, both functionally and symbolically, of the king's authority.

The new fiscal measures were viewed with alarm by Caraqueños. Formerly collection of the alcabala had been farmed to the highest bidder at an annual auction, and that bid had never exceeded 40,000 pesos. A desperate cabildo wrote to Ensenada in 1753 that it would be most difficult to pay 150,000 pesos a year, and added that such a sum was "a painful joke," because the town as a whole was not responsible for the uprising, which had been done by "plebians out of control, without the cooperation of the nobility".[24] Ex-governor Julián de Arriaga did not think that the elite was entirely innocent and he agreed with Ricardos that the alcabala was the appropriate tax to alter, but he felt that an increase of 150 percent was too much. "Much time will pass," he wrote to Ensenada from Cádiz in September 1753, "before the novelty of the tax will be forgotten, and the memory of the reason for the tax will provoke more opposition than the amount collected will be worth." Arriaga recommended that once Caraqueños had been shown "the power and the punishment" of the crown the alcabala should be reduced to its former level.[25] But Ricardos prevailed. As decreed on November 15, 1752, collection of the revised taxes was begun on July 1, 1753, the traditional harvest of San Juan. Thirty years later, according to the report prepared in 1772 by Juan Vicente Bolívar, interim royal accountant, the 5-percent *alcabala de tierra* collected for that year amounted to 104,811 pesos, 26 percent of the revenue entered into the Caracas *caja* of the royal treasury from all sources that year. In 1778, the first full year after the intendancy was established in Caracas, the amount collected for the same tax was 110,799 pesos, 40 percent of total revenue. As was intended, this income covered all or most of the cost of maintaining the battalion of royal troops that was thereafter permanently quartered in Caracas. Including salaries and uniforms, expenditures for the *Batallón Veterano*, as it came to be called, were 96,230 pesos in 1771 and 113,354 pesos in 1778.[26] Clearly Arriaga had been wrong about the sustained controversy he believed the revised tax would provoke. Perhaps the best measure of Ricardos's success was the absence of visible opposition to the far-reaching measures he promulgated to reinstate loyalty and renew royal authority in Caracas. This success was no doubt due in part to the power of his preening personality. On the west side of the still unfinished walled plaza, facing the cabildo, Ricardos ordered inscriptions carved on both sides of the arched entryway. One of them was a poem, a testimony in stone to the arrogance and vanity of a man who could command Caraqueños to thank him for all that he had done for them:

EL EXCmo. Sr. Dn. PHe. RICARDOS
THEte. GRA. D. LOS Rs. EXtos. D. S. M. GOVor.
CAPn. GRA. DESTA PROVa. D. VENEZa.
R OMPA LA FAMA CON CLARIN PARLERO
I GNOTOS CLIMAS Y EN SONORAS VOCES
C LAME A RICARDOS HEROE VERDADERO
A RTICULANDO VICTORES VELOCES
R INDALE ESTA CIUDAD CON PROPIO ESMERO
D EBIDAS GRACIAS POR SUS NUEVOS GOCES
O Y QUE EN LA NUEVA CALLE TANTO AUMENTA
S US PROPIOS EN LOS AUGES DE LA RENTA
Año de 1754[27]

In the end, some of the Caracas planter elite were perhaps willing to accept the new royal order for a reason that was more basic than their fear of the forceful Ricardos and the royal soldiers at his command. Our knowledge of the nature of hacienda labor at mid-century is still very sketchy at best, but it seems that any solution to the increasingly severe labor problems of the elite depended on royal assistance. If the mantuanos desired help from the crown in this, they might have tolerated the new taxes and other reforms as their contribution to a compromise that would lessen their labor difficulties. Royal authorities were aware of and acted to improve the labor situation in Caracas province. In 1758, Remírez de Estenoz, Ricardos's replacement as governor, informed the king that he had taken measures to end tobacco cultivation because it was too labor intensive and there was a general shortage of slaves for work in agriculture. Remírez later wrote to Minister of State Arriaga that this shortage was the principal reason why cacao production had not reached expected levels. "The almost general poverty of the *cosecheros*," he emphasized,

> was due to the fact that they cannot apply the measures needed for its development, that is, due to the great lack of *negros* they have no option other than to turn to peonage, but their costs have become so great that it is more prejudicial than beneficial to plant, and for this reason they are reluctant to plant at all, to the notable detriment of the haciendas. Experience shows them that many haciendas [worked by *peones*] have declined, and for this reason it is every day more necessary to provide them with *negros*.[28]

This letter indicates that although slaves were still much preferred, a difficult transition from slavery to free labor was then underway.

A quarter-century would pass before black slaves again would be brought to Caracas in significant numbers, and in the meantime cacao hacendados, with the century-long boom ended, had no choice but to turn increasingly to wage labor as a substitute. The elite hoped that the crown would soon remedy the slave supply problem, but, while they waited for this to be accomplished, perhaps they saw reason to believe that the enhanced presence of royal authority in Caracas, with new laws that required gainful employment for everyone, would provide workers for their cacao haciendas.

The reformed society engineered by Felipe Ricardos and his superiors in Spain did not destroy the Caracas elite. All of the families of status and local importance, including the Blanco and the Mijares, would be present in 1810 to take sides in the Wars for Independence. The nonelite, however, paid a higher price for their protest, and this was true not just of those who lost their lives or spent time in Spanish jails and African presidios. The stigma of rebellion lived on with the family of Juan Francisco de León. In 1759 Juana Petrona de León, his daughter, complained to the Council of the Indies that no one in the family had been able to marry "anyone of our worth [*esfera*]," nor had they been able to become priests or nuns, because "the monument to our dishonor, which can be seen in the Candelaria plaza, not only makes it impossible for us to do so, but also leaves us without the desire to make the effort."[29]

The reformed *alcabala de tierra*, considered by Ricardos the best form of general punishment because everyone would have to pay, continued to provide for the battalion of royal troops stationed in the city. Since it taxed essential commodities and foodstuffs, the poor were charged virtually the same amount as the rich, but it was a burden they were certainly less able to afford. More basically, although there is no direct evidence that it was conscious policy, the essentially moribund slave trade (combined with Ricardos's strict rules regarding employment) meant that work in the cacao groves of the established planters became the destiny of many canarios and others of Caracas's now increasingly landless underclass. The dream realized by previous generations of ambitious immigrants, to own many slaves and their own cacao haciendas, had faded, to be replaced by work in the groves of others, as only slaves had done before.

The elite fared much better. No one suffered more physical punishment than something less than two years arrest, the trade with Veracruz was freed from the restraints of the alternativa, the cabildo was given at least a formal role in determining cacao prices, and Caracas vecinos were given the opportunity to buy stock in the restored Company and space in Company ships' holds. While the tablet describing León as "an infamous traitor" would remain in the Candelaria plaza until 1811, for the mantuano elite, once the new order was established, there was room for royal magnanimity. Before his death in 1753, the Marqués de Toro had been one of the most inveterate of the elite opponents of the Guipuzcoana Company. In December 1757 a royal order to the directors of the Company commanded them to give his widow, doña Teresa de Ascanio, "space for 150 fanegas of cacao every year" free of charge in Company ships. A similar order in 1758 gave the Conde de San Javier the privilege of sending up to 2000 fanegas of cacao to Veracruz over a period of six years without payment of royal duties. In 1751 Martín de Tovar Blanco had chased Juan Francisco de León and his desperate band along the lower Tuy, and he had provided horses and food for the royal forces who pursued the rebel through Píritu. Twenty years later these services rendered "in the turbulent times of the Governor Castellanos and Governor Felipe Ricardos" were proudly proclaimed as basic reasons why Tovar deserved to be granted a noble title, and in 1771 he became the first Conde de Tovar.[30]

For the elite the fundamental cost of the rebellion they had supported, and in some cases covertly fomented, was not economic and in a sense was intangible. Many of those who were most directly involved had already experienced two decades of difficult times before León and his mob forced a frightened Governor Castellanos to flee to La Guaira in 1749. To cope with shortened material resources, especially slave labor, these elites found that it was necessary to live with their parents into adulthood, unmarried, awaiting the deaths of those parents and their inheritance portion, before they could marry or become hacienda owners in their own right. Such waiting and late marriage meant that elite fathers often died before the marriage of their children, especially their sons, and they had no part in the selection of spouses or the lives of their children's families. To further limit the dispersion of family wealth, many married their first cousins, with men most often marrying women from their mothers' families.[31]

The establishment of the Guipuzcoana Company thus coincided with the beginnings of a discernible attenuation of elite Caracas patrilineages. More than two decades later, the most hard-pressed of these mantuano patriarchs, their ability to influence the shape of the next generation already shrinking, were defeated in a direct confrontation with the Company and the brigadier–governor Ricardos. As an immediate result of this defeat they also lost much of their customary power and prestige in the community.

The arrival of Ricardos and his unrelenting assertion of the royal will marked both the end of the long Caracas cacao bonanza and a substantial reduction of local autonomy. It would not be too much to say that this represented the end of an era, the passing of what might be called Habsburg Caracas, a half-century after the royal dynasty had ended. These events also coincided with the passing of a generation of Caracas mantuanos. Significantly, many of those elites who had been most involved in the attempt to force the Company from the colony died within a few years of the failure of their effort. Luis Arias Altamirano, the only member of the elite for whom Ricardos had concrete evidence of collaboration in the León movement, died in 1752 at age fifty-one, the first of the active protesters of his class to do so. Juan Félix Blanco de Villegas, identified as a clandestine leader of the protest and sent to Spain, died in Madrid the same year at age forty-six. His brother Alejandro, who was pardoned and allowed to return from confinement on his hacienda in 1752, died at age forty-two in 1754. The regidor Pedro Blanco de Ponte and his cousin Antonio Blanco Uribe were similarly released in 1752 and died in 1761, aged sixty and fifty respectively. Two nobles who had led the fight against the Company in the 1740s also died during this transitional period: Francisco Nicolás Mijares, the third Marqués de Mijares, in 1764 at age seventy-one, and Francisco de Paula Rodríguez de Toro, the second Marqués de Toro, in 1753 at age forty. Also dead before Ricardos left Caracas was Lorenzo Ponte Martínez, a signer of the 1744 memorial and veteran of many of Caracas's political battles, who at his death in June 1760 was the oldest male mantuano at seventy-seven.[32]

When the word arrived in Caracas on September 19, 1759, of the demise of Ferdinand VI,[33] many of the reforms generally associated with the policies of his successor Charles III were already well established in Caracas: a substantial contingent of royal troops was permanently quartered there, the militia had been revamped, there were new taxes, and in their daily lives Caraqueños encountered a variety of physical symbols of the strength of royal authority, the wall around the plaza mayor being the most conspicuous. The reforms were largely ineffective at reducing the amount of cacao sold to smugglers, and these illicit sales would continue as long as foreign buyers were willing to pay prices higher than those in the legal market, but in other respects provincial Caracas had changed.

For more than a century the colony had known only steadily expanding cacao production. Land had been cleared and new haciendas planted in the fertile Tuy basin at the individual initiative of canario frontiersmen and Caracas mantuanos, as well as the labor of hundreds of African and creole slaves. With fewer slaves in the cacao groves and many royal troops in the plaza, members of the elite were obliged to collaborate with the king's administrators and his licensed merchants. They paid increased alcabala taxes. They made certain peace with the reformed Guipuzcoana Company, which allowed them to buy shares in the corporation. The traditional trade with New Spain was restored to its original status, and cacao prices were set by the cabildo and the Company factor under the watchful eye of the governor. As a tangible measure of this collaboration, beginning in 1767, many elite young men, including some named Blanco and others named Mijares, took advantage of the opportunity to show their loyalty to the king and joined the Company of Noble Adventurers, created in that year, which gave them the rank and status of cavalry officers in the provincial militia.[34] In the 1750s and 1760s, as their parents' struggle against the Guipuzcoana Company became past history, a new generation of young mantuanos accepted without significant complaint the rise of royal authority and the decline of traditional patriarchy. Their own children would not be so complacent however, and the bond between crown and Caracas elite would only survive until 1810.

Appendix A

Slaves Belonging to the Rodríguez Santos–Escovedo Heirs, 1631

Caracas—Domestic Service

Name	Age	Value (reales)
Juliana	19	2000
Ysabel Angola	22	2000
Carolina Angola	20	2000
Juana Criolla w/infant	20	2240
Ysabel Angola	20	2000
Mencia Angola	30	2000
Magdalena Angola	21	1920
María Angola	20	1760
Doña María Angola	12	1280
Dominga Angola	28	2240
Ysabel	18	2000
Lucrecia w/	27	3120
Juan	6	
Agustine	1	

Source: ARPC, Testamentarías, 1648 RU.
Asterisk (*) = married.

Caracas Valley—Hato

Name	Age	No appraisal of value made of hato slaves
*Antón Quicama	30	
*María w/		
Lucrecia	7	
Ana	15 days	
Sebastián Congo	20	
Miguel	30	
Antonio	12	
Manuel	10	

Name	Age	No appraisal of value made of hato slaves
Francisco	14	
Gaspar (teamster)	35	
Nicolás	10	
Angela w/	20	
Pascual	1	
Gracia w/	25	
Martín	1	

Chacao—Wheat Estancia

Name	Age	Value (reales)
*Pedro Catote Angola	26	2800 (carpenter)
*Dominga Angola w/	28	2400
Nicolás	3	
*Juan Grande Angola	28	2800 ("*capitán*")
*Phelipa w/	30	2880
Antonico	6	
Juanico	nursing	
*Gregorio Monjongo Angola	24	2240
*Juliana	24	2000
*Juan Charaguave Congo	24	2080
*Gracia Conga	30	2080
*Domingo Angola	24	2240
María Angola w/	22	2880
Juan	6	
Francisca	1	
*Domingo Grande Angola	24	2000
*Gracia Angola w/	34	2880
Domingo	6	
María	1	
*Pedro Grengango	34	2000
*Vitoria Angola w/	32	2400
Manuel	2	
*Gonzalo Malemba Angola	40	1920
*Ynés ("*nación engole*") w/	23	2960
Pedro	6	
Juana	3	
*Gonzalo Mochiela Angola	34	2080
*Ynéz Angola	30	2000
*Lucas Cachimba Angola	22	2000

Name	Age	Value (reales)
*Catalina Angola w/	24	2560
Luisa	3	
María	1	
*[Antonico *mulato libre*]		—
*Phelipa Angola	22	2000
*Bartolomé Angola	26	2240
*Ysabel Angola w/	25	2400
Juan	4	
*Francisco Valdivia	30	2000
*Ysabel Angola	40	1920
*Domingo Angola ("lazy")	46	1280
*Ana Angola (pregnant)	25	2000
*Luis Angola	27	2080
*Gracia Angola	26	2000
Single Men and Boys		
Gaspar Pariaguén Angola	20	2000
Pedro Angola	34	2000
Antonio Conga	24	2000
Gregorio Cachimba Angolaz	25	1840

Appendix B

Wheat Buyers, 1634

Winter Wheat (grain: 177 fanegas total)

Buyer	Quantity (fanegas)	Price (reales)
Diego Rodríguez	100	34
Domingo de Liendo	24	32
Rodrigo Sánchez	20	38
Francisco Alvarez	10	38
Benito Fernández "a sacar dinero"	10	40
María Medina	8	36
Blas Correa de Benavides	1	40
María Díaz	1	40
Juan Rodríguez Mendez	2	40
Francesca Mejía	1	40

Summer Wheat (flour: 340 fanegas total)

Buyer	Quantity (arrobas)	Price (reales)
Juan Marcano "vecino Margarita"	100	72
Gerónimo Barbosa "vecino Margarita"	300	68
capitán Sancho de Mendoza	50	68
Antonio Meno	500	68
Don Gerónimo del Gueta	8	64
capitán Marco Pereyra	160	72
Pedro Francisco "vecino Puerto Rico"	150	72
governador Francisco Nuñez Melián	100	64
María de Medina	100	68
Alonso de Jaén	50	72
Francisco de Silva	100	72
Benito Fernández "a sacar dinero"	300	80
Domingo de Liendo	39	64
"gasté en casa"	50	64
padre Francisco Juan	33	64

Source: ARPC, Testamentarías, 1638 R.

Appendix C

Rodríguez Santos Tutela: Estate Operating Costs and Personal Expenditures, 1631–1636 (in reales)

	1631	1632	1633	1634	1635	1636	Annual Mean
Estate Costs	1,349	3,642	11,943	9,192	6,759	6,374	6,543
Germana	774	2,469	[4,157]	[2,956]	[3,181]	[5,300]	3,140
Diego	705	551	939	1,544	2,133	2,082	1,326
Paula	140	708	336	210	1,406	1,450	708
Juan	202	212	627	543	774	1,665	671
Alonso	174	235	330	459	548	1,402	525
Total Costs	3,344	7,817	18,332	14,904	14,801	18,273	12,912

Source: ARPC, Testamentarías, 1638 R. The total operating costs for the estate for 1631–1636 were 39,259 reales (4907 pesos). Doña Germana married Domingo de Liendo in 1632 and the bracketed amounts thereafter represent dowry payments made on her behalf.

Appendix D

Estimated Cash Surplus, 1632–1636 (in reales)

	1632	1633	1634	1635	1636	Annual Mean
Wheat Credits	22,864	37,432	27,147	22,250	31,813	27,701
Expenditures	7,817	18,332	14,904	14,801	18,273	12,912
Cash on Hand (actual)	15,047	19,100	9,243	7,449	13,540	14,789
Cash on Hand (at 1632 prices)	15,047	13,660	5,050	−343	−27	6,675

Source: Wheat Credits are taken from table 9, row Total Income; Expenditures are from appendix C, row Total Costs; Cash on Hand (actual) is derived by subtracting expenditures from credits; Cash on Hand (at 1632 prices) is obtained by multiplying annual harvest information in table 9 by 1632 prices, and then subtracting actual expenditures from these amounts.

Appendix E

Slaves Belonging to the Liendo–Rodríguez Santos Heirs, 1658

Caracas—Domestic Service

Name	Age	Value (reales)
*Antonio Angola	40	3200
*Juliana[1] (died 1652)	40 (1652)	2800 (1648 appraisal)
*Manuel Sacasaca[1]	46	2400
*Magdalena Angola[1]	45	2000
Juana[2]	17	2400
María[2]	13	2000
Juliana[2]	14	2400
Juan	18	3200
Juan Criollo[3]	21	3200
Antonio	13	2000
Diego Criollo[4]	14	2400
*Pedro Ysleño	42	2800
*Magdalena	32	2000
*Maria Malemba[5]	40	2800

Santa Lucía

Name	Age	Value (reales)
Miguel Cacheo	36	3200
*Antonio Carabalí	29	3200
*Lucía w/	30	2800
Nicolás Criollo	3	1600
Nicolás Catoto	25	3200
*Sebastián Congo	33	3200
*María Carabalí w/	30	2800
Germana Criolla	7	1600
Paula Criolla	3	1600
Andrés	40	2800

Name	Age	Value (reales)
Manuel Cacheo	32	2800
Juan Angola	40	2800
Catalina Carabalí w/	30	2800
hija Criolla	2	1040
Juan Criollo	4	1200
Manuel Carabalí	49	2000

Cepi

Name	Age	Value (reales)
*Cristobal Angola	55	1600
*María Angola	50	1200
*Manuel Congo	58	1600
Marta w/	40	2800
Manuel Criollo	16	2800
Dominga Criolla	13	2400
*Mauricio Criollo[6]	30	—
*Josefa Criolla	26	2800
*Francisco Cabaca Angola	56	2400
*Ana Angola w/	50	2400
Francisco Criollo	24	3200
Agustín Criollo	14	2800
*Salvador Angola	58	2000
*Ynés Angola	56	1600
Pedro Gayta Angola w/sons	60	1600
Mateo	18	3200
Hernando	14	2800
Antón Fajaro w/son	70	—
Salvador	15	3200
Andrés Angola w/son	60	—
Francisco	16	2800
Pedro Ynglés Angola	50	2800
Antón Cacuro Angola	50	2000
Pedro Embande	65	—
Juan Catoto Angola	46	2800
Pedro Algorta Angola	46	3200
Pedro Angola[7]	44	—
Nicolás Catoto Criollo	26	2800
Catalina	30	2800
Domingo Criollo	20	3200

Name	Age	Value (reales)
Catalina Criolla	13	2800
Juan Criollo	22	2800

Source: ARPC, Testamentarías, 1653–1655 CL.

Asterisk (*) = married.

[1]These three slaves have been identified (by name and age) on the Rodríguez Santos–Escovedo inventory made in 1631; see appendix A.

[2]These three slaves were resident with Germana, Antonia, and Francisca in the Concepción convent. Juliana's parents, Francisco Cabaca Angola and Ana Angola, lived at Santa Lucía.

[3]Juan's father, Pedro Gayta, lived at Santa Lucía.

[4]Diego Criollo was page to young Santiago de Liendo.

[5]María Malemba's husband, Antón Fajaro, and son, Salvador, resided at Santa Lucía.

[6]"Lame and blind."

[7]"Blind."

Appendix F

Liendo Wards: Estate Operating Costs and Personal Maintenance Expenditures, 1645–1657 (in reales unless noted)

	1645[a]	1646	1647	1648	1649	1650	1651	1652	Monthly Mean[f] 1645–1652 (in pesos)	1653[g]	1654	1655	1656	1657	Monthly Mean[h] 1653–1657 (in pesos)	Monthly Mean[i] 1645–1657 (in pesos)
Estate Costs	5,528	18,479	11,801	10,740	11,980	12,422	11,211	11,801	123.6	888	6,034	5,038	12,160	5,238	68.1	102.3
Santiago	44	1,793	2,209	2,366	2,753	3,901	4,274	2,591	28.7							
Francisca	24	480	579	513	517	612	340	778	5.5							
Germana	12	164	347	440	727	1,239[d]	908	1,172	7.2							
Antonia	9	100	226	308	355	238	407	208	2.6							
Juana	9	100	290	290	356	190	1,499[e]	—	3.9							
Children's Food[b]	900	3,650	3,650	3,650	3,650	3,650	3,108	2,924	36.2							
Domestic Slaves' Food[c]	630	2,555	2,555	2,555	2,555	2,555	2,555	2,555	26.6							
Children's Total	1,628	8,842	9,856	10,122	10,913	12,465	13,086	10,223	110.3	1,592	8,998	7,390	7,570	27,023[j]	121.7	114.9
Total Costs	7,148	19,321	21,657	20,862	22,893	24,887	24,297	22,024	234.3	2,480	15,032	12,428	19,730	32,351	189.8	217.2

Source: ARPC, Testamentarías, 1653–1655 CL

[a] October to December
[b] There was a daily allotment of two reales for each of the wards. This and many other expenditures were not distinguished by individuals during the tutela of Pedro de Liendo (1653–1657), and they have been aggregated in the Children's Total portion of the table for those years.
[c] There was a daily allotment of one real for each of seven domestic slaves from 1645 to 1652. Pedro de Liendo eliminated this expenditure during the period 1653–1657.
[d] Germana began her career as a nun in 1650.
[e] Juana died in 1651; the greater part of these expenditures are funeral costs.
[f] Eighty-seven months.
[g] May to December only; there may be missing data for 1653.
[h] Fifty-four months.
[i] One hundred and forty-one months.
[j] Costs of Santiago's assuming the office of alcalde of the Santa Hermandad, of Francisca's wedding, and of Germana's profession to the Immaculate Conception convent.

Appendix G

Slaves and Slave Dwellings, San Joseph Hacienda, 1728

Slaves		Dwellings	
Name	Age	Dimensions*	Material
Matías Tare	40	16 × 4.5	paja
Andrea Criolla	40		
Joseph	10		
Fabiana	9		
Raymundo	6		
Bacilio Criollo	24	10.5 × 4	paja
Lucía Criolla	20		
Manuel Luango	20	7 × 4	paja
María Josepha Criolla	24		
Gabriel Tare	28	10.5 × 4	gamelote
Isabel Criolla	20		
Bernardo Tare	40	12 × 4	cogollo
María Tare	30		
Joseph Tare	40	8 × 3.5	paja
Isabel Tare	30		
Antonio Tare	30	13 × 4	cogollo
Tomasa Tare	30		
Andrés Mina	40	10 × 4	paja
Antonia Tare	30		
Domingo	14		
María Francisca	7		
María	1		
Joseph Tare	38	11 × 4.5	paja
Gracia Cachea	40		
Gregorio Tare	35	12.5 × 5	gamelote
Lucrecia Luango	25		
Susana	2		
Luis Gregorio	1		
Bernardo Criollo	34	12 × 5	gamelote
Inés Tare	50		
Juan Esteven Criollo	34	10 × 3.5	paja
Josepha Tare	40		

Slaves		Dwellings	
Name	Age	Dimensions*	Material
Alejandro Tare	35	15 × 4.5	paja
Ana María Luango	40		
Luisa Tare (widow)	50	12.5 × 4	cogollo
María Criolla ("broken")	30		
Julian Criollo	28		
Lorenzo Mina	25	3 × 3.5	cogollo
Pedro Criollo (widower)	33	17 × 4	cogollo
Tomás	18		
Juan Francisco	7		
María	12		
Paula María	9		
Francisco Tare	26	11 × 4	paja
Pedro Tare	32	8 × 4	paja
Nicolás Tare	32	4 × 4.5	gamelote

Source: Testamentarías, 1735 P.
*Dimensions are in *varas*; one *vara* is equal to about .83 meters.

Appendix H

"Interesados vecinos, mercaderes y cosecheros" who signed protest memorial asking for royal clemency from the Guipuzcoana Company, 28 November 1744. AGI, Santo Domingo, leg. 787.

Key to Status Designation:
Asterisk (*) = identified elite; 1 = widow/widower in 1744; 2 = unmarried in 1744 and to never marry; 3 = married in 1744; 4 = possible widow/widower in 1744, but death date for spouse unknown, or possibly married in 1744, but marriage date unknown; 5 = to marry after 1744.

Name	Status	Birthdate	Deathdate
*Luisa Martínez de Villegas	1	1675	1756
*Gerónima de Ponte	1	1682	1756
*Isabel Clara de Herrera	1	1710	1789
*Francisca Ana Juana Tovar	1	(?)	(?)
*María Petronila Ibarra	1	1685	1749
*Antonia Ibarra	1	1707	1776
*María Lucía de Bolívar	1	1693	1748
*María Ana Mendoza	1	(?)	(?)
Francisco Zampiao	1		
*Isabela Antonia Blanco	1	1709	1775
*Juana de Bolívar	2	1692	1759
*Violante Blanco	2	1698	1765
*María Josefa Blanco	2	1713	1761
*Adriana Petronila Blanco	2	1716	(?)
*Beatriz Sebastiana Monasterios	2	1691	1764
*María Ana Monasterios	2	1692	1777
*Francisca Monasterios	2	1700	1774
Rosa Santoja			
Josefa Santoja			
*Sebastiana Istúriz	1	1689	(?)

Name	Status	Birthdate	Deathdate
*Juan Ignacio Mijares Solórzano	3	1705	1770
*el Marqués de Mijares (Francisco Nicolás Mijares Tovar)	3	1693	1764
*el Marqués de Toro (Francisco de Paula Toro Istúriz)	3	1713	1753
*Fernando Antonio Lovera	3	1697	1764
*Lorenzo Ponte y Villegas	3	1682	1760
*Ruy Fernandez de Fuenmayor y Tovar	2	1678	(?)
*el Doctor Gabriel de Ibarra	2	1708	1783
*Juan de Ibarra	2	1714	1771
*Joseph de Ibarra	4	1717	1785
*Andrés de Ibarra	3	1717	1770
*Diego de Ibarra	3	1711	1771
*Manuel Antonio Blanco de Villegas	1	1703	1776
*Juan Félix Blanco de Villegas	3	1706	1752
Alejandro Blanco de Villegas	3	1712	1754
*Miguel Blanco de Villegas	5	(?)	1774
*Miguel Blanco y Uribe	3	1699	1769
*Cornelio Blanco y Uribe	1	(?)	1760
Luisa Blanco y Uribe	(?)	(?)	(?)
*Pedro Vicente Blanco y Uribe	2	(?)	1755
*Antonio Alejandro Blanco y Uribe	3	1711	1761
*Pedro Blanco de Ponte	3	1701	1761
*Mateo Blanco de Ponte	5	1711	1780
*Alejandro Pío Blanco de Ponte	5	1714	1792
*Antonio José Pacheco y Mijares	3	(?)	(?)
*Francisco Eustachio Galindo y Tovar	3	1694	(?)
*Pedro de Tovar	2	1699	1769
*Francisco Xavier Mijares	4	1707	1776
*Pedro Mijares	3	1713	1788
*Juan Nicolás de Ponte y Solórzano	3	1713	1787
*Francisco de Ponte y Solórzano	2	1715	1775
*Lorenzo de Ponte y Solórzano	2	1717	1761
*Sebastian Basiliano de Ponte	3	1680	1749
*Bartolomé de Monasterios	3	1704	1750
*Manuel de Monasterios	3	1706	(?)
Andrés de Arteaga			
Miguel de Landaeta			
Antonio Gregorio Landaeta			
*Pedro Miguel de Herrera	1	1700	1769
*Juan Manuel de Herrera	4	1712	1767

Name	Status	Birthdate	Deathdate
*Agustín de Herrera	4	1715	1767
*Juan Primo Ascanio	3	1695	(?)
*Florencio de Plaza	5	1713	(?)
*Luis Arias Altamirano	3	1701	1752
*Fernando de Rada	3	1697	1769
*Joseph Juan de Rada	4	1690	1758
*Silvestre de Liendo	5	(?)	1750
Juan Manuel Alphonso			
Pedro Alvarado Serrano			
*Joseph de Monserrate	4	(?)	(?)
Tomás Garabán			
*Alonso Suarez Aguado	1	(?)	(?)
Francisco González			
*Joseph Miguel Gedler	4	(?)	1760
Domingo Bolián			
Luis Beltrán de Maza			
Joseph de Caraballo			
Juan Rodríguez Camejo			
Juan Antonio Moreno			
*Benito Muro	4	(?)	(?)
*Cayetano Gil Arratia	2	(?)	1766
*Manuel Fernández Feo	3	(?)	(?)
*Bartolomé Naranjo	5	(?)	(?)
*Antonio José Gedler	4	1700	1765
*Antonio Muñoz	4	(?)	(?)
*Joseph Francisco Aristeguieta	4	1711	1779
Diego Mañero			
*Josepha María Blanco	4	1683	1754
*Ana de Liendo	5	1716	1798
*Ana Mariá Plaza	2	1708	1755
*María Plaza	5	1711	1786
*Alejandro Blanco y Uribe	4	1697	1755
*el Conde de San Javier (Juan Jacinto Pacheco Mijares)	5	1720	(?)
*Pedro Francisco Gedler	3	1719	1788

Appendix I

Map 5 illustrates the spatial distribution of the residences of six groups of kin, based on the 1759 household census. Additional information about these selected kin groups and details of the composition of the individual households are provided here.

The six groups are further subdivided into sets; here a "set" of kin is defined as the parents, the children, the siblings, and the children of those siblings, of both husband and wife (or widower or widow) who are heads of the initial household. The patterns shown in Map 4 are centered on the principal households, and each principal household typically has two sets of kin, one for the male head and one for the female head (although the simple principal household of Group Three has but one head and thus one set of kin, while the complex principal household of Group Two has four heads of household and thus four sets). Other than providing a starting point for the analysis, the principal household designation has no particular significance among the several households in each set.

The six groups were chosen from the many that could have been presented for two reasons. First, these surnames appear often in the text (Liendo, Blanco, Tovar, Ponte, Mijares); and second, most of the heads of household in these groups were mature but not aged adults in 1759. By selecting groups of siblings who were at midrange in the life cycle in 1759, who were no longer children but not yet grandparents, a maximum distribution of siblings in distinct households was expected. Younger sets of siblings would find many of them still at home with their parents, and sets of older siblings would find many of them already dead in 1759. If an individual died before the 1759 census but was survived by a widow or widower (with or without children) who was alive in 1759, that individual's household is included here. The thirty-two distinct households that make up the residences of the six sets of kin (some households belonged to more than one set) are but a portion of the eighty-five elite households analyzed in chapter 7.

Birth, death, and marriage dates are given when they are known; children are designated by age when known or by the designation *párvulo* taken from the census. (In canonical terms párvulos had not reached age of reason, which is to say they were not yet ready to be admitted to communion and confession. Ideally this occurred at age seven, but priests probably judged individuals on a case basis.) The term *children* refers to the offspring of the household head or heads. Occasionally these "children" were adults in 1759.

In certain complex households the census taker observed what were described as distinct families (*"otra familia en esta casa"*). This distinction has been noted here.

GROUP ONE

Household 1.1: (RADA LIENDO–LIENDO BLANCO)
Cuadra: "Santíssimos Nombres de Jesús y María"
Location: 2nd blk. north of Cathedral
    Heads: RADA LIENDO, Fernando   b.1697 d.1769
               LIENDO BLANCO, Josefa Clara   b.1700 d.1785
    Marriage date: 1738. These spouses were first cousins.
    Children at home: 4, ages 15 to 26
    Other kin in home: PONTE LIENDO, Josefa. Sister of Fernando Rada's first wife
    Slaves: 15
    Libres: 0

Household 1.2: (LIENDO BLANCO, sister of head hshld. 1.1)
Cuadra: "Nuestra Señora de la Piedad"
Location: 1st blk. east, 2nd blk. north of Cathedral
    Heads: LIENDO BLANCO, Ana María   b.1716 d.1791
              PLAZA BLANCO, Florencio   b.1713 d. (?)
    Marriage date: 1749. These spouses were first cousins.
    Children at home: 6, for párvulos, others 12 and 13
    Other kin at home: none
    Slaves: 9
    Libres: 5

Household 1.3: (LIENDO BLANCO, sister of head hshld. 1.1)
Cuadra: "Los Corazones de Jesús y María"
Location: 2nd blk. west of Cathedral
   Heads: LIENDO BLANCO, Josefa Antonia   b.1706 d.1767
             GALINDO TOVAR, Domingo   b.1692 d.1757
Marriage date: unknown. Josefa Liendo was a widow in 1759.
   Children at home: 4, ages 16 to 26, all unmarried
   Other kin at home: none
   Slaves: 18
   Libres: 2

Household 1.4: (LIENDO BLANCO, brother of head hshld. 1.1)
Cuadra: "Santíssimo Nombres de Jesús y María"
Location: 2nd blk. north of Cathedral
   Heads: LIENDO BLANCO, Silvestre   b. (?)   d.1750
             PLAZA BLANCO, María Josefa   b.1711 d.1786
Marriage date: 1746. María Plaza was a widow in 1759; these spouses were first cousins.
   Children at home: 1, age unknown, unmarried in 1759
   Other kin at home: PLAZA BLANCO, Josefa. Sister of María Plaza
   Slaves: 11
   Libres: 0

Household 1.5: (LIENDO BLANCO, sister of head hshld. 1.1)
Cuadra: "Nuestra Señora de los Mártires" (Altagracia parish)
Location: 2nd blk. north, 1st blk. east of Cathedral
   HEADS: LIENDO BLANCO, Paula María   b. (?)   d.1759
              ARIAS BLANCO, Luis Felipe   b.1701 d.1752
Marriage date: 1738. Paula Liendo was a widow in 1759.
   Children at home: 6, none párvulo, all unmarried in 1759
   Other kin at home: Catalina Arias, sister of deceased Luis Arias; she would never marry (b.1702 d.1767).
   Slaves: 17
   Libres: 0

Group One notes: The male head of household 1.1, Fernando Rada Liendo, had no living siblings in 1759. One other Liendo Blanco sibling is known, Antonio Liendo, who died in 1761, but he was not located in the 1759 Caracas census.

GROUP TWO
Household 2.1: (PACHECO MIJARES–TOVAR BLANCO and
PACHECO MIJARES–MIJARES ASCANIO)
Cuadra: "Los Corazones de Jesús y María"
Location: 2nd blk. west of Cathedral
First family
    Heads: PACHECO MIJARES, Juan Jacinto   b. (?)   d. (?)
               (II Conde de San Javier)
               TOVAR BLANCO, Melchora Ana   b.1729 d.1764
    Marriage date: 1741
    Children at home: 2, both párvulos
Other kin at home: the Conde de San Javier lived with his wife and family in this house together with his sister and her husband and children who are given in the following family. Also listed as belonging to the Conde's family are 5 Pacheco nephews. They are the children of his brother Antonio Pacheco Mijares (uncertain whether he was alive in 1759) and María Toro Istúriz, who died in 1753.
    Others: agregado Félix Rojas, presbítero
    Slaves: 9
    Libras: 1
Second family
    Heads: PACHECO MIJARES, Juana   b. (?)   d. (?)
               MIJARES ASCANIO, Francisco   b.1707 d.1776
    Marriage date: 1737. These spouses were first cousins.
    Children at home: 7, ages 1 to 20, all unmarried
    Other kin at home: those described in the first family in this same household
    Slaves: 25
    Libres: 5

Household 2.2: (TOVAR BLANCO, sibling, and BLANCO
MARTINEZ, mother of head hshld. 2.1)
Cuadra: "Nuestra Señor del Buen Consejo"
Location: 3rd blk. west of Cathedral
First family
    Heads: TOVAR BLANCO, Martin   b.1726 d.1811
               (to become I Conde de Tovar in 1771)
               PONTE MIJARES, María Manuela   b. (?)   d.1814
    Marriage date: 1758

Second family
    Heads: BLANCO MARTINEZ, Catarina   b.1700 d.1767
               TOVAR GALINDO, José Manuel   b.1693 d.1759
    Marriage date: 1721. Catarina Blanco was a widow in 1759. She was the mother of the Tovar Blanco siblings in this household and in household 2.1
    Children at home: 1, Sebastiana Tovar Blanco, age 27
    Other kin at home: none
    Slaves: 29
    Libres: 2

Household 2.3: (MIJARES ASCANIO, brothers of head hshld. 2.1)
Cuadra: "Los Corazones de Jesús y María"
Location: 2nd blk. west of Cathedral
    Heads: MIJARES ASCANIO, Juan Ignacio   b.1705 d.1770
               TOVAR BLANCO, Luisa María   b.1702 d.1786
    Marriage date: 1738
    Children at home: 7, ages 2 to 19, all unmarried
    Other kin at home: Joseph Gabriel Mijares Ponte, half-brother to Mijares Ascanio siblings (b.1722 d.1792)
    Slaves: 15
    Libres: 2

Household 2.4: (MIJARES ASCANIO, brother of head hshld. 2.1)
Cuadra: "Dulce Nombre de María"
Location: 1st blk. south of Cathedral
    Heads: PONTE VILLEGAS, Lorenzo   b.1682 d.1759
               MIJARES TOVAR, Josefa Teresa   b.1691 d.1765
    Marriage date: 1711. This elderly couple were parents to the wife of Pedro José Mijares Ascanio, the Mijares sibling of interest here. Several other adult children of the aged couple lived with them in this household, some with their spouses and children, but these other Ponte Mijares siblings were not distinguished as separate families in the census. On the basis of its composition, reinforced by the census takers' sense that there was but one large family here, this is the only three-generation stem household in Caracas in 1759. This household is fully described in Group Six, household 6.3

Heads: PONTE MIJARES, Cecilia Teresa   b.1721 d.1805
       MIJARES ASCANIO, Pedro José   b.1713 d.1788
Marriage date: 1742. These spouses were first cousins.
Children at home: 8, ages 1 to 16, all unmarried
Other kin at home: parents/grandparents Ponte and Mijares, uncles and aunts Ponte Mijares, their spouses and children
Slaves: 34 (entire household)
Libres: 5
Indians: 2

Household 2.5: (MIJARES ASCANIO, sister of head hshld. 2.1)
Cuadra: "La Visitación de Nuestra Señora"
Location 1st blk. west, 2nd blk. north of Cathedral
Heads: MIJARES TOVAR, Francisco   b.1693 d.1764
       MIJARES ASCANIO, María   b.1719 d.1750
Marriage date: 1736. These spouses were first cousins; Francisco Mijares was a widower in 1759.
Children at home: 4, ages 9 to 19, all unmarried
Other kin at home: none
Others: agregado Alonso Pacheco, presbítero
Slaves: 19
Libres: 11

Household 2.6: (MIJARES ASCANIO, sister of head hshld. 2.1)
Cuadra: "Los Desposarios de Nuestro Señor"
Location: 2nd blk. west, 1st blk. north of Cathedral
Heads: MIJARES ASCANIO, Melchora   b.1712 d.1780
       PONTE MIJARES, Juan Antonio b.1713 d.1787
Marriage date: 1736. These spouses were first cousins.
Children at home: 2, Lorenzo Agustín and José Ignacio Ponte Mijares, adult sons in their twenties, exact ages unknown
Other kin at home: none
Slaves: 7
Libres: 5

Group Two notes: The center or principal source of this kindred in 1759 was the elderly couple who were heads of household 2.4. Lorenzo Ponte Villegas and Josefa Mijares Tovar were grandparents to Maria Ponte Mijares, the wife of Martin Tovar, in household

2.2, and they were the parents of the Ponte Mijares siblings in households 2.2 and 2.4. Without doubt Josefa Mijares was the matriarch of all those named Mijares in this group. The spouses who were first cousins (heads of households 2.1, 2.4, 2.5, and 2.6) were related to each other through her (as mother: the Ponte Mijares; and as aunt: the Pacheco Mijares, the Mijares Ascanio, and the Mijares Tovar). She was the aunt of both Francisco Nicolás Mijares Tovar, the third Marqués de Mijares, and Juan Jacinto Pacheco Mijares, the second Conde de San Javier. By 1760, she was, at age 69, the oldest living blood relative of all these people.

GROUP THREE

Household 3.1: (HERRERA MESONES)
Cuadra: "Nuestra Señora del Pilar de Zaragosa"
Location: same blk. south and 1st blk. east of Cathedral
    Head: HERRERA MESONES, Carlos b.1705   d.1761

Carlos Herrera was canon and treasurer of the Caracas cathedral. He lived in this house, most probably located on the same block, perhaps attached to the cathedral, with six of his sisters. These were all adult, unmarried women.

    Other kin at home:
        HERRERA MESONES, María Rosa b.1696   d.1764
        HERRERA MESONES, Juana Rosa b.1706   d.1770
        HERRERA MESONES, Nicolasa   b.1709   d.1788
        HERRERA MESONES, Francisca   b.1703   d.1768
        HERRERA MESONES, Manuela   b.1701   d.1779
        HERRERA MESONES, Isabel   b.1707   d.1768
Slaves: 31
Libres: 5

Household 3.2: (HERRERA MESONES, brother of head hshld. 3.1)
Cuadra: "Nuestra Señora de Belem"
Location: 1st blk. east, 1st blk. north of Cathedral
    Heads: HERRERA MESONES, Juan Manuel   b.1712 d.1767
              RADA SOTO, Ana María   b. (?)   d.1768
    Marriage date: 1743
    Children at home: 5, two párvulos, others to age 14

Other kin at home: none
Slaves: 13
Libres: 1

Household 3.3: (HERRERA MESONES, brother of head hshld. 3.1)
Cuadra: "Nuestra Señora de Atocha"
Location: 2nd blk. east, same north–south level as Cathedral
    Heads: HERRERA MESONES, Agustín   b.1715 d.1767
               SUAREZ BOLIVAR, Catalina   b. (?) d. (?)
    Marriage date: 1741
    Children at home: 6, three párvulos, others to age 13
    Other kin at home: none
    Slaves: 14
    Libres: 0

GROUP FOUR

Household 4.1: (BLANCO URIBE–BLANCO MARTINEZ)
Cuadra: "Santíssimos Nombres de Jesús y María"
Location: 2nd blk. north of Cathedral
    Heads: BLANCO URIBE, Miguel Ignacio   b.1699 d.1769
               BLANCO MARTINEZ, Francisca   b.1705 d.1770
    Marriage date: 1734
    Children at home: 6, ages uncertain. Four will marry in the 1760s.
    Other kin at home: none
    Slaves: 22
    Libres: 3

Household 4.2: (BLANCO URIBE, sisters of head hshld. 4.1)
Cuadra: "Nuestra Señora de la Luz"
Location: facing the plaza on its west side, opposite the Cathedral.

    The census taker organized this household into five "families," although four of them contained only single individuals (not counting slaves and libres) who were unmarried sisters. The fifth "family" was comprised of another widowed sister and her daughter. The census taker's division is followed here.

First family
　Head: BOLÍVAR URIBE, Juana María　　b.1692　d. (?)
This single woman was half-sister to Miguel Blanco Uribe, head of hshld. 4.1, and half-sister to the Blanco Uribe women in this household.
　Slaves: 4
　Libres: 0
Second family
　Head: BLANCO URIBE, Isabel Antonia　　b.1709　d.1775
　Slaves: 5
　Libres: 0
Third family
　Head: BLANCO URIBE, María Josefa　　b.1713　d.1761
　Slaves: 9
　Libres: 0
Fourth family
　Head: BLANCO URIBE, Adriana　　b.1716　d. (?)
　Slaves: 7
　Libres: 7
Fifth family
　Heads: BLANCO URIBE, Isabel　　b.1709　d.1775
　　　　　BLANCO VASQUEZ, Pedro　　b.1700　d.1750
　Marriage date: 1733. These spouses were first cousins; Isabel Blanco was a widow in 1759.
　Children at home: 1, Luisa Blanco Blanco, age unknown
　Slaves: 4
　Libres: 0

Household 4.3: (BLANCO URIBE, brother to head hshld. 4.1)
Cuadra: "Nuestra Señora del Carmen"
Location: 1st blk. north, 2nd blk. west of Cathedral
　Heads: BLANCO URIBE, Antonio　　b.1711　d.1761
　　　　　PONTE GALINDO, Maria　　b.1714　d.1789
　Marriage date: ?
　Children at home: 5, two párvulos, other ages unknown
　Other kin at home: no
　Slaves: 8
　Libres: 4

Household 4.4: (BLANCO URIBE, brother to head hshld. 4.1)
Cuadra: "Madre de Díos"
Location: 1st blk. north of Cathedral
   Heads: BLANCO URIBE, Cornelio   b. (?)   d.1760
             BLANCO PONTE, Francisca b. (?)   d.1769
   Marriage date: 1744. Cornelio Blanco's first wife died in 1739; some of his children by this first marriage lived in this household.
   Children at home: 5, one párvulo, others of uncertain age
   Other kin at home: none
   Slaves: 8
   Libres: 1

Household 4.5: (BLANCO URIBE, brother to head hshld. 4.1)
Cuadra: "Nuestra Señora del Olvido"
Location: 1st blk. south, 3rd blk. west of Cathedral
   Heads: BLANCO URIBE, Manuel   b.1702 d. (?)
             PONCE BARBOZA, María   b. (?)   d. (?)
   Marriage date: 1733. María Ponce was a widow in 1759.
   Children at home: 5, unmarried adult children of uncertain age
   Other kin at home/Others: four other "families" of single women (surnamed Barboza and Ponte but with no clear links to the principals here), each with her slaves, also lived in this household.
   Slaves: 18
   Libres: 3

Household 4.6: (BLANCO MARTÍNEZ, sister to head hshld. 4.1)
Cuadra: "Nuestra Señora del Buen Consejo"
Location: 3rd blk. west of Cathedral
   Heads: BLANCO MARTÍNEZ, Catarina   b.1700 d.1767
             TOVAR GALINDO, José Manuel   b.1693 d.1759
   Marriage date: 1721. Catarina Blanco was a widow in 1759.
   Children at home: 1, Sebastiana Tovar Blanco, age 27
   Other kin at home: none
   Slaves: 29
   Libres: 2

Household 4.7: (BLANCO MARTÍNEZ, sister to head hshld. 4.1)
Cuadra: "Madre de Diós"
Location: 1st blk. north of Cathedral

Heads: BLANCO MARTÍNEZ, Mariana   b.1711 d.1783
        MONASTERIOS BLANCO, Miguel   b.1706 d. (?)
Marriage date: 1729. These spouses were first cousins.
Children at home: 4, one párvulo, others of uncertain age
Other kin at home: 2 nieces of Mariana Blanco, the daughters of her deceased sister; 1 nephew of Miguel Monasterios, the son of his deceased brother
Slaves: 8
Libres: 6

Household 4.8: (BLANCO MARTÍNEZ, brothers/sister to head hshld. 4.1)
Cuadra: "Los Desposarios de Nuestro Señor"
Location: 2nd blk. west, 1st blk. north of Cathedral

There were three families in this household, all three headed by Blanco Martínez siblings, two of them widowers, the third a widow.

First family
Heads: BLANCO MARTÍNEZ, Cecilia   b.1709 d.1772
        MONASTERIOS BLANCO, Bartolomé b.1704 d.1750
Marriage date: 1728. These spouses were first cousins; Cecilia Blanco was a widow in 1759.
Children at home: 4, eldest aged 30, others of uncertain age
Other kin at home: none
Slaves: 8
Libres: 2

Second family
Heads: BLANCO MARTÍNEZ, Manuel   b.1703 d.1776
        MONASTERIOS BLANCO, María   b.1703 d.1740
Marriage date: 1723. These spouses were first cousins; Manuel Blanco was a widower in 1759.
Children at home: 5, of uncertain age
Slaves: 4
Libres: 4

Third family
Heads: BLANCO MARTÍNEZ, Miguel   b. (?)   d.1774
        PONTE MIJARES, Luisa María   b.1727   d.1756
Marriage date: 1750. Migurel Blanco was a widower in 1759.
Children at home: 3, two párvulos, other young child

Other kin at home: 4 nephews of Miguel Blanco, sons of his deceased brother
Slaves: 9
Libres: 4

GROUP FIVE

Household 5.1: (BLANCO PONTE–PLAZA BLANCO)
Cuadra: "Nuestra Señora del Milagro"
Location: 1st blk. north, 3rd blk. west
    Heads: BLANCO PONTE, Mateo Alejandro   b.1711 d.1780
              PLAZA BLANCO, Petronila   b.1725 d.1767
Marriage date: 1747. These spouses were first cousins.
Children at home: 8, four párvulos, others older
Other kin at home: none
Slaves: 10
Libres: 2

Household 5.2: (BLANCO PONTE, brother of head of hshld. 5.1)
Cuadra: "Nuestra Señora de Loreto"
Location: 1st blk. south, 1st blk. east of Cathedral
    Heads: BLANCO PONTE, Alejandro Pío   b.1714 d.1792
              BLANCO HERRERA, Rosa   b. (?)   d.1803
Marriage date: 1747. These spouses were first cousins.
Children at home: 5, four are párvulos
Other kin at home: none
Slaves: 8
Libres: 1

Household 5.3: (BLANCO PONTE, brother of head of hshld. 5.1)
Cuadra: "Nuestra Señora de la Pureza"
Location: 1st blk. north, 1st blk. east of Cathedral
    Heads: BLANCO PONTE, Pedro José   b.1701 d.1761
              PLAZA BLANCO, Juana   b.1716 d.1787
Marriage date: 1738. These spouses were first cousins.
Children at home: 6, two are párvulos, others of uncertain age
Other kin at home: none

Slaves: 14
Libres: 0

Household 5.4: (BLANCO PONTE, sisters of head of hshld. 5.1)
Cuadra: "Nuestra Señora de Guia"
Location: 1st blk. west, 1st blk. north of Cathedral
    Head: BLANCO PONTE, Josefa María   b.1716 d.1761
    Other kin at home (sister of Josefa Blanco Ponte):
        BLANCO PONTE, Isabel   b.1709 d.1776
Additonal kin at home: Diego Blanco Plaza, nephew to Josefa and Isabel Blanco Ponte, son of their brother, Pedro José Blanco Ponte, resident in hshld. 5.3.
Slaves: 18
Libres: 0

Household 5.5: (PLAZA BLANCO, brother of head of hshld. 5.1)
Cuadra: "Nuestra Señora de la Piedad"
Location: 1st blk. east and 2nd blk. north of Cathedral
    Heads: PLAZA BLANCO, Florencio José   b.1713 d. (?)
             LIENDO BLANCO, Ana María   b.1716 d.1798
Marriage date: 1749. These spouses were first cousins.
Children at home: 6, four párvulos, the others 13 and 14
Other kin at home: none
Slaves: 11
Libres: 5

Household 5.6: (PLAZA BLANCO, brother of head of hshld. 5.1)
Cuadra: "Santíssimos Nombres de Jesús y María"
Location: 2nd blk. north of Cathedral
    Head: PLAZA BLANCO, Manuel   b.1722 d.1791
Other kin at home: none
Other: 2 officers of royal batallion
Slaves: 3
Libres: 13

Household 5.7: (PLAZA BLANCO, sister of head of hshld. 5.1)
This household was already given in this group as household 5.3, part of the Blanco Ponte sibling set; it is given again here as part of the Plaza Blanco set.

Cuadra: "Nuestra Señora de la Pureza"
Location: 1st blk. north, 1st blk. east of Cathedral
    Heads: PLAZA BLANCO, Juana   b.1716 d.1787
               BLANCO PONTE, Pedro José   b.1701 d.1761
Marriage date: 1738. These spouses were first cousins.
Children at home: 6, two are párvulos, others of uncertain age
Other kin at home: none
Slaves: 14
Libres: 0

Household 5.8: (PLAZA BLANCO, brother of head of hshld. 5.1)
Cuadra: "Nuestra Señora de Monserrate" (Altagracia parish)
Location: 2nd blk. north, 1st blk. west of Cathedral
    The primary head of this household was the widowed mother of the wife of Mateo Plaza. The common division into several families was not made in this case, which suggests that in this household Mateo Plaza had secondary authority to his mother-in-law, in whose house he had come to live.
    Heads: ARIAS BLANCO, María Teresa   b.1699 d.1770
               BOLIVAR AGUIRRE, José   b.1693 d.1758
Marriage date: (?) María Arias was a widow in 1759.
Children at home: 7; 6 unmarried adults and Josefa Bolívar.
Other kin at home: BOLIVAR ARIAS, Josefa   b. (?)   d.1779
                           PLAZA BLANCO, Mateo   b.1720 d.1784
Marriage date: 1749
Children at home: 4, all párvulos
Slaves: 15 (entire household)
Libres: 3

GROUP SIX

Household 6.1: (PONTE MIJARES–MIJARES ASCANIO)
Cuadra: "Los Desposarios de Nuestro Señor"
Location: 2nd blk. west, 1st blk. north of Cathedral
    Heads: PONTE MIJARES, Juan Nicolás   b.1713 d.1787
               MIJARES ASCANIO, Melchora   b.1712 d.1780
Marriage date: 1736. These spouses were first cousins.
Children at home: 2 adult sons.
Other kin at home: none

Slaves: 7
Libres: 5

Household 6.2: (PONTE MIJARES, sister of head hshld. 6.1)
Cuadra: "Los Desposarios de Nuestro Señor"
Location: 2nd blk. west, 1st blk. north of Cathedral

There were three families in this household, all three headed by Blanco Martínez siblings, two of them widowers, the third a widow. Luisa María Ponte Mijares, deceased, had been the wife of Miguel Blanco Martínez. Only this family is given here; the entire household is described in Group Four, household 4.8.

    Heads: BLANCO MARTÍNEZ, Miguel   b. (?)   d.1774
               PONTE MIJARES, Luisa María   b.1727 d.1756

Marriage date: 1750. Miguel Blanco was a widower in 1759.
Children at home: 3, two párvulos, other young child
Other kin at home (in this family): 4 nephews of Miguel Blanco, sons of his deceased brother. Two other families in this household, headed by the siblings of Miguel Blanco, are given in Group Four, household 4.8.
Slaves: 9
Libres: 4

Household 6.3: (PONTE MIJARES, parents/siblings of head
                hshld. 6.1)
Cuadra: "Dulce Nombre de María"
Location: 1st blk. south of Cathedral
First family
    Heads: PONTE VILLEGAS, Lorenzo   b.1682 d.1759
               MIJARES TOVAR, Josefa Teresa   b.1691 d.1765

Marriage date: 1711. This elderly couple were the parents of Juan Nicolás Ponte, head of household 6.1. They lived here with all their remaining offspring, including both their single and married children and their grandchildren, as well as other kin. This was the only three-generation, stem household of Caracas elites in 1759. The married children were not identified as separate families, but the two (also elderly) sisters of Lorenzo Ponte Villegas who also lived here were considered to comprised a "family" of their own.

Children at home: 8; 6 single adults, 2 married with children of their own, as follows. These married children and their children were not identified as separate families in the 1759 census, nor were there any slaves or libres identified to them specifically:

    PONTE MIJARES, Antonio José   b.1723   d.1770
    BLANCO MONASTERIOS, Luisa b. (?)   d.1786
    Marriage date: 1751
    Children (grandchildren of heads of hshld.) at home: 2 párvulos.
    PONTE MIJARES, Cecilia Teresa   b.1721   d.1805
    MIJARES ASCANIO, Pedro José   b.1713   d.1788
    Marriage date: 1742. These spouses were first cousins.
    Children (grandchildren of heads of hshld.) at home: 8, ages 1 to 16, all unmarrried
    Other kin at home: 2 granddaughters (Blanco Ponte) of the heads of hshld. They were orphaned by the death of their mother (María Teresa Ponte Mijares) in 1757; their father (Alejandro Blanco Martínez) had died in 1754.
    Slaves: 34 (entire first family)
    Libres: 5

Second family
    Heads: PONTE MARTÍNEZ, Luisa Isabel   b.1681 d.1773
               PONTE MARTÍNEZ, María   b.1696 d.1763
    These women were sisters of head of hshld. Lorenzo Ponte. Luisa Ponte never married. María Ponte had married Lorenzo Sedeño in 1733, but was a widow without children by 1759.
    Slaves: 23
    Libres: 5

Household 6.4: (MIJARES ASCANIO, brothers of head hshld. 6.1)
Cuadra: "Los Corazones de Jesús y María"
Location: 2nd blk. west of Cathedral
    Heads: MIJARES ASCANIO, Juan Ignacio   b.1705 d.1770
               TOVAR BLANCO, Luisa María   b.1702 d.1786
    Marriage date: 1738
    Children at home: 7, ages 2 to 19, all unmarried
    Other kin at home: Joseph Gabriel Mijares Ponte, half-brother to Mijares Ascanio siblings (b.1722 d.1792)
    Slaves: 15
    Libres: 2

Household 6.5: (MIJARES ASCANIO, brother of head hshld. 6.1)
Cuadra: "Dulce Nombre de María"
Location: 1st blk. south of Cathedral

This household was described above in this group, hshld. 6.3, as part of the Ponte Mijares sibling set. It is repeated here because a Mijares Ascanio sibling also lived in it.

    Heads: PONTE VILLEGAS, Lorenzo   b.1682 d.1759
               MIJARES TOVAR, Josefa Teresa b.1691 d.1765

Marriage date: 1711. This elderly couple were parents to the wife of Pedro José Mijares Ascanio, the Mijares sibling of interest here.

    PONTE MIJARES, Cecilia Teresa b.1721   d.1805
    MIJARES ASCANIO, Pedro José b.1713   d.1788

Marriage date: 1742. These spouses were first cousins.

Children at home: 8, ages 1 to 16, all unmarried.

Other kin at home: parents/grandparents Ponte and Mijares, uncles and aunts Ponte Mijares, their spouses and children

Slaves: 34 (entire household)
Libres: 5
Indians: 2

Household 6.6: (MIJARES ASCANIO, sister of head hshld. 6.1)
Cuadra: "La Visitación de Nuestra Señora"
Location: 1st blk. west, 2nd blk. north of Cathedral

    Heads: MIJARES TOVAR, Francisco   b.1693 d.1764
               MIJARES ASCANIO, María   b.1719 d.1750

Marriage date: 1736. These spouses were first cousins; Francisco Mijares was a widower in 1759.

Children at home: 4, ages 9 to 19, all unmarried
Other kin at home: none
Others: agregado Alonso Pacheco, presbítero
Slaves: 19
Libres: 11

Household 6.7: (MIJARES ASCANIO, brother to head hshld. 6.1)
Cuadra: "Los Corazones de Jesús y María"
Location: 2nd blk. west of Cathedral

    Heads: PACHECO MIJARES, Juana   b. (?)   d. (?)
               MIJARES ASCANIO, Francisco b.1707 d.1776

Marriage date: 1737. These spouses were first cousins.

Children at home: 7, ages 1 to 20, all unmarried

Other kin at home: this is the second family in the household headed by the II Conde de San Javier. Juana Pacheco was the sister of the Conde. This household is fully described in Group Two, hshld. 2.2.

Slaves: 25

Libres: 5

Notes

INTRODUCTION

1. Vicente de Amezaga Aresti, *Hombres de la Compañía Guipuzcoana* (Caracas, 1963), 24–31.
2. Magnus Mörner, "Economic Factors and Stratification in Colonial Spanish America with Special Regard to Elites," *Hispanic American Historical Review* 63 (1983): 347.
3. The most recent summary of this literature is Fred Bronner, "Urban Society in Colonial Spanish America: Research Trends," *Latin American Research Review* 21 (1986). See especially pages 35–39.

1. COMMERCE AND CONFLICT: THE FIRST CARACAS ELITE

1. Hermano Nectario María, *Historia de la conquista y fundación de Caracas*, 2d ed. (Madrid, 1966). Juan de Pimentel, "Relación de Nuestra Señora de Caraballeda y Santiago de León (1578)," in Antonio Arellano Moreno, ed., *Relaciones geográficas de Venezuela* (Caracas, 1964), 118. The estimate of Indian population comes from the testimony of Francisco Infante and Garci González de Silva, 3 January 1589, in Archivo General de la Nación, Caracas (hereinafter cited AGN), *Encomiendas*, 5 vols. (Caracas, 1945–1958), 1: 230–232. Peter Boyd-Bowman, "Patterns of Spanish Emigration to the Indies, 1579–1600," *The Americas* 33 (July 1976): 78–95.
2. Domingo Ibarqüen y Vera, "Relación sobre El Dorado y sobre la expedición de Antonio de Berrio (1597)," in Arellano Moreno, ed., *Relaciones geográficas*, 247–257.
3. Those who participated in these ventures stood to share in the spoils; this is what kept the group together and it was contingent on the leader to execute effectively what a modern historian has called "the technique of hope" if he was to maintain order and his own authority. See Mario Góngora, *Studies in the Colonial History of Spanish America* (Cambridge, 1975), 3–5.
4. In Venezuela the New Laws restructuring of the encomienda, including the requirement that tribute be paid rather than labor service, was observed largely in the breach; Eduardo Arcila Farías, *El régimen de la encomienda en Venezuela*, 2d ed. (Caracas, 1966), chaps. 8 and 9. J. A. de Armas Chitty, *Caracas: Origen y trayectoria de una ciudad*, 2 vols. (Caracas, 1967), 1:78–79, 226, 2:135–136. San Sebastián de los Reyes was refounded on several occasions; Lucas Guillermo Castillo Lara, *Materiales para la historia provincial de Aragua* (Caracas, 1977), 268–269, 297–329.

5. Luis A. Sucre, *Gobernadores y capitanes generales de Venezuela*, 2d ed. (Caracas, 1964), 104–105.

6. "Relación de Santiago de León," Arellano Moreno, ed., *Relaciones geográficas*, 120. The accomplishments of these men are given in Archivo de la Academia Nacional de la Historia, Fundadores de Caracas, Méritos y Servicios, II, tomo XIX.

7. Pierre Chaunu, *Séville et l'Amérique: XVIe–XVIIe siècle* (Paris, 1977), 181–186, 296–297. C. H. Haring, *The Buccaneers in the West Indies in the XVII Century*, reprint ed. (Hamden, Conn., 1966), 16.

8. "Relación de Santiago de León," Arellano Moreno, ed., *Relaciones geográficas*, 121.

9. Late sixteenth-century grants of land and water rights, too numerous to be cited individually, can be traced in *Actas del Cabildo de Caracas*, 12 vols. (Caracas, 1943–1975) (hereinafter cited ACC), I, passim. The prominence of wheat mills on the Caracas landscape in the 1590s is reflected in their frequent use as reference points in grant petitions made to the cabildo. Also beginning in the 1590s the cabildo made various attempts to control certain aspects of the wheat trade: the quantity of flour that had to be gotten from a given quantity of grain, the price of bread, and occasional prohibitions on the export of wheat and flour from the city. The present-day depository for colonial notary records is the Archivo del Registro Principal de Caracas (cited here as ARPC). There are two small volumes of synopses of these records for the last years of the sixteenth century: Manuel Pinto C., *Los primeros vecinos de Caracas* (Caracas, 1966); and Agustín Millares Carlo, ed., *Protocolos del siglo XVI* (Caracas, 1966).

10. Haring, *Buccaneers*, 38–39.

11. Academia Nacional de la Historia, *Actas del cabildo eclesiástico de Caracas (1580–1770)*, 2 vols. (Caracas, 1965), 1:64, 78–79; ARPC, Escribanías, June 27 and July 13, 1595. The cabildo ordered all masons and carpenters to work exclusively on the church until it was completely rebuilt; ACC, 1:442 (May 11, 1596).

12. ARPC, Escribanías, June 9 and July 21, 1597.

13. ARPC, Escribanías, February 3, March 24, and September 15, 1599; July 15 and October 30, 1605. Baltasar García's land grant is in ACC, 1:259 (May 24, 1593); and his marriage to the widow Medina is given in Consejo Municipal del Distrito Federal, *El libro parroquial más antiguo de Caracas* (Caracas, 1968), 135.

14. AGN, Real Hacienda, legs. 3, 5, 6. The royal tax recorded in these volumes is the *almojarifazgo*, and Caracas vecinos enjoyed royal exemption from this tax for most of the first half of the seventeenth century. The original cédula granting this favor, dated April 16, 1608, was copied into the cabildo record in 1619; ACC, 4:127–128. The complete record begins in 1603 because an earlier exemption for vecinos lapsed in April of that year; AGN, Real Hacienda, leg. 3, fol. 460 (April 24, 1603).

15. The figure of six *arrobas* of wheat flour from every *fanega* of grain milled is based on the actual yield of the mill belonging to the heirs of Juan Rodríguez Santos; ARPC, Testamentarías, 1638 R, fols. 279–283.

16. In 1578 the climate in the Caracas Valley was described as having a "fresh and humid temperament and with much rain which generally begins in May and ends in December"; "Relación de Santiago de León," in

Arellano Moreno, ed., *Relaciones geográficas*, 117. Records kept at the Cagigal Observatory in Caracas during the course of the twentieth century show an average monthly rainfall of more than 100 millimeters during the months from June to October; Marco-Aurelio Vila, *Aspectos geográficos del Distrito Federal* (Caracas, 1967), 52–84.

17. Fernand Braudel, *The Mediterranean and the Mediterranean World in the Age of Philip II*, 2 vols. (New York, 1972), 1:588–590.

18. Andalusian wheat prices are from Earl J. Hamilton, *American Treasure and the Price Revolution in Spain, 1501–1650* (New York, 1934), 353–357, 376–381. Hamilton's prices are in *maravedís* per fanega of wheat in the grain. For Caracas the single price of four reales per arroba of wheat flour, the price used to calculate the *almojarifazgo* export tax, was used. The following equivalents were necessary to make the comparison: one fanega of grain was equal to six arrobas of wheat flour, and one real equaled thirty-four maravedís. Therefore, the 4-reales price of one arroba of flour was equal to 816 maravedís for one fanega of wheat in the grain ($4 \times 34 \times 6 = 816$). The years between 1580 and 1620 in which Caracas wheat was cheaper than Andalusian were: 1582, 1584, 1589, 1598, 1603, 1604, 1605, 1616, 1617, 1618, and 1619. Wheat exports from Seville are analyzed in Michele Moret, *Aspects de la Société Marchande de Seville au début de XVIIe siècle* (Paris, 1967), 78–79, 95–103. The interesting study by Carla Rahn Phillips, *Six Galleons for the King of Spain: Imperial Defense in the Early Seventeenth Century* (Johns Hopkins Press, 1986), gives a detailed assessment of the procedures and costs of outfitting the fleet. The rising cost of wheat, fivefold during the course of the sixteenth century, is considered (pp. 99–100), and Phillips notes that suppliers of the armada "frequently used local American products to supplement the standard rations" (p. 101). However, the case of Caracas wheat may be the exception to her contention that "In the Indies nearly everything supplied to the fleets cost more and was harder to procure" (ibid.).

19. AGN, Real Hacienda, leg. 3. ARPC, Escribanías, November 16, 1605.

20. Due to its earlier importance as a pearl fishery, and perhaps because of its location as the first landfall after the Atlantic crossing, during the first years of the seventeenth century the island of Margarita still served as a principal depository and center for Spanish merchandise which was reexported for sale all along the Tierra Firme coast. Enrique Otte, comp., *Cedularios de la monarquia española de Margarita, Nueva Andalucia y Caracas (1553–1604)*, 8 vols. (Caracas, 1959–1967), 1:xix–xlvi.

21. Carrasquer's name appears very frequently in the early records of the Caracas notaries. As befitting both his merchant occupation and his place in Caracas society, Carrasquer was the first officer (*castellano*) of the La Guaira fortress; Otte, *Cedularios*, I:xliii. Carrasquer as encomendero can be found in AGN, Encomiendas, I:73. See also Stephanie Blank, "Patrons, Clients, and Kin in Seventeenth-Century Caracas: A Methodological Essay in Spanish American Social History," *The Hispanic American Historical Review* 54 (May 1974): 274–275.

22. Frederick Pike, "Aspects of Cabildo Economic Regulations in Spanish America Under the Hapsburgs," *Inter-American Economic Affairs* 13 (1960): 83.

23. Blank, "Patrons, Clients, and Kin," 260–83. Blank's consensus view is most clearly expressed in her "Societal Integration and Social Stability in a Colonial Spanish American City, Caracas 1595–1627" (Ph.D. Diss., University of Wisconsin, 1971).

24. Sucre, *Gobernadores*, 115–118.

25. ACC, 1:169–171 (October 8, 1591); 1:191 (May 25, 1592); 1:209–211 (September 4, 1593); 1:221 (June 28, 1593); 1:239 (March 30, 1593).

26. Riberos's *sitio de molino* was located near where the Anauco emptied into the Guaire, ACC, 1:374 (June 13, 1594); Lázaro Vásquez's 1597 request for a *toma de agua* was from the Guaire proper, ACC, 1:392 (May 22, 1597). It is possible that the technical problems of irrigating and operating mills on the Guaire—which has as it passes through Caracas only a slight vertical drop, low banks, and therefore a broad flood plain in colonial times—made it unsatisfactory for wheat agriculture and milling. The river typically carries from two to three times more water during the heavy-rain months than it does during the dry months; Marco-Aurelio Vila, *Aspectos geográficos*, 94.

27. ACC, 1:374 (June 13, 1594). The cabildo granted petitions for eleven mill sites during the 1590s, however only four are referred to in the *Actas* as actually in place and functioning (those that were certainly built are marked by an asterisk in the following list; dates refer to the first reference in the source). Anauco: Juan de Villegas Maldonado (September 14, 1592); Juan de Riberos (June 13, 1594); Chacao: *Sebastián Díaz (May 24, 1593); Francisco Olalla (May 24, 1593); Jácome Fantón (May 24, 1593); Diego de Xexas (May 24, 1593); Garci González de Silva (May 24, 1593); Catuche: *Esteban Marmolejo (August 2, 1599); undetermined site: *Alonso Andrea (November 27, 1592); Juan de Guevara (June 6, 1593); *Francisco Sánchez de Córdova (October 24, 1590).

28. ACC, 1:480 (January 8, 1598).

29. The provision which allowed millers one almud for every fanega of wheat that they ground is in ACC, 3:70–71 (January 29, 1607); that an almud was the eighth part of a fanega comes from Hamilton, *American Treasure*, 192.

30. Blank, "Patrons, Clients, and Kin," 267.

31. ACC, 1:298 (November 26, 1593). This history, written by a "poet-soldier" named Ulloa, has been lost.

32. ACC, 1:379–380 (June 15, 1594); 1:383–384 (July 4, 1594) for *ejido*. Figueredo is in ACC, 1:160 (December 3, 1590); 1:380 (June 14, 1594); 2:311–312 (June 14, 1594); 2:313 (September 1, 1594). The first reference to González de Silva's petition for the same land is ACC, 1:511–512 (August 2, 1599). Figueredo's *composición* payment is recorded in AGN, Real Hacienda, leg. 3, fol. 6.

33. González de Silva appears as *padrino* at Figueredo's wedding in February 1759; Consejo Municipal, *El libro más antiguo*, 167. Figueredo's *quinto* payment is in AGN, Real Hacienda, leg. 3, fol. 16; his statement about his respect for González de Silva is in ACC, 2:327–328 (January 24, 1601).

34. ACC, 2:320–329 (January 24 and 29, 1601). Paula and Clara Guevara Díaz de Rojas would marry Baltasar and Gaspar González de Silva Rojas in the 1620s; Carlos Iturriza Guillén, *Algunas familias caraqueñas*, 2 vols. (Caracas, 1967), 1:325–326.

35. ACC, 2:325 (January 29, 1601).
36. ACC, 2:336-339 (April 17, 1608).
37. *Recopilación de Leyes de las Indias*, libro iv, tit. xii, ley xiv, cites a royal cédula of November 1, 1591, which required that land and water not held with adequate title was to revert to the crown. Governors and viceroys could ask to see titles at any time, and they could declare invalid ones null and void. Libro iv, tit. xii, ley xx, cites a cédula dated January 10, 1589, which allowed viceroys and governors to revoke grants made by cabildos if title had not been confirmed by the crown, always after the grant holder had been given opportunity to pay the *composición* fee.
38. ACC, 2:286-290 (July 29, 1609).
39. ACC, 1:183 (September 14, 1592); 3:97-98 (June 28, 1607); 3:163 (June 9, 1609); 3:234-236 (April 9, 1610); 3:273 (March 21, 1611); 4:45 (June 6, 1619).
40. Tulio Febres Cordero, *Archivo de historia y variedades*, 2 vols. (Caracas, 1930), 1:191-194. In 1612 the commerce between San Antonio de Gibraltar on the south side of Lake Maracaibo and the Andean town of Mérida was so extensive that the cabildo of Mérida proposed the establishment of a customs house and warehouses at Gibraltar to protect their wheat shipments; ibid., 1:97.
41. Caracas was at the peak of its wheat boom in 1606 when Maracaibo vecinos sent for help to Governor Sánchez de Alquiza, who had passed through Maracaibo on his arrival in Venezuela that same year and knew first hand of the war between Quiriquires and Motilones and the Maracaiberos. At first Sánchez de Alquiza refused, ordering instead that the lake town's encomenderos had to put down the uprising within four months or lose their grants. A change of heart in 1608 sent Juan Pacheco Maldonado and fifty men, gathered from the Andean town of Trujillo and from Coro, to the succor of Maracaibo. AGI, Santo Domingo, leg. 208.
42. F. Braudel and F. Spooner, "Prices in Europe from 1450 to 1750," chap. 7 in E. E. Rich and C. H. Wilson, eds., *The Cambridge Economic History of Europe* (Cambridge, 1967), 4:471, 477, 484-485.
43. AGI, Contaduria, leg. 1613.
44. ACC, 2:23-233 (December 6, 1605). Eduardo Arcila Farías, *Economía colonial de Venezuela*, 2d ed., 2 vols. (Caracas, 1973), 1:128-129.
45. Sucre, *Gobernadores*, 98-107.
46. Tomás Polanco Martínez, *Esbozo sobre historia económica venezolana* (Madrid, 1960), 109-115. Eduardo Arcila Farías, *Economía colonial de Venezuela* (Mexico, 1946), 289-292.
47. José de Viera y Clavijo, *Noticias de la historia general de las Islas Canarias*, 5 vols. (Madrid, 1772-1783), 4:259.
48. See n. 14 above.
49. AGN, Real Hacienda, legs. 3, 5, 6. For vecino status of shippers, see: Consejo Municipal, *El libro más antiguo*; Carlos Iturriza Guillén, ed., *Matrimonios y velaciones de españoles y criollos blancos celebrados en la catedral de Caracas desde 1615 hasta 1831* (Caracas: Instituto Venezolano de Genealogía, 1974); "Relación de los extrangeros que residen en la ciudad de Santiago de León (1607)," AGI, Santo Domingo, leg. 193; road tax list, ACC, 2:96-99, 118-119.
50. The foreign vecino share of tobacco exports for the period 1604-

1607 was: 1604: 0 of 122 arrobas (0%); 1605: 135 of 1970 arrobas (6.8%); 1606: 995 of 5583 arrobas (17.8%); 1607: 250 of 1362 arrobas (18.3%).

51. Carlos Iturriza Guillén, *Algunas familias valencianas* (Caracas, 1955), 100–104 (Juan de Guevara); Carrasquer, Guevara, and Vásquez de Escovedo were *concuñados*, brothers-in-law by marriage (to the sisters Díaz de Rojas), Carlos Iturriza Guillén, *Familias caraqueñas*, 1:243–249. Baptisms of the Rodríguez Jaramillo and Villanueva children are in Consejo Municipal, *El libro más antiguo*, 17 and 32. Diego de Villanueva was royal treasurer and author of an important survey of the Caracas region, "Relación de Diego de Villaneuva y Gibaja, (1607)," given in Arellano Moreno, ed., *Relaciones geográficas*, 287–301. His marriage to young Catalina Mejía is in Iturriza Guillén, ed., *Matrimonios y velaciones*, 35. The Portuguese traders Caravajal and Diaz León are listed in AGI, Santo Domingo, leg. 193, "Relación de los estrangeros . . . ." Juan de Aguirre can be found in ARPC, Escribanías, August 15, 1605. Alonso Rodríguez Santos and his descendents are in Iturriza Guillén, *Familias caraqueñas*, 2:778–787.

52. ACC, 2:255 (June 26, 1605).

53. Sucre, *Gobernadores*, 106–107; Consejo Municipal, *El libro más antiguo*, passim.

2. CACAO IN THE SEVENTEENTH CENTURY: THE FIRST BOOM

1. An earlier version of this chapter was published as "Encomienda, African Slavery, and Agriculture in Seventeenth-Century Caracas," *Hispanic American Historical Review* 61 (November 1981): 609–635. "Relación de Diego de Villanueva y Gibaja (1607)," in Antonio Arellano Moreno, ed., *Relaciones geográficas de Venezuela* (Caracas, 1964), 287–301. Few Caracas residents received goods on consignment from merchants in Seville. For a list, see AGN, Real Hacienda, leg. 11, fols. 23–25. The illegal entry of slaves is discussed at length in Miguel Acosta Saignes, *Vida de los esclavos negros en Venezuela* (Caracas, 1967), chap. 3. Examples of slave ships allegedly blown off course on their way from Angola to the Canary Islands can be found in AGN, Real Hacienda, leg. 10, September 22, 1613, and June 25, 1618.

2. "Relación de Villanueva," in Arellano Moreno, ed., *Relaciones geográficas*, 280. Thirty leagues was Villanueva's statement of the distance from Caracas to San Sebastián; however, the San Sebastián site was changed five times during the seventeenth century, according to Lucas Guillermo Castillo Lara, *Materiales para la historia provincial de Aragua* (Caracas, 1977), 273–278. The Spanish league used in Caracas was most likely the *legua común* of 5.57 kilometers, judging from the measure of 24 leagues given in Villanueva's report as the distance from Caracas to the stable settlement of Nueva Valencia, a distance of approximately 125 kilometers. Thus the San Sebastián referred to by Villanueva was located about 160 or 170 kilometers south of Caracas. See Roland Chardon, "The Elusive Spanish League: A Problem of Measurement in Sixteenth-Century New Spain," *Hispanic American Historical Review* 60 (May 1980): 294–302.

3. ARPC, Testamentarías, 1653–1655 CL; AGN, Real Hacienda, leg. 14, July 29, 1628. The Ibarra–Ovalle dispute is in Archivo Arquidiocesano, Caracas (hereinafter cited AA), Episcopales, Obispo Gonzalo de Angulo.

Venezuelan historian Eduardo Arcila Fariás suggested that cacao grown on the coast originated in the Andes because cultivation of the plant was recorded in the mountain town of Mérida (Venezuela) in 1579; Eduardo Arcila Fariás, *Economia colonial de Venezuela* (Mexico City, 1946), 88. The designation *árboles de Trujillo* may refer to transplanted Andean cacao, but these trees appeared in the Caracas region after the initial boom was well underway.

4. Murdo J. MacLeod, *Spanish Central America* 117, 241, 378.

5. Arcila Farías first published his data on Caracas commerce in 1946 in *Economía colonial*, 96–101. He made no clear reference to the source of his information, but evidently he used the series entitled *Libro común y general de la tesorería*, AGN, Real Hacienda. The tax record in these volumes is the *almojarifazgo*, and therein lies a problem: Caracas vecinos, who shipped most of the region's cacao, enjoyed royal exemption from this duty during most of the first half of the seventeenth century. The original cédula granting this favor, dated April 16, 1608, was copied into the cabildo record in 1619; ACC, 4:127–128. Arcila Farías was aware of this exemption (*Economía colonial*, 89, 463), but when he compiled his statistics on commerce, he ignored the fact that his source did not include the greater part of all cacao shipped, that which belonged to Caracas vecinos. Due to this error, Arcila Farías's often-cited data give the impression that cacao cultivation and trade developed gradually and steadily over the course of the seventeenth century. In fact, exports were more considerable during the thirty years before 1650 than during the thirty years thereafter. The same flawed data are given in Eduardo Arcila Farías, *Comercio entre Venezuela y México en los siglos xvii y xviii* (Mexico City, 1950), 71–73.

6. The most thorough account of Portuguese Jews who traded Venezuelan cacao in New Spain is by Stanley Mark Hordes, "The Crypto-Jewish Community of New Spain, 1620-1649: A Collective Biography" (Ph.D. Diss., Tulane University, 1980), esp. 81–84, 92, 107–109, 131–132. Also see J. I. Israel, *Race, Class, and Politics in Colonial Mexico, 1610–1670* (Oxford, 1975), 124–130.

7. In 1638 a Portuguese agent in Angola reported that slave traders were packing ships with 700 and 800 Africans rather than the customary 400, with the result that "at sea it causes the death of many hundreds of them because of the excessive crowding and lack of water." Quoted in Herbert S. Klein, *The Middle Passsage: Comparative Studies in the Atlantic Slave Trade* (Princeton, 1978), 200, n. 47. In these circumstances, Caracas's proximity to Africa and its situation as the first significant port after the Atlantic crossing where slave cargoes might be absorbed on a regular basis made it a welcome sighting for ships' captains and crews, and, of course, for the slaves as well. The hypothesis that slaves were used as a medium of exchange to acquire readily sold, highly profitable cacao, and that they were purchased in Caracas by individuals who had only limited immediate labor needs (many were encomenderos), but who needed a market for their cacao beans, supports the argument of Brazilian historian Fernando Novais, who would have it that the slave trade created African slavery in the New World, and not the reverse. Fernando Novais, *Estrutura e Dinâmica do Antigo Sistema Colonial (Séculos XVI–XVIII)*, Caderno CEBRAP, no. 17 (São Paulo, 1974).

8. Eduardo Arcila Farías, *El régimen de la encomienda en Venezuela* (Seville, 1957), chaps. 8, 9.
9. Sucre, *Gobernadores*, 115–118.
10. The ca. 1635 document is in AGN, Fundación de Trujillo, leg. 10, fols. 335–346. The sources listed in n. 50 below were used to fix a date for this document. It was published, dated tentatively but erroneously as sixteenth century, by Guillermo Morón, *Historia de Venzuela*, 5 vols. (Caracas, 1971), 4:631–638. In 1609 the local definition of Indian tributary was established as all men between the ages of twelve and sixty and all women between the ages of ten and sixty inclusive; "Ordenanza de encomiendas de Sancho de Alquiza y de fray Antonio de Alcega de 30 de noviembre de 1609," published in Arcila Farías, *El régimen*, 342–351.
11. AGN, Real Hacienda, leg. 12, fols. 166–167.
12. Cornelius Osgood, *Excavations at Tocorón, Venezuela* (New Haven, Conn., 1943), 49. For the literature on pre-Hispanic Venezuelan culture and civilization, see Mario Sanoja and Iraida Vargas, *Antiguas formaciones y modos de producción venezolanos* (Caracas,, 1974). Climatic information is from J. Sánchez C. and J. García B., "Regiones meso-climáticas en el centro y oriente de Venezuela," *Agronomía Tropical* (Caracas), 18 (October 1968): 429–439. A basic source for identifying Venezuelan place names is the *Gacetilla de nombres geográficos* (Caracas, 1974); Marco-Aurelio Vila, *Antecedentes coloniales de centros poblados de Venezuela* (Caracas, 1978), is also helpful.
13. The trade between Caracas and San Sebastián was too slight in 1609 to interest Hispanic mule-skinners, and an exception to the general prohibition of Indian teamsters was made by Alquiza and Alcega in their ordenanza of that year. So that San Sebastián encomenderos would not keep these drivers at work nearer the coast, the ordenanza required that Indian muleteers return from Caracas within fifteen days; Arcila Farías, *El régimen*, 347. At least until midcentury there was no permanent road between Caracas and San Sebastián. The cattle ranchers of the district offered encomendero Luis de Castro 1000 pesos to open a trail from Paracotos to the Tuy River, midway between the towns; ARPC, Escribanías, April 22, 1649. Evidence of Indian slavery is in ACC, Episcopales, Obispo Mauro de Tovar.
14. Travel in the Aragua Valley is described in Mariano Martí, *Documentos relativos a su visita pastoral de la diócesis de Caracas, 1771–1784*, 7 vols. (Caracas, 1969), 2:286–429. Shipping costs in 1841 are compared in John V. Lombardi, *The Decline and Abolition of Negro Slavery in Venezuela, 1820–1854* (Westport, Conn., 1971), 116, n. 27.
15. ACC, 6:147 (October 9, 1626).
16. MacLeod, *Spanish Central America*, 117. In Yucatan the average encomienda income fell from 1390 pesos in 1607 to 659 pesos in 1666; Manuela Cristina García Bernal, *Yucatán: Población y encomienda bajo los Austrias* (Seville, 1972), 418–419.
17. The actual meaning in the Caracas context of this designation of gentility is not considered here. That the title held significance, although usage varied with time and place, is argued by James Lockhart, *The Men of Cajamarca: A Social and Biographical Study of the First Conquerers of Peru* (Austin, 1972), 31–33, 111, 208.
18. Ovalle's will is in ARPC, Testamentarías, 1650–1653 *sin letra*. The Blanco Ponte family is traced in Iturriza Guillén, *Familias caraqueñas*, 1:161–

180. The first reference to the Blanco Ponte family in the Caracas documentation is ACC, leg. 4, fol. 310 (September 9, 1619). Trade between the Canaries and the Indies is explored in detail in Huguette and Pierre Chaunu, *Séville et l'Atlantique (1504–1650)*, 8 vols. (Paris, 1955–1958), vol. 8, pt. 1, 424–430.

19. Pedro de Liendo's will is in Universidad Central de Venezuela, *La obra pía de Chuao, 1568–1825* (Caracas, 1968), 190–194. The Liendos and don José Rengifo Pimentel are also included in Iturriza Guillén's genealogical study, *Familias caraqueñas*, 2:451–452, 726. Multiple holdings of encomiendas were not unusual in seventeenth-century Caracas; Arcila Farías, *El régimen*, 170–172.

20. ARPC, Testamentarias, 1650–1653 *sin letra;* Ovalle's wife's dowry, 12,565 pesos of 10 reales, is in ARPC, Escribanías, February 21, 1602. His brother Antonio was corregidor in Santo Domingo; ARPC, Escribanías, November 12, 1637. In the absence of other heirs, Ovalle's nephew Juan inherited the valuable Choroní estate, much to the disgust of his wife's Caracas family. Ovalle heads the list of foreigners in "Relación de los estrangeros (April 12, 1607)," Archivo General de Indias, Seville (hereinafter cited AGI), Santo Domingo, leg. 193.

21. AA, Episcopales, Obispo Gonzalo de Angulo.

22. His donation of 1000 reales to aid the expedition against the Indian rebels in Nirgua, at a time when few benefits were to be had from such military activity, could not have been overlooked by his Spanish peers, whose contributions were 10, 25, or 40 reales; ACC, 5:389.

23. ARPC, Testamentarías, 1650–1653 *sin letra*.

24. Antonio de Herrera's *Historia* was a common item in colonial Venezuelan libraries; see Ildefonso Leal, *Libros y bibliotecas en Venezuela colonial*, 2 vols. (Caracas, 1978), 1:cix–cx. Ovalle's small collection does not appear in Leal's extensive inventory.

25. ARPC, Testamentarías, 1650–1653 *sin letra*.

26. No peso value was assigned to the slaves on the Ovalle estate in the inventory of 1653, but the average value of slaves recorded in other inventories taken at about the same time was 250 pesos or more; ARPC, Testamentarías, 1648 RU; 1653–1655 CL.

27. *La obra pía de Chuao*, 191–194.

28. Total sale was 7693 pesos; ARPC, Escribanías, September 21 and 24, 1640.

29. The genealogies of these women's families are traced in Iturriza Guillén, *Familias caraqueñas*. The 1000 pesos were loaned by the Rodríguez Santos family, wheat farmers and merchants; ARPC, Testamentarías, 1638 R, fols. 457–459.

30. Alonso Rodríguez Santos's will is in ARPC, Testamentarías, 1648 RU. Francisco Castillo de Consuegra's will is in ARPC, Testamentarías, 1614–1634 CEFMSU.

31. Baltasar de Escovedo, ARPC, Testamentarías, 1634–1637 MDPACVG; Agustín Pereira, ARPC, Testamentarías, 1656–1657 *sin letra;* ARPC, Escribanías, January 21 and December 23, 1630, May 3 and October 3, 1634.

32. Chap. 3 contains a detailed analysis of the Liendo estate; see table 13 there which includes harvest and price data.

33. ARPC, Escribanías, January 15, 1630; Testamentarías, 1653-1655 CL. The Liendo slaves, with ages and their inventoried peso values, are listed in Appendix E.

34. ARPC, Testamentarías, 1656-1657 *sin letra*, will of Elvira de Campos, states that 1800 fanegas of cacao worth an estimated 50,000 pesos were harvested from the 22,000-tree coastal hacienda of Juan Navarro during an unspecified number of years before 1637.

35. Ibid. The Navarro groves were completely destroyed by the *alhorra*. In 1684 a Caracas escribano wrote: "It should be noted that in the year 1635 there began the *alhorra* in the *arboledas de cacao* that existed then in the valleys of the *costa de la mar arriva y abajo* and others of the *tierra adentro* and because many haciendas were lost it was necessary for some vecinos to plant again, and [although] the said *alhorra* lasted ten years more or less, it still continues [to afflict] the *árboles de la tierra*." AGI, Contaduria, leg. 1613.

36. The best description of the earthquake is Bishop Mauro de Tovar to the king, August 14, 1641, AGI, Santo Domingo, leg. 218. The bishop's colorful career is described in Andrés F. Ponte, *Fray Mauro de Tovar* (Caracas, 1945), and in Manuel Guillermo Díaz, *El agresivo obispado caraqueño de don Fray Mauro de Tovar* (Caracas, 1956).

37. MacLeod, *Spanish Central America*, 251.

38. Ibid., 242-244.

39. Archivo del Consejo Municipal del Distrito Federal, Caracas (hereinafter cited as ACM), Actas del cabildo, Originales, 1669-1672, August 6, 1670.

40. MacLeod, *Spanish Central America*, 280-287.

41. Several millions of pesos were confiscated by the inquisitors according to Hordes, "The Crypto-Jewish Community," 153.

42. ARPC, Testamentarías, 1653-1655 CL.

43. ARPC, Escribanías, Tomás de Ponte, August 5, 1653, fols. 110-116. Occasionally the slave trade itself depended on Mexican credit: Almeyda sold an additional nine slaves to don Manuel Felipe Tovar, knight of the Order of Santiago, for 2790 pesos, 2400 pesos of which were to be paid him in Mexico by Tovar's agent, Luis Pérez de Castro, vecino and alguacil of Veracruz. Escribanías, Juan López Villanueva, June 13 and July 14, 1653, fols. 68-70.

44. Lucas Guillermo Castillo Lara, *Las acciones militares del gobernador Ruy Fernández de Fuenmayor (1637-1644)* (Caracas, 1978), 35, 52-58.

45. ACM, Actas del cabildo, Originales, 1669-1672, May 21, June 20, 1671. If the *mal 'olanda* were the same disease later described as the *mal de Loanda*, then it probably meant scurvy, an infirmity associated with overloading and undersupplying the slave ships. See Joseph C. Miller, "Mortality in the Atlantic Slave Trade: Statistical Evidence on Causality," *The Journal of Interdisciplinary History* 11 (Winter 1981): 412-413.

46. MacLeod, *Spanish Central America*, 363.

47. New appointments to the cabildo are in ACM, Actas del Cabildo, Originales, 1673-1676, February 6, May 16, 1675.

48. The construction of the new seminary is in ACM, Actas del cabildo, Originales, 1673-1676, October 25, 1673; the jail is mentioned on September 2, 1674; and the fort was discussed in the sessions of November 16, 27, and December 1, 1673.

49. This document is in AGI, Contaduría, leg. 1613; it was published in

Revista de Historia (Caracas), 28 (August 1970); 63–81. The effort was made to auction the collection of the alcabala on two occasions, September 25, 1673, and again on June 5, 1675, but no one was willing to bid. ACM, Actas del cabildo, Originales, 1673–1676.

50. Only four of the thirty-eight encomenderos who held encomiendas with an annual *renta* of 1000 pesos or more have not been identified by place of birth and with a descending kindred network. The genealogical studies used are those by Carlos Iturriza Guillén, *Algunas familias caraqueñas*, already cited, and *Algunas familias valencianas* (Caracas, 1955). José Antonio de Sangroniz y Castro, *Familias coloniales de Venezuela* (Caracas, 1943) is serviceable, but lacks the detail and completeness of Iturriza Guillén's work. The marriage registry for the cathedral parish has been published by the Instituto Venezolano de Genealogía, *Matrimonios y velaciones de españoles y criollos blancos celebrados en la catedral de Caracas desde 1615 hasta 1831* (Caracas, 1974).

51. An idea of the size of the slave labor force comes from an estimate of 16,000 slaves in the Caracas region made by Bishop González de Acuña in 1674; Bishop Antonio González de Acuña to the king, June 15, 1675, in Guillermo Figuera, ed., *Documentos para la historia de la iglesia colonial en Venezuela*, 2 vols. (Caracas, 1965, 1967), 2:101–104.

52. Leopoldo de la Rosa, "La emigración canaria a Venezuela en los siglos xvii y xviii," *Anuario de Estudios Atlánticos* (Tenerife), 20 (1976): 617–631.

53. The concentration of canarios in the Candelaria parish is revealed in the "Matrículas de las parroquias de Caracas y demás pueblos de su diócesis, 1759," a manuscript census located in the Biblioteca Nacional, Caracas.

54. Castillo Lara, *Materiales para la historia de Aragua*, 240–244.

55. Guillermo Figuera, ed., *Documentos para la historia de la iglesia*, 2:119–120.

56. The 1690 encomienda census is in AGI, Santo Domingo, leg. 197-B. A copy is in the Archivo de la Academia Nacional de la Historia, Caracas (hereinafter cited AANH), Traslados, Sección Caracas, vol. 138.

57. All encomienda Indians, whether defined as tributaries or not, were counted in 1690.

58. Classified "zambos" by the *Ynforme* compilers, these children of Indian and African parentage were considered Indians for tax purposes.

59. There were virtually no Indians remaining on the coast by 1719. AANH, Misiones de Capuchinos, Trinidad, Guayana y los Llanos de Venezuela, leg. 2, no. 36, fol. 81.

60. ARPC, Civiles, 1730.

61. Mario Góngora, "Urban Social Stratification in Colonial Chile," *The Hispanic American Historical Review* 55 (August 1975): 430–431.

62. Peter J. Bakewell, *Silver Mining and Society in Colonial Mexico: Zacatecas, 1546–1700* (Cambridge, 1971), 208–220.

63. Ibid., 229.

3. WHEAT FARM AND CACAO HACIENDA

1. Kathy Waldron, "A Social History of a Primate City: The Case of Caracas, 1750–1810" (Ph.D. Diss., Indiana University, 1977), 84–85. François Depons, *Viaje a la parte oriental de Tierre Firme en la América Meridional*, 2

vols. (first published in 1806), trans. Enrique Planchart, (Caracas, 1960) 1:232.

2. This combination, which he fears may be a "theoretical monstrosity," is discussed with considerable sophistication for New Spain by Eric Van Young, "Mexican Rural History since Chevalier: The Historiography of the Colonial Hacienda," *Latin American Research Review* 18 (1983): 18–22. The link between town and rural hacienda is not emphasized by Van Young, who assumes that landowners practiced patriarchal or seigneurial status and authority in the countryside where they were constant residents. This may be appropriate for owners of Mexican haciendas, but Caracas cacao hacendados most often made such influence felt from and within their urban residences.

3. This custodianship was known as the *tutela*. Most frequently the guardian was both *tutor* and *curador ad litem* of minor heirs, which meant that he or she was obliged to care for such minors, educate them, and defend them in legal cases that might be brought against their persons or their property.

4. Moreover, the existing historiography of colonial Spanish America does not, to my knowledge, make any use whatsoever of tutela records. This may be due to their rarity. I am certain that these two cases are the only ones for seventeenth-century Caracas for which the set of documents, both guardian's accounts and estate inventories, are extant. Although unwieldy and of short term, they seem to me to be of considerable utility, as this chapter demonstrates.

5. ARPC, Testamentarías, 1648 RU.

6. ARPC, Testamentarías, 1638 R.

7. The Rodríguez Santos estancia was comparable in size to New Spain wheat haciendas at the same time. In Mexico a transition from small farms to large haciendas, of 100 sown fanegas or more, had taken place during the second half of the sixteenth century. Charles Gibson, *The Aztecs Under Spanish Rule: A History of the Indians of the Valley of Mexico, 1519–1810* (Stanford, 1964), 322–325.

8. Iturriza Guillén, *Familias caraqueñas*, 47, 778–779.

9. According to Rivillapuerta's account, bags of one *vara* of *lienzo*, worth four reales, were filled with four *arrobas* of flour; since four arrobas were equivalent to two-thirds of one *fanega* of wheat in the grain (the Rodríguez Santos mill ground six arrobas from every fanega of grain), the added cost for bags was approximately six reales for every fanega ground and bagged.

Compare the estimate of milling earnings of 20 to 30 percent with the cabildo provision that millers receive in payment one-eighth (one *almud* per fanega) of the grain they ground for others in their mills, see n. 29, chap. 1.

10. Escudero's age and the tenure of his service with the Rodríguez Santos is given in ARPC, Tierras, GRS 1637.

11. They were criticized for selling bread in four-pound loaves for two reales rather than the stipulated five-pound loaves for that price; ACC, 5:191 (April 1, 1623) and 6:297 (November 18, 1628).

12. ACC, 6:147 (October 9, 1626).

13. ARPC, Testamentarías, 1638 R.

14. AGN, Real Hacienda, leg. 14, July 29, 1628. Iturriza Guillén, *Familias caraqueñas*, 2:451–452.
15. Universidad Central de Venezuela, *La obra pía de Chuao, 1568–1825* (Caracas, 1968), 183–190.
16.. ARPC, Testamentarías, 1653–1655 CL.
17. Cacao from coastal haciendas located downwind from La Guaira was only rarely brought to that port for sale and reshipment. The custom was for a buyer to make his purchase in Caracas from the hacienda owner, who then wrote a bill of sale that entitled the buyer to either a specified quantity or, more often, all the cacao available at the hacienda when the buyer arrived there. The mayordomo would then fill the order and take a signed receipt for the amount of cacao taken by the buyer, who would then continue on his way down the coast, perhaps stopping to take on cacao from other haciendas before proceeding to New Spain with his purchases. It was not uncommon for buyers to pay for their purchases only after they sold their cacao in New Spain, a payment that was made to the New Spain agent of the Caracas hacienda owner. In 1654 and 1655, with record low prices and no buyers in New Spain due to the currency shortage there, Pedro de Liendo paid five reales the fanega to bring Cepi cacao to La Guaira "to sell it and to give it a market because there was none in Cepi and the cacao was about to be lost, rotting in the storehouse." ARPC, Testamentarías, 1653–1655 CL.
18. Most likely these names referred to cutaneous diseases common to slaves which were caused by nutritional deficiencies, most probably yaws, perhaps pellagra or beriberi. The term *bubas* is discussed in this context in Kenneth F. Kiple, *The Carribean Slave: A Biological History* (Cambridge, 1984), passim.
19. ARPC, Testamentarías, 1653–1655 CL, fols. 385–388.
20. There are no data for the year 1653. An estimate of income was made by multiplying the harvest average for recorded years by the current sale price of cacao (10 pesos). The estimated gross income for 1653 is thus 2137 pesos.
21. In colonial Caracas the value of developed cacao property was determined by the number of cacao trees growing on a given hacienda. The custom was to evaluate every fruit-bearing tree at one peso; trees that had divided at the trunk and were about to bear fruit (known as *horqueteados*) were worth half as much or four reales, while recently planted saplings (*resiembros*) were worth two reales. This method of appraisal was peculiar in that it did not vary over time with the price paid for cacao, and was not, therefore, strictly an assessment of the productive value of the cacao property. Mature trees growing in the rich alluvial soil of the Tuy River valley were usually appraised at one and one-half pesos each, but this was also fixed and did not fluctuate with prices or over time. A survey of cacao haciendas made in 1720 indicated that Tuy River cacao groves then had a much higher yield than did coastal *arboledas*, about 25 fanegas of beans per 1000 trees compared with 10 fanegas per 1000 trees on the coast; Pedro José Olavarriaga, *Instrucción general y particular del estado presente de la provincia de Venezuela en los años de 1720 y 1721*, published by the Academia Nacional de la Historia (Caracas, 1965). Yet the cost of planting cacao in the interior was high, and a portion of the return from higher yields obtained there went

for planting and for transport of cacao beans to market. The one peso per tree assessment (and one and one-half peso per tree in the Tuy) probably provided a quick, rule-of-thumb evaluation of the cost of establishing and maintaining a given grove. It thus functioned as an estimate of the grove's market value, and that is how it is used here. The current price paid for cacao and the cost of slave labor were two factors that determined the income from cacao haciendas, but the fact that these variables had no effect on the appraised value of cacao property seems significant. Could it be that Caracas planters ignored such prices in their estimates of the value of their estates because they could do nothing about them? Was the calculation of estate value with current market prices of cacao and slaves too sophisticated for the accounting techniques of the times, or was it that prices of both cacao and slaves tended to fluctuate around a rather constant mean, and therefore had no significance for Caracas planters?

22. AGN, Real Hacienda, leg. 14, July 29, 1628.
23. The 1684 survey is located in AGI, Contaduría, leg. 1613; it was published in *Revista de Historia* (Caracas), 28 (August 1970): 63–81.
24. ARPC, Tierras, 1681 BGHLV. Cacao holdings in 1720 are from Olavarriaga, *Instrucción general*.

4. THE TUY VALLEY FRONTIER

1. MacLeod, *Spanish Central America*, 241–252.
2. The *padrón* of the rural domain of Caracas taken in 1684 serves as a base census of cacao haciendas; AGI, Contaduría, leg. 1613. This document was published in *Revista de Historia* (Caracas), 28 (August 1970): 63–81. For 1720 the document is Olavarriaga, *Instrucción general*. The original is in the archive of the Academia Nacional. Olavarriaga listed cacao haciendas by geographical location, owner, and number of trees, and also included an assessment of the yield of each hacienda in *fanegas* of cacao beans per 1000 trees. The 1744 listing is in AGN, Caracas, Diversos, XXVII, fols. 348–361.
3. AGI, Santo Domingo, leg. 752. Sucre, *Gobernadores*, 188–194. Iturriza Guillén, *Familias caraqueñas*, 2:700.
4. León, his wife, and ten children comprised the largest canario family on the petition. AGI, Santo Domingo, leg. 793.
5. A detailed summary of the competition between *canarios* and *morenos libres* to get royal permission to settle in Curiepe is in AGI, Santo Domingo, leg. 793. The best general history of the settlement of the barlovento region in Venezuela, based largely on previously unknown materials found in Caracas archives, is Lucas Guillermo Castillo Lara, *Apuntes para la historia colonial de Barlovento* (Caracas, 1981), 337–477.
6. G. Scelle, *La Traite Nègrière aux Indes de Castille*, 2 vols. (Paris, 1906), 2:122–129, 145–158.
7. AGI, Santo Domingo, leg. 793.
8. Sucre contends that Cañas's preference for the lower classes of Caracas society and his abuse and uniform rejection of the elite stemmed from his African upbringing. A man of cruel nature for whatever reason, his excesses (including the hanging of eleven muleteers accused of smuggling) resulted in a secret appeal made by the cabildo's regidores to the

Audiencia in Santo Domingo. In 1714 Jorge Lozano y Peralta, oidor of the Audiencia, arrived in Caracas, arrested Cañas, placed the alcaldes ordinarios of the cabildo in charge of the province, and sent the governor in chains to Spain. In Madrid Cañas was deprived of his membership in the Order of Santiago and sentenced to death. His life was saved by a general pardon issued to celebrate the birth of Prince Charles (1716). Sucre, *Gobernadores*, 207–213.

9. Castillo Lara, *Apuntes*, 350–354.

10. The transfer was ordered by royal decree dated May 27, 1717. In 1726 Venezuela returned to its previous status as an autonomous executive *gobernación* dependent judicially on the Audiencia of Santo Domingo. From 1739 to 1742 Venezuela would again be subordinate in both the executive and judiciary realms to the authority of the viceroyalty of New Granada.

11. Castillo Lara, *Apuntes*, 380–383.

12. Sucre, *Gobernadores*, 229–236.

13. Four of the *corregidor* jurisdictions were on the coast: Choroní, Maiquetía, Cuyagua, and Caraballeda. The interior regions with corregidores were La Vega, Petare-Baruta, Guarenas, and Turmero-Aragua Valley. Otto Pikaza, "Don Gabriel José de Zuloaga en la gobernación de Venezuela (1737-1747)," *Anuario de Estudios Americanos* 19 (Seville, 1962): 522–523, 658–659.

14. Ibid., 523.

15. Castillo Lara, *Apuntes*, 393–418.

16. Ibid., 425–429.

17. Quoted in ibid., 452.

18. Ibid., 455–465.

19. Ibid., 465–468. The details of the foundation of Panaquire are given in Lucas Guillermo Castillo Lara, *La aventura fundacional de los isleños* (Caracas, 1983).

20. Some *doctrina* towns on the lower Tuy created by Dominican and Capuchine missionaries to evangelize Indians were established earlier than frontier settlements located closer to Caracas which were based entirely on cacao production. Capaya, for example, which was somewhat nearer Caracas than Curiepe, was founded by Dominicans in 1712. Castillo Lara, *Apuntes*, chaps. 7–10, details the foundation history of the Tuy settlements.

21. The increase in number of trees from 434,850 trees in 1684 to 3,251,200 trees in 1720 was an average of 78,245 trees per year for the 36-year interval. The average annual increase for the 24 years from 1720 to 1744, when 5,094,200 trees were counted, was 76,792 trees. These numbers directly refute the Guipuzcoana Company claim that cacao productivity in the province went up dramatically after its creation in 1728.

22. In 1764 Pedro Felipe de Llamas, commissioned by the governor to survey certain settlements of the upper Tuy, included in his report from Ocumare del Tuy: "from this pueblo for a distance of twenty leagues [the Tuy] is not navigable, and from there to the point where the river enters into the sea, it would be about twenty-five leagues more or less, it is navigable, and when it is clean canoes that carry sixty to seventy fanegas of cacao can travel on it." AGN, Visitas Públicas, vol. 6.

23. The real cédula, dated 3 July 1735, was issued in response to the

letter of Basque governor Martín de Lardizábal to the king, 18 June 1733. Lardizábal's letter, cited in Ermila Troconis de Veracoechea, *Documentos para el estudio de los esclavos negros en Venezuela* (Caracas, 1969), 250, reads in part:

> ... the many haciendas of cacao in the valleys of Caucagua and Capaya are near enough to the coast, and by allowing a port on that coast cacao will be taken there and all of it will be lost to the foreigners, as already has begun to happen; and, with the hope that in that district a port will be allowed, many haciendas have been established at a great distance from this city, with the objective of later proposing that, because of the resulting high cost of transporting [overland] said cacao, [hacienda owners] will be allowed to ship it from the coast in those parts.

24. Muleskinners' charges in the Tuy are from the accounts of the haciendas of Simón Piñate, ARPC, Testmentarías, 1735 P. Testimony in the disputed sale of a Caucagua cacao hacienda in 1744 provides this information: "... not only is mule travel difficult on the said road, but during certain seasons it is almost impossible, requiring at all times a great deal of work." At the best of times muledrivers would charge twenty reales for each carga of cacao, but during the rainy season no one could be found to do it even for twenty-four reales the carga. At only fourteen reales the carga above Caucagua regardless of the season, mule transportation from the upper Tuy to Caracas was always much cheaper. ARPC, Civiles, 1744 F.

25. Information about English slave sales in Caracas is from Colin A. Palmer, *Human Cargoes: The British Slave Trade to Spanish America, 1700–1739* (Urbana, 1981), chap. 6. The Guipuzcoana Company's record as slave trader is mentioned in Roland D. Hussey, *The Caracas Company, 1728–1784* (Cambridge, Mass., 1934), 172–174.

26. The best discussion of Anglo-Spanish diplomacy and the American trade during this period is Geoffrey J. Walker, *Spanish Politics and Imperial Trade, 1700–1789* (Bloomington and London, 1979), chap. 8. Data on slave sales is from Palmer, *Human Cargoes*, chap. 6.

27. The Piñate data are located in ARPC, Testamentarías, 1735 P.

28. At San Joseph, of thirty-four adult slaves, twenty-six were married and there was one widow and one widower. The slave community was comprised of nineteen dwellings, described in detail in the inventory. The typical hut was ten by four *varas*—about eight and one-half by three and one-third meters—and had two openings for windows. They were most often covered with straw, although the leaves from sugar cane (*cogollo*) or an aquatic plant (*gamelote*) were also used for roofing material. Walls were uniformly of stick-and-mud construction known as *bahareque*. ARPC, Testamentarías, 1735 P. A list of Piñate slaves and further information about their dwellings are given in Appendix G.

29. ARPC, Escribanías of Gaspár Joseph de Salas, 1722–1726.

30. The Liendo data (from October 1645 to December 1656) only cover a period of declining prices in the history of the Cepi hacienda. Were it possible to analyze the decades prior to 1645, given the high prices paid for cacao then, the estimate of net profit given in chap. 3 would have been about three times greater than the calculated 1400 pesos per annum, or a

sum about equal to the estimated income from the Piñate haciendas in the Tuy.

31. The hacienda census data shown in figs. 8 and 9 above demonstrate that the number of trees in the province continued to expand at a steady rate from 1684 to 1744, with no discernible change in the rate of increase from 1720 to 1744, as would be expected if the Company had greatly influenced cacao production. This fact is not to be understood as an entirely new discovery, but even historians who reject the Company's argument that it alone was responsible for the greatly increased planting of cacao in the province have not been certain about the part actually played by the Company in the development of the colony.

The Guipuzcoana Company's claims to substantial stimulation of production were published in its *Manifesto que con incontestables hechos prueba los grandes beneficios que ha producido el establecimiento de la Real Compañía Guipuscoana de Caracas* (Madrid, 1749). The document offered a statistical argument in which an effort was made to show that more cacao was shipped to Spain during the eighteen years from 1730 to 1748 than during the twenty-nine years from 1700 to 1729. Hussey, *Caracas Company*, accepted the veracity of the *Manifesto* in this particular: "Its figures, on the other hand, are chiefly a compilation of certified copies of treasury accounts. It is satisfactory for most purposes as the accounts themselves, and more available for the average reader" (p. 86). Arcila Farías, *Economía colonial*, is much more critical of the Company's manipulation of the export statistics. For Arcila Farías, the numbers are misleading because they do not account for the difficulties of carrying on commerce during the years before the establishment of the Guipuzcoana Company when the War of Succession interfered with high-seas shipping. Nor did the Company care to point out the increase in cacao shipped to New Spain, shipments which were in fact much greater in volume than the Company commerce with Spain and independent of the Company (2:279). Although he did not attempt to document the point, Arcila Farías's instincts accurately told him that "the Company had no right to claim that [the increase in exports from 1730 to 1749] were due to its efforts and not the result of the surge made by the province itself" (2:263). Castillo Lara, *La aventura*, agrees: "All the accomplishments that the Company wanted to take credit for as exclusively the results of its own efforts could have come about without the Company's presence" (p. 266). Castillo Lara's comment, based on the simultaneous increase of commerce with Mexico, is substantiated by the hacienda censuses used here.

32. Palmer, *Human Cargoes*, 170.
33. Ibid., 126–128.

5. LEÓN'S REBELLION

1. Don Prudencio Peníchez, corregidor of Petare and Baruta, to the governor, April 28, 1789, AGN, Gobernación y Capitanía General, leg. 41.
2. Mariano Martí, *Documentos relativos a su visita pastoral de la diócesis de Caracas, 1771–1784*, 7 vols. (Caracas, 1969), 2:609–610.
3. Esteban Fernándes de León to the governor, Sabana de Ocumare, August 1, 1775, AGN, Gobernación y Capitanía General, leg. 38. The

response of the governor, José Carlos de Aguero, noted on the margin of the cited letter, indicates that there was nothing that could be done about the problem besides more vigilant policing. The governor's note does reveal that slaves could work on Saturdays for their own benefit:

> I should say to you . . . that to avoid the theft of cacao, in response to the three points you mention as causes, do not let hacendados give to their slaves any more remuneration than the freedom to work for themselves on Saturday; . . . I say that the first point has a remedy, because every master should give to his slaves what they need or suffer punishment; with the respect to the illegal sale of clothing and other dry goods, I order you to collect all the licenses of this sort and oblige the holders to erect a public store if they want to sell those things; and as far as the *aguardiente de caña* is concerned, you must see to the total extinction of the distilleries.

4. "*Justicia Mayor* era el nombre técnico del delegado del gobernador fuera de Caracas. El que desempeñaba el cargo en las ciudades y villas se denominaba *Teniente y Justicia Mayor*. Se anteponía el nombre de *Corregidor* a quien ejecía funciones análogas en pueblos y comarcas de indios. El nombramiento de ambos corría de cuenta de Gobernador de la provincia, aunque había de estar refrendado por la Audiencia de Santo Domingo," Otto Pikaza, "Don Gabriel José de Zuloaga en la gobernación de Venezuela (1737–1747)," *Anuario de Estudios Americanos* (Seville), 19 (1962): 523.

5. Zuloaga was named governor and captain-general of Venezuela in August 1736, and took possession of the office in Caracas in October 1737. He was first given the right to appoint and to remove tenientes at his independent discretion by a real cédula dated November 7, 1739. AGI, Caracas, leg. 65. His arguments opposing the incorporation of Venezuela to the viceroyalty of New Granada, of which the matter of the tenientes was only a part, are in Zuloaga to the king, September 20, 1740, AGI, Caracas, leg. 66. The provision which provided that the Caracas governor be exempted from the authority of New Granada in the particular naming tenientes is in Crown to Zuloaga, February 12, 1742, AGI, Caracas, leg. 11.

6. Zuloaga to the king, January 1, 1745, AGI, Caracas, leg. 418.

7. The only evidence that would ever be forthcoming was given by Nicolás de León, Juan Francisco's son, who testified after his capture in 1752 that his father

> had written to Don Luis Arias Altamirano [who was then maestre de campo], informing him of the new *Teniente* and the resistance put up by the people of the area, but there was no written response [from the mantuanos], and only by word of mouth did they tell us, especially the said Don Luis, that it was time to throw out that *Teniente* and all the Vizcayans who were dominating the land, and that it would be a good idea to go to Caracas, with everyone carrying arms, to ask for the suspension of the Royal Guipuzcoana Company, and to inform His Majesty [of the widespread opposition to the Company].

Statement of Nicolás de León, February 8, 1752, in Instituto Panamericano de Geografía e Historia, *Documentos relativos a la insurrección de Juan de León* (Caracas, 1947), 188.

8. León to Castellanos, April 4, 1749, AGI, Caracas, leg. 418.

9. Castillo Lara, *Apuntes*, chap. 19. Not until 1773 would the Guipuz-

coana Company begin to load cacao in the Cabo Codera region at the mouth of the Tuy River; ibid., 521.

10. AGI, Caracas, leg. 421. León's letter of explanation, written in December 1751 after the exhausted fugitive had decided to surrender, is given as the prologue in Francisco Morales Padrón, *Rebelión contra la Compañía de Caracas* (Seville, 1955), 7–14.

11. AGI, Caracas, leg. 937. Born in 1682, Lorenzo Ponte was sixty-seven years old in 1749, one of only three sexagenarians among elite men in Caracas at that time. (The other two, Feliciano de Sojo Palacios Gedler and Gabriel Regalado Rada Arias, were both born in 1689). The third Marqués de Mijares, don Francisco Nicolás Mijares de Solórzano y Tovar, was born in 1693. Iturriza Guillén, *Familias caraqueñas*, 1:73 (Rada); 1:308 (Palacios); 2:529 (Mijares); 2:682 (Ponte).

12. Quoted in Castillo Lara, *La aventura*, 221.
13. AGI, Caracas, leg. 418.
14. AGI, Caracas, leg. 419.
15. AGI, Caracas, leg. 418.
16. Castillo Lara, *La aventura*, 231–233.
17. Instituto Panamericano de Geografia e Historia, *Documentos relativos a la insurrección de Juan de León* (Caracas, 1947), 39–40.
18. Cited in Hector García Chuecos, *Historia Documental de Venezuela* (Caracas, 1957), 28.
19. Castillo Lara, *La aventura*, 243. The Company's violations of its original charter are discussed in chap. 6.
20. The best description of these events is in Castillo Lara, *La aventura*, 273–288. León's statement was made in a conversation with lieutenant governor Domingo Aguirre y Castillo, cited in José de Armas Chitty and Manuel Pinto C., eds., *Juan Francisco de León: Diario de una Insurgencia* (Caracas, 1971), 67.
21. Armas Chitty and Pinto C., eds., *Juan Francisco de León*, 80.
22. Ibid., 67.
23. This description of the attack on La Guaira and its immediate aftermath is based on the narrative account in Castillo Lara, *La aventura*, chaps. 13–14.
24. "Recopilación o resumen General de las almas que tiene esta Gobernación de Venezuela y Caracas según consta de las matrículas del año 1750 y 51 de todo el obispado," AGI, Caracas, leg. 367.
25. Castillo Lara, *La aventura*, 341.
26. ARPC, Civiles, 1749 T.
27. One Company ship, the *San Joachin*, made port in Spain in 1750. Its cargo of 4429 fanegas of cacao had most likely been purchased before frightened Company employees fled Caracas in April 1749. The record of Company shipping is given in Hussey, *Caracas Company*, 305–318.
28. Ibid., 135–136.
29. Ensenada was in charge of the ministries of War, Navy, and Indies, and Finance and State. W. N. Hargreaves-Mawdsley, *Eighteenth-Century Spain, 1700–1788: A Political, Diplomatic and Institutional History* (London: Macmillan, 1979), 80–94.
30. Arriaga to Ensenada, January 14 and March 29, 1750, quoted in "La politica del marqués de la Ensenada—asesorado por el ex-virrey Eslava—

en relación con el levantamiento contra la Guipuzcoana," Demetrio Ramos Pérez, *Estudios de Historia Venezolana* (Caracas, 1976), 654–655.

31. Palmer, *Human Cargoes*, chap. 8.

32. Geoffrey J. Walker, *Spanish Politics and Imperial Trade, 1700–1789* (Bloomington and London, 1979), 210–220.

33. Ibid., 111–113, 116, 189, 205.

34. José Campillo y Cossio died in 1744, but he had been in charge of the ministries of Marine, War, and the Indies in 1743 when he wrote in opposition to the slave trade and in favor of encouraging economic growth in the colonies by drawing Indians into the marketplace as a free peasantry, wage laborers who could consume the manufactures of the metropolis. *Nuevo sistema de gobierno económico para la América* (1743) (Madrid, 1789). Campillo is discussed in Peggy K. Liss, *Atlantic Empires: The Network of Trade and Revolution, 1713–1826* (Baltimore and London, 1983), 55–56. If the ministers of empire thought that Indians could replace slaves, certainly they would have considered Canary Islander immigrant farmers as capable substitutes for slaves as well.

35. Letter of Nicolás de León, August 17, 1751, *Documentos relativos a la insurrección de Juan Francisco de León* (Caracas, 1947), 87–88.

36. Hussey identifies these two groups as "liberals," those who favored abolition of the Company and mercy toward the Caracas rebels, and "conservatives," those described here, whose harshness toward Caracas is understood as "what would be expected of those trained in the absolutist school of civil or military command"; *Caracas Company*, 144–150.

37. Quoted in ibid., 148–149.

38. Venezuela was separated from the viceroyalty of New Granada by order of a real cédula signed February 12, 1742. Zuloaga to the king, September 20, 1740, AGI, Caracas, leg. 66.

39. In 1741 he gained widespread fame for successfully defending Cartagena from the English admiral Edward Vernon, and he had earned a flawless reputation for his able management of the new viceroyalty during ten years of constant economic and diplomatic stress. Walker, *Spanish Politics*, 207–216.

40. Ramos, "La politica," 665. The principal purpose of Ramos's article is to affirm Eslava's central role in influencing Ensenada's policy. The Havana Company is summarized in Hussey, *Caracas Company*, 207–214.

41. Walker, *Spanish Politics*, 100. Analola Borges, *Alvarez Abreu y su extraordinaria misión en Indias* (Santa Cruz de Tenerife, 1963), passim.

42. The reasons for Alvarez y Abreu's presence in Caracas were probably public knowledge by this time; he is listed in the cathedral marriage register as "Alcalde Visitador, Abogado de los Reales Consejos." Marriage between families of royal officials on temporary assignment did not violate the prohibitions against marriage between the king's administrators and women of local elite families. In June 1716 the Basque accountant of the Caracas royal treasury, Juan de Vega Arredondo, married a second daughter of the governor, María Josefa de Bertodano, making him and licenciado Alvarez y Abreu brothers-in-law. Instituto Venezolano de Genealogía, *Matrimonios y velaciones*, 367–369. Alberto Bertodano is in Sucre, *Gobernadores*, 216–218.

43. Hargreaves-Mawdsley, *Eighteenth-Century Spain*, 78–87. Alvarez y Abreu's letter to Ensenada is quoted in Hussey, *Caracas Company*, 146.

44. Castillo Lara, *La aventura*, 391.
45. Sucre states that Ricardos was married to doña Leonor Carrillo y Albonorz, daughter of the Duke of Montemar, *Gobernadores*, 275. Montemar's career is traced in Hargreaves-Mawdsley, *Eighteenth-Century Spain*, 67–79. Ensenada had served as Commisary of the Navy during the Orán expedition, and he was made a marquis for his part in the defeat of Naples in 1734–1735; ibid., 80.
46. AGI, Caracas, leg. 57.
47. Castillo Lara, *La aventura*, p. 387.
48. These men were maestre de campo Luis Arias Altamirano, alcalde ordinario for 1751, regidor Pedro Blanco de Ponte, Alejandro and Miguel Blanco Uribe, Antonio Blanco Uribe, Pío Blanco de Ponte, and Miguel de Monasterios. These were mature men in their forties and fifties who had been leaders of the protest against the Guipuzcoana Company for a decade.
49. Ricardos to the king, April 30, 1752, AGI, Caracas, leg. 421.
50. Testimony of Nicolás de León, February 8, 1752, *Documentos relativos a la insurrección de Juan Francisco de León*, 188.
51. Ricardos to Ensenada, October 20, 1752, AGI, Caracas, leg. 421.
52. Ricardos to Ensenada, September 11, 1751, AGI, Caracas, leg. 421.
53. Castillo Lara, *La aventura*, 430–439.
54. Ibid., 468–470.
55. Archivo de la Academia Nacional de la Historia, Caracas, Colección Villanueva, 130, fol. 224.
56. Letter of Antonio Díaz Padrón to Ricardos, August 26, 1751, in *Documentos relativos a la insurrección de Juan Francisco de León*, 93–94.
57. Archivo de la Academia Nacional de la Historia, Caracas, Colección Villanueva, 133, fol. 172.
58. Cited in Castillo Lara, *La aventura*, 494–495.
59. Testimony of Nicolás de León, February 8, 1752, *Documentos relativos a la insurrección de Juan Francisco de León*, 192; AGI, Caracas, leg. 421. John V. Lombardi, *Venezuela: The Search for Order, the Dream of Progress* (New York, 1982), 87–88.
60. Castillo Lara, *La aventura*, chap. 20, passim.
61. Neither Bolívar nor Tovar signed the 1744 memorial protesting the policies of the Guipuzcoana Company; AGI, Santo Domingo, leg. 787.
62. Morales Padrón, *Rebelión contra la Compañía de Caracas*, 7–14.
63. Ibid., 10.
64. Ricardos to Ensenada, April 30, 1752, AGI, Caracas, leg. 421.
65. León and his son surrendered in late January 1752, some weeks after he wrote his apology and defense. While in the Caracas jail Nicolás spoke of the support given them by maestre de campos Luis Arias Altamirano, who was already dead, but otherwise they refused to name their mantuano supporters. The *Santa Bárbara* left La Guaira on March 28, 1752. Ricardos to the king, 29 June 1751, AGI, Caracas, leg. 57; and Ricardos to Ensenada, October 20, 1752, AGI, Caracas, leg. 421.
66. Ricardos to Ensenada, March 2, 1752, AGI, Caracas, leg. 421. Archivo General de la Nación, Insurrección de Juan Francisco de León, vol. 2, fol. 293. Ensenada was informed of León's death by Julián de Arriaga, August 4, 1752, AGI, Caracas, leg. 421.
67. Archivo General de la Nación, Insurrección de Juan Francisco de León, Vol. 2, fol. 293. The Spanish text of the plaque is as follows:

Esta es la Justicia del Rey nuestro Señor, mandada hacer por el Excmo. señor Don Phe. Ricardos Tne. General de los Exceros. de Su Majestad su Govr. y Cap. General desta prova. de Caracas, con Francisco León, amo de esta casa, por pertinaz, rebelde y traidor a la Real Corona y por ello Reo. Que se derribe y siembre de sal pa. perpetua memoria de su Infa.

68. AGI, Santo Domingo, leg. 714. The settlement remained, and according to a census taken in 1758, the year after Felipe Ricardos had been replaced as governor of Caracas, there were 14 households in Panaquire and a total resident population of 264 individuals, of whom 233 were black slaves. "Matrículas de las parróquias de Caracas y demás pueblos de su diócesis, 1759," manuscript census located in the Biblioteca Nacional de Venezuela, Caracas.

69. La Gazeta de Caracas, September 20, 1811. The subsequent history of this copper tablet is given in Aristides Rojas, Estudios históricos: Orígenes Venezolanos (Caracas, 1891), 267–273.

6. THE PROTEST OF THE CARACAS ELITE

1. Domingo Galindo y Sayas, Pedro Ruiz Arquinzones, José Bolívar, Feliciano Sojo Palacios, Agustín Piñango, Miguel de Aristeguieta, Antolín de Liendo, Mateo de Monasterios, and Miguel de Rengifo were described as "peaceful and loyal to the King" by Sebastián de Eslava, ex-viceroy of New Granada. Demetrio Ramos Pérez, "La política de Marqués de la Ensenada—asesorado por el ex-virrey Eslava—en relación con el levantamiento contra la Guipuzcoana," Estudios de Historia Venezolana (Caracas, 1976), 672.

2. A recent attempt to argue that Company profits came mostly at the expense of contraband trade with the Dutch is made in Eugenio Piñero, "The Cacao Economy of the Eighteenth-Century Province of Caracas and the Spanish Cacao Market," Hispanic American Historical Review 68 (February 1988):86–92.

3. This is my understanding of the benefits available to those who were able to ship their cacao in the tercio buque. The custom is briefly outlined in Eduardo Arcila Farías, Economía colonial de Venezuela, 2 vols., 2d ed. (Caracas, 1973), 1:250–254. Several aspects of the process of taking on cargo remain unclear. Once a ship's captain had received a royal license from the governor to receive cargo, both cosecheros and merchants must have appeared to register the cacao they wanted to export. An agent of the royal treasury probably figured their tax obligations at this point. But what is enigmatic is the method by which it was decided who would get the opportunity to ship when there was more cacao for export than the ship could carry. When there was more cosechero cacao for export than could be accommodated in the hacienda owners' tercio buque, how was it determined who would be allowed to load cacao (and thus be able to profit from the sale of those beans in Veracruz) and who would be obliged to sell cacao at Caracas prices to local merchants or the ship's captain? Did the ship's supercargo accept cacao for these reserved portions of the ship on a first-come, first-served basis? Conversely, when all cosecheros who had cacao available for shipment had loaded it on a given vessel, yet their tercio buque had not been filled, who decided whether the remaining space

would be made available to local merchants and not the ship captain? Arcila Farías noted that by order of a royal cédula issued in 1721, before the establishment of the Guipuzcoana Company, it was the cabildo together with the governor who determined the cargo capacity of each ship, and that except in the case of his legitimate incapacity the governor could not delegate his authority in this matter to anyone else. In 1733, with the Company in competition for cargoes with both the English slave *asiento* and colonial shippers who wanted to sell all their beans to Mexico, the Basque governor Lardizábal reserved for himself alone the right to examine the cacao offered for placement in their tercio buque on ships bound for New Spain by cosecheros on their own account, and to reject any cacao that he believed had not originated on the cosecheros' haciendas. *Economía colonial*, 251–253. The powerful role of the governor in this may well have been one reason why the Caracas cabildo, dominated as it was by cosecheros eager to maximize their exports, was always eager to exercise gubernatorial authority in the governor's absence.

4. See the discussion in chap. 4.

5. AGI, Santo Domingo, leg. 787.

6. In June of 1742 word reached Caracas that the price then being paid for cacao at Veracruz was 52.5 pesos; in Caracas at that time the price ranged from 9.5 to 14.5 pesos; Governor Gabriel de Zuloaga to the king, February 26, 1745, AGI, Santo Domingo, leg. 786.

7. The 1744 *padrón* is located in AGN, Diversos, Tomo XXVII. This was the purpose behind the creation of this well-known document, which has not heretofore been analyzed as to its original function. Presumably the colony's haciendas were to be surveyed frequently, but in the aftermath of the rebellion of 1749 the policy was ended and no other censuses were taken.

8. León to Governor Julian de Arriaga, January 1750; quoted in Arcilia Farías, *Economía colonial* (1st ed., 1946), 232.

9. They did not find it in their interest to report that from 1740 to 1742 persistent rains, described by Juan Francisco de León as "a constant deluge," had caused floods "never seen before in this province." Juan Francisco de León to Fernando de Mechinel, "Corregidor, Justicia Mayor, Cabo de Guerra Principal, y Juez de Comisos" of Guarenas, November 12, 1742, published in Andrés Hernández Pino, ed., *Papeles coloniales: Aporte para la historia de los pueblos del Estado Miranda* (Caracas, 1948), 19–20. The fact that exports had tumbled from 1740, when a near-record 63,912 fanegas were carried (a record of 64,829 fanegas had been exported in 1736), to a sixteen-year low of 25,409 fanegas in 1742 (only 16,102 fanegas were exported in 1726), was no doubt due at least in some part to the severe weather that washed away many Tuy cacao groves.

10. Letter of Julián de Arriaga (interim governor of Caracas from 1749 to 1751) to the factors of the Guipuzcoana Company, March 29, 1750, "La política del marqués de la Ensenada—asesorado por el ex-virrey Eslava—en relación con el levantamiento contra la Guipuzcoana," in Ramos Pérez, *Estudios de Historia Venezolana*, 655.

11. Cabildo to the king, January 1745, AGI, Santo Domingo, leg. 786.

12. Examples of Mexican investments in Caracas cacao are included in a Guipuzcoana Company document that lists the ships either lost at sea or

taken by enemy corsairs while traveling between Veracruz and La Guaira from 1733 to 1739. In 1733 the frigate of Gerónimo López Barroso, "uno de las del trajín de la Vera Cruz," sank in the Bermuda Channel with 25,000 pesos lost to Caracas and New Spain investors; in 1734 the frigate of Pedro de Arrieta sank off Grand Cayman with cacao worth 150,000 pesos, much of it purchased by New Spain merchants; in 1734 the frigate of Gabriel de Bezama was lost near the island of Arenas, fifty leagues from Campeche, with 10 percent of its cargo silver coin for Caracas; in 1738 a frigate bound for Caracas was taken near the island of Tortugilla with 100,00 pesos in cash and Mexican merchandise. Interested in discrediting the traditional trade, the Company also gave examples of unscrupulous or inept individuals who had stolen or misspent cash intended for the purchase of Caracas cacao: in 1736 Pedro Ariztoy, maestre, could not account for 12,000 pesos he had been given in Veracruz by Andrés González for "the purchase and return of cacaos"; the previous year captain Lorenzo Hernández de Santiago, vecino of Caracas, was jailed in Veracruz for the loss of 50,000 pesos he had received for the same purpose. The directors of the Royal Guipuzcoana Company to the Council of the Indies, March 17, 1739, AGI, Santo Domingo, leg. 786.

13. The published broadside is entitled: *Segundo Memorial del Conde de San Xavier y de Don Francisco de Ponte en nombre de los vecinos, cosecheros, y cargadores a Nueva España* (Madrid, 1746). The observations about the reluctance of New Spain merchants to invest in the cacao commerce and the departure from Caracas as a result of difficulties caused by the lack of capital there were made in an earlier *memorial* (Madrid, 1745). Copies of these are in AGI, Santo Domingo, leg. 786.

14. The directors of the Royal Guipuzcoana Company to the Council of the Indies, March 17, 1739; Governor Zuloaga to the king, February 26, 1745, AGI, Santo Domingo, leg. 786.

15. AGI, Santo Domingo, leg. 786.

16. AGI, Santo Domingo, leg. 787.

17. The average age at death for these women for whom both birth and death dates are available ($N = 17$) is 69.2 years; for men ($N = 36$) the mean age at death is 62.6. Birth, marriage, and death dates are found in the same sources cited in previous chapters: Iturriza Guillén, *Familias caraqueñas* and *Familias valencianas*; Sangróniz y Castro, *Familias coloniales*; and the marriage registry for the cathedral parish, published by the Instituto Venezolano de Genealogía, *Matrimonios y velaciones*.

18. The 1744 *padrón* of cacao haciendas was made at the request of Governor Gabriel Joseph de Zuloaga. Archivo General de la Nación, Caracas, Sección Diversos, XXVII, fols. 348–361. Haciendas were listed by location, owner, and number of trees.

19. *Documentos relativos a la Insurrección de Juan Francisco de León*, 203. Two known signers contributed to this secret fund: Juan Félix Blanco and Juan Rodríguez Camejo.

20. In summary, thirty-eight individuals with cacao haciendas signed the 1744 document; they owned 781,500 cacao trees on sixty-four haciendas. In addition, eleven owners of 263,000 cacao trees on sixteen other haciendas who did not sign can be associated with the signatories by reason of their close kindred to them and other evidence.

21. Most recently, for example, see Magnus Mörner, "The Rural Economy and Society of Colonial Spanish America," in *The Cambridge History of Latin America* (Cambridge, 1984), 2:201: "Absentee creole landlords concentrated in Caracas formed a homogeneous, ambitious elite which tenaciously fought royal functionaries and Spanish-born merchants, who from 1728 to 1784 monopolized external trade through the Caracas Company."

22. Sucre, *Gobernadores*, 243–245.

23. Real cédula, August 11, 1676, AGI, Caracas, leg. 11; this concession was originally granted to the town of Coro in 1560. The years in which Caracas alcaldes ordinarios acted as governor pro tem were: 1705, 1714, 1715, 1720, 1723, 1724, 1725, and 1726. A royal cédula signed January 17, 1723, reiterated the order of 1676. Sucre, *Gobernadores*, 175–231 passim.

24. Analola Borges, *Isleños en Venezuela: La gobernación de Ponte y Hoyo* (Santa Cruz de Tenerife, 1960); Sucre, *Governadores*, 207–242.

25. The province of Venezuela was transferred from the political jurisdiction of Santo Domingo to that of the viceroy of New Granada in a royal decree signed May 27, 1717; Sucre; *Gobernadores*, 222.

26. Sucre, *Gobernadores*, 229–244.

27. In September 1702 an agent of the Habsburg archduke Charles of Austria, don Bartolomé de Capocelato, count of Antería, was arrested in the coastal valley of Ocumare and jailed in Caracas. In May 1703 he escaped, evidently with the help of the governor, Nicolás Eugenio de Ponte y Hoyo, who was accused of sympathizing with the Habsburg cause. Suffering from a debilitating mental illness, Ponte was replaced in November 1703 by the town's alcaldes, but the act of their taking gubernatorial authority was cause for some considerable concern by many who thought that they would go beyond sympathy and actually declare that the province belonged to a Habsburg sovereign. Evidently no charges were brought against anyone for treason, but among those who were later accused of having denounced the Bourbons in favor of the Habsburg archduke Charles were sargento mayor Juan Blanco Infante, elected alcalde ordinario in 1703; capitán Sebastián Nicolás de Ponte y Ponte; his cousin capitán Pedro de Ponte Ochoa; and the regidores Juan Nicolás de Ponte y Loreto, who was also elected alcalde in 1703, and Alejandro Blanco y Blanco. Some of the details of this rather confusing episode are given in Analola Borges, *La casa de Austria en Venezuela durante la guerra de sucesión española (1702–1715)* (Santa Cruz de Tenerife, 1963). A generation later the descendants of these Blancos and Pontes were conspicuous in their opposition to the Guipuzcoana Company.

28. Factor Goyzueta is quoted in Castillo Lara, *La aventura*, 270–271.

29. The cabildo's response is recorded in AGI, Caracas, leg. 418.

30. The woman who supposedly put events in motion on that occasion is also unknown, but factor Goyzueta may have referred to doña Luisa Catalina Martínez de Villegas, aged sixty-nine in 1744, the oldest of those who signed the protest memorial in November of that year, and the first signature on the list. Doña Luisa had been a widow for twenty years in 1744, and in 1741 she claimed that during this time she had been responsible for the care of "a very extensive family," some forty-four people, "counting only children and grandchildren." AGI, Santo Domingo, leg. 786. Probably her influence in the colony was great: four of her children

also signed the 1744 document, as did members of their spouses' families. Her husband, Alejandro Blanco de Villegas, was regidor of the cabildo and served as alcalde ordinario in 1721 and governor pro tem until May of that year, when a new governor was named for Caracas; Sucre, *Gobernadores*, 227–228. Their son, Juan Félix Blanco de Villegas, a signatory in 1744, was alcalde in 1746, and would be regarded by the Company as one of its most determined opponents. He was arrested and sent to Spain in 1751; AGI, Caracas, leg. 421. It was doña Luisa who put up a determined fight to keep Juan del Rosario and the *morenos libres* out of Curiepe in the 1720s.

31. The alcaldes ordinarios for the Caracas cabildo from 1700 to 1749 are given in Sucre, *Gobernadores*, 200–268, passim.

32. The following men were either fathers of 1744 signatories or signers themselves: Juan Luis Arias Altamirano, the governor pro tem in 1714; Francisco Felipe Mijares de Solórzano (who was the Marqués de Mijares) and Juan de Ibarra in 1715; Francisco Gil de Arratia in 1716; Antonio Alejandro Blanco Infante and Mateo Gedler in 1720; Francisco Carlos Herrera and Ruy Fernández de Fuenmayor in 1724 and again in 1725.

In 1705 Francisco Felipe Tovar y Mijares and Francisco de Meneses comprised the third set of alcaldes ordinarios who governed in the absence of Nicolás de Ponte y Hoyo, who had fallen seriously ill in 1703. The children of these men were among those cacao hacendados who did not sign the 1744 letter to the king. Much later, in 1723, Miguel Ascanio Tovar was elected alcalde and became governor pro tem, and in January 1726 Domingo Antonio Tovar and Diego de Liendo were chosen for the position, with the expressed understanding that, because they did not belong to the factions opposed to Diego de Portales y Meneses, they could facilitate Portales's return to office. These three men did not sign the 1744 protest either.

33. AGI, Santa Domingo, leg. 787. "Rolde de los deudores a la Rl. Ca. Guipuzcoana, 10 de diciembre de 1744."

34. The genealogy of the Condes de San Javier is given in Alejandro Mario Capriles, *Coronas de Castilla en Venezuela* (Madrid, 1967), 275–279.

35. "Relación y noticia de todas las haciendas de trapiche que a la fecha de ésta se hallan en esta Provincia de Venezuela," April 25, 1752, AGI, Caracas, leg. 368.

36. The 1684 count is found in AGI, Contaduría, leg. 1613; the 1720 census is from Pedro José de Olavarriaga, *Instrucción General y Particular del Estado Presente de la Provincia de Venezuela en los años 1720 y 1721* (Caracas, 1965); and the 1744 count is in AGN, Caracas, Sección Diversos, XXVII.

37. The relevant genealogical information is in Iturriza Guillén, *Familias caraqueñas*, 1:164–168, 211–212.

38. The yield in fanegas per 1000 trees was given on a valley-by-valley basis by Olavarriaga in the 1720 *Instrucción*; the 1744 yields are assumed to have been the same as they were in 1720.

39. The relevant genealogical information is in Iturriza Guillén, *Familias caraqueñas*, 1:202–208.

40. Iturriza Guillén, *Familias caraqueñas*, 1:203. Ricardos to the king, April 30, 1752, AGI, Caracas, leg. 421.

41. Sucre, *Gobernadores*, 279–283. In the margin of this letter the secretary of the Navy and Indies in the Council of the Indies, former Caracas

governor Julian de Arriaga, noted: "It is understood what he says to me about the *contador mayor*, and I have always been persuaded that in royal offices it is best to have a European, but not a Vizcayan." José Solano to Arriaga, May 20, 1768, AGI, Caracas, leg. 57. In 1772 Juan Bolívar was still only interim *contador*, AGI, Santo Domingo, leg. 549.

42. Iturriza Guillén, *Familias caraqueñas*, 2:603–616, AGI, Contaduría, leg. 1613.

43. This was probably the San Matheo estate where Simón Bolívar and other elites gathered in 1808 to discuss their discontent with Caracas's place in Spain's empire. "Real Audiencia (Caracas) a Juan de Casas y Berrera, Gobernador de Venezuela," November 24, 1808, manuscript in the Lilly Library, Indiana University. "Relación y noticia de todas las haciendas de trapiche," AGI, Caracas, leg. 368.

7. FIRST FAMILIES

1. Waldron, "Social History," 105 and 303–304 (appendix 1); chap. 3 of Waldron's dissertation is a comprehensive general study of this census. Some of Waldron's conclusions differ from those of the present study, however. The census document is in the Biblioteca Nacional de Venezuela, Caracas. "Matrículas de las parróquias de Caracas y demás pueblos de su diócecis, 1759." In 1750, according to the summary provided by cabildo regidor Fernando Lovera, there had been 18,008 individuals in Caracas and 179,716 in the province as a whole. "Recopilación o resumen Gral. de las Almas que tiene esta Gobernación de Venezuela y Caracas según consta de las matrículas del año 1750 y 51 de todo el obispado," April 22, 1752. AGI, Caracas, leg. 368.

2. This definition of elite is different from one based on the composition of the household that was used by Waldron. For her, an elite household was one headed by a white individual called *don* or *doña* by the census taker, and in which resided many more than the average number of both whites and slaves. Waldron, "Social History," 50–51. In 1759 there were many individuals of impeccable elite status, office holders with wealth and established social prominence, who lived with only a spouse and a few children or other relatives (and many slaves, to be sure). The households of these people, because of the small number of whites in them, would be overlooked if the composition of the household is used as a definition of elite residence.

3. For the city as a whole in 1759 Waldron notes that only 13 percent of all households were extended either vertically or laterally, and that only 8 percent of all households were "extended patriarchal," that is both extended and headed by men. Many of these households, she found, were residences of the elite. Ibid., 116–118. The several studies which show that wealthy whites commonly lived in nuclear-family households are discussed in Linda Greenow, "Microgeographic Analysis as an Index to Family Structure and Networks," *Journal of Family History* 10 (Fall, 1985): 277.

4. In eighty-two of eighty-five elite households the head of household or the spouse of the head of household had at least one sibling living elsewhere in Caracas in 1759. Two blocks was the average distance be-

tween these eighty-two households and the residences of all the siblings of the eighty-two heads of household and their spouses.

Genealogical and demographic data used in the family reconstitutions, the identification of broader networks of kindred, and the study of cousin marriage on which the rest of this chapter depends come from the same sources cited in previous chapters: Iturriza Guillén, *Familias caraqueñas* and *Familias valencianas*. Less useful is Sangróniz y Castro, *Familias coloniales*.

Analysis of the spatial dimension of elite residence presented several problems. The priest who took the census in 1759 identified households by the *cuadra* on which they were located. Each block received a religious name, for example, the cuadra between the cathedral and the plaza was "Nuestra Señora de Venezuela y Santa Ana," while the next block to the south on the same street, where the residence of ex-governor Felipe Ricardos was located, was called "Dulce Nombre de María." However, the cuadra composed both sides of a street from one corner to the next; consequently it is not possible to determine on which side of the street any given house was located. A more fundamental problem was the difficulty in locating the cuadras on a street map of the city. The census takers did not follow any consistent pattern in their canvas of the city. The key to the solution of this problem proved to be a description, "Plano de la Ciudad Mariana de Caracas," prepared by the bishop Antonio Diez Madroñero in 1766. The document follows each street from beginning to end as it crossed the city, giving the name of each cuadra in succession. An abbreviated version of the "Plano" is published in Enrique Bernardo Núñez, *La ciudad de los Techos Rojos*, 4th ed. (Caracas, 1973), 168–173.

5. The research on kin household clusters is surveyed in Greenow, "Micrographic Analysis," 277–278.

6. This couple lived in the cuadra "Nuestra Señora de las Lágrimas," located in the southwest corner of the parish, five blocks from the plaza mayor. Juan Mijares's legitimate half-brother, the third Marqués de Mijares, and Melchora Tovar's sister, María Josefa Tovar, were residents in houses on the block "La Visitación de Nuestra Señora," located two blocks north of the plaza.

7. This count was made easier by the publication of the marriage registry for the cathedral parish, Instituto Venezolano de Genealogía, *Matrimonios y velaciones*.

8. Susan Migden Socolow, "Marriage, Birth and Inheritance: The Merchants of Eighteenth-Century Buenos Aires," *Hispanic American Historical Review* 60 (August 1980): 390. This difference is most likely due to the fact that, although in Buenos Aires resident merchants were eager to marry their daughters to immigrants with strong commercial connections in Spain, in Caracas such competition was not the rule because the Guipuzcoana Company controlled the European market for Caracas produce, there were few immigrant merchants, and most elite marriages were between men and women from established planter families. As is argued here, with time the number of individuals who were members of families with claims to elite status increased more rapidly than the cacao economy could expand, thus in this sense there was no particular incentive or advantage to early marriage.

9. Because these calculations are made on the basis of averages of all children without regard for the rank order of their birth, firstborn offspring would have been more likely than the average interval suggests to marry while their fathers and mothers were alive, last-born less likely.

10. This is because the genealogical studies of Iturriza Guillén and Sangróniz y Castro rarely include birth dates for individuals born in the seventeenth century. The 296 cases are all those elites listed in these genealogies, both married and unmarried, who lived to adulthood and for whom both a birth date and a death date are known.

11. Waldron describes the epidemic, although she mistakenly identifies it as measles; "Social History," 25–27.

12. Both the structure and the frequency of first-cousin marriages are influenced by the size of the pool of cousins who are at risk of marriage. Here the structure of first-cousin marriage does not consider the size or composition of this pool. The large number of cases considered, taken as they are from the entire century, gives credence to the argument that the high incidence of mother's brother's daughter marriages was due to strategic choices, and not the result of a consistently greater number of cousins of this type at risk of marriage. In the anthropological idiom, cousins who marry are cross-cousins if their related parents are siblings of unlike sex. Matrilateral cross-cousin marriages are those in which a man marries his mother's brother's daughter, and this form was the preferred one in eighteenth-century Caracas. In the structuralist view of Lévi-Strauss, matrilateral cross-cousin marriage functions to regularize the exchange of women between or among several patrilineages (men give their daughters to their sister's sons for brides, and receive daughters for their sons from their wives' patrilineage), which produces interdependence and social solidarity among groups that might otherwise be antagonistic to one another. Claude Lévi-Strauss, *The Elementary Structure of Kinship*, rev. ed. (Boston, 1969). Although in colonial Caracas matrilateral cross-cousin marriage was merely preferred by the elite, and was not prescriptive, it did serve to connect patrilineages to one another, defusing the intergenerational authority of patriarchs.

13. The thirteen remaining elite households were headed by single individuals or by several unmarried siblings.

14. Of the twelve households in which the heads were cousins alive in 1759, the structure of the relationship of the husband to wife was:

Father's Brother's Daughter:	2	Mother's Brother's Daughter:	4
Father's Sisters's Daughter:	2	Mother's Sister's Daughter:	4

Of the nineteen households in which the heads were either cousins who were both alive in 1759 or widows and widowers whose cousin–spouses had died, the structure of the relationship of husband to wife was:

Father's Brother's Daughter:	5	Mother's Brother's Daughter:	5
Father's Sister's Daughter:	2	Mother's Sister's Daughter:	7

15. By decade, the following surnames were linked in first-cousin elite marriages:

1720s: Aguirre, Blanco (3), Herrera, Loreto, Lovera (2), Mijares, Obelmejía, Rengifo, Tovar

1730s: Aguirre, Blanco, Ibarra, Liendo (3), Mijares (2), Ponte

1740s: Blanco (4), Bolívar, Gedler, Hidalgo, Mijares, Tovar (2)

This information comes from Iturriza Guillén, ed., *Matrimonios y velaciones*.

16. In a printed broadsheet received by the Council of the Indies in March 1739, the Guipuzcoana Company accused the Marqués de Toro and the Conde de San Javier of being "the only, or the principal merchants, who for themselves, or on commission for merchants in Veracruz" control the cacao trade between Caracas and New Spain. The Basque monopolists accused them of wanting to keep the Company out of this lucrative commerce. The Company claimed that because Toro and San Javier monopolized this exchange they were able to buy cheaply in Caracas and sell at a high price in Mexico. *Los directores de la Rl. Compañía Guipuzcoana de Caracas*, copy in AGI, Santo Domingo, leg. 786. Zuloaga to the king, February 26, 1745, ibid.

17. No Blanco married a Mijares (Marqués de Mijares), a Pacheco (Conde de San Javier), a Berroterán (Marqués del Valle de Santiago), or a Rodríguez de Toro (Marqués del Toro). In 1721 Catarina Blanco y Martínez de Villegas married José Tovar Galindo, and their son, Martín Tovar Blanco, became the first Conde de Tovar in 1771.

18. Ricardos to the king, August 1, 1751, AGI, Caracas, leg. 421.

19. Hussey confused the two men and believed that the count of San Javier was Alejandro Blanco Uribe. *Caracas Company*, 118, 356.

20. AGI, Caracas, leg. 421. Hussey quotes an unidentified minister who claimed that the count of San Javier could not contain his pleasure ("*se le soltaba la risa*") when he came before authorities after the news of the 1749 rebellion reached Spain; *Caracas Company*, 139.

21. The list is credited to Sebastián de Eslava, ex-viceroy of New Granada, by Demetrio Ramos Pérez, "La politica de Marqués de la Ensenada—asesorado por el ex-virrey Eslava—en relación con el levantamiento contra la Guipuzcoana," in his *Estudios de Historia Venezolana*, 672.

22. There had been three such marriages in the Liendo family, including that of Antolín de Liendo, in 1738. Liendo's self-interest kept him close to the royal cause and out of the camp of the protesters. His is the exceptional case that proves the rule: his wife–cousin was his mother's sister's daughter, a Blanco, but also the daughter of the royal accountant, Martín Madera de los Rios. He was a lawyer, representative in Caracas of the Audiencia of New Granada when he married, and later a close collaborator of Ricardos's. Arriaga to Ensenada, March 26, 1753, AGI, Caracas, leg. 421. Liendo did not use the Blanco part of his surname, but his younger brother, Silvestre Liendo Blanco, did. Silvestre Liendo signed the 1744 memorial, and he also married a Blanco first-cousin.

8. THE KING IN CARACAS: THE BOURBON REFORMS

1. D. A. Brading, "Bourbon Spain and Its American Empire," in *The Cambridge History of Latin America* (Cambridge, 1984), 1:397–401.

2. Brading points out Arriaga's American experience in ibid., 397. Early in 1752 it was Arriaga, then serving as the intendant for Cádiz, who imprisoned Juan Francisco de León and the other accused insurgents when they arrived from Venezuela. In Caracas in 1750 he had pardoned these men for threats against the Guipuzcoana Company and their attack on La Guaira. In August 1752 Arriaga, then president of the Casa de la Contratación, wrote to inform the marquis de la Ensenada that León had died in the Hospital Real in Cádiz. Sucre, *Gobernadores*, 269–271. Arriaga to Ensenada, August 4, 1752, AGI, Caracas, leg. 421. It was Arriaga who suggested that Nicolás de León be sent to serve in the royal regiment at the African presidio of Orán; Arriaga to Ensenada, February 9, 1753, AGI, Caracas, 421.

3. Arriaga to the king, January 14, 1750, AGI, Caracas, 421.

4. Brading, "Bourbon Spain," 404.

5. Ricardos to the king, April 30, 1752, AGI, Caracas, leg. 421. Other elites recommended for recognition for their collaboration were Juan Manuel Herrera and *maestro de campo* Domingo Galindo.

6. Solano to Arriaga, May 20, 1768, AGI, Caracas, 57. Juan Bolívar's petition was denied, and he was still *contador interino* in 1772; AGI, Santo Domingo, leg. 549.

7. The stock issue, the price-setting policy, and the provision allowing Caracas cosecheros space for their cacao on Company ships were innovations. Perhaps none of these reforms was more significant than the decision agreed to by the Company's directors at their 1752 meeting in Guipúzcoa that a new issue of Company stock be made, doubling it in quantity, and that this stock be offered to Caracas residents. The proposal, which may have been more in the nature of a royal order, was made to the directors by the king's representative, ex-governor Julián de Arriaga. Information about this meeting comes from Jules Humbert, Spanish edition, *Los orígenes venezolanos* (Caracas, 1976), 112; original edition, *Les origines vénézuéliennes* (Bordeaux, 1905). Otherwise the reformed Company was simply obliged to return to the conditions of its original charter, which did not include the *alternativa* privilege or the right to restrict seaborne cacao transport. Notice of the reforms was published in *Real cédula de fundación de la Real Compañía Guipuzcoana de Caracas y Reglas económicas de buen gobierno . . . con adición de las posteriores declaraciones de Su Majestad sobre varios puntos, hasta el año 1753* (Madrid, 1765). A copy of this document is in AGI, Caracas, leg. 950-B. Hussey gives a general account of these changes in *Caracas Company*, chap. 6.

8. Arriaga to the king, January 14, 1750, AGI, Caracas, leg. 421.

9. "Resolución del Rey sobre la Provincia de Caracas y su Compañía," March 6, 1751, AGI, Caracas, leg. 57. Arriaga had brought a total of 1200 soldiers and cavalry with him from Spain; AGI, Caracas, leg. 418.

10. In 1751 the population of Caracas proper, limited to its several parishes and exclusive of its immediate rural hinterland, was 18,008 persons of all ages and sexes, not including the soldiers. "Recopilación o resumen Gral. de las Almas que tiene esta Gobernación de Venezuela y Caracas según consta de las matrículas del año 1750 y 51 de todo el obispado," April 22, 1752, AGI Caracas, leg. 368.

11. AGI, Caracas, leg. 57.

12. Ricardos to Ensenada, September 11, 1751, AGI, Caracas, leg. 421.

13. Prior to this, alcaldes ordinarios had repeated in office only when they had been elected in midyear to finish the incomplete term of a predecessor, or when they had taken, as was their privilege, the responsibility of the governor in the event of his unexpected absence and the failure of a new appointee to arrive by the beginning of the next year when elections were held. Alcaldes were reelected for both of these reasons during the difficult years from 1725 to 1727. See Sucre, *Gobernadores*, 240–242. The alcaldes ordinarios elected from 1752 to 1754 were Francisco Palacios Gedler and Diego de Ibarra. Palacios had less reason to quarrel with the Guipuzcoana Company than did other Caracas elites; see the estimate of his family's cacao holdings in chap. 6.

14. The expansion of cabildo offices is described in Waldron, "Social History," 203–219. No one has studied the records of the late eighteenth-century Caracas cabildo more closely than Waldron, who is certainly correct in her observation that the increased preoccupation with good government after midcentury

> ... reveals a shift away from concern with municipal regularity and towards a concern with the personal conduct of the city's inhabitants. Earlier, the cabildo focused on controlling the use of water, assuring an adequate supply of fresh meat, and maintaining streets and solares, but in the ensuing years, with the regulation of these matters well-established, a greater interest in the economic and social behavior of private citizens is detectable. (Ibid., 200–201)

Waldron errs, however, in assuming that this shift was a kind of natural evolution away from Spanish control due to population and economic growth of Caracas: "During the sixteenth and seventeenth centuries when the city remained no more than a town it was quite possible to manage the daily affairs of Caracas from laws originating in Spain. In the eighteenth century, however, when the city grew most rapidly and expanded its activities significantly, it was no longer feasible or desirable to rely on Spain for direction." Ibid., 199–200. To the contrary, as undesirable as it was for Caraqueños, the increase in town government in the 1750s was precisely the result of the increased interest of the crown in controlling the behavior of its Caracas subjects.

15. José Luis de Cisneros, *Descripción exacta de la Provincia de Benezuela* (Valencia, 1764; facsimile edition, Caracas, 1950), 43.

16. See, for example, Sucre, *Gobernadores*, 273; Núñez, *La ciudad*, 17, 245; and Waldron, "Social History," 205–206. The foremost historian of colonial Venezuelan architecture, Graziano Gasparini, gives no explanation of Ricardos's motives in his *Caracas: La ciudad colonial y Guzmancista* (Caracas, 1978), 59: "Para la historia de la ciudad, el nombre de Ricardos está ligado a las tiendas que mandó construir en 1755 alrededor de la Plaza Mayor, las cuales—poco más de un siglo después—fueron demolidas por orden de Guzmán Blanco a fin de convertir la Plaza Mayor en Plaza Bolívar."

17. Waldron notes that it was very unusual for the cabildo to undertake an enterprise as costly as this, but she is unaware of the role of Ricardos when she states that "Given the large amount of money involved it is evident that the city believed the improvement of its plaza and market facilities essential." Waldron, "Social History," 205–206.

18. Report of Lorenzo Rosel de Lugo to Ricardos, January 31, 1752, AGI, Caracas, leg. 421.
19. Ricardos to Ensenada, May 1, 1752, AGI, Caracas, leg. 368.
20. "Instrucción pública" promulgated by Ricardos, November 15, 1752; and revision of the tax schedules issued April 28, 1753, AGI, Caracas, leg. 368.
21. Ricardos to Ensenada, May 1, 1752, AGI, Caracas, leg. 368.
22. In 1751 the cabildo voted public funds to build three new *carnicerías*, bringing the total number to four. Waldron suggests that this major increase in slaughterhouses might have been done "to keep abreast of population growth and the physical extension of the city"; "Social History," 249. It would seem more likely, however, that the cabildo was persuaded to quadruple its processing facilities so that meat could be more efficiently taxed. In its own estimate of the productive capacity of the province, done to illustrate to the Crown that 150,000 pesos in revenue could not be gotten from the reformed alcabala, the cabildo assumed that 137,000 head of cattle were consumed province-wide per year, but it was acknowledged that this figure was far from certain, "due to the irregularity of the butchering and sale [of cattle] in the countryside at a distance from the community because of the lack of *mataderos* and *carnicerías*." Cabildo to Ensenada, April 28, 1753, AGI, Caracas, leg. 368.
23. The Guipuzcoana Company blamed Dutch smugglers, who could undersell them by as much as 35 percent and whose ships could not be stopped by their inferior coast-guard vessels, for the busy contraband trade which caused the Company to operate at a deficit of 350,000 pesos for the period January 1752 to November 1755. Hussey, *Caracas Company*, 180–183. The prohibition on shipping cacao by sea from sites located upwind from La Guaira, while it forced cacao growers to send their beans to port overland by expensive muletrain, was intended to stop contraband on the coast. Permission to renew seaborne transport of cacao, granted as part of the reform which returned to Guipuzcoana Company to the conditions of its original charter, may have given new impetus to smuggling.
24. *Auto* of Ricardos, April 28, 1753; Cabildo to Ensenada, May 28, 1753, AGI, Caracas, leg. 368.
25. Arriaga to Ensenada, September 11, 1753, AGI, Caracas, leg. 368.
26. A summary of the credits and debits of the Real Hacienda for the province of Caracas for 1771 and 1772 are in AGI, Caracas, leg. 33. The record for the last months of 1777 and 1778 are published in Mario Briceño-Iragorry, ed., *Orígenes de la Hacienda en Venezuela (documentos inéditos de la época colonial)* (Caracas, 1942), 187–208. The revised alcabala taxes are identified by Ricardos's name in the entries in both cases, although there is a discrepancy as to when the policy was decreed. The 1772 document reads: "Por el Real Derecho de Alcabala de tierra que según instrucción formada por don Felipe Ricardos, Gob. y Capitán General que fue de esta Provincia en veinte y cinco de abril de mil setecientos cincuenta y tres con facultad y aprobación Real . . . "; in 1778 the date for the origin of the policy is some months earlier: "Este Ramo se cobra por Real Orden de 15 de noviembre de 1752, conforme a la Instrucción formada por el Excmo. Sr. Dn. Felipe Ricardos, Gobernador y Capitán General que fué de esta Provincia con facultades reales."

27. In good baroque style, the first letters of each line were arranged as an acrostic to form the word "RICARDOS," and they were carved perpendicular to the horizontal so that their meaning could not be missed. A rather free translation of the tablet follows:

> THE VERY EXCELLENT SENOR DON PHELIPE RICARDOS
> LIEUTENANT GENERAL OF THE ROYAL ARMIES OF HIS MAJESTY GOVERNOR
> CAPTAIN GENERAL OF THIS PROVINCE OF VENEZUELA
> CALL ON FAME WITH SHOUTING HORN
> IN UNKNOWN CLIMES AND RESOUNDING VOICES
> PROCLAIM RICARDOS A TRUE HERO
> REALIZING RAPID VICTORIES
> RENDER HIM THIS CITY WITH FITTING CARE
> DUE THANKS FOR YOUR NEW PLEASURES
> TODAY IN THIS NEW STREET THERE IS SO MUCH IMPROVEMENT
> OF YOUR PROPERTIES WITH THE INCREASING REVENUES
>
> YEAR 1754

Of course the governor's message did not mention that the increasing revenues went to pay for a standing army in the city. This inscription is quoted or a photograph of the tablet is shown in Sucre, *Gobernadores*, 274; Núñez, *La ciudad*, 18; and Gasparini, *Caracas*, 60, but only as a curiosity. None of these authors make any critical comment about the Ricardos poem.

28. Remírez to Arriaga, March 14, 1761. Twice before Remírez had written to the king on this matter, first in response to a royal order to reduce tobacco farming (issued on July 25, 1757) on April 6, 1758, and again on March 25, 1759; AGI, Caracas, leg. 57.

29. AGI, Caracas, leg. 367.

30. Arriaga to Remírez, October 24, 1758, AGI, Caracas, leg. 57. That association with the rebellion left no lasting stain on the Rodríguez de Toro family may have been due in part to the fact that Bernardo José Rodríguez de Toro, the younger brother of the deceased marquis, was oidor in the Audiencia of New Spain, a post that had been purchased for him for 15,000 pesos in 1741, the year before the death of his father, the first Marqués de Toro. Mark A. Burkholder and D. S. Chandler, *Biographical Dictionary of Audiencia Ministers in the Americas, 1687–1821* (Westport, Conn., 1982), 297. This was the highest position in Spain's imperial bureaucracy ever obtained by a Caracas native son. There is no record of the outcome of a second request made by the widow Ascanio in 1760. She wrote to the king that she had been given legal guardianship by her husband of their ten children, and that without royal help she would be unable to keep their house "in the decency and character" with which his majesty had endowed it. Her request was to be allowed to make five voyages to Veracruz and one to Spain with cacao, paying only one-third the royal duties in each case. She also asked to be allowed to send the same ship to *colonias amigas* to buy 100 slaves for her haciendas and those of her children, and she asked that her son be allowed to assume the title and mayorazgo of the marquisate without paying the *media anata* tax. Theresa de Ascanio, Marquesa de Toro, to the king, May 25, 1760, AGI, Caracas,

leg. 367. The grant of the title of count to Martín de Tovar is discussed in Núñez, *La ciudad*, 259.

31. Unlike societies where inheritance divisions were discretionary and obedient children could expect material rewards in a father's will for their services, this extended period of waiting in the father's home did not provide a commensurate increase in paternal authority, for in elite Caracas homes slaves did the work and the bipartible inheritance rule ensured an equal share for every heir.

32. Born in 1682, don Lorenzo was probably the only elite man in Caracas in 1759 who had clear, firsthand recollections of the first years of the War of Spanish Succession and the short-lived movement in 1702 and 1703 led by some of the Caracas elite, including his father, to reject the sovereignty of the Bourbon Philip of Anjou in favor of the Habsburg Archduke Charles of Austria. The details of this event remain obscure; see Analola Borges, *La casa de Austria en Venezuela durante la guerra de sucesión española (1702–1715)* (Santa Cruz de Tenerife, 1963). In April 1759, the oldest elite woman died, Francisca Tovar Mijares, aged eighty-eight; she had already married twice, in 1691 and again in 1698, before the death of Charles II brought an end to Habsburg rule in the Spanish world.

33. AGI, Caracas, leg. 57. He died August 10, 1759.

34. The Company of Noble Adventurers was initiated by don José Solano y Bote, governor of Caracas from 1763 to 1771; Sucre, *Gobernadores*, 279–281. "Compañía de Nobles Aventureros Acaballo de la ciudad de Santiago de León de Caracas, formada de sus hijos nobles," 25 July 1768, AGI, Caracas, leg. 850.

Glossary

ACTAS. Acts or proceedings.
AGUARDIENTE. Liquor made from sugar cane.
ALBAÑIL. Bricklayer or stone mason.
ACHAQUE. Physical infirmity, especially habitual illness associated with old age.
ALCALDE ORDINARIO. Annually elected judge of municipal council.
ALCABALA. Sales tax.
ALFÉREZ MAYOR. Senior *regidor;* municipal standard-bearer.
ALHORRA. Crop blight.
ALMAJORIFAZGO. Tax on imports and exports.
ALMUD. Unit of measure; one-twelfth of a *fanega*.
ALTERNATIVA. System of loading ships on basis of their arrival at port. First arrival must load and depart before next could receive cargo.
ARBOLEDA. Grove of cacao trees.
ÁRBOLES DE LA TIERRA. Indigenous cacao trees.
ARROBA. Unit of measure; about 11.5 kilograms or 25 pounds.
ASIENTISTA. Holder of *asiento;* slave factor.
ASIENTO. A contract. The contract to supply slaves to the colony.
AUDIENCIA. The court or governing body of a region.
BACHILLER. Lowest academic degree, below master and doctor.
BAHAREQUE. Stick-and-mud building material.
BALANDRA. Small boat with a single mast.
BARLOVENTO. Windward.
CABALGADA. Armed expedition to capture slaves or booty.
CABILDO. Municipal council
CABO. Corporal; subordinate to *teniente de justicia mayor*.
CACIQUE. Indian chief.
CANARIO. Canary Islander.
CANASTILLA. Small shop built in wall of central plaza.
CANOA. Canoe or trough.
CAPITÁN. Head of a company, commander of a sailing vessel.
CARAQUEÑO. Person from Caracas.
CARGA. A load; a *fanega* and a half of dried cacao beans.
CARNICERÍA. Slaughterhouse.
CARRERA DE VERACRUZ. Cacao trade between Caracas and Mexico.
CASTELLANO. Governor's lieutenant in charge of royal fort at La Guaira.

Glossary

CÉDULA. Royal order or instruction.
CIMARRÓN. Fugitive or runaway slave.
COGOLLO. Building material made of sugar cane stalks.
COMPADRAZGO. Relationship through godparents.
COMPADRE. Godparent.
COMPOSICIÓN DE TIERRAS. Legalization of land titles by payment of a fee.
CONCUÑADOS. Men who are brothers-in-law because they are married to sisters.
CONTRABANDISTA. Smuggler.
CORREGIDOR DE INDIOS. Official in charge of an Indian district.
COSECHERO. Cacao planter.
CRIOLLO. Individual or item of American or colonial origin.
CUADRA. Portion of street from one corner to the next; the houses on both sides of that portion of the street.
CURANDERA. Healer, herbalist.
DIEZMOS. Any tax of 10 percent; the church tithe.
ENCOMENDERO. The holder or an *encomienda*.
ENCOMIENDA. Royal grant of Indians for labor or tribute.
ESCRIBANO. Public notary.
ESCRIBANÍA. Office of notary.
ESTANCIA. In Caracas context, a wheat farm.
EJIDO. Land held communally by township.
FANEGA. A dry measure; in Caracas context 1.5 bushels.
FANEGADA DE SEMBRADURA. Area planted with one *fanega* of seed.
FLOTA. Fleet; Spain's transatlantic convoy system.
FORASTERO. Outsider, nonresident.
FORTALEZA. Fort.
FRAZADA MESTIZA. Woolen blanket made in Mexico.
GAMELOTE. Leaf of an aquatic plant; used for roofing material.
GOLETA. Small, double-masted ship.
GRANDES CACAOS. Elite cacao planters.
HACENDADO. Owner of a hacienda.
HACIENDA DE CACAO. Cacao estate.
HATO. A cattle ranch.
HIDALGUÍA. Quality of nobility.
HIPOTECA. Mortgage.
ISLEÑO. Canary Islander.
JUEZ DE COMISOS. Official responsible for contraband goods.
JUNTA GENERAL. Open or public town meeting; *cabildo abierto*.
LADINO. A Spanish-speaking, Hispanicized individual.
LABRADOR. Spanish farmer.
LEGAJO. Bundle of documents.
LEGUA. League; in Caracas context, a distance of about 5.7 kilometers.
LETRADO. Lawyer; holder of a law degree.
LIENZO. Common cotton cloth.
MAESTRE DE CAMPO. Superior militia officer.

MAJORDOMO. Estate overseer or manager.
MANDADOR. Leader or driver of a slave gang.
MANTUANO. Member of elite Caracas family.
MATALOTAJE. Expenses paid to muleteers.
MAYORAZGO. An entailed property.
MERCADER. Large-scale merchant.
MESTIZAJE. Miscegenation.
MOLINO. Mill; in Caracas context, water-powered mill to grind wheat to flour.
MORENO LIBRE. Free person of color.
NEGRO. Black; person of African ancestry.
OBRA PÍA. Pious donation.
OIDOR. *Audiencia* judge.
PADRÓN. A census or listing of individuals or property.
PAJA. Dried grass, straw.
PAQUETES. Small shops built in wall of central plaza.
PARDO. Person of mixed African and Hispanic descent
PESO. Monetary unit; 8 *reales*.
PROTOCOLOS. Notary records.
PULPERÍA. General retail store.
RANCHOS. Small, wooden, tent-covered retail stalls in central plaza.
REAL. Monetary unit; the *peso* was divided into eight silver *reales*.
REAL HACIENDA. Royal treasury.
REGIDOR. Council member of a *cabildo*.
RELACIONES GEOGRÁFICAS. Geographical surveys.
RENTA. Income.
REPARTIMIENTO POR PADRÓN. System, based on number of cacao trees owned, of determining amount of cacao a *hacendado* could ship in *tercio buque*.
SERVICIO PERSONAL. Primitive *encomienda*; labor provided by Indians without official assignment or contract directly to *encomendero*.
TIERRA ADENTRO. The interior.
TENIENTE; TENIENTE DE JUSTICIA MAYOR. Governor's lieutenant in rural district; justice of the peace.
TERCIO BUQUE. The third part of a ship's cargo hold.
TRAPICHE. Small sugar estate and mill.
TUTELA. Legal custodianship of minor children.
VARA. Distance equivalent to .83 meter.
VECINO. Full citizen or resident of a town; householder.
VELLÓN. Copper money.
VISITADOR. Inspector.
VIZCAÍNO. A person from the province of Vizcaya, a Vizcayan; in eighteenth-century Caracas idiom any person of Basque origin.
VIUDA. Widow.
ZAMBO. A person of African and Indian ancestry.

Bibliography

ABBREVIATIONS USED IN NOTES AND BIBLIOGRAPHY

AA   Archivo Arquidiocesano, Caracas
AANH   Archivo de la Academia Nacional de la Historia, Caracas
ACC   *Actas del Cabildo de Caracas*, 12 vols. (Caracas, 1943–1975).
ACM   Archivo del Consejo Municipal de Distrito Federal, Caracas
AGI   Archivo General de Indias, Seville
AGN   Archivo General de la Nación, Caracas
ARPC   Archivo del Registro Principal de Caracas

The history of early Venezuela remains among the least studied of Spain's American colonies. The city and province of Caracas are better known than the rest of the region comprised by the modern Venezuelan nation, yet here too historians have shown only modest interest. Therefore the present study necessarily relies principally on unpublished materials. The manuscript documents cited in this book are housed in the following archives: in Caracas, the Archivo del Registro Principal de Caracas; the Archivo de la Academia Nacional de la Historia; the Archivo General de la Nación; the Archivo de Consejo Municipal del Distrito Federal; the Archivo Arquidiocesano; and the Sección Libros Raros y Antiguos of the Biblioteca Nacional. In Spain, the Archivo General de Indias was also consulted extensively.

The Archivo del Registro Principal de Caracas is the depository where most of the unwritten past of colonial Caracas, both town and province, awaits discovery. There are four important colonial collections in this archive. The section *Escribanías* contains notary records that are complete from 1595 through most of the nineteenth century. Wills and estate inventories are located in *Testamentarías*, but these records often include most useful inheritance cases tried at law and the division of estates. The ledgers used for the analyses of the wheat estancia and cacao haciendas in chapter 3 and the Piñate cacao haciendas in chapter 4 were found attached to Testamentarías wills. *Tierras* contains documents from the early seventeenth century pertaining to cases brought to law over property and water rights. None of the collections in the Registro Principal has a serviceable index, but, with the exception of *Civiles*, they are arranged in chronological order and, if the researcher has physical access to the stacks, they can be consulted with reasonable efficiency. This is not the case with *Civiles*, a section that comprises a vast quantity of materials, much of which is contained in black cardboard cartons identified only as *Cajas Negras*. These documents treat for the most part a wide variety of legal cases, many of them judged originally by the cabildo's alcaldes ordinarios, but the section is in general disorder and it has almost never been consulted by historians.

The Archivo de la Academia Nacional de la Historia has a useful collection of copies of documents pertaining to Caracas, *Traslados*, the originals of which are in the Archivo General de las Indias, Seville. Other sections utilized in this study are: *Fundadores de Caracas*, *Caracas*, and *Misiones de Capuchinos*. The continuing series of monographs and document collections published by the National Academy, the Biblioteca de la Academia Nacional de la Historia, has made a most important contribution to the study of colonial Venezuela. The volumes of this series used in this study are listed in the appropriate section of this bibliography.

The Archivo General de la Nación is the principal historical archive in Venezuela. Especially useful were the sections *Encomiendas*, *Real Hacienda*, and *Diversos*. In the Archivo Arquidiocesano I consulted the sections *Episcopales*, which is arranged in chronological order by bishop, *Obras pías*, and *Matrimoniales*, in which are recorded many of the dispensations given by the Church to allow cousins to marry. Several manuscripts from the colonial period are to be found in the Sección Libros Raros y Antiguos of the Biblioteca Nacional, including the important household census, "Matrículas de las parróquias de Caracas y demás pueblos de su diócesis, 1759." Finally, the archive of the Consejo Municipal de Distrito Federal has the manuscript of the records of the town council. These have been published through the year 1668; thereafter they must be consulted in the Consejo archive, and this collection is referred to in the notes as Archivo del Consejo Municipal (ACM), Actas del Cabildo, Originales.

In the Archivo General de Indias, Seville, important material was located in the following sections: Santo Domingo, Caracas, Santa Fe, and Contaduría.

The following are the articles, books, and published documents cited in the text and the notes.

Acosta Saignes, Miguel. *Vida de los esclavos negros en Venezuela*. Caracas: Hespérides, 1967.

Actas del cabildo de Caracas. 12 vols. Caracas: Tipografía Vargas, 1943–1975.

Actas del cabildo eclesiástico de Caracas. 2 vols. Biblioteca de la Academia Nacional de la Historia, nos. 65–66. Caracas: Italgráfica, 1965.

Amezaga Aresti, Vicente de. *Hombres de Compañía Guipuzcoana*. Colección histórico-económica venezolana, vol. 9. Caracas: Banco Central de Venezuela, 1963.

Arcila Farías, Eduardo. *Economía colonial de Venezuela*. 2 vols. Caracas: Italgráfica, 1973; Mexico City: Fondo de Cultura Económica, 1946.

———. *El régimen de la encomienda en Venezuela*. Seville: Escuela de Estudios Hispano-Americanos, 1957.

———. *Comercio entre Venezuela y México en los siglos xvii y xviii*. Mexico City: El Colegio de México, 1950.

———et al., eds. and comps. *La obra pía de Chuao, 1568–1825*. Universidad Central de Venezuela. Caracas: Imprenta Universitaria, 1968.

Bakewell, Peter J. *Silver Mining and Society in Colonial Mexico: Zacatecas, 1546–1700*. Cambridge: Cambridge University Press, 1971.

Blank, Stephanie. "Patrons, Clients, and Kin in Seventeenth-Century Caracas: A Methodological Essay in Spanish American Social History." *Hispanic American Historical Review* 54 (1974): 260–283.

———. "Societal Integration and Social Stability in a Colonial Spanish American City, Caracas 1595–1627." Ph.D. diss., University of Wisconsin, Madison, 1971.

Borges, Analola. *La casa de Austria en Venezuela durante la guerra de sucesión española (1702–1715)*. Santa Cruz de Tenerife: Goya Artes Gráficas, 1963.

———. *Alvarez Abreu y su extraordinaria misión en Indias*. Santa Cruz de Tenerife: Goya Artes Gráficas, 1963.

———. *Isleños en Venezuela: La gobernación de Ponte y Hoyo*. Santa Cruz de Tenerife: Goya Artes Gráficas, 1960.

Boyd-Bowman, Peter. "Patterns in Spanish Emigration to the Indies, 1579–1600." *The Americas* 33 (1976): 78–95.
Brading, David A. "Bourbon Spain and Its American Empire." In *The Cambridge History of Latin America*, vol. 1, ed. Leslie Bethell, 384–439. New York: Cambridge University Press, 1984.
Braudel, Fernand, and F. Spooner. "Prices in Europe from 1450 to 1750." In *The Cambridge Economic History of Europe*, vol. 4, ed. E. E. Rich and C. H. Wilson,, chap. 7. New York: Cambridge University Press, 1967.
———. *The Mediterranean and the Mediterranean World in the Age of Philip II*. 2 Vols. New York: Harper & Row, 1972.
Briceño-Iragorry, Mario, ed. *Orígenes de la hacienda en Venezuela (documentos inéditos de la época colonial)*. Caracas: Imprenta Nacional, 1942.
Bronner, Fred. "Urban Society in Colonial Spanish America: Research Trends." *Latin American Research Review* 21 (1986): 3–72.
Burkholder, Mark A., and D. S. Chandler. *Biographical Dictionary of Audiencia Ministers in the Americas, 1687–1821*. Westport, Conn.: Greenwood Press, 1982.
Campillo y Cosio, José. *Nuevo sistema de gobierno económico para la América*. [1743]. Madrid: Imprenta de B. Cano, 1789.
Capriles, Alejandro Mario. *Coronas de Castilla en Venezuela*. Madrid: Gráficas Orbe, 1967.
Castillo Lara, Lucas Guillermo. *Materiales para la historia provincial de Aragua*. Biblioteca de la Academia Nacional de la Historia, no. 128. Caracas: Italgráfica, 1977.
———. *Las acciones militares del gobernador Ruy Fernández de Fuenmayor (1637–1644)*. Biblioteca de la Academia Nacional de la Historia, no. 134. Caracas: Italgráfica, 1978.
———. *Apuntes para la historia colonial de Barlovento*. Biblioteca de la Academia Nacional de la Historia, no. 151. Caracas: Italgráfica, 1981.
———. *La aventura fundacional de los isleños*. Biblioteca de la Academia Nacional de la Historia, no. 163. Caracas: Italgráfica, 1983.
Cedularios de la monarquiá española de Margarita, Nueva Andalucia y Caracas (1553–1604). 8 vols. Enrique Otte, comp. Caracas, 1959–1967.
Chardon, Roland. "The Elusive Spanish League: A Problem of Measurement in Sixteenth-Century New Spain." *Hispanic American Historical Review* 60 (1980): 294–302.
Chaunu, Pierre. *Séville et l'Amerique: XVI–XVIIe siècle*. Paris: A. Colin, 1977.
Chaunu, Huguette, and Pierre Chaunu. *Séville et l'Atlantique (1504–1650)*. 8 vols. Paris: A. Colin, 1955–1958.
Cisneros, José Luis de. *Descripción exacta de la Provincia de Benezuela (1764)*. Caracas: Editorial Avila Gráfica, 1950.
De Armas Chitty, José Antonio. *Caracas: Origen y trayectoria de una ciudad*. 2 vols. Caracas, 1967.
———, and Manuel Pinto C., eds. *Juan Francisco de León: Diaro de una insurgencia*. Caracas, 1971.

De la Rosa, Leopoldo. "La emigración canaria a Venezuela en los siglos xvii y xviii." *Anuario de Estudios Atlánticos* (Tenerife), 20 (1976): 617–631.
Depons, François. *Viaje a la parte oriental de Tierra Firme en la América Meridional.* 2 vols. Enrique Planchart, trans. Caracas, 1960.
Díaz, Manuel Guillermo. *El agresivo obispado caraqueño de don Fray Mauro de Tovar.* Caracas: Tipografía Vargas, 1956.
Documentos relativos a la insurrección de Juan Francisco de León. Buenos Aires: Instituto Panamericano de Geografía e Historia, 1949.
Documentos para el estudio de los esclavos negros en Venezuela. Selection and commentary by Ermila Troconis de Veracoechea. Biblioteca de la Academia Nacional de la Historia, no. 103. Caracas: Italgráfica, 1969.
Documentos para la historia de la iglesia colonial en Venezuela. 2 vols. Guillermo Figuera, ed. Biblioteca de la Academia Nacional de la Historia, nos. 74 and 75. Caracas: Italgráfica, 1965.
Encomiendas. Archivo General de la Nación. 5 vols. Caracas, 1945–1958.
Febres Cordero, Tulio. *Archivo de historia y variedades.* 2 vols. Caracas: Editorial Sur América, 1930–1931.
Ferry, Robert J. "Encomienda, African Slavery, and Agriculture in Seventeenth-Century Caracas." *Hispanic American Historical Review* 61 (1981): 609–635.
Gacetilla de nombres geográficos. Caracas: Ministerio de Obras Públicas, 1974.
García Bernal, Cristina. *Yucatán: Poblacíon y encomienda bajo los Austrias.* Seville, 1972.
García Chuecos, Hector. *Historia documental de Venezuela.* Caracas: Editorial Rex, 1957.
Gasparini, Graziano. *Caracas: La ciudad colonial y Guzmancista.* Caracas: E. Armitano, 1978.
Gibson, Charles. *The Aztecs Under Spanish Rule: A History of the Indians of the Valley of Mexico, 1519–1810.* Stanford, Calif: Stanford University Press, 1964.
Góngora, Mario. "Urban Social Stratification in Colonial Chile." *Hispanic American Historical Review* 55 (1975): 421–446.
———. *Studies in the Colonial History of Spanish America.* New York: Cambridge University Press, 1975.
Greenow, Linda. "Microgeographic Analysis as an Index to Family Structure and Networks." *Journal of Family History* 10 (1985): 272–283.
Hamilton, Earl J. *American Treasure and the Price Revolution in Spain, 1501–1650.* Cambridge, Mass.: Harvard University Press, 1934.
Hargreaves-Mawdsley, W. N. *Eighteenth-Century Spain 1700–1788: A Political, Diplomatic and Institutional History.* Totowa, N.J.: Rowman and Littlefield, 1979.
Haring, C. H. *The Buccaneers in the West Indies in the XVII Century.* Reprint ed. Hamden, Conn.: Archon Books, 1966.
Hernández Pino, Andrés, ed. *Papeles coloniales; Aporte para la historia de los pueblos del Estado Miranda.* Caracas: Editorial Venezuela, 1948.

Hordes, Stanley Mark. "The Crypto-Jewish Community of New Spain, 1620–1649: A Collective Biography." Ph.D. diss., Tulane University, 1980.
Humbert, Julián. *Los orígenes venezolanos (Ensayo sobre la colonización española en Venezuela.* Biblioteca de la Academia Nacional de la Historia, no. 127. Caracas: Italgráfica, 1976.
Humboldt, Alexander von. *Personal Narrative of Travels to Equinoctial Regions of America during the Years 1799–1804.* 7 vols. Reprint. New York, 1966.
Hussey, Roland D. *The Caracas Company, 1728–1784: A Study in the History of Spanish Monopolistic Trade.* Cambridge, Mass.: Harvard University Press, 1934.
Israel, Jonathan Irvine. *Race, Class, and Politics in Colonial Mexico, 1610–1670.* New York: Oxford University Press, 1975.
Iturriza Guillén, Carlos. *Algunas familias caraqueñas.* 2 vols. Caracas: Escuela Técnica Industria Salsiana, 1967.
———. *Algunas familias valencianas.* Caracas, 1955.
———, ed. *Matrimonios y velaciones de españoles y criollos blancos celebrados en la catedral de Caracas desde 1615 hasta 1831.* Instituto Venezolano de Genealogía. Caracas: Italgráfica, 1974.
Kipple, Kenneth F. *The Caribbean Slave: A Biological History.* New York: Cambridge University Press, 1984.
Klein, Herbert S. *The Middle Passage: Comparative Studies in the Atlantic Slave Trade.* Princeton: Princeton University Press, 1978.
Leal, Ildefonso. *Libros y bibliotecas en Venezuela colonial (1633–1767).* 2 vols. Biblioteca de la Academia Nacional de la Historia, nos. 132 and 133. Caracas: Italgráfica, 1978.
Lévi-Strauss, Claude. *The Elementary Structure of Kinship.* Boston: Beacon Press, 1969.
El libro parroquial más antiguo de Caracas. Caracas: Consejo Municipal del Distrito Federal, 1968.
Liss, Peggy K. *Atlantic Empires: The Network of Trade and Revolution, 1713–1826.* Baltimore and London: The Johns Hopkins University Press, 1983.
Lockhart, James. *The Men of Cajamarca: A Social and Biographical Study of the First Conquerors of Peru.* Austin: University of Texas Press, 1972.
Lombardi, John V. *The Decline and Abolition of Negro Slavery in Venezuela, 1820–1854.* Westport, Conn.: Greenwood Press, 1971.
———. *Venezuela: The Search for Order, the Dream of Progress.* New York: Oxford University Press, 1982.
MacLeod, Murdo J. *Spanish Central America: A Socio-Economic History, 1520–1720.* Berkeley: University of California Press, 1973.
Manifiesto que con incontestables hechos prueba los grandes beneficios que ha producido el establecimiento de la Real Compañía Guipuscoana de Caracas. Madrid, 1749.

María, Nectario. *Historia de la conquista y fundación de Caracas.* 2d. ed. Madrid: Escuelas Profesionales Sagrado Corazón de Jesús, 1966.
Martí, Mariano. *Documentos relativos a su visita pastoral de la diócesis de Caracas, 1771–1784.* 7 vols. Biblioteca de la Academia Nacional de la Historia, nos. 95–101. Caracas: Italgráfica, 1969.
Miller, Gary Michael. "Status and Loyalty in Colonial Spanish America: A Social History of Regular Army Officers in Venezuela, 1750–1810." Ph.D. diss., University of Florida, 1985.
Miller, Joseph C. "Mortality in the Atlantic Slave Trade: Statistical Evidence on Causality." *The Journal of Interdisciplinary History* 11 (1981): 385–423.
Morales Padrón, Francisco. *Rebelión contra la Compañía de Caracas.* Seville: Escuela de Estudios Hispano-Americanos, 1955.
Moret, Michele. *Aspects de la Société Marchande de Seville au début de XVIIe siècle.* Paris: M. Rivère et Cie., 1967.
Mörner, Magnus. "Economic Factors and Stratification in Colonial Spanish America with Special Regard to Elites." *Hispanic American Historical Review* 63 (1983): 335–369.
———. "The Rural Economy and Society in Colonial Spanish America." In *The Cambridge History of Latin America*, vol. 2, ed. Leslie Bethell, 189–217. New York: Cambridge University Press, 1984.
Morón, Guillermo. *Historia de Venezuela.* 5 vols. Caracas, 1971.
Protocolos del siglo XVI, ed. Agustín Millares Carlo. Biblioteca de la Academia Nacional de la Historia, no. 80. Caracas: Italgráfica, 1966.
Novais, Fernando. *Estrutura e dinâmica do antigo sistema colonial (séculos XVI–XVIII).* Caderno CEBRAP, no. 17. São Paulo: Editora Brasiliense, 1974.
Núñez, Enrique Bernardo. *La ciudad de los techos rojos.* 4th ed. Caracas: Litografía La Bodoniana, 1973.
Olavarriaga, Pedro José. *Instrucción general y particular del estado presente de la provincia de Venezuela en los años de 1720 y 1721.* Biblioteca de la Academia Nacional de la Historia, no. 76. Caracas: Italgráfica, 1965.
Osgood, Cornelius. *Excavations at Tocorón, Venezuela.* New Haven, Conn.: Yale University Press, 1943.
Palmer, Colin A. *Human Cargoes: The British Slave Trade to Spanish America, 1700–1739.* Urbana, Ill.: University of Illinois Press, 1981.
Phillips, Carla Rahn. *Six Galleons for the King of Spain: Imperial Defense in the Early Seventeenth Century.* Baltimore: The Johns Hopkins University Press, 1986.
Pikaza, Otto. "Don Gabriel José de Zuloaga en la gobernación de Venezuela (1737–1747)." *Anuario de Estudios Americanos* (Seville), 19 (1962): 501–693.
Pike, Frederick. "Aspects of Cabildo Economic Regulations in Spanish America Under the Hapsburgs." *Inter-American Economic Affairs* 13 (1960): 67–86.
Pimentel, Juan de. "Relación de Nuestra Señora de Caraballeda y Santiago

de León [1578]." In *Relaciones geográficas de Venezuela*, ed. Antonio Arellano Moreno. Caracas: Italgráfica, 1964.

Pinto C., Manuel. *Los primeros vecinos de Caracas*. Caracas: Comisión Nacional del Cuatricentenario de la Fundación de Caracas, 1966.

Piñero, Eugenio. "The Cacao Economy of the Eighteenth-Century Province of Caracas and the Spanish Cacao Market." *Hispanic American Historical Review* 68 (1988): 75–100.

Polanco Martínez, Tomás. *Esbozo sobre historia económica venezolana*. Madrid: Ediciones Guadarrama, 1960.

Ponte, Andrés F. *Fray Mauro de Tovar*. Caracas: Impresores Unidos, 1945.

Ramos Pérez, Demetrio. "La politica del marqués de la Ensenada—asesorado por el ex-virrey Eslava—en relación con el levantamiento contra la Guipuzcoana." In his *Estudios de historia Venezolana*, 651–674. Biblioteca de la Academia Nacional de la Historia, no. 126. Caracas: Italgráfica, 1976.

Relaciones geográficas de Venezuela durante los siglos XVI, XVII y XVIII, ed. Antonio Arellano Moreno. Biblioteca de la Academia Nacional de la Historia, no. 70. Caracas: Italgráfica, 1964.

Rojas, Arístides. *Estudios históricos: Orígenes Venezolanos*. Caracas: Imprenta del Gobierno Nacional, 1891.

J. Sánchez, C., and J. García, B. "Regiones meso-climáticas en el centro y oriente de Venezuela." *Agronomía Tropical* (Caracas), 18 (1968): 429–439.

Sangroniz y Castro, José Antonio. *Familias coloniales de Venezuela*. Caracas: Editorial Bolívar, 1943.

Sanoja, Mario, and Iraida Vargas. *Antiguas formaciones y modos de producción venezolanos*. Caracas: Monte Avila Editores, 1974.

Scelle, G. *La traite negriére aux Indes de Castille*. 2 vols. Paris: L. Larose and L. Tenin, 1906.

Socolow, Susan Migden. "Marriage, Birth and Inheritance: The Merchants of Eighteenth-Century Buenos Aires." *Hispanic American Historical Review* 60 (1980): 387–406.

Sucre, Luis A. *Gobernadores y capitanes generales de Venezuela*. Caracas: Litografía del Comercio, 1928.

Van Young, Eric. "Mexican Rural History since Chevalier: The Historiography of the Colonial Hacienda." *Latin American Research Review* 18 (1983): 5–61.

Viera y Clavijo, José de. *Noticias de la historia general de las Islas Canarias*. 5 vols. Madrid: Imprenta de Blas Román, 1772–1783.

Vila, Marco Aurelio. *Antecedentes coloniales de centros poblados de Venezuela*. Caracas: Universidad Central de Venezuela, 1978.

———. *Aspectos geográficos del Distrito Federal*. Caracas: Corporación Venezolana de Fomento, 1967.

Waldron, Kathy. "A Social History of a Primate City: The Case of Caracas, 1750–1810." Ph.D. diss., Indiana University, 1977.

Walker, Geoffrey J. *Spanish Politics and Imperial Trade, 1700–1789*. Bloomington and London: Indiana University Press, 1979.

Index

Aguado Lovera, Fernando de, 193, 203
Aguirre, Juan de, 39, 41
Aguirre y Castillo, Domingo, 150–151, 166
Aix-la-Chapelle, Peace treaty of, 158, 165
Aizpurua, Nicolás de, 202
Alas, Martín de las, 43
Alcabala, 66, 247–249, 251
Alfinger, Ambrose, 2
Alhorra (crop blight), 59, 61–62, 66, 92, 95, 97
Alquiza, Sancho de, 34, 43
Alternativa, 155, 157, 165, 181–182, 184, 189
Alvarez y Abreu, Antonio José de, 114–115, 117–118, 161–164, 180
Anauco (stream), 25, 26, 28
Angola (Africa), 56
Aragua (valley), 51–52, 67–70, 145, 155, 213
Araguita (valley), 185
Arcila Farías, Eduardo, 34, 47–48
Arechederra Tovar, Sebastián, 196
Arias, Francisco, 165
Arias Altamirano, Luis, 165, 167, 253
Arias Blanco, Maria Teresa, 209
Arias de Aquilena, Francisco, 56
Aristeguiete Lovera, Miguel, 193, 239
Aroa (valley), 205
Arriaga y Rivera, Julián de, 153–159, 166, 168, 172, 241–244, 246, 249–250
Ascanio Herrera, María Teresa, 252
Asiento. See Slave trade
Audiencia: Santa Fe de Bogotá, 113–115, 117–118, 160; Santo Domingo, 31, 34, 111–113, 117–120, 141, 152, 197

Barbary coast, 13
Barquisimeto, 2, 4
Baruta (valley), 23, 69
Basques, denied colonial administrative appointments, 242–243

Batallón Veterano, 249, 251
Beato, Pedro Martín de, 114–115, 117, 163
Bengoechea, Sabastián de, 22, 41
Berrotarán, Francisco de, 108–109
Berrotarán Tovar, Miguel, 109
Betancourt y Castro, Marcos, 114–115, 117, 162–163, 197
Blanco, 1759 households of, 219–221
Blanco de Ponte, Alejandro Pío, 239
Blanco de Ponte, Pedro (17th century), 39, 56
Blanco de Ponte, Pedro (18th century), 165, 167, 239, 253
Blanco de Villegas, Alejandro (father), 112, 118, 238–239
Blanco de Villegas, Alejandro (son), 239, 253
Blanco de Villegas, Juan, 110, 119–120
Blanco de Villegas, Juan Félix, 165–166, 239, 253
Blanco de Villegas, Miguel, 239
Blanco de Villegas kin, 120, 128, 238–239
Blanco Ochoa, Antonio, 205–208
Blanco Ponte, Alejandro, 54, 56–57
Blanco Uribe, Alejandro Antonio, 143, 205–208, 213–215, 239, 253
Blanco Uribe, Cornelio, 214
Blanco Uribe, María Josefa, 214
Blanco Uribe, Miguel, 165, 207, 214
Blanco Uribe kin, 205, 208, 213–215, 238–240
Blank, Stephanie, 24–25, 28
Bolívar, Simón (16th century), 22
Bolívar, Simón (the "Liberator"), 6, 208–209
Bolívar Aguirre, José, 171, 196, 205, 209–211, 213–215, 239, 242
Bolívar Aguirre kin, 205, 214–215, 239–240
Bolívar Arias, Josefa, 196
Bolívar Arias, Juan, 210–211, 242
Bolívar Arias, Teresa, 196

Bolívar Martínez, Juan, 209
Bolívar Ponte, María Jacinta, 192
Bolívar Uribe, Juana, 206
Bolívar Uribe, María, 206
Borburata (valley), 191
Bourbon Reforms, 5, 9, 236, 241–243; policies in Caracas, 244–245, 254
Braudel, Fernand, 21
Buenos Aires, merchant marriages, 222

Cabalgada, 14–15
Cabildo, 23, 35, 141. *See also* Caracas cabildo
Cacao: farming, 33–34, 46, 63, 73–74, 86, 91–93, 95–96, 100, 105–106, 121, 125, 132–135; hacienda censuses, 8; impact on Caracas society, 53, 65; prices, 60–62, 91–93, 126, 137–138, 148, 155, 165, 185–186, 189, 203, 208, 243–244; *1684* hacienda census, 66–68, 70, 99, 100, 106, 121, 204; *1720* hacienda census, 67, 100, 106–107, 121–123, 126–127, 204; *1744* hacienda census, 67, 106–107, 121–123, 126–127, 182; trade, 3–6, 42, 44–45, 48–49, 52, 55, 62–65, 70–71, 99, 148, 155, 157, 165, 179–187, 242; transportation to La Guaira, 55, 124–125, 132–133, 144, 160, 243; trees indigenous to Caracas region, 3. *See also Alternativa; Repartimiento por padrón; Tercio buque*
Cádiz, 4
Caldera, María Candelaria, cacao haciendas of, 129–136
Canal, Bartolomé de la, 18
Canarios. *See* Canary Islanders
Canary Islanders: immigrants to Caracas, 4, 54, 106; place in Caracas province society, 67, 106, 122, 125–128, 138, 159–160, 174–175, 251; role in 1749 rebellion, 5, 143–148, 168; struggle for land in Tuy Valley, 109–111, 119–120
Cañas y Merino, José Francisco, 112, 197
Candelaria. *See* Caracas, Candelaria parish
Capaya (valley), 144, 185, 191
Caraballeda (valley), 49, 57, 69
Caracas, 49, 61, 69; Altagracia parish, 217; Candelaria parish, 67, 146–148, 152, 154, 168, 173–175, 251; Cathedral parish, 217, 220, 224, 238; climate, 15–16, 20–21, 49, 80; ejido, 26, 29, 31, 33, 43; foundation, 1, 13; plaza reconstruction, 246–247; 1759 household census, 8, 72–73, 217–218; trapiches in region (1752), 204. *See also* Elites; Portuguese
Caracas cabildo: activities during cacao period, 65–66, 95–96; activities during wheat period, 14–16, 18, 23–24, 28–35 passim, 41–43, 52, 86–88; gubernatorial authority, struggle for, 114–117, 163, 196–200; León's rebellion, role in, 145–146, 148–150, 152–156, 163; protest against Basque policies, 181–182, 186–187; Ricardos's policies against, 244–247, 249, 317 n. 3
Caracas Company. *See* Guipuzcoana Company
Carrasquer, Nofre, 22–23, 40–41, 43
Carrasquer Rada, Ana, 193
Carrillo y Andrade, Lope, 196, 198
Cartagena, 3, 15, 18, 21–23, 28, 32–33, 39–43, 45, 56–58, 78
Castellanos, Luis, 143–144, 146–153, 155
Castillo, Francisco, 58
Cata (valley), 206
Cattle ranching, 51, 66, 68, 79
Catuche (stream), 25, 28–31
Caucagua (valley), 121–122, 124–125, 139, 143–145, 185, 206–208, 212
Cepi (valley), 46, 59–60, 63, 87–97, 209
Chacao (stream), 25, 26, 28, 76, 79
Charles III, 241, 254
Charles V, 2
Choroní (valley), 47, 54–56
Chuao (valley), 56–57, 64–65, 87, 99, 170
Chuspa (valley), 49, 100, 113, 211
Cisneros, Joseph Luis de, 246
Collado, Pablo, 1
Compadrazgo, 25
Company of Noble Adventurers, 9, 254
Conception convent, 88–89, 98–99
Coro, 2, 18, 111–112, 197
Council of the Indies, 120, 153, 157–158, 163, 174, 177, 184, 187–188
Cubagua, 1
Cumaná, 171
Cumanagoto (Indians), 14, 29
Curaçao, 64, 111–112, 156, 170. *See also* Dutch traders; Smuggling
Curiepe (valley), 108–114, 117–121, 144, 185, 239
Cuyuagua (valley), 196

Index   339

Díaz de Alfaro, Sebastián, 14, 26, 30
Depons, François, 72
Drake, Francis, 18
Dutch traders, 64, 169–170. *See also* Curaçao; Smuggling

Earthquake (1641), 59, 61–62
Echeverría, Martín de, 143–145, 167
Ejido. See Caracas, *ejido*
El Dorado, 13
Elites: alcaldes ordinarios, 200–202; Basque parentage, 195–196; cacao haciendas of, 121–123, 125–128, 187–188, 190–191, 237–238; consumption patterns, 56, 85, 97–101; cousin marriage, 231–233, 239–240, 253; death of protest generation, 253; debts with Guipuzcoana Company, 202–203, 214–215; defined, 10, 194, 217; grandparents, 228, 234; impact of reforms upon, 252–254; inheritance laws, impact upon, 6, 7, 230–231, 235, 238, 252; marriage patterns, 8, 67, 216, 219–235, 238, 252; political activism of, 24–25, 33–35, 42–44, 197–201; protest against Guipuzcoana Company, 177–178, 187–206, 214–215, 236, 239–240; punishment for 1749 rebellion, 216, 236, 243–244, 247–251; role in 1749 rebellion, 145, 148–151, 154, 156–157, 165–168, 175, 177–178; trapiches owned by, 204; urban residence of, 72–74, 216–219; 233–235; widows, 188–189, 193, 234. *See also* Protest memorials
El Tocuyo, 2, 23
Encomienda, 1, 3, 13, 25, 43, 48–53, 55, 57–59, 67–70, 87
Ensenada, Marqués de la, 157–161, 164–165, 173, 243, 249
Escovedo, Francisca de, 78, 85
Eslava, Sebastián de, 160–161, 164, 177
Estancias de trigo. See Wheat

Fajardo, Francisco, 1
Ferdinand VI, 157, 165, 241, 254
Ferigo, Leonardo, 30–33
Figueredo, Manoel, 29–33
Flota, 3, 21, 158
Fortalezas, 13
Francia, Nicolás de, 203

Galindo Quiñones y Barrientos, Francisco, 152–153
Galindo y Sayas, Domingo, 239

Gámez, Francisca, 57
García Pineda, Alsono, 25–26
Gedler, Isabel María, 211
Gedler Ponte, Pedro Francisco, 192, 193
Gibraltar (Venezuela), 32, 63
Gil de Aguirre, Isabel, 212
Goizueta, Juan Manuel, 143, 145
Góngora, Mario, 70
González de Silva, Garci, 14, 24, 26, 28–31, 33, 39–41
Goyzueta, Juan Manuel, 199
Guaiguaza (valley), 206
Guaire (river, valley), 16, 20, 49, 52, 88, 95, 124
Guarenas (river, valley), 49, 69
Guayana jungle, 13
Guayaquil, 47, 62
Guevara, Juan de, 19, 30, 40–41
Guipúzcoa (Spain), 4
Guipuzcoana Company: debts owed to, 202–204, 212–215; commercial policies in favor of, 178–187 passim; establishment, 4, 5, 106; impact on Caracas economy, 136–138, 311 n. 31; protests against, 8, 142–165 passim, 172; reformed, 175, 243–244, 254; and slave trade, 125–126; viewed from 1811, 174. *See also* Francia; Goyzueta; Lardizábal; Protest memorials; Zuloaga

Hatos. See Cattle ranching
Havana, 3, 5, 241
Havana Company, 161
Herrera, Antonio de, 56
Herrera, 1759 households of, 219–221
Higuerote (bay), 113, 119

Ibarra, Juan de, 47, 55
Ibarra, María Petronila, 191
Ibarra y Herrera, Diego, 191
Ibarra y Ibarra, Ana Josefa, 191
Ibarra y Ibarra, Antonia, 191
Indians, 1, 3, 13–14, 32, 49, 67, 84, 94–95, 145, 148, 151, 168. *See also* Cumanagoto; Encomienda; Tomusa
Infante, Francisca, 57
Inquisition, 48, 58, 62
Isleños. See Canary Islanders
Izalcos, 47

Labor, wages paid as substitute for slavery, 250–251
La Grita, 33

La Guaira, 1, 5, 16, 22, 47, 52, 55, 74, 112–113, 116; governor Castellanos takes refuge there, 145–147, 149–150; León attacks fortress, 151; round-trip to Veracruz from, 181–182
Landaeta, Antonio Gregorio, 203
Lardizábal, Martin de, 120, 144, 156, 184–185, 198, 200
La Vega (valley), 69
León, Juana Petrona de, 251
León, Juan Francisco de: comment about *repartimento por padrón*, 183; Curiepe, conflict over land, 110, 119; Panaquire settlement, 120, 138; protest and rebellion, 143–156, 159, 165, 167–170, 199, 213; surrender and punishment, 171–175, 251
León, Nicolás de, 159, 167, 171–173
Liendo, Domingo de, 54, 59, 87–88, 95, 97, 99, 100
Liendo, Juan de, 99, 100
Liendo, Pedro de, 46, 54, 56–57, 59, 87–88, 97–100
Liendo, Santiago de, 54, 63, 87–88, 90, 94–95, 97–100
Liendo Blanco, Antolín de, 239–240
Liendo Blanco, Antonio, 193
Liendo Blanco, Josefa Clara, 192
Liendo Cepi cacao hacienda, 75–76, 86–101, 128, 134–136
Liendo Gedler, Germana, 196
Losada, Diego de, 13
Lovera y Bolívar, Juan, 193
Lovera y Bolívar, Juana Josefa, 211–212

MacLeod, Murdo, 47, 62
Maiquetía (valley), 69
Mamporal (valley), 144, 185
Mantuanos. See Elites
Maracaibo, 32–33, 43
Margarita, 1, 22, 41, 63
Marmolejo, Esteban, 29
Martí, Mariano, 139
Martínez de Villegas, Juan, 51
Martínez de Villegas, Luisa Catalina, 118–120, 239
Matriarchy, 230–235. *See also* Patriarchy
Mérida, 33
Mexía, Catalina, 57
Mexico, 3, 4, 6, 22, 46, 56, 99, 113, 186
Mexico, cacao market, 42, 48, 62–64, 70–71, 87, 100, 105, 179, 186
Mijares, Juan Antonio, 219
Mijares, Marqués de. *See* Mijares Tovar, Francisco Nicolás

Mijares Ascanio, Melchora Ana, 234
Mijares kin, 238–240
Mijares Tovar, Francisco Nicolás (III Marqués de Mijares), 146, 166, 239, 253
Mijares Tovar, Josefa, 234
Monasterios Renjifo, Francisco Domingo de, 118
Monasterios Sartucho, Mateo, 239
Morenos libres, 110–114, 118–120, 122, 138, 148
Muleteers. *See* Cacao, transportation to La Guaira

Naiguatá (valley), 69
New Granada, 14–15; viceroyalty of, 113–116, 142, 160, 162, 180, 197–198. *See also* Audiencia, Santa Fe de Bogotá
New Spain. *See* Mexico
Nirgua, 14

Ocumare de la Costa (valley), 206
Ocumare del Tuy (valley), 116, 121, 140, 149
Olavarriaga, Pedro José de, 114–115, 117, 163
Osgood, Cornelius, 51
Ovalle, Diego de, 40, 42, 47, 54–56

Pacheco Mijares, Juan Jacinto (II Conde de San Javier), 143, 146, 166, 167, 183–187, 192, 202, 238–239
Pacheco Mijares, 1759 households of, 219–221
Palacios, Juana Teresa, 211
Palacios Gil, Feliciano, 213
Palacios kin, 205, 214–215
Palacios Lovera, José de, 195, 205, 212–214
Palacios y Gedler, Feliciano de, 195, 205, 211–215, 239
Palacios y Palacios, Ana Juana, 212
Palacios y Sojo, Bernabé de, 211
Palacios Zárate, José, 211
Pamplona, 33
Panama, 1, 15
Panaquire (valley), 120–122, 125, 128, 143–145, 155, 160, 168–169, 171, 173–174, 182, 185
Panezillo, 1
Patanemo (valley), 191
Patriarchy, 8, 74, 192, 222, 229–233, 253–254. *See also* Elites
Peru, 3, 15, 62

Petare, 69
Philip II, 16
Philip V, 156, 164, 198
Pike, Frederick, 23, 35
Pimentel, Juan de, 16, 17
Pirates, 34
Píritu, 171, 173, 244
Piñango, Augustín, 239
Piñate, Joseph Silvestre, 131, 133
Piñate, Simón, 129–136
Polanco Martínez, Tomás, 34
Ponte, Juan Nicolás, 165–167
Ponte Marín, María Petronila, 193, 209
Ponte Marín, Pedro, 109
Ponte Villegas, Lorenzo de, 146, 192, 228, 253
Ponte y Andrade, Pedro de, 108–109
Ponte y Hoyo, Nicolás, 197
Ponte y Mijares, Francisco de, 143, 166–167, 183–187
Portales y Meneses, Diego, 115–117, 119, 163, 197
Portobelo, 3, 15
Portuguese: Caracas vecinos, 34; slaves-for-cacao traders, 48, 62; tobacco traders, 35, 42–43
Preston, Aymas, 16
Protest memorials: *1741*, 188, 205, 235; *1744*, 189–194, 196, 200–203, 235, 239
Puerto Cabello, 49
Puerto Rico, 32, 40, 41

Rada Arias, José, 192
Rada Liendo, Fernando, 192
Real Compañía Guipuzcoana de Caracas. See Guipuzcoana Company
Rebellion (1749), 136, 138, 142–155, 159, 168–171, 241; royal reaction to, 157–161, 163–169, 171–174, 236, 243–249
Relaciones Geográficas, 16, 45
Remírez de Estenoz, Felipe, 250
Rengifo Pimentel, José, 54, 56, 57
Renjifo Mendoza, Miguel Gerónimo de, 239–240
Repartimiento por padrón, 182–184, 189. See also Cacao, 1744 hacienda census
Riberos, Juan de, 18, 26, 27
Ricardos, Felipe, 164–175, 177, 210, 217, 235–236, 243–251, 253
Rivillapuerta, Bartolomé, 78–87, 94, 96
Rodríguez de la Madrid, Domingo, 195
Rodríguez de la Madrid Vásquez, Andrés, 195
Rodríguez de la Madrid y Liendo, Salvador, 196

Rodríguez de la Madrid y Liendo, Santiago, 196
Rodríguez del Toro, Bernardo (I Marqués de Toro), 183–184, 186–187
Rodríguez del Toro y Istúriz, Francisco de Paula (II Marqués del Toro), 166, 192, 252–253
Rodríguez del Toro y Istúriz, María Teresa, 191–192
Rodríguez Santos, Alonso, 39, 41, 43, 58, 77
Rodríguez Santos, Juan, 58, 77–78, 85
Rodríguez Santos wheat estancia, 75–94, 96, 97, 100–101, 134
Rosario Blanco, Juan del, 112–114, 117–120, 138
Ruiz Arguinzones, Pedro, 239

San Javier, Conde de. See Pacheco Mijares, Juan Jacinto
San Matheo (valley), 100
San Sebastián (Spain), 4
San Sebastián de los Reyes, 14, 26, 45, 49, 51, 53, 68, 145
Santa Lucía (valley), 88–90, 95–99, 116, 121
Santo Domingo, 5, 32, 41, 54, 111–112, 118. See also Audiencia, Santo Domingo
Seven Years War, 241
Seville, 21, 33, 39–40, 55, 57, 78
Sierpe, Gil de la, 49
Slavery: African, 3–4, 6; control of Tuy slaves, 139–140; domestic, 72–73, 79, 89–90; and elite status, 128, 138; impact of declining prices on, 186, 188; Indian, 1–2, 51; Liendo-Rodríguez Santos slaves, 88–90, 93–96; and *morenos libres*, 110–112; Piñate-Caldera slaves, 130–131; Rodríguez Santos-Escovedo slaves, 79, 84, 87, 93; transition from encomienda labor to, 43, 56–58, 64–65, 67–70. See also Indians; Slave trade
Slave trade, 6, 7, 45; from Curaçao, 64, 71; early slave imports, 57–58, 97; English asiento, 9, 124–139 passim, 158–159, 163, 188; French asiento, 111–112; Portuguese asiento, 109, 111
Smuggling: tobacco, 34–35; cacao, 5, 124, 156, 169–170, 186, 327 n. 23; and *tenientes de justicia*, 139–142. See also Curaçao; Dutch traders
Soconusco, 47
Sojo Palacios. See Palacios

Solano y Bote, José, 211, 242–243
Sosa Betancourt, Manuel de, 146–147, 166
Soto Ibarra, Isabel, 192
South Sea Company. *See* Slave trade, English asiento
Spanish Succession, War of the, 198
Spira, Georg, 2
Sugar, 66, 68–70, 100, 190; *trapiches* in Caracas province (1752), 204

Tácata (valley), 121
Taguasa (valley), 209
Tenerife, 35, 54
Tenientes de justicia mayor, 116–117, 140–144, 149, 169, 171, 173
Tercio buque, 179–183, 215
Tierra adentro, 2
Tierra Firme, 3, 15, 33
Tobacco: ban on, 34–35, 42–43; farming, 33–34; trade, 20, 24, 34–39, 41–42; traders, 35–39, 41–42
Tócome, 145–146, 153
Tomusa (Indians), 108
Toro, I Marqués de. *See* Rodríguez del Toro, Bernardo
Toro, II Marqués de. *See* Rodríguez del Toro y Istúriz, Francisco de Paula
Tovar, Antonio, 70
Tovar, Mauro de, 61
Tovar, 1759 households of, 219–221
Tovar Blanco, Martín (I Conde de Tovar), 171, 252
Tovar Galindo, Ana Juana, 203
Tovar Galindo, Fernando, 196
Tovar Galindo, José Domingo, 196
Tovar Galindo, José Manuel, 196
Tovar Galindo, Martín, 196
Tovar kin, 69
Tovar Mijares, Antonio, 196
Tovar Mijares, Luisa Catalina, 196
Tovar Mijares, Mauro, 196

Tovar Mijares, Melchora, 219
Tribiño Guillamas, Juan de, 49
Tunja, 33
Turmero (valley), 51, 69
Tutela (guardianship), 76–77, 100–101
Tuy (river, region), 4, 5; closing of frontier, 135–139, 254; expansion of cacao haciendas to, 66–67, 74, 105–144 passim, 185; productivity of haciendas in 1744, 207; trapiches, 204

Unare (river), 171
Urbina, Andrés de, 180
Uribe y Gaviola, Isabel de, 205–207

Valencia (town, valley) 2, 14, 49, 51, 53, 58, 67–69, 164; trapiches, 204
Vasconcelos de Acuña, Francisco, 56
Vásquez de Escobedo, Diego, 40, 41
Vásquez de Rojas, Juan, 56
Vellón (copper coinage), 63
Vera Ibargoyen, Melchora, 42
Villalonga, Jorge de, 114
Villanueva, Diego de, 41, 45

Waldron, Kathy, 72
War of Jenkins' Ear, 158
Welsers, 2
Wheat: farming, 3, 16, 20, 32–33, 66, 68, 70, 73, 77–86, 93, 96–97, 100; flour mills and milling, 26–28, 30–31, 78–82, 100; trade, 3, 15–16, 18–20, 22, 31–32, 34, 36–38, 40–46, 80–86; traders, 35–38, 40–42

Ynforme (report on Indian population in 1690), 68–69

Zambos, 69
Zuloaga, Gabriel José de, 142–144, 156, 160–161, 164, 182–183, 187, 198, 200, 238

Designer: U.C. Press Staff
Compositor: Huron Valley Graphics
Text: 10/13 Palatino
Display: Palatino

www.ingramcontent.com/pod-product-compliance
Lightning Source LLC
Chambersburg PA
CBHW031433230426
43668CB00007B/518